Tiger Stadium

McFarland Historic Ballparks

1. *Forbes Field: Essays and Memories of the Pirates' Historic Ballpark, 1909–1971.*
Edited by David Cicotello and Angelo J. Louisa. 2007

2. *Ebbets Field: Essays and Memories of Brooklyn's Historic Ballpark, 1913–1960.*
Edited by John G. Zinn and Paul G. Zinn. 2013

3. *Old Comiskey Park: Essays and Memories of the Historic Home of the Chicago White Sox, 1910–1991.*
Edited by Floyd Sullivan. 2014

4. *Tiger Stadium: Essays and Memories of Detroit's Historic Ballpark, 1912–2009.*
Edited by Michael Betzold, John Davids, Bill Dow, John Pastier and Frank Rashid. 2018

Tiger Stadium

Essays and Memories of Detroit's Historic Ballpark, 1912–2009

Edited by MICHAEL BETZOLD,
JOHN DAVIDS, BILL DOW,
JOHN PASTIER, *and* FRANK RASHID

MCFARLAND HISTORIC BALLPARKS, 4
Series Editors David Cicotello *and* Angelo J. Louisa

McFarland & Company, Inc., Publishers
Jefferson, North Carolina

LIBRARY OF CONGRESS CATALOGUING-IN-PUBLICATION DATA

Names: Betzold, Michael, editor.
Title: Tiger Stadium : essays and memories of Detroit's historic ballpark, 1912–2009 / edited by Michael Betzold, John Davids, Bill Dow, John Pastier and Frank Rashid.
Description: Jefferson, North Carolina : McFarland & Company, Inc., Publishers, 2018. | Series: Mcfarland historic ballparks ; 4 | Includes bibliographical references and index.
Identifiers: LCCN 2018001697 | ISBN 9780786464487 (softcover : acid free paper) ∞
Subjects: LCSH: Tiger Stadium (Detroit, Mich.)—History. | Detroit Tigers (Baseball team)—History.
Classification: LCC GV417.T54 T55 2018 | DDC 796.35706/877434—dc23
LC record available at https://lccn.loc.gov/2018001697

BRITISH LIBRARY CATALOGUING DATA ARE AVAILABLE

ISBN (print) 978-0-7864-6448-7
ISBN (ebook) 978-1-4766-3114-1

© 2018 Michael Betzold, John Davids, Bill Dow, John Pastier and Frank Rashid. All rights reserved

No part of this book may be reproduced or transmitted in any form or by any means, electronic or mechanical, including photocopying or recording, or by any information storage and retrieval system, without permission in writing from the publisher.

Front cover: A photograph of Briggs Stadium, as it was known then, viewed from the corner of Michigan and Trumbull Avenues in Detroit, circa 1940s (Superior View Studio)

Printed in the United States of America

McFarland & Company, Inc., Publishers
Box 611, Jefferson, North Carolina 28640
www.mcfarlandpub.com

In memory of Catherine Darin (1920–2009)
and Eva Navarro (1951–2001)

Downtown stadiums like this … seem to hold and intensify the sounds and hopes and intimate oneness of their crowds, and when you're inside, watching your team (in its brilliant home whites, with the same famous, old-timey gothic initial) violently at play, it's possible to wonder for a moment which decade you are in and which wonderful, hero-strewn lineup is on view down there, in the instant of its passing from action to history.—Roger Angell

* * *

In Detroit, there's a cozy seat at the railing in the second deck where you can lean forward and hear the swish of the bat when the on-deck hitter swings. When there's an argument at the plate, you don't have to ask the players afterward what was said. This is the best place I've found to grasp the central aspect of the sport, the tense business being conducted by the pitcher and the hitter....

[F]rom that spot in Tiger Stadium I sensed the paradoxical physics of pitching. It's as physically difficult to hit a slow pitch after *seeing* a fast one thrown with the same delivery as it is hard to hit a laser-beam heater.... Whitey Ford said he had the hitter's front foot on a string and could jerk that lead foot off stride whenever he wanted. In Detroit from that seat you can feel what he meant.—Thomas Boswell

* * *

No better spectator park exists. By actual measurement, [Tiger Stadium's] seating proximity to the field surpasses all other parks, old or new.... As design, it is a rare specimen of the Golden Age of ballparks, full of complexity, and miraculously combining both monumentality and human scale.—John Pastier

View from the upper deck along the first base side on a sunny afternoon at Tiger Stadium in 1999 (© Rebecca Cook).

Table of Contents

Acknowledgments	ix
Introduction	1

Part I: History and Background

A Century on Common Ground I: Bennett Park and Navin Field MICHAEL BETZOLD	7
A Century on Common Ground II: Briggs Stadium and Tiger Stadium MICHAEL BETZOLD	30
Detroit Lions Roar at Briggs Stadium BILL DOW	64
Longevity and Adaptability: Tiger Stadium's Evolution, Architecture, Functionality, Structure and Urban Context JOHN PASTIER WITH DRAWINGS BY JOHN DAVIDS	68
The Mallparking of America: Tiger Stadium and the Subsidy Game NEIL deMAUSE	121
Losing Tiger Stadium, 1987–1997 FRANK RASHID	129
The Battle for Sacred Ground, 1998–2011 REBECCA LONG with a 2016 Postscript by MICHAEL BETZOLD	153

Part II: Memories

Tiger Stadium Souvenirs BILL DOW	167
Tiger Stadium in Literature MICHAEL P. GRUBER	178
Tiger Stadium Memories and Stories *(Interviews were conducted and edited by Bill Dow)*	
• From the Stands	187
• From the Workers	204
• From the Booth	213

- From the Gridiron ... 216
- From the Diamond ... 219

"The Biggest House in the Neighborhood": Living Near Tiger Stadium ... 229
  FRANK RASHID

The Stadium: An Essay in Memory of George Cantor ... 238
  TOM DELISLE

For the Love of the Game ... 244
  KAREN ELIZABETH BUSH

Closer ... 247
  TODD JONES

Reflections on the Closing of Tiger Stadium
- The Final Opener ... 251
  KIM STROUD

- The Final Week ... 251
  JUDY DAVIDS

- The Navin Field Grounds Crew ... 252
  JOHN DAVIDS

- Elegy for Tiger Stadium ... 255
  JIM DANIELS

Appendix 1: 161 Baseball Hall of Famers Who Played at the Tiger Stadium Site ... 259
  BILL DOW

Appendix 2: The 15 All-Star Game Home Runs Hit at Briggs/Tiger Stadium ... 261
  BILL DOW

Appendix 3: The Lions' Most Memorable Games at Tiger Stadium ... 262
  BILL DOW

A Select Bibliography of Works About Tiger Stadium ... 263
  COMPILED BY FRANK RASHID

About the Contributors ... 267

Index ... 269

Acknowledgments

Many have contributed to this book. We are grateful to all whose essays, reflections, and memories appear in it. We thank Andrew Clem for creating the most accurate and comprehensive graphic and statistical database of 20th- and 21st-century baseball parks' physical characteristics, which has been invaluable for developing a context for Tiger Stadium's evolution; Ethan Casey for allowing us to draw on his research about Tiger Stadium's history; and Michael Gruber for saving and providing Tiger Stadium Fan Club documents. Jerry Lemenu, Dave Mesrey, Kevin Rashid, Gary Gillette, and Kim Stroud made helpful comments and suggestions, in particular, about preliminary drafts of "Losing Tiger Stadium." Tom Goldstein answered questions about Tiger Stadium sources, especially in the *Elysian Fields Quarterly*. Rick Ruffner, Robert Wright, and Jason Thompson helped with the selection and processing of stadium photographs from the extensive collection at Avanti Press. We received authorization to include photographs and drawings from several sources. Joseph E. Duggan, executor of the estate of Mrs. Ruth Murphy, granted permission to use Gene Mack's 1946 drawing of Tiger Stadium. Jerry Lemenu allowed us to reprint his cartoon from the 1990s. Longtime Detroit sports photographer Rebecca Cook not only let us use her wonderful Tiger Stadium photographs but also spent many hours helping us to select and prepare them for publication. Photographer Michelle Andonian and artist Lowell Boileau graciously consented to having their images placed in our book. And Patricia Muldoon, Sarah Derry, Tom Derry, Karen Elizabeth Bush, and Tom DeLisle provided photographs from their personal collections.

We thank Penguin Random House for permission to quote from Philip Levine's poem "A Walk with Tom Jefferson" in Michael P. Gruber's essay "Tiger Stadium in Literature." Jim Daniels, Jan Mordenski, and Richard Behm also graciously allowed Gruber to quote from their poems in his essay. We also are deeply grateful to Jim Daniels for giving permission to use his "Elegy for Tiger Stadium."

We were also assisted by staff members of the following libraries and collections: Mark Bowden, Dawn Eurich, and Romie Minor of the Burton Historical Collection and the Ernie Harwell Collection at the Detroit Public Library; Deborah Rice and Mary J. Wallace of the Walter Reuther Library at Wayne State University; Danielle Kaltz, digital asset manager of the *Detroit News*; and Gene Myers, sports editor, and Kathy Kieliszewski, visuals director, of the *Detroit Free Press*. In addition, the staff of the Marygrove College library assisted us. Linnea Dudley provided historical materials, Jennifer Meacham gave invaluable technical assistance, and Christine Malmsten, formerly of the Marygrove library and now at the library of Oakland Community College, answered questions and helped us to locate older Detroit maps.

Acknowledgments

Marygrove deans Donald Levin and Judith Heinen and professors Darcy Brandel, Audrey Becker, Loretta Woodard, Michael Martin, Thomas Klug, Ellen Duncan, Mary Byrnes, Steven Engel, and Nikhil Gupta offered support and advice to Frank Rashid. Clemson University professors Robert Russell, Barry Stiefel, and James Ward gave invaluable suggestions and guidance to Rebecca Long as she researched grassroots efforts to preserve Tiger Stadium. Long also thanks Peter Comstock Riley and Gary Gillette for granting extensive interviews and serving as resources.

Financial assistance came from the Marygrove College Faculty Development Fund. We thank the members of the college's Faculty Development Committee: professors Michael Martin, Nikhil Gupta, Leona Mickles-Burns, and Steven Patterson. The following persons responded to our request for financial support, mostly through a Kickstarter fundraising campaign: Steven Thomas, Suzanne Antisdel, James Karagon, Rose DeSloover, Darcy L. Brandel, Anne Rashid, Judith Heinen, Marie Lemenu, Ellen Duncan, Carl Gladstone, Tony and Mary Campbell, Laurie LePain Kopack, David Cicotello, Laura Janssen, Francis Grunow, Audrey Becker, Mike and Megan Brady, Kenny Hemler, Mike Malley, Tom Meyer Klipsch, Will Alberts, Peggy Bach, Tom Craft, and Chris Davis. Their generous support allowed us to purchase photograph rights from library archives, newspapers, and private vendors.

We thank David Cicotello and Angelo J. Louisa for their extreme patience and good counsel. And finally, we are grateful to Tom Derry and the Navin Field Grounds Crew for carrying on.

Introduction

>   Shortly after her 1946 arrival in Detroit from County Cork, Ireland, Catherine Darin attended her first baseball game at Briggs Stadium. She knew nothing about baseball but reveled in the excitement surrounding "Mr. Greenberg" and his teammates, and, though a stranger to the city and its people, she immediately felt she was part of the Detroit crowd.
>
>   A daughter of Mexican American immigrants, Eva Navarro traced her love of Tiger Stadium to her late father, who took her to games in the 1960s and shared her fondness for the Tigers' colorful first baseman Stormin' Norman Cash. As for Darin and dozens of others, memory and principle later led to her activism on behalf of the stadium.
>
>   The son of Lebanese American immigrants, Frederick Rashid, homesick for his small Illinois hometown after his family moved to Depression-era Detroit, absorbed himself in baseball, took refuge in the games at Navin Field, and, during the 1934 and 1935 championship seasons, accepted his new identity as a Detroiter.
>
>   The daughter of an African American family, Detroit City Councilwoman JoAnn Watson in 2008 and 2009 tried to prevent the abandoned stadium's demolition partly because it was where her parents had met and fallen in love. "If it weren't for Briggs Stadium," she often said, "I wouldn't be here."

In 1988, when the committee of Tiger Stadium Fan Club members led by Michael P. Gruber nominated Tiger Stadium for inclusion on the National Register of Historic Places, they decided to emphasize not only the stadium's architectural significance and its role in the history of sport, but also its social history: its role in the ethnic, racial, and cultural life of the city. The ballpark eventually known as Tiger Stadium, they asserted, was a significant historic site because of what happened in the stands as well as on the field. The stadium was related to the city every bit as much by the social forces influencing Detroit life as by the streets circumscribing its design. Its myriad connections to the physical and social landscape created a distinctively recognizable urban space.

The urban philosopher Lewis Mumford describes the "social drama" that happens in urban spaces and defines the city as "a geographic plexus, an economic organization, an institutional process, a theater of social action, and an aesthetic symbol of collective unity." He adds, "It is in the city, the city as theater, that man's more purposive activities are focused, and work out, through conflicting and cooperating personalities, events, groups, into more significant culminations."[1] For more than a century, the "social action" of Detroit life in all of its complexity played out on the property at the corner of Michigan and Trumbull Avenues.

And it was drama, not light entertainment; the "significant culminations" were not always as inclusive as those experienced by Darin, Navarro, Rashid, and Watson. The stadium is often popularly regarded as a "symbol of collective unity," and many happy, even magical moments happened there, but so did moments of individual and collective madness. In its design, this ballpark was among the most democratic professional sports venues, with plenty of affordable seats throughout the stadium, and so it provided opportunities for negotiating the conflicts present in the rest of the society. Racial segregation was practiced, confronted, and at least to some extent overcome on the field and in the stands. Of necessity, members of different economic classes came into close contact at the ballpark, although it was not entirely free of barriers. (Occupants of the bleachers, in particular, were prevented from roaming to the rest of the ballpark.) Other conflicts were merely personal. Before management watered down the beer sold to the patrons—and raised its price—there were many more fights between fans than among players. The ballpark's magic did not immunize it from the perverse behavior often displayed by people in crowds; fans were as capable of pummeling as of embracing, as capable of forcing St. Louis Cardinal Ducky Medwick into the dugout after pelting him with trash in the 1934 World Series as of coaxing Mark Fidrych from the dugout for a curtain call during their memorable 1976 love-in with him. The fans demanded attention, sometimes vying for it with the players, as in the 1980s when people in both the upper and lower decks simultaneously performed the Wave, a collective activity perfected in Tiger Stadium because of the ballpark's full double-decking. "Detroit fans," wrote Roger Angell in 1984, "certainly know how to express themselves."[2] Streakers, strippers, trippers, tipplers, brawlers, preachers, huggers, hucksters, and wavers all played their part in a long-running and multifaceted "social drama."

But what impact, finally, did Tiger Stadium and the game that was played there have on the community? There is a popular notion that the undeniably wonderful 1968 baseball season—featuring an integrated group of players engaging in miraculous comebacks cheered on by racially diverse crowds, culminating in a joyous celebration of collective unity after a miraculous, come-from-behind World Series victory—brought healing to a city torn apart by the racial and economic distress leading to the insurrection of 1967. Although this enchanting narrative is still often repeated in and around our city, the following decades proved it more a temporary illusion than a lasting reality. After 1968, metro Detroit continued year after year to become increasingly segregated by race and class, unaffected by what happened in and around Tiger Stadium in that fantastic season. The narrative becomes still more complicated when the joyous celebration of 1968 is compared with the mayhem outside Tiger Stadium that followed the team's 1984 World Series victory when the celebration turned ugly, destructive, and violent.[3] Perhaps what happened inside Tiger Stadium, a structure distinctively isolated from its surroundings, had little connection with life beyond its great gray walls.

Nevertheless, to those who experienced them, the wonders of 1968—like the experiences of Darin, Navarro, Rashid, and Watson—show that society's shortcomings can be at least temporarily addressed if people share common ground and a collective unifying goal, even if it is just a "dramatic" diversion. Detroit baseball fans and others so often point to 1968 not because it really changed anything, but because it inspired a vision of a more harmonious society. The ballpark's distinctive design focused our attention not just on the field but on one another. As we grew further apart, as metropolitan Detroit was spreading out, as its residents increasingly chose single-family over multiple-unit dwellings and private transportation over public, as gated communities proliferated and social and economic barriers became more formidable, Tiger Stadium continued to bring us together and became by default one of the metropolitan area's last remaining pieces of common ground. Over the years, as the stadium expanded, its architects and engineers had figured out how to jam 53,000 fans and a baseball field onto slightly more than eight-and-a-half acres. In this gritty urban space, in its crammed seats and crowded concourses, close encounters with "the other" were inevitable. In the resulting drama, we were all players. We had to be.

But no longer. The owners of professional sports franchises seek to increase their profits by creating exclusive seating in luxury boxes and club sections, explicitly separating customers by class, and patrons in these sections have more amenities and eat different food. Moreover, the owners prefer to have fewer cheap seats—if they can still be called "cheap" at $18–$23 each. Comerica Park has fewer than half as many bleacher seats as did Tiger Stadium and holds 11,000 fewer people overall, yet it takes up considerably more space, just over 12 acres.[4] John Pastier has determined that when expanded in 1938, Briggs Stadium had 6,308 seats per acre; when opened in 2000, Comerica Park had 3,307 seats per acre. This is not just a matter of roomier seating areas. By eliminating view-obstructing posts—which in Tiger Stadium allowed the upper deck to sit directly on top of the lower deck—and by limiting outfield seating, contemporary baseball stadiums like Comerica Park necessarily have larger footprints and necessarily create upper decks much further removed from the action. The back row of Tiger Stadium's upper deck was as close to the field as the front row of the upper decks in most stadiums built in the last 40 years. With its extra space and many distractions such as a merry-go-round, Comerica Park diverts attention from the game. Tiger Stadium was essentially a different space, promoting a very different collective experience that was focused on the game itself rather than on revenue-producing gimmickry.

This book concentrates primarily not on the amazing exploits of colorful and talented athletes but more pointedly on the people who cheered and booed them and on the increasingly devastated city that fewer and fewer of them called home. In his retelling of the stadium's history, "A Century on Common Ground," Michael Betzold leads off Part I: History and Background, demonstrating how the different Detroit Tigers owners represented the changing economics of the city, its graduation from a light to a heavy industrial economy and eventually to the low end of the service economy. From small businessmen to a powerful industrialist to a media mogul to pizza purveyors, the successive Tigers owners reflected the city's changing conditions. Their interests, priorities, and prejudices reflected those of the larger culture. The blatant racism of Walter Briggs, Sr., determined who could play on his teams, yet he never asked the public to pay for his place of business. Mike Ilitch is clearly much more open to a diverse group of players and fans, yet he has priced most African American Detroiters out of the game, even though as taxpayers they have subsidized his stadium and other enterprises. The owners' values affected the design, construction, modification, and ultimate abandonment of Tiger Stadium.

Often overlooked in the Tiger Stadium story is the effect of the stadium's attributes on the game of football. In "Detroit Lions Roar at Briggs Stadium," Bill Dow argues that while not often regarded as an ideal venue, Tiger Stadium lent a distinctive quality to that sport's experience in its 36 years as Detroit's home for professional football.

John Pastier, with the help of John Davids's drawings, illustrates this evolution over time, its effect on the game and on the experience of those in the stands, in "Longevity and Adaptability: Tiger Stadium's Evolution, Architecture, Functionality, Structure and Urban Context." Pastier and Davids uncover little-known and hitherto unpublished aspects of the stadium's development and design. In addition, Pastier emphasizes Tiger Stadium's proximity to the city's center; it was the closest to its home city's downtown of all the historic ballparks. In its design and location, Tiger Stadium was both hospitable and accessible. Davids's drawings graphically document the organic transformation of the ballpark over nearly 90 years, from initial construction through two major periods of expansion. The stadium's development reflects both Detroit's population explosion in the 20th century and baseball's increasing popularity. Significantly, the changes in the 1930s produced the largest bleacher seating section of any major league ballpark, directly reflecting the growth of the city's working middle class, which, in turn, was caused largely by the automotive industry's growth. The drawings reveal interesting details of the temporary facilities built in 1934 and 1935 to meet the rapidly increasing demand to see one of baseball's most dynamic back-to-back pennant winners—the latter of which also captured the World Series—as well as one small change made to protect the future of the Tigers' first bonus baby, Al Kaline. The Cochrane Plan demonstrates what could have been the ballpark's third major expansion and remodeling. This proposal was drawn up in close collaboration with the members of the Tiger Stadium Fan Club and expressed their desire to maintain (and improve where possible) the distinctively intimate character and seating proximity of the old stadium while providing the modern amenities the ball club sought in a new structure. It proved that both goals were achievable, showing one more time the remarkable flexibility and adaptability of one of America's great ballparks.

Honoring the prolonged and sometimes bitter stadium fight and the editors' heavy involvement in that struggle, we include four essays emphasizing different aspects of the issue. Neil deMause, in "The Mallparking of America: Tiger Stadium and the Subsidy Game," puts the issue in a national context, showing how the availability of public money after the 1960s affected the design and funding of major league baseball stadiums leading up to the Tigers' decision to replace Tiger Stadium. In "Losing Tiger Stadium, 1987–1997," Frank Rashid examines the issue in its unique local circumstances, relating it to other attempts to redevelop Detroit in response to the city's loss of its industry and population in the decades following World War II and detailing the efforts of the Tiger Stadium Fan Club (TSFC) to persuade the Tigers to stay in Tiger Stadium. In "The Battle for Sacred Ground, 1998–2011," Rebecca Long discusses the efforts of several groups to redevelop and/or reuse all or part of Tiger Stadium after the Detroit Tigers abandoned the ballpark. Long details several proposals developed in response to the City of Detroit Requests for Proposals that ended up thwarted by the Mayor's Office or the Detroit Economic Growth Corporation. Noteworthy in her work are the efforts of Peter Comstock Riley, the Old Tiger Stadium Conservancy, and the Navin Field Grounds Crew. Her essay ends with a 2016 postscript by Michael Betzold.

Part II: Memories, edited by Bill Dow, focuses on the testimony of those who cheered, played, and worked at Tiger Stadium. Dow's "Tiger Stadium Souvenirs" covers key moments in baseball and football from the 1930s to the 1980s. In "Tiger Stadium in Literature," Michael P. Gruber examines the portrayal of the ballpark in poems and stories, most of which reflect the "social drama" played out in the stands. "Tiger Stadium Memories and Stories" is composed of short pieces based on interviews Dow conducted with fans, players, broadcasters, vendors, and others. "The Biggest House in the Neighborhood:

Living Near Tiger Stadium" consists of responses by longtime Corktown residents to Frank Rashid's questions about life near a major league baseball stadium. Three pieces—one each by a journalist, a well-known Tiger fan, and a player—follow. In "The Stadium: An Essay in Memory of George Cantor," Tom DeLisle writes of his sense of loss after Tiger Stadium was abandoned and then destroyed. In "For Love of the Game," Karen Elizabeth Bush, known to many Tigers fans as "The Lady in Blue," offers reflections based on decades of experience at Michigan and Trumbull. The section's closing essay, fittingly written by former Tiger closer Todd Jones, reveals the interaction between fans and players and the effect of the stadium's closing on the Tigers themselves.

In many ways, this book is an elegy. It pays tribute to and mourns the loss of a significant place and time. Its editors and most of its contributors are unabashed Tiger Stadium fans who fought to keep it as the home of the Detroit Tigers or save it from destruction once the franchise abandoned it. The book's concluding pieces by TSFC members Kim Stroud, Judy Davids, and John Davids, and a poem by Jim Daniels, the ballpark's most prolific poet, reflect our desire to draw some understanding from what is for us a sad, even tragic story. We therefore conclude if not with hope at least with solace. As we completed this work, we still occupied this common ground where memories of Mr. Greenberg and Stormin' Norman mingle with those of our parents and friends, even with the ashes of those who fought by our side.

View from the upper deck along the third base side looking towards right field, late September 1999 (© Rebecca Cook).

6 Introduction

NOTES

1. Lewis Mumford, "What Is a City?" *Architectural Record* 82 (1937) rpt. *The City Reader*, eds. Richard T. LeGates and Frederick Stout (New York: Routledge, 1996), 185.

2. Roger Angell, "Tiger, Tiger," *The New Yorker* (December 3, 1984), 97. Angell adds:

> Over the summer, the turned-on Tiger-made throngs evolved simultaneous clockwise and counter-clockwise Waves in the upper and lower decks, which then somehow reversed themselves. Sometimes there came a funny, slow-motion Wave in the center field bleachers (always a place of great humor and invention this summer), which would be succeeded by a right-to-left sprint Wave that could circle the stadium (I checked it) in 27 seconds flat. There was also the foolish, comical business of the two bleacher sectors' yelling a beer commercial back and forth ("TASTES GREAT!" from one side, and then "LESS FILLING" from the other) while brandishing fingers and programs at each other.

3. This 1984 mayhem, often erroneously considered an instance of "Detroit" violence, should be seen in context. Few of its participants lived in the city. Many in the crowd were attracted by the rare occurrence of three consecutive celebrations (for the division championship, the American League pennant, and the World Series), each more raucous than the next, for sports victories all happening in the home city. When victories take place on the road, the celebrations tend to be spread out and less intense. When at home, the celebratory activity concentrates around the stadium.

4. As John Pastier and John Davids have discovered, the exact acreage of the stadium sites can be measured in different ways. Nevertheless, all else being equal, Comerica Park, which holds 11,000 fewer people than did Tiger Stadium, takes up about 30 percent more space.

PART I. HISTORY AND BACKGROUND

A Century on Common Ground I
Bennett Park and Navin Field

MICHAEL BETZOLD

Full Circle

They appear in the spring, with lawn tractors, rakes, and shovels. They cut the grass, pull the weeds, and smooth the lumpy infield dirt.

Afterwards, they play a little pickup ball. A first baseman stands where Norm Cash once clowned, a shortstop crouches where Billy Rogell once roamed, a batter imitates Mickey Tettleton's statue-still stance, a prankster slides into third, imaginary spikes high, like a man named Cobb.

Folks driving by on Michigan Avenue stop to snap pictures. Sometimes they pull a mitt out of their trunk and join in the game.

They keep coming all summer, despite Detroit cops who sometimes chase the grounds crew and players off what is still city property—even though the city stopped tending it more than a decade earlier.

It is just a game. No one is making money. Nothing is at stake. And the stadium itself is gone to dust. But this is a fitting activity for this patch of ground where professional baseball was played for 104 summers—longer than anywhere else in the country.

The tract of land started as a gathering place for common people and eventually became one of *the* gathering places for common people—one of the premier proletarian baseball stadiums in the land—though while it operated, few, even in Detroit, recognized it as such. Now the cobbled-together structure that lured well over a hundred million fans is a heap of history, the grandeur of the glory days just a memory. But some folks still like to play catch with the ghosts here and lay claim to it again.

In the small city of Detroit, the first recorded baseball game, between two local gentlemen's clubs, took place in the summer of 1859.[1] From its disparate origins as a descendant of the British game of rounders and other similar pastimes, the game of baseball as we recognize it was from the start an urban phenomenon. Research is continually unearthing earlier mentions of the game. In 1791, a bylaw in Pittsfield, Massachusetts, regulated where baseball could be played in the town square.[2] Newspaper articles in 1823 detailed an organized form of the game played in Manhattan.[3] The first known baseball club was founded in New York in 1837, two years before baseball's phony creation myth put Abner Doubleday in Cooperstown, and eight years before Alexander Cartwright, a

Manhattan bank clerk and volunteer fireman, supervised what was until recently thought to be the first game in the Elysian Fields in Hoboken, New Jersey.[4] Thus, though its mythology casts baseball as a pastoral pursuit, by birth it is a city game. These days, it is at home in towns big and small across North America and, increasingly, on both American continents, Asian islands, and even, via reverse migration, some places in Europe.

The Civil War was a major impetus for baseball's becoming the national pastime. As the conflict was tearing the nation apart, a game was uniting all corners of the country. Soldiers on each side often played ball, and the sport's popularity spread far and wide after the troops returned to their hometowns.

In its early days baseball was strictly a gentleman's hobby, with local clubs playing by regional rules. After the Cincinnati Red Stockings turned into a professional squad and the National Association was formed in 1871, followed five years later by the National League (NL), the paid players, to the chagrin of the sport's original purists, gradually supplanted the amateurs in most towns as the objects of spectators' fervent attention. And Detroit was no different.

Detroit's National League club, the Wolverines, took up play in 1881, replacing, of all clubs, the pioneering squad in Cincinnati, which had temporarily folded. The Wolverines played at Recreation Park on what was then the northeast edge of town and in 1887 won the league championship; two years later, however, the franchise moved to Cleveland.[5] Still, interest in baseball remained high in Detroit, by then a major stove-manufacturing city. In 1894, a city team joined the Western League, a "minor league" professional association. The new club played its first two seasons at the small eastside Boulevard Park while seeking a plot of land for a bigger venue.[6]

By the mid–1890s, the northwest corner of Michigan and Trumbull was a well-known site in Detroit. Originally the land there was part of the Navarre Farm, the first plot deeded to the west of Fort Pontchartrain, the stronghold French settlers had built in founding the city in 1701. The farm eventually passed to William Woodbridge, a judge and Michigan governor. After the city annexed it over Woodbridge's objections, he divided it into plots that in subsequent years became the homes of Irish immigrants from County Cork in a neighborhood that naturally came to be known as Corktown. The old Sauk Trail that followed a native pathway from Detroit to Chicago became Michigan Avenue, and Woodbridge named an intersecting road after his famous father-in-law, poet John Trumbull. Woodbridge kept a grove on the northwest corner of the two streets at Michigan and Trumbull and deeded it to his heirs. By the time baseball was first played in Detroit at the end of the 1850s, the beautiful wooded spot, with its tall trees, had already become a popular picnic ground on the edge of the city. In 1875, Woodbridge's son Dudley leased the grove to the city, which cut down the trees in the first of many changes that some viewed as desecrations and others as improvements. This transformed the grounds into a farmers' wood and hay market that came to be known as Western Market.[7] Its counterpart across town, Eastern Market, would later become and remain to this day the city's landmark farmers' market, while Western Market would move a few blocks north to make way for a different type of commerce and community activity.

Over the winter of 1895–1896, the Detroit baseball club's owner, George Vanderbeck, spent $10,000[8] to build a ballpark on the site of the old Woodbridge grove on the northwest corner of Michigan and Trumbull.

Philadelphia Athletics vs. Detroit Tigers, Bennett Park, May 21, 1911 (Ernie Harwell Sports Collection, courtesy Burton Historical Collection, Detroit Public Library).

Bennett Park

Beginnings

By the opening day of the season in the spring of 1896, Vanderbeck had constructed a large L-shaped wooden grandstand with an unusual peaked roof behind home plate and along the third-base line. A vast improvement in size and amenities over the club's eastside fields, Vanderbeck's park marked a solid commitment from the Detroit club to become a permanent fixture in the rapidly expanding ranks of professional baseball. The game would be played on the site for the next 104 summers, still to date the longest period of continuous occupancy for baseball, and one of the longest in the world for any sport.

Vanderbeck's low-budget park was not envisioned to be anywhere near so long-lived. The grounds were fashioned hastily by covering the cobblestones of the old hay market with a thin layer of topsoil and then putting down a bit of sod in the outfield. This seat-of-the-pants landscaping produced a treacherous playing surface that degraded the games; cobblestones often resurfaced in the infield, making routine ground balls take perilous bounces. No field of that era was very well groomed, but the home of the Detroit club was notoriously rocky and rough, especially in its first seasons. After even moderate rainfalls the outfield was marshy; no provisions had been made to drain it.

The stands were ramshackle, in particular a set of bleachers that ran down the first base line along Trumbull and brought the park's overall capacity to around 5,000.[9] The playing field's orientation was a major miscalculation. Home plate was planted near the corner of Michigan and Trumbull, facing roughly northwest. In that era, professional games were always played in the mid-to-late afternoon. Batters stared into the blazing summer sun as it made its descent from zenith to horizon, making it sometimes difficult to see the pitches.

Originally the park was called Woodbridge Grove or the Haymarket. But from the very first game at the field on April 28, 1896—when Detroit routed the visiting Columbus Senators, 17–2—and every year thereafter until his death in 1927, Charlie Bennett caught the first pitch of each season at Michigan and Trumbull. The catcher on the Wolverines' National League teams of the 1880s, Bennett had lost his legs in a train accident in 1894 and afterwards became a living symbol of the spirit of competition, one of the city's biggest sports legends. In tribute, the field became known as Bennett Park.

Bennett Park's outfield fences were roughly 300 feet down the left field line, 400 feet to center, and 360 feet down the right field line.[10] Overflow crowds were allowed to park themselves in front of those barriers when the stands were full for big games. While the seats inside the fences were only sometimes filled to capacity, "wildcat bleachers" soon sprang up in the alley behind the homes along National Street, which ran north from Michigan, a block west of Trumbull.[11] Seats in the upper rows of the tall, rickety structures afforded good if somewhat precarious views of the game over the left field fence. Homeowners charged from five to 15 cents for those outlaw seats in the first of many decades' worth of independent entrepreneurial schemes in the neighborhood that sought to profit from the baseball venue in its midst.[12] And the wildcat bleachers were an early example of what would be another long-lived conflict, common in many cities: the struggle between the ball club and those outside the park who capitalized on its activity without club authorization.

It was not just that the homeowners were taking revenue from the ball club by selling their own seats; their patrons were also having a deleterious effect on the game. Despite years of effort, the ball club could not control the drunken and vocal crowds outside the fence. Soon raucous fans filled other wildcat bleachers along Cherry Street in right field, in front of a lumber mill.

The club made repeated efforts to thwart the wildcatters, including hanging canvas strips to impede their view, but that only enraged the rowdy fans more. They would often hurl vegetables and fruit at the players from behind the ribbons of canvas. This, too, would presage incidents of fan interference in games in Detroit decades in the future.[13]

Wildcat stands overlooking left field in Bennett Park in about 1909 or 1910 (Ernie Harwell Sports Collection, courtesy Burton Historical Collection, Detroit Public Library).

New Major League Franchise

By the 1890s, baseball had acquired a well-deserved reputation as a rough-and-tumble, even mercenary game; it was certainly no longer the province of gentlemen. The sport's crass culture was epitomized by the Baltimore Orioles, especially its third baseman, John McGraw, who lorded over a slashing, no-holds-barred style of play. (Baltimore's star shortstop was Hughie Jennings, who would be the manager of the Detroit teams from 1907 through 1920.) Through this part of the professional era until the 1920s, quite a few baseball players associated with gamblers and other unsavory characters.

Despite the sport's reputation, it attracted patrons of all classes and both genders. Baseball was rapidly increasing in popularity nationwide. In 1900, the Western League was renamed the American League (AL), and its president, the shrewd and ambitious Ban Johnson, began bidding to challenge the hegemony of the long-established National League.

Detroit was one of the American League's eight charter franchises. Even though its market size was well below league average, its 146,000 season attendance was third highest in the league in 1900. The next year, Johnson worked out a deal to make the upstart American League officially a major league, on paper (if not yet in reputation or stature) the coequal of the National League. This act marks the beginning of what is known as the modern era in baseball. In response to its ascendancy to the big leagues, Detroit's club added two short sets of bleachers in left and right fields, bringing the capacity to 8,500.[14] Of the 11 cities with major league teams in 1901, Detroit, with a population of 286,000, was slightly larger than only two others—Milwaukee and Washington, D.C.—and smaller than three others without any club: Buffalo, San Francisco, and New Orleans.

By the time they started playing at Bennett Park, the Detroit club had become known as the Tigers, named after the famed Michigan Light Guard infantry unit whose armory was in the city. At times, the players even wore orange-and-white socks. When the Tigers took the field for their inaugural home game on April 20, 1901, it would be the start of 99 consecutive major league seasons for the club at the same location. For the opener, the stands were filled, as were the "official" bleachers and the wildcat bleachers, and an overflow crowd of more than a thousand stood in the far reaches of the outfield, behind ropes. Attendance was announced at 10,023.[15]

The first major league home game for the Tigers is still unique in major league history, and the fans played a large part in the remarkable result. With the home team committing a horrible seven errors and being embarrassed by the visiting Milwaukee Brewers, many fans in the stands left early. But the patrons standing in the outfield had no egress until the game was over. The Tigers came to bat in the bottom of the ninth inning trailing 13–4. The team then staged the greatest last-at-bat rally that would ever occur in major league baseball.[16] As the crowd in the outfield, though somewhat restrained by the ropes, surged forward, the Tigers hit ball after ball into the standing fans, and all such drives were ruled doubles. The Tigers ended up winning 14–13, with the crowning blow being a bases-loaded pop-up down the foul line that landed a few feet fair in the encroaching crowd. It was the first, and certainly the most improbable, of many game-winning rallies at the corner of Michigan and Trumbull. In the next two days, more eighth- and ninth-inning rallies secured wins for the upstart Tigers, who, buoyed by this phenomenal opening series, surged to a 14–4 start before later falling back to earth and out of first place for good.

The parks of this era were wooden and susceptible to combustion, and several suffered fire damage or even burned down altogether. In this respect, Bennett Park, though a largely wooden structure, was lucky: it never was harmed by flames.

The stands were usually packed with men getting out of work, and the crowds grew gradually as late afternoon games progressed. Until 1910, Detroit had blue laws that banned Sunday baseball, so Tiger home games on the Christian Sabbath were played just outside the southwest city limits near the city's stockyards at Burns Park, which was named after sheriff, hotel owner, and club president James D. Burns.

Manager George Stallings frequently feuded with Burns during that first season of 1901, and league boss Johnson, flexing his autocratic powers, booted them both out of his enterprise. The Tigers became the property of Samuel Angus, a successful local insurance agent, who immediately made his presence felt: he built a new clubhouse for the 1902 season and moved the box seats to the rear of the grandstand in a sort of precursor to suite seating.

Despite these improvements, in 1902 attendance plummeted by nearly 30 percent, and Johnson almost moved the club to Pittsburgh. But he was blocked by the National League, which did not want a team competing against its franchise in that city.[17]

After the 1903 season, Angus sold his interest in the ball club to Michigan lumber magnate William C. Yawkey, the state's richest businessman. The sale brought into the picture another man, Frank Navin, who would control the Tigers for more than 30 years.

Two Men of Their Times

Navin, born in Adrian, Michigan, was the son of Irish immigrant farmers. Like his older brother Thomas Jr., who was eventually imprisoned for embezzlement, Navin earned a law degree in Detroit.[18] But he abandoned his interest in the legal profession after failing in a campaign to be elected justice of the peace. He turned next to selling insurance and soon started keeping accounts for Angus. Thus, when Angus acquired the Tigers, Navin, known for his attention to detail, became the club's business manager. It was not long before he assumed day-to-day control of the club because Angus was too preoccupied with other endeavors. After acquiring the Tigers, Yawkey insisted that Navin be put in charge of the club's business affairs. After Yawkey died suddenly, his playboy son William H. inherited the club, but he had even less interest in baseball. (William H.'s nephew Thomas A. did, however; he eventually became the owner of the Boston Red Sox.) Under the younger Yawkey, Navin exercised even more control of the club, becoming the *de facto* club president.

It took three lean years for Navin to build up the franchise. At first, he maintained a hard line financially, skimping on player contracts and frills and selling increasing amounts of space on outfield fences for advertising over the objections of players who claimed the signs distracted them. Then he began to assemble a winning team, learning about baseball talent as he went along in a rather hit-and-miss fashion. His smart moves included poaching from the National League both pitcher Wild Bill Donovan and outfielder Wahoo Sam Crawford, a power hitter who led the league in triples six times (and still holds the all-time record for three-baggers, with 309); in those days, with distant outfield fences in most parks, triples were more common than home runs and were the hallmark of a power hitter. But on the opposite side of the ledger, Navin sold pitcher Carl Hubbell, a future Hall of Famer, to the Giants and refused to sign a young player named Walter Johnson, who would go on to join the Washington Senators and become arguably the best pitcher in baseball history. And it took his team's manager to persuade the stubborn Navin to sign crowd-pleasing shortstop Germany Schaefer in 1904. (Schaefer at least once stole second base, then first base, just to rattle the pitcher, thus giving rise to a rule barring players from running the bases backwards so as not to make a "travesty" of the game.)[19] Then, in August 1905, the Augusta, Georgia, minor league club owed the Tigers a player to complete a deal. Navin wanted catcher Clyde Engel, but manager Bill Armour talked him into selecting an unheralded prospect instead. This outfielder would change Detroit baseball forever.

Tyrus Raymond Cobb joined a struggling team, and from the first game lit a fire under it with his all-out, no-holds-barred style of play. The 19-year-old from Georgia played ball like a man possessed—and indeed he was. A mere week before he was called up from the Augusta club, he had suffered an unimaginable personal tragedy when his mother shot his father to death while he was climbing a ladder into her bedroom window to try to catch her in an adulterous embrace with another man. Cobb's devils can be traced to his stormy relationship with his autocratic father, who wanted him to be a respectable man—a lawyer, or a doctor like himself. Cobb had plenty to prove on the baseball diamond, and he played the game with a relentless determination that bordered on a pathological will to win by whatever means necessary. His tactics of intimidation were legendary, as was his mastery of the tactics necessary to enhance his growing reputation as a player to be feared. Cobb allowed the story to spread that he sharpened his spikes before each game; it was at the most an exaggeration and probably an outright falsehood. He habitually slid into bases spikes high, and he was so fast and reckless that his mere presence on the basepaths caused havoc, for he was ready and willing to steal second, third, or home on any occasion. During his long career, he set many records that lasted for 50 or more years, and some have never been eclipsed—most notably his .366 lifetime batting average and his 54 steals of home.[20] When he retired, he was widely considered to be the best all-around player the game had ever seen, for (although some available records indicate otherwise) his defense in center field was considered as daring, spectacular, cunning, and effective as his offensive skills.

Cobb's latter-day reputation for dastardly play and personal amorality is somewhat overblown: he was not the only racist to play the game in that era and not by a long shot the sport's only megalomaniacal personality.[21] During his time with the Tigers, in fact, he was a fan favorite; he was a thrilling performer and catapulted the team to the top of the league. His teammates may not all have liked him personally, but they certainly preferred playing with him to playing against him. When, during the 1912 season, he was suspended for attacking a fan in the stands in Philadelphia, the players even went on strike in support of him. Cobb was spectacularly self-absorbed and driven by demons, but he epitomized the way the game was played during the so-called Deadball Era.

Cobb arrived during the nadir of the fledgling franchise. From 1904 to 1906, while the rest of the American League was starting to flourish, the Detroit club was drawing well under half of the league's average home attendance. The owners of the Cleveland franchise, who wanted Detroit as their minor league club, waged a new campaign to boot the Tigers out of the league, but Ban Johnson saw that Navin was laying the groundwork to turn things around in Detroit, so he stayed the course.

The winter of 1906–1907 was a real turning point. Navin shrewdly snatched player-manager Hughie Jennings from Baltimore and used Yawkey's money to buy property along Cherry Street, north of the park's right field wall, raze the lumber mill there, and move those fences back to create more on-field standing room for overflow crowds.

From then on, the extra room would be much needed. While Jennings brayed "Ee-yah!" like a mule from the third base coach's box and Schaefer entertained with his antics, Cobb and Crawford put on a speed-and-power show, and the Tigers won the American League championship in 1907, with Cobb leading the league with a .350 batting average and attendance finally topping the 1901 high-water mark. Temporary bleachers were set up in the outfield for the World Series, but the Tigers were swept by the powerful Chicago Cubs. An embarrassingly small crowd of 7,370 showed up to watch Detroit lose the last game.

Nevertheless, Navin was optimistic about the club he increasingly controlled. For the 1908 season, Bennett Park was expanded to seat 10,500.[22] Navin could afford to do so because he continued to pinch pennies on player salaries, with Cobb and Crawford getting only $8,000 combined for the year. He also continued to buy up stock, and during 1908, became nearly a half-owner, according to some accounts by winning the pot in a poker game against Yawkey. The Tigers captured the league pennant again in 1908, with attendance rising by 150 percent over 1906 (helped by an expanded site and a 24 percent seating expansion), and again were beaten by the Cubs in the World Series. The Detroit club had gone from moribund to center stage, and by winning the pennant for a third time in 1909, it accomplished a trifecta that would be matched only by two American League clubs—the Athletics and the Orioles—in the next 100-plus years and exceeded

The original caption from an unknown source reads: "Bennett Park from the grandstand. This picture was taken in the seventh inning of the final game of the New York series, with Crawford at bat. It was just after Cobb had made his steal of home with Sweeney holding the ball." The date was May 12, 1911 (Ernie Harwell Sports Collection, courtesy Burton Historical Collection, Detroit Public Library).

for sustained dominance only by the Yankees. In 1909, baseball's two greatest stars, Cobb and Pittsburgh's Honus Wagner, faced off against each other in the World Series; Pittsburgh prevailed, but somehow an average of nearly 16,000 paying customers packed into Bennett Park for Detroit's four home games.

Yet another expansion for the 1910 season increased seating by 33 percent to 14,000.[23] But the three single-deck covered grandstands and a small set of bleachers in the right field corner were beginning to strain the capacity of the 5.5-acre site.[24] Navin's plans for still further expansion the next winter were blocked by property owners along Cherry Street.

Attendance reflected the increasing enthusiasm for the new powerhouse Tigers, who had become a source of civic pride. After drawing 259,000 fans in their inaugural 1901 season, they lagged far below the league average and did not admit a quarter-million again until 1907. But with their league championships, they started drawing more than double the crowds compared to their pre-title years. In 1909 and 1911, they came close to a half-million tickets sold and finally exceeded the league's average attendance, even while remaining one of the smallest cities in the majors.

The Tigers were now poised for a breakthrough. In the person of Cobb, they had arguably the game's most exciting player, and the club he led was a perennial contender. Imagine what he could have done while batting at home with the sun never in his eyes. It was time to fix the home grounds' unfortunate field orientation and join the stampede of ball clubs that were building modern urban sports palaces. Starting in 1909, imposing concrete-and-steel structures were replacing wooden ballparks in Philadelphia, Pittsburgh, Cleveland, St. Louis, New York, Boston, Cincinnati, Chicago, and Washington. Now, Detroit itself was ready for such a change: Henry Ford's revolutionary innovations—the assembly line and, later, the $5-a-day wage—would fuel the incredible boom that would over the course of three decades expand Detroit from a small but bustling stove-manufacturing city of 286,000 in 1900 to an exploding metropolis of 1.6 million that would be the world capital of automobile production. Detroit needed a new ballpark that would match its competitors' and fit its stature and that of its baseball club. Fortunately, the right man stood at the helm of the Tigers: Frank Navin.

Navin Field

The Old Stone Face

"Old Stone Face" was one of the nicknames that the Tiger players liked to call owner Frank Navin. It acknowledged his customarily stoic demeanor and seemingly inflexible personality, on display annually in contract negotiations and in many of his dealings with the public. The sobriquet was to prove to be emblematic. The facade he left as his legacy—the back wall of the sturdy concrete-and-steel grandstands at the corner of Michigan and National—would stand for nearly a century as the implacable face of Tiger baseball.

By pinching pennies on player contracts and frills (among other things, making the Tigers buy their own uniforms), and by assembling a winning team through trial and error and shrewd deals, Navin had turned around a franchise that had in its early years been the subject of frequent threats to be moved to a different town. After the three consecutive pennants catapulted it to the front ranks of the American League, the franchise's value was estimated at $650,000. Navin invested his hard-won profits in a new ballpark built between the 1911 and 1912 seasons by the Osborn Engineering Company of Cleveland. Osborn was the dominant design firm during the era's ballpark boom and into the 1950s. The new park's general contractor, Hunkin and Conkey, was also based in Cleveland.

The cornerstone of Navin's plan was reorienting the diamond to place home plate in the southwest rather than the northwest corner of the property so that the batters would no longer be squinting into the late-afternoon summer sun. All else flowed from this practical decision that eliminated Bennett Park's most obvious design flaw. The new grandstands would, naturally, embrace the new configuration of the ballfield. The club also expanded its grounds to nearly 6.7 acres by finally buying out the Cherry Street lumber yard proprietors and National Street homeowners who had benefited from the wildcat bleachers on their properties. The acquisition of that land allowed more room for the construction of an impressive grandstand behind the new home plate near the corner of Michigan and National. The extra property along National provided room for the spacious grandstand and its concourse, while still leaving a generous distance from home plate to the new right field fence along Trumbull Avenue. The new stadium, like Fenway Park in Boston, Ebbets Field in Brooklyn, and others erected in urban neighborhoods in the era, had to fit into the confines of existing street patterns, though in Detroit these constraints were not daunting. With Detroit booming, no longer was Michigan and Trumbull at the edge of the city: it was in the middle of the thriving Corktown neighborhood just a mile or so from a growing downtown.

The price of the new construction was $300,000, and not one cent of taxpayer money went into it. No one at the time believed that a baseball stadium was anything but a private business venue that should be paid for entirely by the club owners. Yawkey and Navin sought nothing from the city or its citizens except a little more room to grow.

The new single-deck grandstand was deep and had ample seating. It cradled the infield in a close embrace that extended down both foul lines past first and third base. Well-built, sturdy, and spacious, it would outlast the life spans of Cobb and his legions of fans by many decades; in fact, it would continue to stand after the start of the following century, a long lifetime in the future. Along with roofed pavilions that extended further down the lines, the new construction increased the capacity of the Tigers' home to a comfortable 23,000.

With Charlie Bennett still being a fixture on Opening Day each season, many traditionalists wanted to keep the name Bennett Park, but the park was fittingly renamed Navin Field. After all, nothing remained of the old, ill-sited wooden ballpark that had awkwardly birthed one of the American League's charter franchises. The main entrance to the field, however, remained at Michigan and Trumbull, the corner still marking the club's street address and the location of its detached office building and ticket office, because there was much more room there than at Michigan and National. But that main gate along Trumbull was now located near the grounds' right field corner. The new entrance behind home plate was smaller and much less grand.[25]

Inside the stadium, the seats were at first painted yellow and the fences gray. The customary advertisements covered the outfield fences, and left field featured a large scoreboard with room for out-of-town scores, quite an innovation at the time. Center field provided another welcome feature: a large green wall to provide a good visual background for hitters.[26] With fences that were 340 and 365 feet down the lines and about 465 feet to center, one might think that this was a pitcher's park.[27] But with power alleys about 360 feet deep, temporary bleachers encroaching upon both sides of the outfield at various times, its great hitters' background, and a well-manicured outfield, this was a park better suited for offense than Bennett Park had been, and it would become even more so in subsequent reincarnations until its dying days: a great hitters' park though far from a bandbox.

Opening Day of the 1912 season was scheduled to be Thursday, April 18. But it rained, and the game was postponed. Navin was superstitious and did not want to christen the stadium on a Friday. So the opener was delayed until April 20, and that became significant years later, because it was the very same day the Red Sox played their first game at the new Fenway Park. (After the earlier parks of that era were demolished, the two stadiums in Boston and Detroit would stand for years, tied in a dead heat for the honor of oldest venue in baseball.)

Civic leaders, members of the visiting Indians and the Tigers, and hundreds of fans paraded from downtown to the stadium, led by a marching band. Charlie Bennett caught the ceremonial 3 p.m. first pitch. And, fittingly, the first run was scored when Ty Cobb stole home. Cobb, making his mark on the new venue immediately and indelibly, also made two sensational catches in center field. The official attendance was announced at 24,382 as extra fans camped in the deep outfield and in a small set of temporary "circus bleachers" set up in right field. Navin Field, like Bennett Park, saw an auspicious start for its tenants: the home team won, dramatically, in 11 innings.

Cobb's Lake and His Nemesis

With its modern, well-appointed facilities and amenities, Navin Field made Bennett Park look like the poorly disguised old hay market grounds that it was. And, with its new home venue sparkling and solid, Detroit settled in for a long run as a contending if not championship-caliber club. The team played consistently exciting ball, but a pennant eluded the Tigers' grasp year after year, despite the stalwart contributions of Cobb, hailed during much of his career as the greatest offensive force the sport had ever known—at least until Babe Ruth started hitting home runs and stealing his thunder.

If Yankee Stadium was soon to become "the house that Ruth built," Navin Field was the ballpark built for Cobb. Groundskeepers even hosed down the area in front of home plate to create a swamp suitable for his bunts to drown in; it became known as "Cobb's lake." With the stands close to the field, it was easy for fans to see their star's exploits and to hear his opponents' curses in reaction—not to mention Ee-yah Jennings's braying cheers from the third base coach's box.

The new park became the premier gathering place for sports entertainment in the rapidly growing city, which was now swelling with newcomers from the South and from Europe. Year after year they came to work in the new auto factories, grabbing those good-paying $5-a-day low-skilled dream jobs.

Most fans of the time either walked or took trolleys to the games at Michigan and Trumbull. Even so, seeing the handwriting of the future on the wall, some people living in shacks on streets around the ballpark tore them down and rented the vacant lots for parking for the increasing number of fans who drove to the game. Others simply parked fans' cars on their front lawns on game days and charged what the market would bear. Navin had built no public parking of his own; there was no place to do so on his property. But the traffic was coming, since Henry Ford's motorcars were becoming more and more affordable.

Detroit was undergoing incredibly rapid growth and transformation. The city's land area more than quadrupled; apart from the river and lakes that formed the border with Canada to the south and east, there were few if any topographical obstacles to mobility and development, and neighborhoods spawned newer neighborhoods along the major roads laid out like the spokes of a wheel into the hinterlands. The city was alive with immigrants, and though the sport was new to them, many of them took quickly to baseball, which was seen as a badge of Americanization. News of the team's exploits was a prominent feature in all the Detroit papers; the star players became demigods of a sort. The Tigers were a source of civic pride, the club's rise mirroring the ascendancy of the city itself, a new industrial behemoth for a new age, a relative paradise of sorts for a newly created middle class just recently removed from lives of grinding poverty in the South or repression overseas in Europe.

Yet the game still was mired in its unsavory past. Increasingly, gamblers and shady operators mingled with businessmen in the stands, hoping to take advantage of the immigrants and the naïve new fans who mixed with the older, more seasoned spectators. The atmosphere at the ballpark rarely was sedate, and sometimes it turned downright rowdy. One day in 1915, the crowd got so incensed when George Moriarty of the Tigers was called out at home on a game-ending double play and then was spat on during the ensuing brouhaha by Boston's player-manager Bill Carrigan that fans stuck around and formed a kind of lynch mob outside the visitors' clubhouse after the game, and Carrigan had to don a disguise to escape.

The games also customarily included some on-field clowning as part of the entertainment. Tricks and pranks and dirty play were all part of the spectacle; the games were usually quickly played, and they were mesmerizing for fans seated so close to the field that they could see the players scratch and spit, hear them yell and curse, and delight in antics such as the hidden ball trick, bunts, hard slides, steals, and the routine style of roughhouse play that only decades later would come to be sanitized a bit and known generically as "small ball."

Yawkey died in 1918, and Navin finally became a 50 percent owner with the acquisition of the necessary 15 shares from the Yawkey estate. (The Yawkey family never again played a role in running the Tigers, though they continued to be the dominant force in the operations of the Boston Red Sox for decades to come.) Navin remained the club's president, with complete control over club operations, but, in order to keep a strong financial force behind the club, the remaining 50 percent of shares in the franchise were sold to automobile magnates John Kelsey and Walter O. Briggs. Briggs was delighted; he reportedly had been unable to procure a ticket for a 1907 World Series game and had vowed at the time to own the club eventually.

Briggs, a prominent Catholic, was perhaps a factor behind one of the most remarkable events ever held at Michigan and Trumbull. On October 31, 1920, Catholics in Detroit rallied their forces to insure a defeat of a statewide proposal on the ballot two days later that would have amounted to requiring most children to attend public schools, dealing a death blow to parochial schools in Michigan. After a massive parade through the streets of Detroit that included 50,000 schoolchildren, Catholics gathered at Navin Field for an open-air Mass and rally. Nuns in their habits filled entire sections at the park in what was reputedly the first such public appearance by large groups of the "sisters" in the history of the nation. One source estimates the crowd at 85,000 to 100,000 and another at more than 100,000; by either measure, even if the figures were inflated, it was certainly the largest crowd ever to gather for any purpose at Michigan and Trumbull.[28]

Throughout the second decade of the century, attendance at Navin Field rose and fell with the Tigers' performance and the country's financial and wartime fortunes. In its first four seasons, Navin Field could not even match the club's fan totals for 1909 and 1911 at Bennett Park. In 1916, however, after a thrilling 1915 season in which the Tigers almost won the pennant, attendance jumped to more than 616,000. Two years later, the club was abysmal, the nation was embroiled in World War I, major league schedules were truncated, and crowds shrank by two-thirds. With the war over, in 1919 attendance more than tripled at Navin Field to over 643,000.

Baseball underwent its most momentous transformation at the dawn of the Roaring Twenties. It was precipitated by the biggest betting scandal in American sports history—the throwing of the 1919 World Series by the Chicago White Sox to the Cincinnati Reds at the behest of Chicago and New York gamblers. This was the epitome, though by no means the absolute end, of the corrosive influence of gamblers on the sport. The fallout was widespread: Eight members of the team that would come to be forever known as the Black Sox were banned for life, including Shoeless Joe Jackson, a marvelously talented rube who is to this day permanently barred from the Hall of Fame. Baseball appointed Judge Kenesaw Mountain Landis to become its all-powerful commissioner and clean up the sport's tarnished reputation. At the same juncture, Babe Ruth was transformed from a dominating Red Sox pitcher to an unmatched Yankee slugger and the nation's biggest celebrity. His power blossomed naturally but it helped that the ball was, according to all

The inserted text reads: "Demonstration Given by 100,000 People at Navin Field. Against the School Amendment. Sunday, October 31, 1920" (original photograph by Spencer & Wyckoff, Library of Congress).

available evidence, "juiced up" to attract fans back to the tarnished sport. In any event, the low-scoring Deadball Era ended in a barrage of Ruthian homers, to Cobb's everlasting chagrin. (He despised the power game as inauthentic.) In Detroit, changes also rocked the team: Jennings was dismissed after the 1920 season and Cobb was named manager.

As a manager, the autocratic, temperamental Cobb often berated his own players. (Many superstars do not make good skippers, because they do not understand a talent level far below their own.) He also tried to gain whatever advantage he could from his home ballpark. When a power-hitting opponent came to town, suddenly temporary bleachers would often appear in the outfield, in order to turn long drives into ground-rule doubles. But despite his shenanigans, having fan favorite Cobb at the helm was good for Tiger attendance as the country shook off its wartime woes and entered the Roaring Twenties: it increased for four straight seasons starting in 1921, reaching over one million in 1924 for the first time in franchise history.

Additional expansions under Navin's ownership helped accommodate the growing crowds. After the 1922 season, Navin built new single-deck pavilions down both the first base and third base lines and placed a large second deck on the main grandstand behind home plate. These significant improvements, paid for by Navin, brought the stadium into the major league mainstream, where all but three parks were double- or even triple-decked. The new seating tier in the main grandstand was built atop square steel columns placed halfway back in the lower grandstand. This cantilever construction technique, standard for that era, enabled the second deck to be placed almost directly atop the lower, putting even the higher-level seats remarkably close to the field. As a result, the seats in the upper deck behind home plate would be considered by well-traveled baseball observers as among the best vantage points in baseball: the action on the infield took place almost directly below, and the effect was almost like viewing an opera from a theater box. Many fans for generations to come preferred these seats, most of which remained reasonably priced, to any others in the park, though Detroiters who did not visit stadiums in other cities had no idea just how remarkable and rare those seats were. They came at a trade-off, however, because the columns created partially obstructed views for some fans sitting in the rear rows of the upper and lower decks. (The upper-deck columns were needed to support the roof.) Such obstructions were common in venues of the time, and few complained about them. The prior generation of wooden ballparks had a far higher proportion of column-obstructed views.

Navin Field in 1930: A *Detroit News* **aerial photograph (Ernie Harwell Sports Collection, courtesy Burton Historical Collection, Detroit Public Library).**

With the city's auto factories bustling, fans flocked to the corner of Michigan and Trumbull for a beer and a hot dog and a glimpse of their heroes. The new middle class, created by the automobile industry, was populating neighborhoods spreading throughout the city, but all roads led to the ballpark.

When Babe Ruth came to Detroit with the Yankees, he would usually hog the headlines, having supplanted Cobb as the game's biggest star; in fact, the gregarious Yankee soon became the nation's biggest celebrity of any kind. Once in the Motor City, Ruth would take the interurban rail line to nearby Mount Clemens, a spa town known for its mineral baths and attendant delights. Such Ruthian exploits were never allowed by the press to tarnish the Babe as a role model. During the 1924 season, the Tigers twice drew overflow crowds of 40,000 or more for games against the Yankees.

Cobb was growing increasingly bitter at the changes Ruth and Landis were bringing to the game by burying the Deadball Era. Cobb hated Ruth so much that he would run in from center field to tell his hurler what kind of pitch to throw the slugger, usually to no avail.[29] The Cobb-Ruth jousting fueled a longtime rivalry between the two squads, and for decades to come, young Detroiters would be raised on hatred for the Yankees. In one game in 1924, a brawl on the field between the two clubs spilled over into the stands. Some fans rushed onto the field to join the fight, while others actually threw their seats onto the field.

On June 8, 1926, Ruth hit a ball that rocketed over the center field wall and landed in the intersection of Trumbull and Cherry Street. According to William Jenkinson, the foremost chronicler of Ruth's home runs, this shot travelled perhaps 575 feet on the fly and is in his estimation (and by legend) the longest home run in baseball history.[30]

During Cobb's time at the helm of the team, pennants continued to elude the Tigers, and by the mid–1920s Cobb was publicly blasting Navin for failing to acquire the top-notch pitching needed to complement Detroit's productive offense. But Navin had become a close friend and confidante of Commissioner Landis, who often consulted him, and Landis's crusade against the influence of gambling almost netted him a few high-profile catches: Cleveland outfielder Tris Speaker and Cobb himself, who barely escaped scandal after accusations (never proven) that they had conspired to throw games. Navin finally canned Cobb in 1926 and traded him, ending his long Tiger career. Ironically, Navin himself was a huge presence at local racetracks, squandering his money on his habit of playing the horses. Meanwhile, in the background, Briggs was still quietly buying up stock in the Tigers and by 1927 had bought out Kelsey to become co-owner of the club, though Navin remained its public face.

Baseball was not the only attraction at Navin Field. There were frequent boxing matches in the evening: the ring would be set up at second base with lights above it and temporary bleachers hauled out to be placed around it. A similar arrangement was made for *Opera Under the Stars*. Anything that might turn a buck was fair game: even barnstorming teams came to town, like the bearded House of David, whose players would sometimes ride donkeys around the bases. And for decades to come Michigan and Trumbull would host various political and religious rallies, including a speech by presidential candidate Alf Landon in 1936, an appearance by preacher Billy Graham that drew a reported 42,000 in the early 1950s,[31] a rally for Democratic presidential nominee contender Eugene McCarthy in 1968, and a speech by Nelson Mandela in 1990.

Ducky, Black Mike and the Goose

In the early 1930s, gambling losses and the effects of the great stock market crash diminished Navin's fortunes, and it was Briggs' money that saw the club through the lean early years of the Great Depression, when the team's seasonal standing sagged along with the economy and attendance plummeted, returning to Bennett-Park-like levels and bottoming out at 320,972 in 1933. Most folks were too concerned about getting their next meal to consider wasting money on a ticket to a ball game, especially since the Tigers without Cobb had become a much less exciting squad. They finished in the second division for six years in a row ending in 1933. That year, Navin resorted to putting up a screen in front of the left field stands to thwart Philadelphia Athletics slugger Jimmy Foxx, who hit only two home runs in Detroit out of a total of 48 that year.[32]

Luckily, Briggs' fortune was secure—he had expanded his profitable holdings in many directions, from his original enterprise of manufacturing automobile bodies for Ford to making bathroom fixtures to real estate investments. Briggs' companies owned many factories and employed many thousands of workers.

Both Briggs and Navin knew the Depression-socked city was desperate for a distraction. It had been a quarter-century since the Tigers had won a pennant. After the 1933 season, Navin offered the manager's job to Babe Ruth, who turned it down. In

An *Opera Under the Stars* performance, probably in 1935 (Walter P. Reuther Library, Archives of Labor and Urban Affairs, Wayne State University).

Top: The program cover for the *Opera Under the Stars* performance of *Naughty Marietta*, August 1935 (Program courtesy Linnea Dudley, Marygrove College Library. Photograph by Frank Rashid). *Bottom:* Alf Landon speaks at Navin Field on October 13, 1936 (Walter P. Reuther Library, Archives of Labor and Urban Affairs, Wayne State University).

Top: Boxing at Briggs: Joe Louis defeats Bob Pastor on September 20, 1939. *Bottom:* The Reverend Billy Graham preaches at Briggs Stadium in 1954 (both photographs, Walter P. Reuther Library, Archives of Labor and Urban Affairs, Wayne State University).

hiladelphia, Connie Mack was holding a fire sale of the players that remained from his championship teams of 1929–1931, and Navin used Briggs' money to buy catcher Mickey Cochrane for the then-princely sum of $100,000 and make him the new skipper.

Cochrane, nicknamed "Black Mike," was as hard-nosed as Cobb if not nearly as ill-tempered and unforgiving of his charges. He took the reins just as the team was beginning to rise again and led by example. Cochrane immediately became a fan favorite, but the Tigers had other stars, too: second baseman Charlie Gehringer, a Michigan native, and newly acquired Goose Goslin.

Everything turned around in a hurry under Cochrane. In 1934, the Tigers returned to first place, and attendance nearly tripled. In fact, Detroit alone attracted nearly a third of the American League's fans. The town was baseball crazy, and the game was a welcome relief from the persistent hard times of the Great Depression.

Excited by their prospects for sellout crowds, Navin and Briggs put up a huge set of temporary bleachers along Cherry Street in left field. These stands held some 17,000 fans, many of whom brought their own lunches to the game to save money. Vendors also supplied the crowd in the bleachers.

An overflow crowd for a 1934 game between the Tigers and the St. Louis Browns. Note that the scoreboard is in left field and that housing remains beyond the left field fence (*Detroit News* from a print provided by Avanti Press).

The World Series against St. Louis went to a deciding seventh game in Detroit. The Cardinals were routing the Tigers late in the game when St. Louis left fielder Ducky Medwick slid into Detroit third baseman Marv Owen in a fashion that frustrated Tiger fans saw as too rough. When Medwick tried to return to his position after the inning, denizens of the bleachers routed him with a barrage of tasty produce. He was pelted so hard he sought refuge in the dugout. After two attempts to return to left field, Medwick retreated, and Commissioner Landis, who was on hand, ordered St. Louis to replace him to avoid a forfeit. The Tigers lost, 11–0, and the franchise was not only winless in four World Series appearances, it was now embarrassed.

The following season, Cochrane vowed to take the team all the way. The 1935 Tigers were the toast of the town, drawing over a million fans and capturing the pennant by storm. The season literally electrified the city: for the first time, crowds in downtown Detroit followed World Series games on an electric display set up on the side of a building. In the sixth game against the Chicago Cubs, Cochrane scored the winning run on a single

A view from Trumbull Avenue of the temporary bleachers set up for the 1934 World Series. The back of the scoreboard—relocated from left field—is in the foreground. An enterprising homeowner has sold advertising space on the roof of his home in center field. The ad is for Roesink's Pant Store on Monroe Avenue in downtown Detroit. Notice the telephone pole sitters looking over the right field bleachers, the mounted police on the sidewalk, and what appears to be a blimp in the upper right corner. (*Detroit News* from a print provided by Avanti Press).

After the sixth and deciding game of the 1935 World Series, won by the Tigers, 4–3, fans leave Navin Field via the right field exit (Ernie Harwell Sports Collection, courtesy Burton Historical Collection, Detroit Public Library).

by Goslin, sending the city into an all-night, horn-honking celebration of the club's first World Series championship after three-and-a-half decades of falling short. Even the normally reserved Navin joined the celebration in the dugout. A few weeks later, however, he suffered a heart attack while riding his horse at a local stable, fell from his mount, and died. It was a dramatic end to Navin's tenure as the man who had brought the Tigers from a nearly stillborn infancy to the pinnacle of baseball.

NOTES

1. This first reference occurs in the *Detroit Free Press*, August 8 and 9, 1859.
2. John Thorn made this discovery in 2004. See John Pastier, *Historic Ballparks: A Panoramic Vision* (Edison, New Jersey: Chartwell Books, 2006), 8.
3. A New York University librarian discovered these articles in 2001. See Pastier, 8.
4. Recent scholarship has discredited the assertions of Harold Peterson in *The Man Who Invented Baseball* (New York: Scribner, 1973) that detail Cartwright's contributions, including the 90-foot distance between bases. See most recently John Thorn's *Baseball in the Garden of Eden: The Secret Early History of the Game* (New York: Simon & Schuster, 2011).
5. Michael Betzold and Ethan Casey, *Queen of Diamonds: The Tiger Stadium Story* (West Bloomfield, Michigan: Altwerger and Mandel, 1992), 25–27.
6. *Ibid.*, 27–28.
7. Don Voelker, "Michigan and Trumbull Before Baseball," *Michigan History* (July/August 1989), 24–

31. See also *ibid.*, 21–22, and Richard Bak, *A Place for Summer: A Narrative History of Tiger Stadium* (Detroit: Wayne State University Press, 1998), 51–57.
    8. Tiger Stadium Fan Club (TSFC), *Tiger Stadium, Where Baseball Belongs* (Detroit, 1988), 2.
    9. Ron Selter, "Bennett Park Historical Analysis," http://www.baseball-almanac.com.
    10. TSFC, 3, and Selter, "Bennett Park Historical Analysis."
    11. For extended examinations of Bennett Park, see Betzold and Casey, 29–38, and Bak, 51–115.
    12. Michael Benson, *The Ballparks of North America: A Comprehensive Historical Reference to Baseball Grounds, Yards, and Stadiums, 1845 to Present* (Jefferson, North Carolina: McFarland, 1989).
    13. The most notorious example is the pelting of St. Louis Cardinal leftfielder Joe "Ducky" Medwick in the seventh game of the 1934 World Series (see p. 27).
    14. Almost all ballpark sources agree that Bennett's capacity was 8,500 in 1901. Only Philip J. Lowry seems conflicted. In the 1992 edition of his *Green Cathedrals: The Ultimate Celebration of All 271 Major League and Negro League Ballparks, Past and Present* (Reading, Massachusetts: Addison-Wesley, 1992), he agrees with Selter and others. However, in the later edition, titled *Green Cathedrals: The Ultimate Celebration of Major League and Negro League Ballparks*, rev. ed. (New York: Walker, 2006), he gives the 1901 capacity as 7,000.
    15. Betzold and Casey, 33, and Bak, 73.
    16. This rally was well covered in the Detroit newspapers as recounted in Betzold and Casey, 33, and Bak, 73–74. This is the only recorded instance of a ten-run ninth-inning comeback in major league baseball history.
    17. Bak, 78–79.
    18. Marc Okkonen and David Jones, "Frank Navin," SABR Baseball Biography Project, http://sabr.org/bioproject. The biography was previously published in David Jones, ed., *Deadball Stars of the American League* (Dulles, Virginia: Potomac Books, 2006).
    19. Dan Holmes, "Germany Schaefer," SABR Baseball Biography Project, http://sabr.org/bioproject, previously published in Jones.
    20. "Stealing Home Base Records," http://www.baseball-almanac.com.
    21. The revisionist extreme vilification of Cobb is epitomized by Ron Shelton's 1994 movie *Cobb*, which exaggerates his faults in the hindsight of modern days. Many players of his era and later were just as venomous in their racism. Leerhsen, Charles, *Ty Cobb: A Terrible Beauty* (New York: Simon & Schuster, 2016).
    22. Ronald M. Selter's *Ballparks of the Deadball Era: A Comprehensive Study of Their Dimension, Configurations and Effects on Batting, 1901–1919* (Jefferson, North Carolina: McFarland, 2009), 95.
    23. *Ibid.* See also Selter, "Bennett Park Historical Analysis," http://www.baseball-almanac.com.
    24. Selter, *Ballparks of the Deadball Era*, 95.
    25. This discrepancy in space at each end of the block along Michigan occupied by the stadium is due to Michigan Avenue heading more to the west-northwest rather than straight west as it leaves downtown—and Trumbull and National not bisecting it exactly perpendicularly.
    26. The first recorded use of a center field backdrop to aid the batter's vision was at Piedmont Park in 1906. See Paul Dickson, *The Dickson Baseball Dictionary*, 3rd ed. (New York: Norton, 2009), 86.
    27. Andrew Clem's diagrams of the period give the center field distance at 467 feet, which is plausible. See "Tiger Stadium, Former Home of the Detroit Tigers (1912–1999)," *Clem's Baseball: Our National Pastime*, http://www.andrewclem.com/Baseball/TigerStadium.html#diag.
    28. More than 100,000 were said to be in attendance. See Leslie Woodcock Tentler, *Seasons of Grace: A History of the Catholic Archdiocese of Detroit* (Detroit: Wayne State University Press, 1990), 447–448. "A crowd estimated at between eighty-five and a hundred thousand attended an outdoor mass." See JoEllen McNergney Vinyard, *For Faith and Fortune: The Education of Catholic Immigrants in Detroit, 1805–1925* (Urbana: University of Illinois Press, 1998), 235.
    29. In fact, Ruth hit more homers (123) and had a higher career slugging percentage (.744) against the Tigers than against any other club. See the "Babe Ruth Player Page," http://www.baseball-reference.com.
    30. But note this comment by William J. Jenkinson, one of Babe Ruth's greatest admirers: "Not surprisingly, all of the great true distance hitters have also been the source of the greatest exaggerations. Despite his extraordinary accomplishments, Babe Ruth is not immune. His tremendous blow to right-center field in Detroit on June 8, 1926, has often been reported as traveling over 600 feet. Certainly, this drive was propelled somewhere around 500 feet in the air, which makes it legitimately historic, but proof that it traveled 600 feet cannot be found." William J. Jenkinson, "Long Distance Home Runs," http://www.baseball-almanac.com. Jenkinson's essay originally appeared in the Society for American Baseball Research's *The Home Run Encyclopedia: The Who, What, and Where of Every Home Run Hit Since 1876*, Bob McConnell and David Vincent, eds. (New York: Macmillan, 1996).
    31. The attendance for the Billy Graham rally is mentioned in J. DeWitt Fox, M.D., "How Billy Graham Keeps Healthy," *Life and Health: The National Health Journal* (May 1954): 28.
    32. "Jimmie Foxx," http://www.baseball-reference.com.

A Century on Common Ground II
Briggs Stadium and Tiger Stadium

Michael Betzold

Briggs Stadium

A Workingman's Ballpark

Walter Briggs made Detroit Tigers baseball tremendously accessible to working families by turning Navin Field within the space of a few years into a massive stadium with the largest number of good, affordable seats in the history of professional baseball, before or since. The Tigers had electrified his city by winning the 1935 World Series and in so doing had enriched Briggs even more. Because Briggs was a prototype of the wealthy businessman who became a club owner, he did not need the money from baseball. He wanted the club to be profitable, surely, but he wanted most of all to be able to spend whatever he needed to keep his club as contenders. And by so doing, he wanted the club to remain popular and to be a source of pride to Detroit and a reflection of his own achievements.

To do this, Briggs nearly doubled the capacity of his ballpark, named it after himself, and basked in its glory, and long after his death, the stadium he built became a monument to the unadulterated experience of watching a game of baseball. In that, it was perhaps unmatched. Briggs' plan made his stadium a place where the greatest possible number of fans could afford to get a good view of the game. Whatever his motives, he built a stadium that maximized access for the working-class men who toiled in his and the city's other automobile factories—and their families.

Briggs was known for paying low wages and for his opposition to organized labor. In 1926, a fire at one of his factories highlighted substandard working conditions, and his plants were often embroiled in strikes and protests.[1] And, though he did employ many black workers, by nature and practice the automobile magnate, like many white men of the era, was a racist. Of course, in the mid–1930s, major league baseball was, by custom and tradition but also by its own unwritten yet firm laws, a pastime for white people. Blacks played on their own teams in their own leagues; none but the most progressive, farsighted people dreamed it could or should be otherwise.[2]

Nonetheless, Briggs' expansion plan was ambitious and far-reaching, and the result was something that would stand the test of time long after the virulent racism of his day had abated. He made a park that was a sort of enclosed al fresco theater, a baseball-only

Briggs Stadium became the site for worker demonstrations against Briggs Manufacturing Company. Here picketers gather beneath the Trumbull Avenue sidewalk overhang on May 27, 1939 (Walter P. Reuther Library, Archives of Labor and Urban Affairs, Wayne State University).

world, accessible from the outside world and in the open air but almost completely cut off from the surrounding workaday world of the big city. It was a place to be transported to baseball heaven on earth. In many respects then, it became, for adherents of the game of baseball, a "green cathedral": separate from the world while yet still in it.

To accomplish this transformation, Briggs retained the grandstand and pavilions of Navin Field, the sturdy heart of the stadium, and expanded the place both up and out to fully enclose yet still closely embrace the field of play. Using the same basic construction technique Osborn Engineering had employed for Navin Field and for many other parks of the era—columns in the stands to anchor a cantilevered upper deck almost directly above the lower deck—Briggs set out to double-deck the entire stadium, extending what Navin had done to the original grandstands behind home plate.

The project proceeded in stages over more than two years, yet nonetheless resulted in an edifice that was structurally unified and, despite some quirkiness, visually coherent.[3] Briggs, already entertaining the possibility of an expansion even before Navin's death, had toured ballparks in other cities to gather ideas, including Chicago's Wrigley Field

32   Part I: History and Background

Tiger radio broadcasting legend Ty Tyson announcing from the third deck in 1936. The stadium is in transition: The temporary bleachers are gone, and the scoreboard has been moved from right field back to left field (*Detroit News* from a print provided by Avanti Press).

and Comiskey Park, with Comiskey being the stadium his expanded park in Detroit would end up resembling the most.

In the winter of 1935–1936, Briggs began work down the first base side of the field. When it was completed for the new season, a double-decked seating area extended all the way to the right field corner, and a new double-decked grandstand was built in right field. What had been a grandstand and a separate pavilion down the first base line was now tied together with an unbroken exterior wall and concourses below the seating areas in both the upper and lower decks, and this, in turn, was tied into the new right field grandstand.

In this initial phase of expansion, Briggs created what would become the park's most famous feature: the right field upper-deck "overhang." It was not a quirk for the sake of novelty: it was a creative engineering solution to a difficult physical problem, the proximity of Trumbull Avenue to the right field fence. Navin Field's home plate could not be moved much if at all if Briggs wanted to keep his original grandstand, double-decked since 1923. Replacing this grandstand would have been not only unnecessary and wasteful but prohibitively expensive and impractical: its back wall already almost grazed the corner of Michigan and National, allowing barely sufficient room for pedestrian ingress and egress. The distance from home plate to the right field fence was thus constrained by the distance between National and Trumbull. But Briggs wanted to make room for the maximum amount of seating in the space available, and this included putting a second deck in the outfield stands as well. The solution was to build the back wall of the lower right field section of the grandstand at the Trumbull Avenue property line, leaving room only for a wide sidewalk. Then the upper-deck wall was erected to protrude a few feet out over the sidewalk to the rear and also ten feet over the field on the other side. This configuration of seating, rather innovative for its time, allowed a reasonably deep right field upper-deck grandstand that accommodated enough seats to justify its construction. The columns supporting the upper deck were aligned with the edge of the right field fence. Four rows of upper-deck seats projected ten feet forward of the fence line. Because of this configuration, a high fly ball with a sharp downward trajectory would occasionally graze the upper deck or even land in its first or second row. Either result would mean a home run for the batter, even as the right fielder camped at the fence vainly waiting for the ball to settle in his glove for an out. Since the upper-deck right field corner was only 315 feet from home plate, the overhang was a tempting target for left-handed sluggers and an irritant for fly-ball pitchers. (In the absence of hard data, however, it is difficult to assess this near-legendary feature's actual effect on games.) The overhang's iconic status was such that it was purportedly duplicated in the stadium the Texas Rangers built for the 21st century. But what Rangers' management misguidedly marketed as a "home run porch" did not overhang its lower deck and was not the product of a confined site. (The Arlington ballpark stood in a vast open field and thus bore no similarity to Detroit's right field quirk.) Like Fenway Park's much more famous Green Monster, the Tigers' jutting upper deck was designed not for the sake of distinctiveness but to mitigate a space shortage caused by the unyielding street grid of an established urban neighborhood.

Two years later, Briggs completed his project by doing much the same thing on the opposite side of the field. Again, the existing grandstand behind home plate was linked to the old single-decked pavilion built for the 1923 season. The resulting entirely double-decked structure was then tied into a new double-decked grandstand that started in left field foul territory, turned the corner, and extended into deep left field. Again, the exterior walls and the concourses beneath the stands were unified into a coherent whole. Also, in center field, Osborn constructed a double-decked bleacher section that seated more than 11,000. What had been six disparate sections of the stadium built in somewhat piecemeal fashion from the end of the 1911 season to the beginning of the 1938 season—the original grandstand of Navin Field that hugged the infield, the two pavilions down the foul lines, the two new outfield pavilions, and the center field bleachers—were all joined together in a reasonably coherent structure. There were some interesting pragmatic departures from geometric purity at the junctures between the sections—you could not walk through the stands themselves all the way around the stadium, but you could make that trip through the concourses beneath the stands on both decks where rest rooms, concessions, and various other facilities were located (though access to the bleacher section was blocked by interior metal gates which were locked to fans). This structure would remain essentially unchanged for the more than six decades of the life of the stadium that were to follow—and, if you were a fan who had never seen the old Navin Field and did not know the history of the construction, you would never have suspected that the stadium you were in had grown by accretion. It was, to all casual appearances, a coherent whole: one mammoth enclosed stadium with a capacity of about 54,000, one huge building almost completely taking up a full city block.

Building so many seats in the outfield was unusual, as was a double deck of bleachers. These approximately 24,000 outfield seats were an integral part of Briggs' concept. Since they were distant from home plate, they could not conceivably be sold for more than a general admission price, and the bleacher seats would be discounted even more. But what they could not generate in revenue per seat, they made up for in their quantity and quality. Fans could enjoy a reasonably good if somewhat distant view of a ball game for an affordable price, and the club could make a small profit from the tickets as well as the concessions. In Briggs' calculation, the more seats there were for all types of fans, the better: more beer and hot dogs would be sold.

This concept was something of a gamble, especially considering that memories of the Ducky Medwick incident were still fresh. Briggs was welcoming in the rabble who had thrown fruit, vegetables, and litter onto Navin Field on that occasion—and on many others. Yet despite his reputation for mistreatment of his factory workers, his stadium did embody, in many respects, a democratic impulse. With the exception of the bleachers, any fan could walk unimpeded all around the stadium, sampling the higher-priced views everywhere. Until the 1990s, no guards would stop fans from slipping into the more expensive seats behind home plate if they were vacant late in the game.

The bleachers would indeed spawn rowdy behavior over the years to come, and, as in all ballparks, fans sometimes threw things on the field or even climbed over fences and onto the field, either as a prank or in celebration. But, overall, the stadium built by Briggs engendered in its very design a unifying effect. Entering it was truly like arriving in a separate world. Especially for children and other first-time visitors, the initial view upon walking up a ramp from a concourse and seeing the interior was awe-inspiring: a vast expanse of green surrounded by impressive banks of seats (in the Briggs era and beyond, themselves dark green). Except for a limited vantage point at the rear of the right-center upper bleachers, there were no panoramic views from within the stadium of the city outside it. This was its own municipality: the land of Tiger baseball, and no matter what was going on outside the gates, the game was always center stage and the focus of all attention.

This was true, of course, only if you were welcomed inside the gates. While Briggs never had any official policy of segregation, many black Detroiters felt unwelcome there. Throughout his tenure as owner, some African Americans felt mistreated and unwelcome at Michigan and Trumbull. Because of this unfortunate legacy, Briggs' stadium was for many Detroiters a painful symbol of prejudice and exclusion.[4] Documented incidents are hard to find, but stories of mistreatment were passed down for generations in the African American community—and the club color bar held firm for a decade after Jackie Robinson made his historic debut with the Dodgers.

With white Detroiters, though, the new stadium was a hit from the start. It was a suitably grand edifice, and for many years to come, it would be known as one of the best maintained and most well-appointed venues in all of baseball. The stadium was not architecturally flashy or fancy; it did not have the obviously quirky configuration of Fenway or the charms of Wrigley; it was utilitarian, and nothing competed with the game for the attention of the fans.

Because of the double deck, all the seats were close to the field, even those in the outfield and especially those in the right field overhang. Upper-deck bleacherites enjoyed the feeling of being lords of all they surveyed: an expansive kingdom stretched below and in front of them. Behind home plate and down the lines, foul territory was scant, giving the fans in both decks a close look at the players when they were on the field and when they were entering and exiting the dugouts.

The stands did partially block the sun in some sections at various times of day, especially in the late afternoon, creating shadows that cut in various ways across the infield; this, too, was a natural part of the experience for the players and the patrons. For the fans, many seats were shaded from the sun by the upper deck or the roof of the third deck, which housed the press box and sometimes, as for the rare World Series games, special boxes for the press, club officials, or members of the public.

In case of rain, it was usually easy to find shelter: fans could sit out rain delays by scurrying to the back rows of the lower deck or by huddling in the concourses, which varied from cramped (behind home plate, down the first base line, and in right field) to spacious (under the left field stands, where the outside street configuration provided much more room).

Built to Last but Stuck in the Past

The new stadium was what Detroit needed to cement its new reputation as a major city with a baseball franchise to be reckoned with. Detroit's population had soared to the fourth largest in the nation, and Briggs Stadium's expanded seating capacity and attendance reflected this lofty position. It was the world's second-most capacious baseball park, after Yankee Stadium.[5](Cleveland's Municipal Stadium was larger than either but was a multisport venue rather than a place designed primarily for the national pastime.)

The Tigers drew more than a million fans even before Briggs had completed the expansion, and afterward, they regularly attracted well above the league average in home attendance. The club had crammed over a million patrons into Navin Field in 1924 and 1935 and at Briggs Stadium in 1937 and in 1940, when the team won its sixth American League championship and lost the World Series for the fifth time. World War II then suppressed attendance figures, but after the war, the stadium fell short of a million fans only in 1953, when the club was an abysmal last-place team, and in 1963 and 1964, when it was again rebuilding.

For most of its tenure as Briggs Stadium, the Tigers' home was easily outdrawing the league average attendance as well. In its first two seasons, in 1936 and 1937, it attracted nearly double the average for the AL; and for the rest of its official existence as Briggs Stadium, through 1960, the Tigers exceeded the league average in every single season except 1952, when the team had the worst winning percentage in franchise history, .325; even then, the annual attendance was just 11,000 below league average.

From 1936 through 1950, the Tigers were a winning franchise, barely under .500 in only two of those seasons and regularly among major league baseball's attendance leaders. From 1951 through 1960, though, the Tigers were lousy, finishing slightly above .500 only three times and the rest of the time buried deep down in the standings. Yet the popularity of their stadium sustained the franchise even in those lean years. Tiger fans were loyal, and part of the reason was the enjoyable experience of attending games at Michigan and Trumbull.

The first year of the completely expanded Briggs Stadium, 1938, was also the last year that a major league team played in a 19th-century ballpark—in mid-season the

Phillies left the Baker Bowl to play at Shibe Park. That fall, the Detroit Lions of the new National Football League (NFL) played for the first time at Briggs Stadium, and they would continue to make it their home field through 1974, when they moved to a domed stadium in suburban Pontiac.

While the Tigers were competing in the American League, Detroit also had a club in the Negro Leagues during the long era of segregated baseball. The Detroit Stars were formed in 1910 and began playing at eastside Mack Park in 1914. The park was built by the club's Jewish owner, haberdasher John Roesink, who owned a downtown clothing store. In 1919, Rube Foster officially created the Negro National League, and the Stars were a charter member, playing at Mack Park until a blaze broke out in 1929 and the grandstand collapsed; after that, the club landed in the enclave of Hamtramck in the 1930s.

In the 1930s, the Tigers produced a new star who became a hero for Detroit's Jewish community: Hank Greenberg, who made a run at Babe Ruth's single-season home run record in 1938, finishing with 58. In 1940, he led the team to first place and became a Hall of Famer after an illustrious career.

Briggs, a devout Catholic, frequently gave away tickets to priests and other clergy at the ecumenical Detroit Council of Churches; they sat together in a block of seats at the stadium. He also gave tickets to children at free or discounted prices, some say to the tune of 100,000 a year. This charitable impulse was not entirely altruistic: it also bred many eventual adult paying customers for the Tigers.

Kids clamor for autographs on Opening Day in 1949 (*Detroit News* from a print provided by Avanti Press).

In May 1939, Lou Gehrig ended his famous consecutive-games-played streak of 2,130 in Detroit, finally sitting out due to the first effects of the fatal illness, amyotrophic lateral sclerosis (ALS), which after his death became popularly known by his name. The record would last until Cal Ripken, Jr., broke it in the 1990s.

In the 1940 World Series, the games in Detroit, with an average attendance of more than 54,000, nearly doubled the

Right: Scoreboard workers changing the numbers by hand (*Detroit News* from a print provided by Avanti Press). *Below:* Lou Gehrig in the visitors' dugout after removing himself from the lineup on May 2, 1939 (Ernie Harwell Sports Collection, courtesy Burton Historical Collection, Detroit Public Library).

The center field scoreboard in 1944. With minor modifications, this appears to be the field-level scoreboard (moved from left field to right field and back again) in the 1930s. (See pages 26, 27, 28, and 32.) Number 26 belonged to right fielder Ned Harris, probably being honored for military service in World War II (*Detroit News* from a print provided by Avanti Press).

crowds at the games played in Cincinnati, even though the Reds won the series. The fifth game in Detroit drew a standing-room-only crowd of 55,189. In 1941, the first of three All-Star Games played at the stadium drew 54,674 fans, with people being packed into nooks and crannies and ending up sitting in the aisles or standing in the concourses behind the back rows of seats.[6]

During the Second World War, Greenberg and many other stars joined the military for the fight. Baseball took a backseat to the war effort but still provided a diversion on the home front. When Greenberg returned in 1945, the Tigers were locked in another tight pennant race, and his grand slam homer on the last day of the season sent them to their seventh World Series. Still operating under wartime travel restrictions, Detroit and the Chicago Cubs made only one road trip in the series, and the Tigers won their second World Series in a seventh game at Wrigley Field. Because of the war, the celebration was much more subdued. The Tigers then entered another quarter-century of play without a pennant.

With the war ended, the crowds returned to the ballpark. In the 1940s, the club occasionally opened the stadium's third deck to accommodate overflow crowds and frequently set new single-game records: on July 20, 1947, they resorted to the old practice of having fans stand in the outfield during a doubleheader with the Yankees that drew an all-time record crowd of 58,369.[7]

Games in Detroit had traditionally started at 3:00 p.m. just as the day shift at the factories was ending. Briggs, being a factory owner, saw no reason to change this, even as night baseball, which started in 1935 in Cincinnati, spread around the majors. By 1948,

The functional and, by today's standards, spartan Tiger clubhouse in 1946 (*Detroit News* from a print provided by Avanti Press).

the only parks without lights were Briggs Stadium and Wrigley Field. Purists—and Briggs was certainly one of them—believed baseball was meant to be played in the sunshine, but times were changing, and after-dark leisure pursuits were more and more common, especially as prosperity finally returned to the nation following the war. Briggs even tried games starting at 5:00 or 6:00 p.m. during the war, but the diminishing daylight was problematic for the players. Finally, it took his son, Walter Jr., known as Spike, to persuade his traditionalist father to relent. The first night game at Briggs Stadium was played June 15, 1948, and was a huge success, drawing 54,480, and the Tigers drew more than 600,000 fans to 14 games under the lights, the maximum allowed by the league that year.[8]

In a sinister sense, Briggs was a traditionalist, too, on the matter of race. Despite Jackie Robinson's entrance into the major leagues in 1947 with the Brooklyn Dodgers that finally shattered baseball's longstanding color bar, Briggs refused to consider black players for the Tigers. When Cleveland signed Larry Doby later in 1947 as the American League's first black player, African Americans finally came out in droves to Briggs Stadium, congregating in the lower-deck grandstand in right field to be close to him, waving their hands through and above the fence in unabashed admiration for a visiting team's player. For decades afterwards, black fans self-segregated themselves at Briggs Stadium

40 Part I: History and Background

A Briggs Stadium night game in 1955. Note the unusual configuration of the infield skin in foul territory (*Detroit News* **from a print provided by Avanti Press**).

in those lower-deck right field stands or in the less popular bleacher seats in the lower deck in center field. Those were the only parts of the place where many of them felt comfortable and were left largely undisturbed. For generations to come, the word kept spreading throughout the African American community of incidents of mistreatment at the home of the Tigers, whether in the form of outright slurs from white fans, refusal of equal treatment by ushers or at the concession stands, or other manifestations of lingering racism. Tellingly, the Tigers were the second-to-last club to integrate, and it did not happen until 1958 when a dark-skinned Latin third baseman, Ozzie Virgil, joined the team. (The Boston Red Sox finally followed suit in 1959 with a player named Pumpsie Green.) Virgil's signing was probably a response to a community pressure group called the Briggs Stadium Boycott Commission.[9] Virgil got five hits in five at-bats in his debut at Briggs Stadium but otherwise proved to be a mediocre hitter, batting .244 for the season. Late in the following season, Doby, near the end of his career, played 18 games for the Tigers.

After the Patriarchy

Years before, in 1951, Briggs Stadium had again hosted the All-Star Game, jumping ahead of its next turn because major league baseball wanted to help the City of Detroit celebrate its 250th birthday. This indicates how important the Detroit franchise had become and the high regard major league baseball officials had for Briggs Stadium. The following year, however, was a sad one: the Tigers finished last for the first time in franchise history, with a terrible 50–104 record. Walter Briggs died before the season started, ending nearly a half-century of his involvement with the club. Spike Briggs, quite appropriately, became the club president, a position he had been filling informally for years. But the disposition of his father's stock in the club, willed to his estate, soon became contentious. Even with the dismal showing of 1952, the Tigers continued to be profitable, and according to an IRS ruling were worth $2.1 million. But federal courts ruled that a baseball franchise was not a prudent investment for a family trust and that Spike Briggs should get no special consideration in the legal battle for control of the club. After some squabbling in the courts among the heirs, it was eventually determined that the club should be put up for sale.

Among the bidders, quite naturally, were the Detroit Lions and their owners. In the 1950s, the Lions, led by quarterback Bobby Layne, were one of the most successful franchises in the National Football League. They prospered at Briggs Stadium, usually playing to sellout crowds. The football field was laid out across the baseball diamond each fall, with one end zone near the left field fence and the other in foul territory beyond first base. The football field of 100 yards plus two ten-yard end zones just barely fit the field in this configuration, with about 20 feet to spare at each end. Preferred seats for football games included those down the third base line and in right field, with the upper-deck seats affording the best views, but even then, the first-row seats in those locations were about 110 feet from the sidelines. During September, the baseball and football line markings conflicted and the infield dirt cut across the football playing field, but that was not unusual in those days: many football teams played in stadiums erected for baseball. The Lions played in NFL championship games in 1952, 1953, 1954, and 1957, losing only in 1954. In these years the Lions were the sports champs of Detroit and the Tigers the chumps, but both clubs continued to draw well at Briggs Stadium.

At the beginning of 1956, there were 20 bidders for the Tigers, but the National Football League forbade the owners of the Lions from buying a baseball franchise, ending that possibility. Among the top bidders reportedly were Fred Knorr, a local radio-TV executive and a business associate of Spike Briggs, and Bill Veeck, perhaps the most flamboyant executive in baseball history. Veeck, a war veteran who carved an ashtray in the knee area of his wooden leg, was known for his showmanship and outlandish promotions. In the most famous stunt in baseball history, as owner of the sad-sack St. Louis Browns, he had a three-foot-seven-inch man named Eddie Gaedel bat against the Tigers, drawing a walk on four pitches.[10] Veeck was also a progressive, forward-thinking visionary: in the 1940s he had petitioned the commissioner of baseball to allow him to move the Browns to the West Coast, a full decade before two legendary New York City franchises, the Dodgers and the Giants, moved to Los Angeles and San Francisco. The maverick Veeck was a misfit in the family of baseball bosses: the other owners and the two leagues' officials considered him dangerously revolutionary. In his autobiography, *Veeck—As in Wreck,* Veeck claimed he had submitted the top bid for the Tigers, $6 million, but was nixed by the baseball establishment and by Spike Briggs himself, who sold the club to a syndicate headed by Knorr for $5.6 million.

The new owners installed Knorr as club president, and the new boss, though nowhere near the innovator Veeck was, still seemed light-years ahead of the hidebound

The upper deck center field bleachers with a view of the downtown skyline around 1950. The flagpole was the tallest point in play in the major leagues (Walter P. Reuther Library, Archives of Labor and Urban Affairs, Wayne State University).

traditionalists of the Briggs regime. Not only were the Tigers integrated within two years of Knorr's taking over the helm, Knorr raised ticket prices, opened Tiger ticket offices outstate, doubled the club's mail-order ticket sales, and most importantly, increased night games, which drew nearly triple the attendance of weekday day games. Knorr kept Spike Briggs on as general manager, but Briggs could not stand how Knorr was modernizing the club and resigned after a year.

The most significant change of all in the new ownership was simply its distancing itself from the Briggs name, which was anathema to black Detroiters. With the signing of Doby in 1959, the Tigers signaled a new openness. And even the minor, more cosmetic changes that Knorr made in the ticket sales operations were more welcoming to black customers.

By the end of the disappointing decade that was the 1950s—the worst for the club ever in terms of on-field performance—the fans were becoming restless. The management was in flux as well, with revolving-door managers and general managers and different forces asserting influence within the Knorr syndicate. Briggs had been the last man in the old patriarchal family tradition of ownership, for good and ill leaving his traditionalist stamp on the teams, the franchise, and the stadium. Now the management had become a corporation of faceless individuals: more modern but less personal. The transition from a family concern where the owner would give away tickets to clergymen and kids to a business conglomerate was soon evident. Frank DeWitt was lured from the Yankees to become club president late in 1959, and longtime Tiger scout and farm team director Rick Ferrell was retained as general manager. DeWitt and Ferrell shocked the baseball world in April 1960 by trading batting champion Harvey Kuenn to the Cleveland Indians for Rocky Colavito, the league home run champion, even though Kuenn was a fan favorite. (Kuenn's career faltered in his new setting, and slugger Colavito soon surpassed him in the Detroit fans' affection.) Things became ugly during the 1960 season when bleacher fans waged war with emotionally troubled Cleveland outfielder Jimmy Piersall. The bleacher creatures eventually started throwing things onto the field at other visiting players as well. It got to the point that Kuenn, the league's player representative, demanded order be restored in Detroit. Late in the season, in another highly unusual transaction, the Tigers and Indians swapped managers.

This same year, at the dawn of a new and extremely significant decade in the life of the nation, a radio-TV executive who had made his mark in outstate Michigan and the Midwest at large emerged from the confusing ownership syndicate to take two-thirds control of the Tigers' stock and become club president. He was John Fetzer, largely unknown at the time. First, he bought out Kenyon Brown, a one-third owner, to take control of the team during the season.

Fetzer saw that another important symbolic act needed to take place to finally sever the sometimes poisonous connection the club had with Walter Briggs, Sr. On December 27, 1960, Knorr, a one-third owner, died, and two days later, Fetzer, now completely in control of the club, changed the name of Briggs Stadium to reflect a sense of shared community ownership for its team. Henceforth, it would simply be Tiger Stadium.

Tiger Stadium

The Voice at the Corner

The year 1961 was transformational for professional baseball. For 60 years the two major leagues, the National and the American, had operated with eight clubs, each playing 154 games, and the league champions meeting in the World Series. In 1961, two new clubs were added to the American League, and the next year the NL followed suit. Also, the schedule was expanded to 162 games. The effect of the expansion was immediate and

Often-Remodeled Briggs Stadium ∴ Now Called 'Dream Field' of Majors

dramatic: hitters went on a tear against the diluted pitching staffs of the opposition. In New York, Mickey Mantle and Roger Maris both chased Babe Ruth's home run record, with Maris ending up eclipsing it by virtue of the additional eight games on the schedule. In Detroit, the prankster first baseman Norm Cash, who never hit .300 before or after, led the league with a lusty .361 batting average, aided, by his own admission, by a doctored bat.[11] That year, manager Bob Scheffing's regular lineup featured leadoff batter and second baseman Jake Wood and center fielder Billy Bruton, the first African Americans to be everyday position players for the Tigers. In another indicator of changing times, the first Saturday night game ever was played at Michigan and Trumbull. In 1961, the Tigers had their best regular season since 1934, winning 101 games, yet still lost the pennant by eight games to the hated Yankees.

In the rest of the turbulent decade, the Tigers would finish under .500 only once—in 1963. Their biggest star was a holdover from the 1950s. Al Kaline, a kid from Baltimore who had never played a game in the minor leagues, won the batting title in 1955 as a 20-year-old and played a fluid right field with a famously strong arm. Around this dependably consistent superstar, new fan favorites were being groomed, some of them local, including for the first time in Tiger history a black player from the city of Detroit: Willie Horton, a standout athlete at Northwestern High School, just a few miles from Tiger Stadium.

The stadium became more and more the city's favorite field of athletic play and the choice site for other non-athletic events, a sort of outdoor community center. Besides the Tigers and the perennially contending NFL Lions, Michigan and Trumbull hosted high school baseball and football championship games, some college and semipro games, and occasional cultural, religious, or even political events. And the 1960s introduced the voice of Ernie Harwell, who soon became a welcome and familiar daily presence in households all over Michigan, thanks to his superb radio broadcasts of Tiger games. Harwell became the club's ambassador to the masses, linking fans whether casual or ardent of all ages, races, places, and backgrounds.

Harwell's play-by-play accounts were the next best thing to being at the ballpark. Because he and his radio partners sat at microphones in a radio booth hung from the upper deck right behind home plate and added another microphone that hung down from the booth above the stands, listeners could hear the crack of the bat, the explosion of a fastball in a catcher's mitt, players' shouts on the field, cheers and even curses in the stands, the cries of vendors hawking their wares in the seats—a clear sound picture that vividly conveyed the ambience of Tiger Stadium, and all of it with narration by the smooth-voiced, polite, self-effacing gentleman from Georgia, who became, as the years went by, the unmistakable voice of the Tigers. Harwell eventually was so essential to the experience of a Tiger game that fans would bring transistors to the ballpark to tune into his broadcast. It was as if a game, even at the park, was not complete without the familiar voice at your side.

Harwell had already built a notable career before coming to Detroit. He remains the only broadcaster in history ever traded for a player, coming to the Brooklyn Dodgers in 1948 from his position as play-by-play man for the Atlanta Crackers in exchange for minor-league catcher Cliff Dapper.[12] In New York, he moved on to the Giants and broadcast the

Opposite: **Gene Mack's rendering of Briggs Stadium c. 1946, one of the series of Mack's popular cartoon drawings of major league stadiums (used by permission of Joseph E. Duggan, executor of the Estate of Ruth Murphy).**

most famous home run in baseball history, Bobby Thompson's game-winning homer, the so-called "Shot Heard 'Round the World" that won the pennant for the Giants in a season-ending playoff game—but Harwell's call was for national television (and few homes had TV sets then) and has never been preserved, unlike Russ Hodges' famous radio call. Harwell worked next for the Baltimore Orioles before Fetzer, who as a radio station owner knew something about voice talent, snatched him for the Tigers.

Harwell's broadcasting philosophy was simply to let the game itself take center stage. He frequently reminded listeners of the essentials—the inning, the score, the number of outs, where runners were on base, who was the batter and the pitcher, and the balls-and-strikes count. He described the action on any balls put into play and otherwise remained mostly silent. Unlike other broadcasters, especially of later days, he was not afraid of "dead air"; he knew the ambient sounds from the always buzzing, intimate stadium would fill the void and make listeners at home feel they were sitting right behind the plate in the best seats in the house, next to him. When there was a lull in the action, he would sometimes provide thumbnail sketches, quick anecdotes, or quirky but colorful tidbits from baseball history. Before a broadcast, he would bring index cards with such stories jotted on them so he could weave them seamlessly into his day's narrative.

Under Fetzer's ownership, the Tigers' radio network expanded throughout Michigan and northern Ohio, and WJR radio's broadcasts were aired on a powerful frequency. They could be heard all over the Midwest and even, on clear nights, as far as some places on the East Coast. Harwell's voice became a widely shared entrance point to the team's growing popularity. Outstate fans made group bus trips to Tiger Stadium once or twice a year. The great out-migration that would become characterized as "white flight" and

Three Detroit Hall of Famers: Ernie Harwell, George Kell, and Al Kaline in 1999 (© Rebecca Cook).

would empty out the city of Detroit over the ensuing decades was already well under way by the 1960s, as the auto industry's decentralization, the construction of freeways radiating out from the city center, and government-subsidized long-term mortgages fostered massive suburbanization and the development of a sprawling metropolitan area.[13] Many ex-residents of Detroit still remained loyal Tiger fans, even though the Tigers competed for loyalty with the Chicago Cubs in western Michigan and with the Cleveland Indians in northern Ohio (though putting a top Detroit farm team in Toledo kept many northwestern Ohio fans loyal to the Tigers). Thus, at the same time the Tigers were by virtue of hiring black players becoming more interesting to African American Detroiters, they were becoming more of a statewide and regional team as well thanks to the influences of Fetzer and Harwell. Harwell cemented that kind of connection by starting an idiosyncratic practice meant to be humorous but taken seriously by many: when a foul ball would land in the grandstand, he would announce that it was caught by "a young man from Kalamazoo" or "a woman from Flushing" or "a fan from St. Clair Shores." He sounded so authoritative that some listeners actually thought Harwell had some sort of coded fan seating chart, when in fact he simply embellished imaginatively on the spot. Nevertheless, this signature bit was yet another factor knitting the Tigers' followers into a statewide fan community centered upon metropolitan Detroit. And for fans who had moved away from Detroit, Harwell's broadcasts solidified their memories of their visits to Michigan and Trumbull.

The Sixties Trip

The stadium was not altered in any way when it was renamed. In fact, after Briggs completed his renovation in the 1930s, almost nothing of significance (other than the installation of lights) changed structurally for decades. A few seats were removed down the right field foul line in what was known as Kaline's Corner to make more room for the rangy star to track down fly balls and protect him from further injury after repeated collisions with those stands. The flagpole remained planted in deep center field. For decades, the wooden seats remained deep green and were periodically painted with a fresh coat. The flags of the other American League clubs remained flying atop the roof of the third deck between the imposing light towers.

As the conservative 1950s gave way to the increasingly tumultuous 1960s, the Tigers were also modernizing in other ways. New black players, including pitcher Earl Wilson and reserve Gates Brown, joined a squad largely composed of up-and-coming stars like Jim Northrup, Mickey Lolich, Dick McAuliffe, Bill Freehan, and Mickey Stanley, all groomed in the Tigers' minor league system. Pitcher Denny McLain was snatched from the Chicago White Sox farm system. Years of losing gave way to the gradual assembling, at long last, of a contending club as these players entered their prime years. After a long period of frequently rotating on-field managers, control of the team was settling down, and finally an unassuming man named Mayo Smith was hired as skipper. He inherited a team so good that he could simply let his players play with little interference.

In late July 1967, as racial tensions intensified throughout the country, the Tigers were battling for a pennant. On Sunday, July 23, the team was playing a home game when plumes of smoke became visible even from the stadium. They came from fires blazing over parts of the city, especially from a neighborhood only a few miles away from Michigan and Trumbull. In the early hours of the previous night, a police raid on a "blind pig"

Kaline's Corner and the right field overhang as seen from the centerfield bleachers, late summer 1999 (© Rebecca Cook).

after-hours club had ignited a powder keg that would result in a five-day urban conflagration in which 43 people died, one of the bloodiest social disturbances in the nation's history.[14] After the game on that first day of the riots, outfielder Willie Horton left the stadium in uniform to try to calm people in the streets in his old high school neighborhood.[15] While racial tensions in the Detroit area continued to boil, the Tigers in the summer of 1967 played as a unified, diverse team; many of the players were from the Detroit area, and most made their off-season homes there, and all were concerned about what was happening around them in their communities. They knew their job was simply to play baseball, even though sport seemed less and less consequential to many in light of the city's and country's turmoil. Unfortunately, the baseball season ended in disappointment, as the Tigers on the last day lost a chance to finish in first at the very end of a thrilling three-team fight for the pennant. During the final home loss, a fan came onto the field and knelt and prayed in front of the Tigers' dugout as others vented their frustration in an on-field riot. But there would be no divine intervention, not for the team nor the city.

The next season, however, seemed in many ways karmic. Playing in a troubled city, the Tigers, just by being a multiracial team with obvious camaraderie, seemed to embody what Detroit most needed: a spirit of hope. They were a team of optimistic underdogs who played with a carefree intensity and whose members all contributed their parts. In fact, in front of packed houses, they staged a series of improbable late-inning comebacks and come-from-behind wins, with seemingly a different hero contributing every day with game-winning hits, including not only reliable pinch-hitters like Gates Brown, but also even slugging pitcher Earl Wilson and unlikely light-hitting utility infielder Tommy

Matchick. Their exploits were on display daily at the stadium and heard incessantly on car radios or transistors at the beach or park as the summer progressed. It was a terribly tumultuous and tragic time for the nation, as the spring saw the horrific assassinations of Martin Luther King, Jr., and Robert Kennedy, and the summer was marred by the police riot at the Democratic nominating convention in Chicago. Populist Democratic presidential candidate Eugene McCarthy held a huge rally at Tiger Stadium that summer.

Through it all, the Tigers provided a welcome diversion. Players were frequently seen at watering holes around town; the Tigers themselves seemed a part of what was happening in Detroit. Pitcher Denny McLain, who won an astounding 31 games that summer, played his organ at gigs in the area. Norm Cash was a regular at the Lindell Athletic Club, a bar down the street from the stadium on Michigan Avenue, and after the game, fans were likely to spot other players who dropped in there. Even with the loss of Kaline to injury, the Tigers romped through the pennant race and finished first by 12 games, touching off a celebration unlike any in the city since the end of World War II. It had been a long drought of 23 years since their last pennant, just a year less than the lengthy dry spell between their 1909 and 1934 league championships. A new generation of post-war Tiger fans, the Baby Boomers, had been raised on trips to Michigan and Trumbull as Cub Scouts, Girl Scouts, altar boys, or safety patrol members, or on family outings, and now their dreams were at last coming true.

In the World Series, the Tigers faced the powerful St. Louis Cardinals and their intimidating pitching ace Bob Gibson. The year 1968 would be known as the "Year of the Pitcher." For a number of reasons, team offenses were at a nadir and pitching dominated in a fashion that had not been seen since the Deadball Era. In the series opener in St. Louis, Gibson set a record by striking out 17 Tigers; Detroit won the second game but disastrously dropped the next two in Detroit, and the Tigers, underdogs to begin with, now faced a seemingly insurmountable three-games-to-one deficit.

Game Five at Tiger Stadium was a memorable turning point. Singer-guitarist Jose Feliciano, who was selected by Ernie Harwell to perform, sang an unusual folk version of the National Anthem. In the fifth inning, the Tigers were trailing when Cardinals speedster Lou Brock flew home from second base on a single to left. Supremely confident he would be safe at home, Brock did not even slide. But catcher Bill Freehan blocked the plate, and Willie Horton's dead-on throw nipped Brock in a close, controversial call. The packed house roared, and two innings later, a now-healthy Kaline drove in the go-ahead run. Only a few teams had ever come down from a three-games-to-one deficit to win the World Series, but the Tigers were used to making incredible comebacks. In St. Louis, Detroit won Game Six in a rout, and Mayo Smith sent out Mickey Lolich, not McLain, to face Gibson in the decisive finale. Aided by a Jim Northrup triple misjudged by the usually outstanding center fielder Curt Flood, the Tigers triumphed.

The ensuing celebration eclipsed even the pennant-clinching party. Downtown was flooded with honking cars as Detroiters, eager for good news, jammed the streets. Blacks and whites partied together, and for one night at least the tensions tearing the city apart were overcome.

The Doomed Dome

In many respects, 1968 was the end of an era. The next year saw another round of major league expansion and the institution of divisional playoffs after the end of the regular season. Thus, the Tigers were the last World Series champions coming out of the long-established schedule in which the season's long grind, not a short playoff series, determined the league pennant winners. The winds of change also blew strongly in the offices of major league baseball executives and officials of the cities that hosted teams. Football, increasing rapidly in popularity, would no longer take a backseat to baseball, which was fading from its prominence as the national pastime. In Detroit, the Lions had long been chafing at their status as renters at Michigan and Trumbull. Also in Detroit, as well as in many other cities, club owners and politicians began to envision new stadiums that would have roofs, like the Houston Astrodome, and would be built to accommodate both baseball and football. These "multipurpose" stadiums would be large, circular, and multidecked, and the seats would have to be far more distant from the diamond and the gridiron than those in the stadiums they replaced.

In February 1969, the Detroit Chamber of Commerce endorsed a plan backed by progressive Democratic mayor Jerome Cavanaugh to build a new two-sport dome on the city's riverfront. But the situation in Detroit was more complicated than in other cities building new multipurpose oval stadiums—Cincinnati, Pittsburgh, Philadelphia, and St. Louis. The legacy of the 1967 riots, Detroit officials correctly feared, would accelerate white flight, and many interests, including most importantly the Lions, favored a suburban site for any new stadium that might be built. Much political maneuvering ensued.

Talk of a new stadium in Detroit dated back decades—to 1948, in fact, when city officials had advanced the idea of a huge facility to lure the Olympics to the city. And in the 1950s, some other leaders had spoken of a 100,000-seat stadium to host the games of the Lions, Tigers, and Wayne State University. During the early 1960s, Detroit and state officials concocted another plan to lure the 1968 Olympics, and the state legislature even imposed a tax on betting at racetracks in order to raise seed money for a multipurpose stadium to be built at the state fairgrounds along Eight Mile Road at the boundary between the suburbs and the city. Once again, these stadium plans fell through when Mexico City was selected to host the Olympics, but the idea of a new sports stadium continued to enthrall some civic leaders. Mayor Cavanaugh formed his own study committee to look at stadium sites, including the fairgrounds, the riverfront, and the decaying neighborhood north of Tiger Stadium that had become known as the Briggs community. Lions owner William Clay Ford, a scion of the famous automobile family, spoke frequently of his desire to escape Tiger Stadium, denigrating it as too small for football and berating its bleacher seats and other facilities as outdated and cramped—and Cavanaugh's main goal was to keep the Lions from moving out of the city. Although Tiger Stadium continued to draw fans who loved its intimacy and long tradition and continued to generate revenues, its future was becoming uncertain.

By the end of the Tigers' 1969 season, the state's lawmakers were backing a stadium at the fairgrounds (a solution that would keep the two clubs in Detroit yet at a place where white suburbanites afraid to venture downtown might feel more comfortable). The Lions, however, became attracted to a plan pushed by the city of Pontiac, north of Detroit, for side-by-side football and baseball stadiums, while Cavanaugh and city officials backed a riverfront site. That plan became the most palatable political solution.

By the following year, the vision of the riverfront dome had continued to expand to include not only concerts and other entertainment and civic events that could be held in a multipurpose stadium but also riverfront residential, retail, and office development anchored by the stadium. Lost in the discussion was how a domed stadium with artificial turf and a circular seating pattern would affect not only the game of baseball itself but the fans' enjoyment of it. Not until a generation later, after immense circular multipurpose stadiums were constructed in several cities, did their damage to the sport become clear and the wrongheaded concepts of the stadium building era of the 1960s and early 1970s fall out of fashion. But, at the time, few raised any aesthetic or business objections, and the planning went full speed ahead: a Wayne County Stadium Authority was created; private businesses contributed money for architectural studies in what was viewed as a civic-minded project; the state hoped to funnel horse racing revenue to the stadium; the city investigated land acquisition; and by 1970, John Fetzer even said he would donate Tiger Stadium to charity (!) if the club were to move to a new stadium. While all this talk of moving out of Tiger Stadium was percolating, the Tigers drew more than 1.5 million fans in the 1969, 1970, and 1971 seasons as the club remained a credible pennant contender, even though failing to repeat its 1968 glory.

Lion owner William C. Ford, however, continued to play a game of chicken, telling the city of Pontiac he would be willing to break his lease with Fetzer for the right deal. Meanwhile, the City of Detroit had trouble assembling the land along the river needed for its grandiose project. By 1971, Ford was also publicly citing his quite valid concerns about traffic congestion at the cramped riverfront site. The Lions absorbed some criticism, and there was even talk among the Lions' many black fans of a boycott if the team were to desert Detroit like so many other businesses had done. For his part, Fetzer had no interest in moving to Pontiac; he felt the Tigers belonged in the city. Finally, in early 1972, Fetzer signed a 40-year lease to play in the envisioned riverfront dome, agreeing to an annual rent of around half a million dollars. The stadium authority announced a 40-year bond scheme to raise $126 million for the publicly funded project.

Despite the gushing support from prominent power brokers, there were a few critics: community leaders who questioned public subsidies for a new stadium when the decaying city was battling poverty, a housing crisis, and rampant crime; and skeptics who questioned the stadium backers' rosy revenue projections that buttressed the bond sale. Even so, construction bids were taken and the bond sale was approved. But county auditors warned taxpayers could be left holding the bag because revenue projections were shaky, and Wall Street responded by lowering the city's credit rating. Despite that, it looked like the train had already left the station—until a local attorney, Ron Prebenda, and financial analyst Marc Alan decided to file a last-minute lawsuit to stop the bond sale. Besides the major financial concerns, they objected to provisions for essentially free office space for the Tigers in the new stadium.

Soon the litigants were joined by the attorney for the small nearby city of Belleville, objecting to the county's stadium authority filing levies on its residents to pay for the bond issue. The two sets of plaintiffs combined forces in one lawsuit. These men were Davids against a Goliath of civic leaders, lenders, sports and entertainment interests, and businessmen. Because of the heavy political backing for the project, the Michigan governor, Republican William Milliken, in an unprecedented step, ordered an expedited ruling from the state Supreme Court. There, to the dismay of the entire power structure of the city of Detroit and the state of Michigan, the deal was quickly struck down. The judge found duplicity in the bond prospectus—the financial instruments were advertised to buyers as revenue bonds but in fact were general obligation bonds, which meant, just as the county auditors had warned, taxpayers would be responsible for the stadium debt if and when the wildly optimistic revenue projections—such as 100,000 fans for rodeos or tennis matches to be held at the riverfront dome—failed to materialize. It was found that officials had even tried to bribe one of the litigants, Alan, with season box seat tickets, while threatening Prebenda, who said he was asked, "Do you want your kids to remember you as the man who destroyed the city of Detroit?"[16]

In fact, it was public officials' eagerness to sign onto new stadium plans, both in the poverty-plagued, cash-strapped city of Detroit and in the nearly equally destitute majority-black city of Pontiac, that helped drive a wedge between the ownership of the Lions and the Tigers and also cast a pall over the baseball seasons at Michigan and Trumbull in the early 1970s. Fresh off the 1968 World Series championship that many observers had characterized as uniting metropolitan Detroit and the state of Michigan, the Tigers were suddenly cast as the unfortunate tenants of an outdated stadium. The idea that new downtown stadiums could revitalize industrial cities abandoned by manufacturing and neglected by political leaders would be a recurring hope in years to come. But, with few exceptions such as (arguably) Baltimore, the hope was vastly overstated.

The Bird's Perch

After the Tigers plummeted into the American League's second division by 1970, Fetzer's management team corralled a combative field manager: the innovative and gregarious loose cannon Billy Martin, later to achieve fame when he was fired four separate times by flamboyant Yankee owner George Steinbrenner. Martin was creative and a great motivator with a burning will to win, but he was also an unpredictable maverick with an anger management problem and a propensity for burning out his pitchers' arms.[17] The fiery brand of baseball he instilled in his team was reminiscent in some ways of the reigns of Mickey Cochrane and Ty Cobb.

In 1971, the third All-Star Game in 30 years was played at Michigan and Trumbull, featuring a flurry of home runs including a memorable rooftop blast off a right field light tower by the Oakland Athletic slugger Reggie Jackson. Since the stadium's 1938 reconfiguration, some 30 balls were hit entirely out of the park over the right field roof, a prodigious but still achievable shot. This does not count the drives, like the one by Jackson, that would rattle off a rooftop light tower and bounce back into the stands or onto the roof or the field. The left field roof, about 50 feet more distant than in right field, required a mammoth drive to clear it, and only four home runs ever went over it, including just one by a Tiger—Cecil Fielder, on August 25, 1990.

Martin rallied the Tigers to contend again in 1971 and took his veteran team to the division title in 1972 by winning on the last day of the strike-shortened season. Though McLain had been dealt away, ostensibly because of his associations with gamblers but probably actually because his overworked pitching arm was going dead, most of the nucleus of the 1968 champions remained, and Martin led them toward the pennant in one last hurrah. But to get to the World Series, they had to win a playoff series against the Oakland As. It was a bizarre series beset by the unsettled mood of the era. The Tigers lost the deciding game at home as the crowd littered center field with bottles, cans, and other debris launched from the upper-deck bleachers. The atmosphere was very different from four years prior.

Martin was canned with the club still in contention during the 1973 season, and, with the championship team of 1968 fading into baseball old age, the underbelly of the Tigers' franchise was exposed. In the glory days while the crop of stars groomed in the early 1960s had matured, the management had not properly nurtured its farm system, neglecting the future to pour too many of its resources into the present. Most sports franchises fall into such cycles, except for perennially wealthy ones such as the Yankees, and the Tigers slid fast, hitting bottom in 1975 with only the second 100-loss season in club history. Attendance stayed above a million a year but declined to an 11-year low, and for only the fourth time in the four decades since Briggs expanded the stadium, it dipped a little under the league average. With just four years below league average attendance in those four decades—and this during a period when the club won the league pennant only three times—Detroit's attendance history certainly was a testament to the loyalty of fans to the franchise, but it also had much to do with the attractiveness of the ballpark, especially to a working-class metropolis with an appreciation for watching the sport up close without frills or gimmickry. Briggs' strategy of maximizing seating while maintaining intimacy had created enduring value and kept attendance healthy even when the team was sickly.

Baseball at Michigan and Trumbull had always pushed the limits of pleasure derived from a communal experience. In 1976, innocence returned in the person of a gangly, unheralded, frizzy-haired young pitcher named Mark Fidrych. And that summer burst the known bounds of shared joy among fervent crowds in a baseball park.

Fidrych was a naïve young man from Worcester, Massachusetts, blessed with a good arm if not really overpowering stuff. He was not a much-publicized prospect, and few expected him to make much of an impact, but he opened eyes immediately by pitching no-hit ball against the Cleveland Indians for six innings in his first major league start. When his good pitching continued game after game, the word started to spread, and crowds started coming out to see him. And no one had ever seen anyone in a baseball park quite like Fidrych before.

He was tagged with the nickname "The Bird," because his moptop of frizzy blond hair and his tall, skinny, slightly awkward demeanor reminded observers of the *Sesame Street* puppet Big Bird. But it was his unvarnished enthusiasm for the game that really turned on the crowd. The Bird would talk to himself on the mound while holding the ball in his hand, psyching himself up with words like "stay low." (His success was mainly due to a consistent sinker ball that stayed at the bottom of the strike zone where hitters would beat it into the dirt for easy ground ball outs.) People started saying that he was talking to the ball. At the start of each inning, and sometimes during an inning, he would get down on his hands and knees and pat down the dirt to keep the mound manicured to his liking. After his fielders made a play, he would shout out a hearty thanks to them and even sometimes bounce over and shake their hands. All of it was more than a little goofy, but it was no act: Fidrych's behavior flowed naturally from a genuine boyish delight in playing the game, and fans at Tiger Stadium, close to the stage where the Bird perched, instantly responded. In an age when salaries in all sports were starting to skyrocket and players were beginning to seem more like well-traveled mercenaries, shifting from club to club, and the sport itself, with its publicly subsidized new stadiums and schedules geared to the dictates of television, seemed more and more like a soulless business, the Bird embodied pure enjoyment, acting like any fan might if he or she were suddenly plucked from the stands and thrust onto the diamond. Fidrych was a regular guy with a flair for unabashed pleasure, expressing sheer joy at earning a living by playing a game. He was the embodiment of every little kid playing baseball. Fans soon packed the house whenever he pitched, in Detroit or on the road. In a nationally televised game against the Yankees on June 28, he beat them, took a curtain call (unheard of in those days), and became a star on the national stage. On July 13 he was the American League starter in the All-Star Game. Fidrych ended up going 19–9 and was voted Rookie of the Year.

And in that same year—with the Lions having fled the city of Detroit to their own domed stadium in Pontiac, there to encounter several decades of futility—the Tigers got a new boost. After the baseball season, Coleman Young, the first African American mayor of Detroit, determined not to lose another professional sports franchise to the suburbs, announced two significant plans. The first envisioned a new publicly financed hockey facility for the NHL's Red Wings, Joe Louis Arena, on a riverfront parcel that had been part of the site for the doomed domed multiuse stadium. The second was the city's purchase of Tiger Stadium from Fetzer as part of a scheme to secure federal funding for a stadium renovation. The Wings' old facility, Olympia, was just as beloved a historic structure as Tiger Stadium, having served the city for 67 years. It had hosted not only seven Stanley Cup championships for the Wings (one of the league's original six franchises) but also the NBA Pistons and the likes of Frank Sinatra, Elvis Presley, and the Beatles.[18] Still, city leaders were in agreement on their plans to replace it. With Fetzer publicly arguing that the facilities at Tiger Stadium needed an upgrade, he and Young worked out a different but no less promising solution for the baseball team. The city would buy the stadium for $1, lease it back to the club, and obtain $5 million in federal urban renewal grants to renovate it.

At first the plan hit a snag as some federal officials questioned the use of public funding for such a purpose, but after some months of political arm-twisting the deal was finalized in July 1977. The plan had become even more urgent after a fire of undetermined origin destroyed the press box at Tiger Stadium that February. In October, Fetzer signed a 30-year lease with options for three subsequent 10-year renewals. The city then issued bonds for $8.5 million to pay for the renovations. They would be repaid with a 50-cents-a-ticket surcharge.

The first plan for the stadium renovations by the architectural firm Rossetti Associates was announced in May 1978. Presented to the city with a price tag of $23 million, it would have replaced the prime front rows of upper deck seating around the infield with a mezzanine level of luxury suites, the boxes for entertaining corporate clients that were, along with club seating decks, the new cash cows of sports facilities nationwide. Exterior escalators would replace the old ramps to the upper levels of the park; parking structures would arch over nearby freeways; and concessions, clubhouses, rest rooms, and maintenance and other facilities would be expanded and modernized. But the plan was never realized.

Instead, repairs to the concrete decking ate up most of the bond money. Ice, snow, and salt spread generously in the stands during Lions games were said to have eaten holes in the foundations—though this assertion would be later debunked. There was not enough money left for a new mezzanine level; instead, a new press box was built on the facing of the third deck, and new radio and TV broadcast booths were built hanging down from the second deck behind home plate. The old hand-operated scoreboard was replaced with a large electronic one placed above the stadium wall behind the upper-deck center field bleachers. The old light towers from 1948 were replaced by new, smaller ones, making it easier for homers to fly unobstructed out of the park. The club also improved the electrical and plumbing systems, rest rooms, clubhouses, and other facilities. The dark green wooden seats were torn out and made their way into many collectors' homes; they were replaced by light blue or orange plastic chairs, creating a more modern but more garish and much less soothing appearance.

Just as the stadium was getting a makeover in the late 1970s and early 1980s, so was the team. Mark Fidrych had suffered a series of arm injuries right after his magical rookie season and despite several comeback attempts never regained his form. His 58-game career left Detroit fans with nothing much more than memories of his incredible rookie year. But soon the team was revitalized by a new crop of talent from the Tigers' farm system—most importantly, a double-play combination that would anchor the team for two decades: shortstop Alan Trammell and second baseman Lou Whitaker. They were smooth defensively and significant contributors offensively—and solid Hall of Famers if, alas, they had only played in New York, Los Angeles, Boston, or some other big media market. As it was, they labored in Midwestern obscurity for more than 20 seasons, their one-club careers a real rarity in the late 20th century. Joining them were homegrown pitchers Jack Morris and Dan Petry, catcher Lance Parrish, and a Michigan State University product, outfielder Kirk Gibson. Brought on to manage the promising young team was a garrulous skipper who had won World Series championships in Cincinnati a few years earlier: Sparky Anderson.

Monaghan's Mistake

In his nearly three decades as principal Tiger owner, John Fetzer had seen the value of his franchise increase tenfold. In the 1980s, baseball was entering the most lucrative period of its growth to date. Having secured the Tigers a place in the city of Detroit for at least the foreseeable future, during a time when the Lions and the National Basketball Association's Pistons had both moved out of Detroit for custom-built facilities in the far northern suburbs, Fetzer was content to turn over most of the operations of the franchise to general manager Jim Campbell. As Fetzer reached his early eighties, he started looking to sell the club. Befitting the new era, the two main suitors were both men who had made their fortunes selling pizza. Little Caesars boss Mike Ilitch now owned the Red Wings. Tom Monaghan, the multimillionaire founder and CEO of Domino's Pizza, lived in nearby Ann Arbor.

Ilitch would have been the clear favorite and logical choice had not the somewhat reclusive Fetzer, who had become a devotee of Eastern spirituality, taken to the even more reclusive and publicly awkward Monaghan, a devout Catholic with archconservative political and social beliefs. In October 1983, when it was announced he was buying the club for $53 million, Monaghan, a self-described lifelong Tiger fan, said publicly: "As long as I own this team, we will not build a new stadium." In matters of baseball as well as politics, he was a staunch traditionalist, he told the media. He even pledged to bring back the old green wooden seats and old painted brick exterior walls of the stadium, which had been clad with a metal siding during a second phase of stadium renovations that were completed for the 1984 season. (The new work brought the total price tag for the renovations to $18 million, and the ticket surcharge was raised from 50 to 90 cents to pay for it.) Monaghan later said he had offered to buy the stadium back from the city, but Mayor Coleman Young and his administration had refused.

Monaghan quickly proved his financial commitment to the team by engineering the first major free agent signing the Tigers had ever made. (Fetzer and Campbell had always resisted this kind of checkbook approach to team building.) The player acquired, first

The Tiger Stadium marquee in 1984. It remained characteristically plain and functional even at World Series time until the Ilitches bought the Tigers in 1992 and, in the following year, installed the Tiger Plaza and a new marquee (Frank Rashid).

baseman Darrell Evans, was the last piece needed in assembling a powerhouse team. When the Tigers skyrocketed to an incredible 35–5 start in 1984, Monaghan seemed like the luckiest grown-up little boy in town with a lucrative new toy. The stadium was freshly wrapped in a new exterior, and the fast start made Tiger tickets a hot item all over the state. The team ended up drawing a record 2.7 million fans in a yearlong carnival atmosphere. Detroit, beset by new rounds of auto industry layoffs and plant closings and troubled by its persistent image as a city beset by poverty and crime, thumbed its nose at the rest of the baseball world. The brash, cocky Gibson led the charge, and the Tigers led their division wire-to-wire. In the postseason, the Tigers made quick work of the Kansas City Royals, the American League's Western Division champs, and then awaited a rematch with their most frequent World Series foes, the Chicago Cubs. Instead, the Cubs were upset by the San Diego Padres, a team that proved no match for Detroit. Indeed, by the fifth game of the World Series, the Tigers were poised to clinch the championship in front of a raucous sellout crowd. As thousands of other fans watched the game in bars near the stadium, Gibson put the exclamation point on the season with a mammoth home run that provided some insurance runs after reliever Goose Gossage had convinced his manager, Dick Williams, in a conference at the mound not to walk him intentionally. The win touched off a wild "dancing in the streets" celebration outside the stadium, but it turned ugly when a stoned suburban kid, sort of an anti–Bird, torched a police car at Michigan and Trumbull.

The mid–1980s were another period of perennial success for the Motor City Kitties, but Tiger management again made the usual mistake of a contender: cashing in all its chips for another last hurrah while neglecting investment in the long-term health of the club, in its farm system, and scouting. In 1987, Anderson found himself with an aging collection of veterans; in a way, that squad was to the '84 champions much like the 1972 team was to the '68 winners. And they met a similar fate. After a lackluster start in which the Tigers were overshadowed and often outdrawn by the Red Wings, whose perennial playoff series usually dragged into May and June, the baseball team turned it around and began a long, exciting climb from last into a battle for first place, passing rivals one by one.

Meanwhile, however, Monaghan had begun waffling on his pledge not to replace Tiger Stadium. His general manager, Jim Campbell, was openly saying the club needed a new facility. Even the old rejected Rossetti architectural plan of years past was revived, this time with a new twist: somehow adding a retractable dome to the stadium (though this was probably a red herring meant to make the cost of building a completely new open-air stadium seem reasonable by comparison).

The regular season ended with a three-game showdown at Tiger Stadium against the Toronto Blue Jays for the Eastern Division title. The Tigers, who had clawed their way back into contention, needed to sweep the series to clinch the crown and managed to do so with three taut one-run triumphs. The exciting climax to an unlikely season, however, seemed to exhaust the team's last energies, and the veteran club lost a disappointing league playoff series to the Minnesota Twins.

Early in 1988, the city of Detroit announced it would entertain proposals for renovation or replacement of Tiger Stadium. Soon an unobtainable and possibly nonexistent "engineering study" was publicized by the Tigers that pegged the cost of renovation at $45-$100 million, but that turned out to be a seat-of-the-pants estimate that included a new fabric roof.

What followed was a protracted battle over the future of the ballpark that consisted of numerous renovation plans; studies both legitimate and highly contested; conflicting claims about maintenance costs; the organization of an official stadium preservation group, the Tiger Stadium Fan Club; and even two stadium "hugs" in April 1988 and June 1990. (See Frank Rashid's, p. 129, for discussion of this protracted and contentious struggle.)

In 1989, Tiger Stadium was included for the first time on the National Register of Historic Places. Two years later it was named by the National Trust for Historical Preservation as one of the country's 11 most important endangered sites. The fan club's Cochrane Plan demonstrated that renovation—similar to what had been done at Wrigley Field and would be done at Fenway Park—could be accomplished for $26.1 million, a fraction of the cost of a new facility. But Mayor Young was dead set on a new stadium.

Before the 1990 season, Monaghan named Bo Schembechler as the new club president. Schembechler, the longtime and much-lauded former University of Michigan football coach, knew nothing about running a professional baseball team, and the duo of the ex–gridiron boss and the ultrareligious pizza man proved problematic. Monaghan, an outsider not connected to the power structure in Detroit, became increasingly absorbed in faith-based projects. (Eventually, he would build his own college, law school, and even a new town in Florida to construct his own isolated world of ultraconservative Catholicism.) The battle over the stadium's future was wearying to him, and he left Schembechler as his point man, but the old coach was also tone deaf to baseball and to the culture and politics of Detroit. Shockingly, Schembechler, badly overplaying his hand as the cocky team boss, did the unthinkable—he fired the most popular man in Michigan, the radio voice of the Tigers for three decades, Ernie Harwell.

When Harwell announced that 1991 would be his last season as the play-by-play announcer due to a forced retirement, a firestorm of unheard-of proportions was unleashed. Harwell, though a loyal company man, was torn. He professed his affection for Tiger Stadium and embodied the very tradition the stadium represented. He appeared at a Tiger Stadium Fan Club event and invited one of its spokesmen to be on a pregame radio show, though stopping well short of becoming a fervent opponent of the push for a new stadium. And as a beloved figure who would be welcome in nearly every home in the state of Michigan, whose humble demeanor and kindness were evident in everything he said, and whose keen understanding of what baseball, in its traditional form, meant to all his listeners, especially the many longtime Tigers loyalists among them, Harwell was an iconic yet highly approachable figure. Thus, his absence from the radio booth was a loss of something vital. To the far-flung "nation" of Detroiters and ex-Michiganders, Harwell represented a time and a place they could remember, embodying a powerful and irreplaceable connection to home. And the home that Ernie Harwell spoke of, whenever his voice was heard in a baseball broadcast or other context, was located at what he liked to call simply "The Corner"—Michigan and Trumbull.

Schembechler's dismissal of Harwell was the one great mistake that insured the end of Monaghan's tenure as the Tiger owner. For a time, the controversy over Harwell leaving the broadcast booth overshadowed the controversy about the stadium. It tarnished Schembechler's reputation, and it destroyed Monaghan's credibility as the club owner. While Tiger management threatened to leave town if they did not get a new publicly financed stadium, after Harwell's canning the Monaghan regime became less viable.

Ilitch Seals the Deal

When Mike Ilitch bought the club in 1992 for a reported $82 million, it was a simple matter to garner instant goodwill by bringing back Harwell and by making the customary initial statements that he would try to save and renovate the stadium. But Ilitch did not really need much additional goodwill. By preserving and renovating the Fox Theater downtown, the grandest of Detroit's many ornate pre–Depression-era movie palaces, Ilitch was already a civic hero. He also had garnered much praise for bucking the trend toward abandonment of the city and keeping his headquarters for Little Caesars in downtown Detroit. He was the only prominent white business leader who was willing to stay in the city, and he would reap tremendous benefits for that in the form of a publicly subsidized downtown sports-and-entertainment empire that, though confined to a portion of downtown and having no effect on the residential areas of the city, would be the core showcase of rebuilding efforts for Detroit.

In the 1990s, meanwhile, the Tigers ended the Sparky Anderson era by turning from a perennial contender to a chronically losing ball club again. In 1992 Ilitch oversaw the last renovation at the corner of Michigan and Trumbull, which included an open-air merchandising bazaar called "Tiger Plaza" inside a new entrance at Michigan and Trumbull—the new owner's first effort to take some souvenir revenue away from the traditional vendors outside his facility. Another low-cost change was sprucing up the lower-deck seats behind home plate to become the "Tiger Den," a VIP seating area complete with waitstaff bringing food and drinks. Otherwise, the Tigers and the City of Detroit continued to make only minimal efforts to maintain the facilities at Tiger Stadium.

After 1996, when Ilitch finally prevailed in his fight to replace Tiger Stadium and ground was broken at a new site across Woodward Avenue from the Fox Theater entertainment district, club officials suddenly began to emphasize the tradition and history of the building they had denigrated and neglected for years. The stadium that club personnel had so often decried for years as inadequate, deficient, and unprofitable was repackaged from a marketing standpoint. Since it was evolving into a nostalgia item, there was money to be made from it, and, as he had shown at the Fox Theater, Ilitch knew how to market nostalgia. With the new stadium to be built near the Fox, his empire would expand into several city blocks of sports and entertainment venues, bars and restaurants, souvenir shops, and parking lots where his companies would capture all possible revenues. With this coup, Ilitch had taken control of about a sixth of downtown Detroit.[19]

In the final years of Tiger Stadium's existence as the home park for the Detroit baseball club, there was money to be milked from it. The ball club had neither difficulty nor shame in selling tickets to the place they were eviscerating, touting it as a beautiful "historic ballpark" to which everyone in the region should make at least one, and preferably several, final pilgrimages, and purchase the nostalgic merchandise for sale—hats, pennants, T-shirts, and other items commemorating the stadium, its history, and its famous players. The marketing pitch continued to ramp up until it reached a feverish frenzy in the final season and then, in the weeks leading up to the "historic last game at Michigan and Trumbull," the atmosphere of some sort of morbid circus.

If the stadium were so wonderful, why was the club leaving it? Well, the club marketers continued to say, it had outlived its time, but boy, what a "grand old lady" it was! Among those who thronged to see the Tigers in their final season at The Corner in 1999, as the century of their tenancy as an American League charter franchise wound down, were many who recognized what was being discarded. Fathers and sons, grandfathers and daughters, husband and wives, groups of old schoolmates, and young people eager to see the insides of another grand old Detroit landmark before its abandonment walked up to the gates and entered to soak up for one last time its breathtaking views, drinking in memories all the more valuable for their evocation of generations past. They snapped countless photographs. How might the ball club have prospered if it had continued this marketing approach as it refurbished and repaired the stadium and kept it alive? With many more seats than Fenway Park and Wrigley Field, the only two structures of its era that have been allowed to remain, Tiger Stadium might have been as profitable as those two beloved ballparks, which have continued to attract reliable sellout crowds of baseball fans, both local and out-of-town, who long to connect with a living embodiment of the sport's celebrated history. Fenway and Wrigley, well into the next century, have remained acclaimed, useful, attractive, and extremely profitable venues for their owners. The Red Sox's cramped but beautiful old park would help them remain perennial contenders by generating uninterrupted capacity crowds year after year. And Wrigley's proven effectiveness as a major drawing card for a perennially noncontending club would make that franchise exceptionally valuable and continue to generate activity that sustained the life of a vibrant urban neighborhood where local businesses—bars and restaurants and souvenir shops and parking lots independently owned and operated—thrived.

Instead, in Detroit, the Tigers were selling tickets to the performance of a melodramatic, prolonged, excruciating public execution, cheered by adoring patrons in their ringside seats. They were abandoning the building but squeezing every last drop of money from its death throes. From 1990 to 1995, the Tigers collected at least $7 million in ticket surcharges that were supposed to go to the city for stadium maintenance under the terms of their 1977 30-year lease. The club failed to account for all its expenses, and some of the money went to buy Little Caesars pizza pans, according to reports in the *Detroit Sunday Journal*.[20] Imagine a doctor withdrawing life support from an elderly patient—and charging admission to watch this homicide while managing lucrative concessions at the bedside. Like a certain notorious pathologist operating in the region in the same era, the Detroit ball club was marketing an "assisted suicide" as a charitable act. At least Jack Kevorkian did not charge admission and sell merchandise while doing his macabre experiments in social engineering. And the demise of Tiger Stadium, despite the club's protestations to the contrary, was no "mercy killing." It was, in fact, a merciless and misguided business decision—a massive transfer of wealth from taxpayers to the coffers of a multimillionaire businessman.

As the 1999 season progressed, the crowds increased at Tiger Stadium along with the team's ineptitude. This, too, was part of the plan. Though never overtly acknowledged by the club, it was clear to many knowledgeable baseball fans what the strategy was. The Tigers were following a blueprint executed in many other cities where the public had gifted its ballclub a new stadium: they seemed to be skimping on player contracts and free agent offers in anticipation of a new surge of revenue. They were counting on an infusion of capital from their new stadium to resurrect the team. In the case of the Tigers, however, the scheme would, at least initially, fail miserably.

Some fans refused to participate in the nostalgia orgy of the final game, finding the whole thing repugnant. They said their quiet farewells on their own, in meaningless games in a meaningless season, just like so many others that they had witnessed in previous seasons just for the pleasure of an afternoon or evening at the park. Some refused even to watch the last game on television, picking up only secondhand the news of the game won, 8–2, and climaxing with the final one of more than 11,000 homers at Michigan and Trumbull, a grand slam roof shot to right by catcher Robert Fick that seemed so fitting as almost to be scripted. Ceremonies followed in which former Tiger greats stood at their old positions on the field and during which tears were visible on the face of Willie Horton in left field, standing in the area where he unleashed the astounding throw that nailed Lou Brock at home plate in October 1968 and turned around the World Series, probably in close vicinity to where produce aimed at Ducky Medwick landed during the 1934 Series. Finally, home plate was dug up to be taken to the club's new field of play, a facility named for the bank that offered the most money in the high rollers' naming game.

The Grounds Left Behind

For nearly a decade after the Tigers moved, Tiger Stadium remained largely untouched. In 2000, a film was shot on location there—the HBO movie *61**, about the Maris-Mantle home run chase of 1961. The stadium stood in for Yankee Stadium, with seats painted to match the Bronx ballpark. On July 24, 2001, as Detroit celebrated its 300th birthday, the stadium hosted a Great Lakes Summer Collegiate League game between the Motor City Marauders and the Lake Erie Monarchs. It was staged by a local sports management company hoping to convince the city to permit a club in the Frontier League (an independent minor league not associated with Major League Baseball [MLB]) to play at The Corner. The following spring the Tigers held a fantasy camp there run by former players.

In subsequent years maintenance was neglected. The city still owned the stadium, though the money generated by the old ticket surcharge was not being spent by the city but funneled instead to Ilitch—a final posthumous insult. Small trees started growing up through Frank Navin's old grandstand. The place flooded in rainstorms, and the weather was left to wreak its havoc all winter and summer. The cash-strapped city said it had no money to demolish it.

The city floated requests for proposals for reuse of the stadium, and several plans were received. The plans varied in how practical or fanciful they were, and many proposals were creative and sought to capitalize in some way on the site's heritage, incorporating a baseball museum, for instance, or using the field of play for amateur, semipro, or collegiate competition. But officials did not really take any of them seriously, and the whole exercise came to resemble a charade.[21] Many observers speculated that Ilitch would never countenance any plans for athletic reuse of the field. Ideas that called for the Tigers to place a minor league franchise at Michigan and Trumbull and to continue to use the field as it had been in the past for high school and college athletics or possibly for amateur baseball or softball might have seemed dangerous to the Tiger owner; he had surely known that an independent minor league team in St. Paul had occasionally outdrawn the Minnesota Twins in 1995.[22] The last thing Ilitch probably wanted was to have baseball fans return to Tiger Stadium to experience firsthand how great it still was to watch baseball there. This was especially true because it was not going so well for the club at the new stadium. After a modest initial attendance surge in the opening season of 2000, average crowds fell off by 44 percent from 30,106 in the inaugural year to 16,892 three years later, both embarrassingly low for a new park of that era.[23] Fans complained about distant seating, exposure to the sun or rain, the circus atmosphere (complete with a Ferris wheel and merry-go-round), and general dissimilarity to Tiger Stadium. Baseball fans, especially those Detroiters and Michiganders who had not visited many stadiums elsewhere, suffered from a bad case of "You don't know what you've got till it's gone."

Since the projected new revenues did not materialize, the club was thrown into disarray, plummeting to new depths in the disastrous season of 2003, when the team lost an incredible 119 games. That year, an independent minor league franchise at Tiger Stadium might have outdrawn the Tigers on certain days. Thus, Tiger Stadium was caught in limbo. It could not get a proper burial because of lack of money. The city said it could not afford the costs of demolition, and it could not afford the costs of maintenance, and it would not buy any ideas for its creative reuse. And it could not be revived, even temporarily, because it was still too great a place to watch baseball and would threaten the huge investment already made, both by the public and by Ilitch, to build Comerica Park. So, like many grand old buildings in Detroit—from public facilities like the train station and hotels and movie theaters to factories and other workplaces to magnificent private homes—it stood there abandoned, vandalized, fallen to ruins, and decaying. (These places, including Tiger Stadium, first became immortalized on artist Lowell Boileau's website *The Fabulous Ruins of Detroit*, and in subsequent years several documentaries and books have also emphasized the spectacular demise of the city.[24] Many of the "ruins" achieved underground cult status, often illegally visited by suburban youth.)

Individuals and groups, most notably the Old Tiger Stadium Conservancy, sprang up, offering to find and fund a solution for Michigan and Trumbull. Creative minds interested in preserving the best of Detroit and perhaps aiding in its revival continued to submit proposals and tried to get them publicized. They were stonewalled by the city for years. Detroit could have been the first city to find a viable new use for an abandoned major league baseball stadium.[25] But the powerful forces that had for decades squabbled over the fate of Tiger Stadium and then finally coalesced on a scheme for its abandonment and replacement had given little thought to what to do with the place after they signed its death sentence.

Finally, in 2009, a demolition firm decided it could sell what remained of the place for scrap and got a contract from the city to tear the place down. It was done in stages, so that for many months all that stood was a dismembered double-deck portion behind home plate, that is, most of Frank Navin's original structure and the flagpole in center field. The grandstand looked even taller and more commanding than it had when it was part of the whole enclosed structure, and now, exposed to the outside world, it really did look like an ancient ruin.

And then it too was torn down and bulldozed and carted away, a pile of twisted beams and slabs and rotten innards, till all that remained was the overgrown field.

Even many years after it vanished, Tiger Stadium is still so closely identified with the Detroit club that many continue to invoke it, intentionally or not: for example, during the nationally televised broadcast of a 2012 American League Championship Series game, an announcer remarked that Detroit centerfielder Austin Jackson, who had just run a long way to make a catch at the "new" Yankee Stadium, was adept at covering the spacious center field grounds in his home park, "Tiger Stadium." Many Michiganders, too, in casual conversations, remark that they are going to a game at Tiger Stadium, when they mean to say Comerica Park. It might be because, even though the century-old address of the Detroit baseball club is now a vacant field, in the minds of followers of the Tigers and baseball fans everywhere—and even for Detroiters who are not baseball fans—Tiger Stadium remains an indelible place.[26]

In April 2012, while Boston celebrated the centennial of its world-famous and beloved Fenway Park, a few dozen people in Detroit gathered on the 100th anniversary of Navin Field. They brought old stadium seats with dark green peeling paint, cooked hot dogs on a grill, and tossed a ball around the infield. Folks for several seasons now have raked and maintained the infield, mowed grass in the outfield, and played sandlot games. People driving by on Michigan Avenue continue to honk, wave, or stop and gawk. It is again just a pasture, that old hay market, once a forested grove, always a gathering spot for people who feel a connection with an enchanted patch of ground.

Notes

1. For information on working conditions and labor battles in the Briggs plants, see Steve Babson's *Working Detroit: The Making of a Union Town* (Detroit: Wayne State University Press, 1984), 61–63. See also Mark Theobald's 2004 essay "Briggs Mfg. Co." for the website Coachbuilt, http://www.coachbuilt.com/bui/b/briggs/briggs.htm.

2. Navin Field had occasionally been rented by black teams "as early as 1916." In the early years of World War II, several Negro League teams played at Briggs Stadium. See Richard Bak's *A Place for Summer: A Narrative History of Tiger Stadium* (Detroit: Wayne State University Press, 1998), 142, 202–203.

3. Later in this book, John Pastier details the way the project proceeded, including Osborn Engineering's role in the stadium's expansion.

4. As one Detroiter wrote during the 1999 season, when the media were filled with nostalgic accounts of the stadium's last days: "To a substantial number of Detroiters, Tiger Stadium stands as a symbol of past racism ... I am talking about a team that did business in a way that was morally reprehensible for a very long time." http://thewaynefontesexperience.blogspot.com/2008/07/i-refuse-to-go-into-mourning-over-pile.html.

5. Standard reference works of the period most commonly list Briggs Stadium's capacity as 58,000 and the Polo Grounds' as either 55,000 or 56,000. All of these are most likely incorrect. A more realistic number for Briggs is 54,000, and an analysis of big-game attendance figures (opening days, World Series games, and All-Star games) for both parks show the Polo Grounds' capacity to be lower than Briggs.'

6. "All Star Game Attendance," http://www.baseball-almanac.com.

7. Bill Shannon and George Kalinsky, *The Ballparks* (New York: Hawthorn Books, 1975), 255.

8. For other accounts of the first night game, see Michael Betzold and Ethan Casey, *Queen of Diamonds: The Tiger Stadium Story* (West Bloomfield, Michigan: Altwerger and Mandel, 1992), 67; Bak, *A Place for Summer: A Narrative History of Tiger Stadium*, 215–217; and Bak's blog entry, "The Tigers Were Last American League Team to Install Lights," http://blog.detroitathletic.com/2012/06/15/when-night-baseball-came-to-detroit/.

9. Bak, *A Place for Summer: A Narrative History of Tiger Stadium*, 240–241.

10. Brian McKenna, "Eddie Gaedel," SABR Baseball Biography Project, http://sabr.org/bioproject.

11. Maxwell Kates, "Norman Cash," SABR Baseball Biography Project, http://sabr.org/bioproject.

12. Ernie Harwell, *Tuned to Baseball* (South Bend, Indiana: Diamond Communications, 1985), 56–57. See also Houston Mitchell, "Was a Dodger Player Once Traded for Announcer Ernie Harwell?" *Los Angeles Times*, June 27, 2012.

13. For an excellent analysis of the combination of forces that led to Detroit's abandonment, see Thomas J. Sugrue, *The Origins of the Urban Crisis: Race and Inequality in Postwar Detroit* (Princeton: Princeton University Press, 1996). See also Frank Rashid's "Losing Tiger Stadium" in this volume.

14. For thorough analysis of the 1967 uprising, see Sidney Fine, *Violence in the Model City: The Cavanagh Administration, Race Relations, and the Riot of 1967* (East Lansing: Michigan State University Press, 2007) and Sugrue.

15. Horton's account of his actions can be found in Jason Beck's "Horton's Heroics Went Far Beyond the Diamond," *Detroit Tigers*, February 14, 2012, *http://detroit.tigers.mlb.com/news/article.jsp?ymd=20120214&content_id=26687178&vkey=news_det&c_id=det*.

16. See also Betzold and Casey, 95–100.

17. Bill James, "Abuse and Durability," in Bill James and Rob Neyer, *The Neyer/James Guide to Pitchers: An Historical Compendium of Pitching, Pitchers, and Pitches* (New York: Simon & Schuster, 2008), 449.

18. Robert Wimmer, *Detroit's Olympia Stadium* (Chicago: Arcadia, 2000) and Robert Wimmer, *Remembering Detroit's Olympia Stadium* (Chicago: Arcadia, 2001).

19. Curt Guyette, "Render unto Caesar: The Devil's in the Details and Pizza Man Mike Ilitch Got One Hell of a Deal," *Metro Times*, April 23, 1997.

20. Bill McGraw, Robert Ourlian, and Paige St. John, "Ilitch Collects, City Trusts: Audit Finds Detroit Hasn't Forced Him to Live up to Contracts," *The Detroit Sunday Journal*, November 26, 1995, and Paige St. John, "Ilitch Spends Repair Funds on Pizza Gear: City Auditor Examines How Tigers Ticket Surcharge Was Spent," *The Detroit Sunday Journal*, December 24, 1995.

21. See Rebecca Long's "The Battle for Sacred Ground, 1998–2011," p. 153.

22. Kevin Lukow, "20 Years of St. Paul Saints Memories by the Year ... 1995," The Tenth Inning Stretch, July 31, 2012, http://10thinningstretch.blogspot.com/2012/07/20-years-of-st-paul-saints-memories-by_31.html.

23. "Detroit Tigers Attendance, Stadiums, and Park Factors," http://www.baseball-reference.com.

24. Boileau developed *The Fabulous Ruins of Detroit* in the late 1990s long before the current fascination with urban ruins. Visit the site at http://www.detroityes.com/fabulous-ruins-of-detroit/home.php.

25. In the 1970s, Troy West, a Pittsburgh architect, unsuccessfully proposed a nonsports reuse plan for Forbes Field.

26. Even in 2013, one commentator, Jonah Keri, still ranked Tiger Stadium number one on a list of 36 ballparks, old and new, that he visited:

This is what baseball looks like in movies, and these are the ancient features that strike a visceral chord in a way that even the most picturesque new parks can't.... There's no perfectly objective way to say that Tiger Stadium outshined Oriole Park, AT&T, or any of the other amenity-stuffed palaces built with modern-day creature comforts in mind. But when you walk into a ballpark and instantly feel like you've been transported to a point in the distant past, when the sport was first rising to popularity and the first steel cathedrals were going up, that transcends any other point in a competing park's favor.

Excerpted from http://grantland.com/the-triangle/ranking-the-best-ballpark-experiences-part-2/.

Detroit Lions Roar at Briggs Stadium

Bill Dow

When a syndicate of local businessmen led by WJR radio magnate G.A. Richards purchased the NFL's bankrupt Portsmouth Spartans in 1934 for $23,000, the newly christened Detroit Lions looked to a local university to host professional football in a city mired in the Great Depression. At a rental cost of $400 a game, Dinan Field, a 25,000-seat concrete stadium for the University of Detroit Titans, became the stage for a hungry and talent-laden team led by quarterback Earl "Dutch" Clark and his explosive running mates Ace Gutowsky and Ernie Caddel.[1]

When the Lions captured their first NFL the following year by defeating the Giants 26–7 at the campus on McNichols Road and Livernois, Lions football had caught hold. After the average attendance for the 1937 season reached above 19,000, the club realized that the growing popularity of professional football necessitated acquiring a bigger facility.[2] They quickly found out that the Detroit Tigers would be willing to share their newly enlarged stadium.

In 1938, Detroit Tigers owner Walter Briggs was happy to make his newly expanded ballpark one of the nation's premiere multipurpose facilities, and he agreed to lease Briggs Stadium to the Lions. After seeing the damage professional football had done to his prized diamond, however, he forced the Lions to return to University of Detroit for the 1940 season. Subsequently, the Lions would lease Briggs/Tiger Stadium from the Tigers for the next 35 seasons.

The Lions fell to the Redskins, 7–5, on October 16, 1938, in their first contest at Briggs Stadium before a huge crowd of 42,855 fans, who had paid ticket prices ranging from 55 cents to $2.20.[3] With an average attendance of 30,000 in their first season at the new venue, the Lions' decision to relocate was more than validated. By the end of the 1940s, when the club won a total of ten games in four years, the Lions threatened to close shop after reporting a combined loss of $206,000 for the 1948 and 1949 seasons, and the average attendance had plummeted to 17,300.[4]

The club's fortunes finally turned in 1950 when the Lions drafted Heisman Trophy winners Doak Walker, the elusive back from Southern Methodist University, and Notre Dame's giant end Leon Hart, and, in a trade with the New York Bulldogs, acquired blond-haired quarterback Bobby Layne, the team's colorful general. After Raymond "Buddy" Parker was elevated to head coach in 1951, the Lions let out a roar heard around the coun-

Doak Walker at Briggs Stadium in 1951 (original *Detroit Times* photograph; collection of Bill Dow).

try. Two years later, rookie middle linebacker Joe Schmidt became the leader of a tenacious defense. By decade's end, the Lions had captured three NFL championships in 1952, 1953, and 1957. Detroit defeated Cleveland in their first two championship meetings in 1952 and 1953, and in 1957 the Lions had revenge on their minds for the 1954 title game that saw the Browns slaughter them, 56–10.

On a sunny 32-degree day before a sold-out Briggs Stadium crowd of 55,263 fans who paid $4 to $10 for tickets, the Lions' Jim Martin kicked off and booted the ball completely over the Cleveland end zone at the 365-foot left field distance marker as the Lion band played the team's fight song, "Gridiron Heroes."[5] The chilly fans at Briggs Stadium and the Detroit area television pirates then witnessed a massacre of historic proportions. When the gun sounded off with a 59–14 Detroit victory, hundreds of fans stormed the field and carried off Joe Schmidt and quarterback Tobin Rote on their shoulders.

One of those fans later became a famous collegiate head coach. A week later, 18-year-old Riverview High School senior Bill McCartney was delighted to open up his *Sports Illustrated* issue to see himself (identified by his varsity jacket) in the crowd carrying Schmidt off the field: "My high school band was invited to play at the game, and the director asked me if I would like to come along, so I got in without a ticket and stood on the field," the former head football coach at the University of Colorado, Boulder, recalls. "I was a linebacker, and Joe Schmidt was my hero, so I immediately ran to him at the end of that unforgettable game. It was such a thrill to be there on the field with Schmidt and later showing everyone the *Sports Illustrated* photo."[6]

The sellout crowds at Michigan and Trumbull in the 1950s cemented a loyal fan base still evident today. The fond memory of being huddled with his family at Tiger Stadium in inclement weather continues to linger with Craig Miner of suburban Birmingham, whose parents held season tickets: "I'll always remember as a little kid sitting in the lower deck in right field behind the benches in the late '60s, zipped up in a fur-lined bag with hand warmers and barely able to look over the screen," Miner says. "Lions football is entrenched in our family's blood from those days. When there is a snowstorm, my mother always said the Lions should be playing outside. You kind of miss the mud games, the cold and the flurries."[7]

Former Detroit Lions offensive guard Bob Kowalkowski remembered the inclement weather at Tiger Stadium: "Playing at Tiger Stadium with all its tradition was great, but it could be difficult at times," Kowalkowski told the *Free Press*. "I'll never forget playing the Eagles in the '68 Thanksgiving Day game in a driving rainstorm. I pulled out on a sweep and lost my shoe. The referee called a time out so we could look in the mud for it. Then all the ruts froze after the game, so that week we practiced at Wayne State, the State Fair Coliseum right after a rodeo, and the basement of the Cobo [Hall] garage in our tennis shoes."[8]

The Lions of the early 1960s were perennial runners-up, but they featured a swarming defense led by captain and middle linebacker Joe Schmidt and Detroit's famous front line, the "Fearsome Foursome," that featured Alex Karras, Roger Brown, Darris McCord, and Sam Williams.

One of the greatest games in Lions history occurred on Thanksgiving Day 1962 at Tiger Stadium. After losing a heartbreaker, 9–7, in the last minute in their earlier game at Green Bay, on Thanksgiving Day the Lions mauled the Packers in a 26–14 victory as Packer quarterback Bart Starr was sacked 11 times, six of those by Brown.[9] In addition to causing Starr to fumble a ball that was taken in for a touchdown by Sam Williams, Brown scored his second safety of the year and end Gail Cogdill hauled in two touchdown catches.

By the late 1960s owner William Clay Ford wanted a larger and modern domed facility with luxury-suite revenue, but after a few years of discussion with local officials, he rejected the proposal of a riverfront stadium, instead preferring a football-only stadium near Michigan and Trumbull. As protracted negotiations broke down, the Lions looked north to Pontiac.

On Thanksgiving Day, November 28, 1974, in front of a crowd of 51,157 fans, the era of Lion football in the great outdoors at Tiger Stadium ended when the team lost to Denver, 31–27, and also lost their star fullback Steve Owens to a career-ending knee injury. It was an unhappy conclusion to the 36 years at the stadium where the Lions had their glory days in the 1950s. Despite its rich football history at the ballpark, there was little fanfare about the last professional football game played at Tiger Stadium.

Thanks to the residents of Pontiac, who passed by a margin of just 393 votes a bond issue to finance construction of a $55 million domed facility, the Lions got their wish. Tomahawk Hill, a motorcycle playground on the corner of M-59 and Pontiac, was quickly transformed into the 80,494-seat Pontiac Metropolitan Stadium in 1975. Just 25 years later the Lions returned to the city of Detroit when Ford Field opened next to Comerica Park at an estimated cost of $430 million to build, financed through private money, public money, and the sale of the naming rights.[10]

Notes

1. For detail about the history of football at Michigan and Trumbull, including early efforts to establish the game at Navin Field, see Richard Bak, *A Place for Summer: A Narrative History of Tiger Stadium* (Detroit: Wayne State University Press, 1998), 247–289.

2. The Lions had six home games and a home attendance of 114,673, for an average of 19,112 per game. See the "NFL Attendance Index," Rodney Fort's Sports Business Data, updated May 24, 2013, https://umich.app.box.com/s/41707f0b2619c0107b8b/1/320026115/2560908089/1.

3. Bak, 258–259. The October 16 game against Washington was the second home game of the season. The Lions had beaten the Pittsburgh Pirates, 16–7, on Friday, September 9, at the University of Detroit. This was not to avoid a conflict with the Tigers, who played at Cleveland on that day, but presumably because Briggs did not want the field damaged by football during the baseball season. As Bak points out, baseball came first at Briggs Stadium, and schedule conflicts made it necessary for the Lions to play occasionally at the University of Detroit until 1950.

4. In 1949, the Lions drew only 104,057 fans, for an average of 17,343 fans per game. See "NFL Attendance Index."

5. Despite the sellout, NFL Commissioner Bert Bell created a fan firestorm by ruling that the title game scheduled to be played four days after Christmas would be blacked out to television viewers in the Detroit area. Bell refused to relent, even after last-minute appeals from hundreds of fans as well as Michigan governor G. Mennen Williams. For those not lucky enough to attend the game, a number of clever fans defeated Bell's 70-mile-wide TV blackout by jury-rigging antennas in order to pick up Lansing's NBC signal and the national telecast by Van Patrick and Ken Coleman.

6. Bill Dow, "Roar Golden Roar: In Their 1957 Championship Year, the Lions Were Truly a Team of Destiny," *Detroit Free Press*, September 28, 2007.

7. Bill Dow, "An Ode to the Former Lions Dens," *Detroit Free Press*, August 21, 2002.

8. *Ibid.*

9. Most sources agree that Starr was sacked 11 times, but "Green Bay Packers 14 at Detroit Lions 26," www.pro-football-reference.com says that Starr was sacked "only" ten times, and the National Football League records do not include Detroit's performance on their list of teams that have had 11 sacks in a game. Also, official NFL statistics for individual sacks were not kept until 1982.

10. See Frank Rashid's "Losing Tiger Stadium, 1987–1997," p. 129, for more on the financing of Ford Field.

Longevity and Adaptability
Tiger Stadium's Evolution, Architecture, Functionality, Structure and Urban Context

JOHN PASTIER WITH DRAWINGS BY JOHN DAVIDS

Under three successive names, and in perhaps a dozen configurations, Tiger Stadium was one of the three longest-serving ballparks in major league history, bested only by its still-active cohorts, Fenway Park and Wrigley Field.[1] Indeed, during the final decade of the 20th century, it was tied with Fenway Park as the all-time record holder for longest major league service. At the time of its abandonment, it had hosted big-league action for 88 seasons, and stood intact for nine more, until its owner, the city of Detroit, began a demolition process that dragged out over the next several years.

Location

Its site, which had also served its predecessor, Bennett Park, from 1896 to 1911, was the major league leader in games played during the 20th century, as well as in total professional baseball seasons and games, dating back to the 19th.[2] The northwest corner of Michigan and Trumbull avenues was the first American location to continuously house an important professional team sports venue for more than a century, logging 104 consecutive years as a minor league and major league baseball facility, in addition to serving as a professional football stadium and a professional boxing venue. After that, it stood as a historic monument, at first intact but essentially empty, and later partially demolished, yet still forming an impressive double-decked backdrop for sandlot games until its final demolition a decade later in September 2009.[3] And until 2016, with its last structural remnants gone, the site still played host to informal games, 120 years after baseball activity began there.

Even without counting any activity at Bennett Park, Tiger Stadium was the first ballpark to log 10,000 regular-season home runs, and it drew about 125 million customers through its turnstiles—109 million for regular season and postseason major league baseball, 11 million for professional football, and millions more for boxing, amateur sports, concerts, religious gatherings, political rallies,[4] and other public events. During its heyday—1912–1988, from the opening of Navin Field until club management alienated fans by disparaging the old ballpark and aggressively seeking a new one—the Tigers drew 88

Downtown Detroit over the right field stands, August 29, 1999 (© Rebecca Cook).

million customers, or 29 percent more than the 68 million average of contemporaneous American League clubs.[5]

Much of this success in attracting patronage grew out of a remarkably convenient location. Its two main boundary streets, Michigan and Trumbull avenues, were well served by electric trolley lines when that was the most ubiquitous form of public transit in American cities. Later on, as the automobile came to dominate Detroit's transportation mix, the ballpark was eventually accessible from four freeways.

This site was a mile from the heart of downtown, making it the most centrally located classic ballpark. It is a common misconception that the old parks were often located downtown, but strictly speaking, none of the first steel-and-concrete generation structures were, with the possible exception of Detroit's. The average classic park was more than three miles from the center of town, and two of the most famous, the Polo Grounds and Yankee Stadium, were almost eight miles from their city hall. All of them occupied urban settings, however.

Michigan and Trumbull's nearness to the heart of Detroit allowed patrons to get to games quickly and easily; this rapidity combined with late afternoon starting times allowed them to see games without losing a full afternoon's work or missing much of the action. It also afforded convenient access from the city's densest population centers. Writing in the 1930s, Sam Greene, a veteran Detroit sportswriter, called Navin Field "the only downtown baseball park in the two major leagues, [located] less than ten minutes' ride by street car from the city hall and the leading hotels. It is so close to the center of the city that many fans leaving stores and offices a half hour before game time can walk leisurely to the park before the umpire dusts off home plate."[6]

It was no lucky accident that the Tigers had such a well-situated home ground. Their

Table 1: The Classic Ballparks' Proximity to the Center of Downtown

Miles[7]	Ballpark	City	First Baseball Use of Site
1.0	Tiger Stadium	Detroit	1896
1.4	Griffith Stadium	Washington	1891
1.7	Redland/Crosley Field	Cincinnati	1884
2.3	Fenway Park	Boston	1912
2.4	Forbes Field	Pittsburgh	1909
2.6	League Park	Cleveland	1891
2.7	Ebbets Field	Brooklyn	1913
2.7	Sportsman's Park	St. Louis	1875
2.8	Baker Bowl	Philadelphia	1887
2.9	Shibe Park	Philadelphia	1909
3.4	Comiskey Park	Chicago	1910
3.7	Braves Field	Boston	1914
4.9	Wrigley Field	Chicago	1914
7.8	Polo Grounds	New York	1890
7.9	Yankee Stadium	New York	1923
3.5	Average of 14 Parks[8]		1901

owner, George Vanderbeck, was a capable but somewhat disreputable entrepreneur,[9] who moved the Tigers there in 1896 from the inadequate and distant digs of a small park outside the city, and managed to make them profitable during a major economic depression. At the time, the Michigan and Trumbull site was being used as "the location of the [municipal] hay scales, wood market, the sawing ground for cedar paving blocks, and the city stone pile."[10] During his four years at The Corner, he embraced innovation. Upon leasing the grounds, he told *Sporting Life* magazine that he envisioned "a ball park [*sic*] in summer, a skating rink in winter, [that] will be lighted with electricity, and something will be going on there day and night the year through. Summer evenings there will be band concerts fireworks and spectacular effects, and … in the winter there will be carnivals galore."[11] *Sporting Life* further reported that "President Vanderbeck will erect a modern steel grand stand in his new park at Michigan and Trumbull avenues. It will be equipped with opera chairs and all conveniences. The bleachers may be covered for rain protection, but the rays of the sun will be unobstructed."[12]

Other than the seemingly impossible final item, it appears that Vanderbeck was able to deliver, at least to a degree, on almost all of his ambitious promises. When Bennett Park was built, he definitely provided iron posts to support the roof, rather than thicker, more visually obtrusive wooden timbers.[13] It is also possible that the roof structure itself was iron or steel, but that cannot be verified. This seems to have been just the third use of metal structural elements in a ballpark, the second being at Philadelphia's cutting-edge Baker Bowl a year earlier, and the first at Staten Island's St. George Cricket Grounds in 1886. After the 1896 season was over, Vanderbeck experimented with a night exhibition game versus the Cincinnati Reds on September 24.[14] While not the first, and not technically successful, it was a rare 19th century example of night baseball. And in 1897, he used the grounds for ice skating during the Christmas holidays.[15]

Vanderbeck's prime contribution to the franchise was not so much his willingness to experiment programmatically or structurally, however. It resided in his astute decision to move the Tigers from a relatively remote and unpromising plot east of the city limits to The Corner, the major leagues' best-located home for most of the 20th century. That logistical advantage was clear even before Bennett Park's debut, when *Sporting Life* magazine noted that the field "is a short [five or six] minutes' ride from the center of the city on five [street]car lines."[16] For all his ethical failings, locating the park so advantageously was George Vanderbeck's impressive legacy to a century of Detroit fans, players, and owners.

While Bennett Park was in the right place, it was not originally the right size, or facing in the right direction. Fortunately, the site was eventually expandable to the west and north, and the park's wooden structure, like all others of the era, was not built for the ages. A high degree of adaptability complemented The Corner's locational advantages, allowing the site and stadium to grow into their purpose over several generations. During its first four decades of existence, the park found itself in a somewhat uncomfortable relationship with a less than ideally sized and oriented property, until finally a satisfying equilibrium between land and structure was reached in the late 1930s. That balance lasted for more than six decades.

As shown below, its site nearly doubled in size through at least three property expansions over nearly four decades before reaching ultimate stability. Before Navin Field was built in 1912, the Michigan and Trumbull site was smaller than the major league average; after 1934, it was larger, until the post–1950 building boom, when suburban stadiums sprung up on sites unconstrained by traditional city street grids. By 1938, the Tigers' site had essentially attained its final size and shape.

Table 2: Growth of Ballpark Site Area and Seating Density at Michigan and Trumbull

Year	Acres	Major League Average[17]	Seats	Seats/Acre	Venue
1896	4.40	Unknown	5,000	1,136	Bennett Park (minor league)
1901	4.40[18]	5.44	7,000 or 8,500[19]	1,591	Bennett Park (major league)
1908	5.50[20]	5.83	10,500[21]	1,909	Expanded Bennett Park
1912	6.66[22]	6.47	23,000[23]	3,433	Navin Field
1923	6.66	7.05	29,500[24]	4,429	Navin, partly double-decked
1934	8.18[25]	7.05	44,500	5,440	Navin with temporary World Series bleachers
1935	8.37[26]	7.05	47,095	5,627	With larger temporary bleachers
1938	8.56[27]	7.23	54,000[28]	6,308	Briggs Stadium, fully double-decked

In comparison, Detroit's Comerica Park opened in 2000 with a seating capacity of 40,000, on a site of roughly 12 acres, and with a density of about 3,300 seats per acre, fewer than Navin Field's smallest configuration.

Michigan and Trumbull was home to baseball's most greatly expanded series of ballpark structures, both proportionally and in absolute numbers of added seats. As shown in the table below, its final configuration provided more than ten times the seating capacity of the original Bennett Park construction, adding nearly 50,000 seats over the years. During that period, stands accommodating roughly 110,000 seating places were cumulatively built and removed at various times.[29]

Table 3: Evolution of Baseball Seating Capacity at Michigan and Trumbull

Year	Seats[30]	Ballpark Name	Comments
1896	5,000[31]	Bennett Park	Original wooden structure, minor league park
1901	7,000 or 8,500[32]	Bennett Park	First expansion, now a major league park
1908	10,500[33]	Bennett Park	Site and seating expanded
1910	14,000[34]	Bennett Park	Permanent bleachers built in left field[35]
1912	23,000[36]	Navin Field	New reoriented fireproof park on expanded site
1923	29,500[37]	Navin Field	Main grandstand is double-decked
1934	44,500	Navin Field	Includes large temporary 1934 World Series bleachers
1935	47,200[38]	Navin Field	Includes larger temporary bleachers for 1935 World Series
1936	36,000[39] or 36,440[40]	Navin Field	Temporary bleachers and right field pavilion razed, new right-side double-deck stands built from old pavilion location to center field
1936	38,000[41]	Navin Field	Alternative capacity figure
1938	54,000[42] or 58,000[43]	Briggs Stadium	Left field pavilion razed, new left-side double-deck stands built from old pavilion location to center field, expansion completed
1953	54,000[44]	Briggs Stadium	Almost certainly more accurate than the more common 1938 figure
1961	52,904[45]	Tiger Stadium	
1962	52,850[46]	Tiger Stadium	
1969	54,220[47]	Tiger Stadium	
1981	52,687[48]	Tiger Stadium	
1983	52,806[49]	Tiger Stadium	1969 capacity reduced by renovations
1997	46,846[50]	Tiger Stadium	
1999	52,416[51]	Tiger Stadium	Comerica Park opened in 2000 with only 40,000 seats[52]

This dramatic growth mirrored Detroit's own: The city joined major league baseball in 1901 as one of its least populated franchises and, fueled primarily by motor vehicle manufacturing, quickly accelerated to fourth position by 1920. While the other major league towns were growing 104 percent on average between 1900 and 1950, Detroit was exploding by 547 percent. By 1920, it was baseball's largest single-team city. By 1950, it was at least twice as populous as any other in that class and in fact was also double the size of the two-team cities of Boston and St. Louis.[53] This period was one of absolute franchise stability throughout the major leagues; starting in the mid-'50s there would be radical club relocations reflecting changing national demographics. Detroit, one of the runts of the litter at the time of its major league debut at the turn of the century, was never in danger of losing its team after 1903, largely because its market had expanded faster than any of the other major league cities[54] and because its ballpark had evolved repeatedly and substantially to accommodate that market.

Table 4: Detroit Compared to Average Major League City Population, 1900–1950[55]

Year	Detroit Population	Rank Among 10 Major League Cities	Major League Average[56]	Detroit's Percentage of Major League Average
1900	286,000	9th	622,000[57]	46.0%
1910	466,000	8th	757,000	61.5%

Year	Detroit Population	Rank Among 10 Major League Cities	Major League Average	Detroit's Percentage of Major League Average
1920	993,000	4th	930,000	106.7%
1930	1,569,000	4th	1,121,000	139.9%
1940	1,623,000	4th	1,167,000	139.1%
1950	1,850,000	4th	1,249,000	148.1%
50-Year Gain	1,564,000	1st	627,000	249.4%

Bennett Park

Bennett Park was the first ball ground to occupy Woodbridge Grove, the former lumber and hay market at the intersection of Michigan and Trumbull avenues. It was immediately north of Corktown, named after Ireland's County Cork,[58] and the city's oldest remaining residential neighborhood. This single-deck, under-5,000-seat[59] grouping of three separate wooden structures was originally built for the Detroit Wolverines of the Western League in 1896.

Home plate occupied the southeast corner of the site.[60] The catchers, batters, and home-plate umpires faced roughly west-northwest, which was both difficult and dangerous for those players and officials, since games started at mid-to-late afternoon, and the summer sun set in that general direction at Detroit's latitude. Still, there were urbanistic and geometric advantages to this orientation. For one, it placed the main entrance at the corner closest to downtown, which was also the junction of the site's two primary thoroughfares—the streets that handled the most vehicular and pedestrian traffic and were served directly by streetcar lines.[61] Second, Michigan and Trumbull met at an acute angle (about 68 degrees), and placing home plate within that angle allowed a set of seating structures that converged with the foul lines—a functionally satisfying configuration in terms of spectator field proximity, horizontal sight lines, and the shape of foul territory.

The Western League continued through 1899 and then renamed itself the American League in 1900 while retaining its minor league status. In 1901, it became a major league, and Bennett Park was expanded to about either 7,000 or 8,500 seats for the occasion, depending on the source. Its 4.4-acre site[62] was small even for the Deadball Era, being about a fourth less than the average major league venue.[63] Its seating capacity was also subpar; by 1907, the average major league park had about 50 percent more seats, and when the World Series first came to Detroit that year, attendance was embarrassingly small—11,306 and 7,370 for the two games. The total and the average were the worst gates recorded in any World Series before or since, and the latter figure also (briefly) set a record for a single-game low. This suggested not only insufficient seating capacity but also poor fan support for a team that boasted the league's best hitter, best base stealer, and most exciting player, Ty Cobb.

However, full attendance figures were not reflected in the official totals during the Bennett Park years, since many fans saw games from several precarious "wildcat bleachers" built beyond the fences in left and right fields. Because the income from these cut-rate seats went to adjoining property owners rather than to the club, the Tigers often installed tall curtains of canvas strips to block views of the field.[64] Tiger President Frank Navin claimed that these bleachers could cost the club as many as 400 admissions per game when full,[65] but his estimate seems unrealistic, since not every five- or 10-cent wildcat

74   Part I: History and Background

ticket holder would have been willing or able to pay several times that amount for an authorized seat inside the ballpark.

In 1908, Bennett Park's physical arrangements changed. With another World Series on the horizon, its site was expanded northward to roughly 5.5 acres by the purchase of property beyond right field, and seating was increased to about 10,500 by filling in gaps between the three previously disconnected seating structures. Also, several rows were added in front of the old stands, and home plate was moved outward by about 40 feet.[66]

Despite the expanded seating and the somewhat improved viewing conditions, the final World Series contest in Detroit that fall drew only 6,210, more than 40 percent below official capacity in a situation where overflow crowds were customary. This set an unbreakable record for the worst single-game attendance ever in the fall classic.[67]

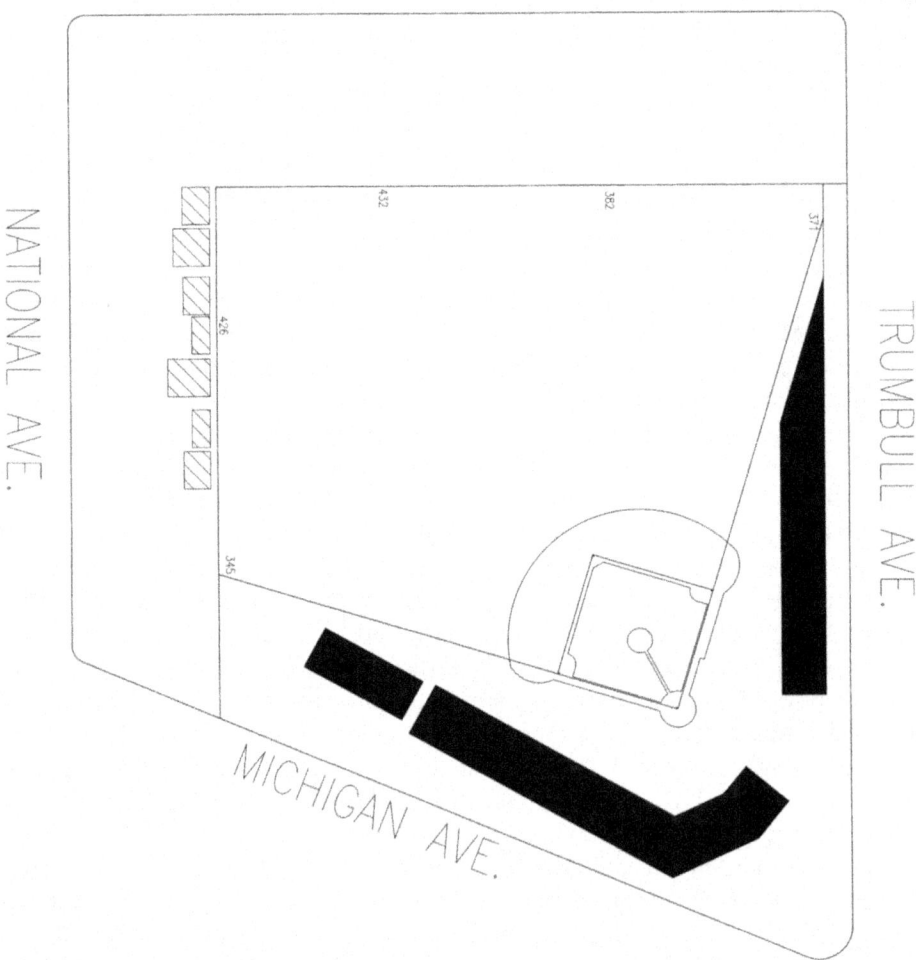

The Bennett Park site plan showing the location of the "wildcat bleachers" beyond left field, built by residents of National Avenue in their backyards. This diagram illustrates the park's final configuration, with bleacher seating in both left and right fields (© John Davids).

Winds of Change

By 1909, it was clear to Navin that a major change was in order. The arrangements at Bennett Park were problematic, and the baseball world was entering a renaissance in the form of new and immensely improved ballparks. To facilitate that change, Navin first secured full control of his leased real estate, buying the property in two stages from multiple owners for nearly $60,000. In May, *Sporting Life* revealed the club's expansion plan and timetable. It mentioned that half the site had been bought, and "upon the purchase of all the land at Bennett Park plans will be immediately be set in motion for a double-deck grandstand … of concrete and steel, of modern style, and will be situated at the northwest corner of the lot, exactly reversing the layout of the present diamond. The work may be done next fall if the required property can be obtained by that time. Arrangements for seating 20,000 persons, with an overflow space which will not interfere with the progress of the game, form [Navin's] general line of intent."[68]

As it happened, only two of these seven steps unfolded as envisioned. The Tigers completed their land purchase in June, paying $97,500 in total.[69] But rather than being immediately set into motion, the plans seemed to go into hibernation. In November, *Sporting Life* reported that Navin "was still undecided regarding the improvement of Bennett Park. The matter had been in the hands of the architects for several months now, but they have as yet failed to come forward with a design for increasing the capacity of the field on a basis which will conserve the size of the playing portion and fulfill the need which the club president has in mind. That a most material increase in the seating capacity will be necessary next year goes without saying.… Just how remains a doubtful matter still, but the management has all winter to decide on the most acceptable means."[70]

Thus, in Navin's mind, the lot size seemed to stand in the way of a new, larger structure. This is puzzling, because a year earlier he had increased the grounds from definitely substandard to a respectable 94 percent of the major league average. Clearly, there were only three ways to increase seating capacity while still preserving the playing field acreage: build a double-deck park as announced, acquire more property, or ban overflow crowds from the field.[71] Each of these would either cost money or diminish revenue, and for a frugal accountant such as Navin, the choice must have been agonizing, since he did not make up his mind for more than two years. In an era when substantial ballparks could be built in a few months, this indecision must have seemed like an eternity. Eventually, Navin opted to buy a strip of additional land on the western edge of his property, bringing its size to 6.7 acres, a bit more than the ever-growing major league norm.

Navin's protracted decision-making process began in a year that marked a great watershed in the history of ballpark design. Shibe Park and Forbes Field opened in 1909,[72] setting off an intense seven-year ballpark-building boom and providing a striking new paradigm for club owners. Their architecture was grand and ambitious, and their main grandstands were built of steel, concrete, brick, and terra-cotta, and were thus far more resistant to the fires that had plagued wooden parks for decades. Compared to wood, the strength of steel meant that columns could be more widely spaced, reducing the incidence of obstructed views; steel allowed larger stands with higher seating capacities and permitted cantilever construction, which meant that many more seats could be placed in front of the view-blocking upper and lower deck column lines.

These new structures were immense by the standards of their day, exceeding 20,000 seats, making them about twice the size of their wooden counterparts. Their cost, measuring well into the hundreds of thousands of dollars,[73] was also unprecedented, reflecting their size, structural complexity, often-impressive materials, and well-wrought details. Not all the new parks were architectural showpieces, but several, particularly Forbes, Ebbets, and Shibe, were. The seven years from 1909 onward produced what we now consider the first generation of classic parks,[74] summarized below:

Table 5: The "Jewel Box" Ballparks of the First Two Decades of the 1900s

City	Park	First Game	Initial Seats	Architectural Rating	Designer of Initial Structure
Philadelphia	Shibe Park	4/12/09	23,000	A+	William Steele & Sons
St. Louis	Sportsman's Park	4/14/09	24,040	D	Uncertain[75]
Pittsburgh	Forbes Field	6/30/09	23,000	A	Charles W. Leavitt, Jr.
Cleveland	League Park	4/21/10	21,400	B+	Osborn Engineering Co.
Chicago	Comiskey Park	7/1/10	35,000	B	Zachary Taylor Davis
Washington	Griffith Stadium	4/12/11	15,000	D	Osborn Engineering Co.
New York	Polo Grounds	6/28/11	34,000	B-	Henry B. Herts and Osborn Engineering Co.
Cincinnati	Redland Field	4/11/12	25,000	C+	Harry Hake
Boston	Fenway Park	4/20/12	23,000	C+	Charles E. McLaughlin
Detroit	Navin Field	4/20/12	23,000	C	Osborn Engineering Co.
Brooklyn	Ebbets Field	4/9/13	24,000	A	Clarence R. Van Buskirk
Chicago	Weeghman Park	4/23/14	14,000	C	Zachary Taylor Davis
Boston	Braves Field	8/8/15	40,000	D	Osborn Engineering Co.

(Architectural Rating is the author's assessment of the quality of the park's initial design.)

Navin Field's Debut

The corner of Michigan and Trumbull underwent a dramatic transformation when steel-and-concrete Navin Field replaced the mostly wooden Bennett Park between the 1911 and 1912 seasons.[76] Writing in *Sporting Life* ten weeks before opening day, Detroit correspondent Paul H. Bruske enthused: "From the office of the Detroit executive have gone forth the orders relative to the rehabilitation of Bennett Park and the construction of the finest baseball plant in the country."[77]

Eleven weeks later, he declared the opening of the new park to be "the most momentous occasion in the history of Michigan base ball.... For the first time in history, Detroit has a ball yard worthy of its rank among the cities."[78] (In 1912, that rank would have been about eighth out of the ten major league towns.)[79]

The new park accomplished several things. It replaced a flammable structure with a fire-resistant one, correcting a significant safety concern. It corrected a problematic orientation, eliminating another safety concern (and a quality-of-play problem). As noted earlier, batters, catchers, and umpires had to battle the late afternoon sun at Bennett Park. Navin Field solved that problem by relocating the playing field and reorienting it a little less than a quarter-turn clockwise (not a half turn, as Navin forecast), so that the batter and catcher safely faced north-northeast. Now only the right fielders had to battle the low late afternoon sun. (Similar quarter-turn reorientations were also made in Cincinnati and St. Louis when those clubs built their fireproof parks on existing sites during this period.) Finally, the field reorientation and a concurrent site expansion reduced the wildcat bleacher problem.

Longevity and Adaptability (Pastier with J. Davids) 77

The site's western boundary was shifted further westward, from the alley east of National to the eastern edge of that street itself. To effect this, the Tigers bought the properties that had harbored most of the wildcat bleachers and demolished the houses there, thus adding about 1.2 acres to the stadium property, giving more space for seating and the playing field. At this point, the size of the Tigers' property surpassed the major league average for the first time. Although displaced from the vicinity of National Avenue, some wildcat bleachers remained near Cherry Street beyond the new left field.

The new ballpark's home plate entrance was now less prominently located at the corner of Michigan and National, and the roughly 112-degree obtuse angle of that intersection meant that the main grandstand no longer had a "natural" acute angle to cradle the foul lines. Now, the main stands were at right angles to each other but for some reason were not quite square with the foul lines—in the vicinity of the infield and for about another 60 feet beyond it, the third base line converged slightly with the left-side grandstand, and the first base foul line diverged slightly from the right-side stands. Farther down the lines, the detached pavilions angled to converge more sharply with their respective foul corners. Similarly, the outfield fences were not square to the foul lines, forming an angle of about 88 degrees in left and about 92 degrees in right.[80] This subtle angular asymmetry would persist for nearly nine decades through several expansions and renovations, until the very end of the ballpark's life.

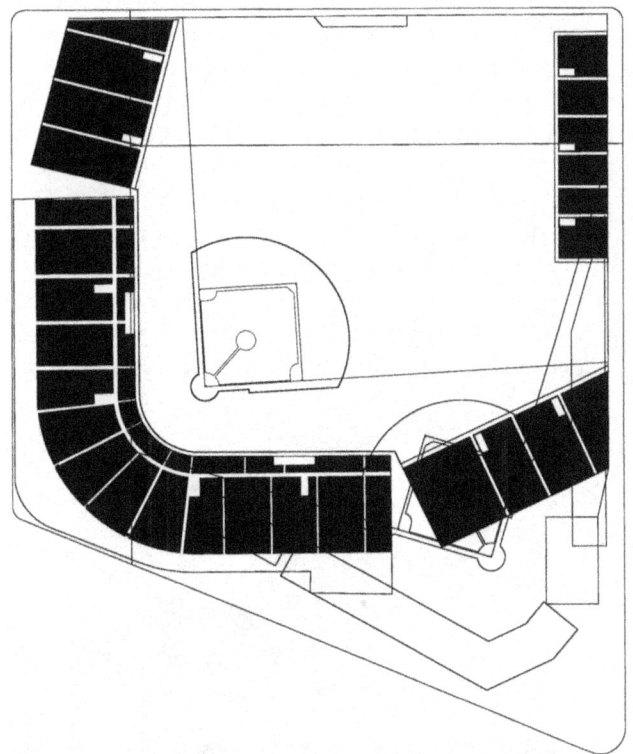

The 112-degree obtuse angle[81] formed by Michigan and National, occupied by the new right-angled main grandstand paralleling National and a new skewed right field pavilion, created an open property remnant at Michigan and Trumbull, which was partly filled by a new office and ticketing building along Trumbull. Eventually, this vacant area became an open-air food court.

Although Navin Field was only single-decked initially, its seating capacity was nearly 65 percent greater than its predecessor. Along with Fenway Park, which opened on the same day, it was the first classic steel-and-concrete ballpark to debut as a mere single-decker[82]; all the others up until then—Baker Bowl, Shibe Park, Forbes Field, Sportsman's Park, Redland Field,

The Navin Field site plan in 1912, based on the 1897 Sanborn Insurance Company map, showing the new location of the field and seating, with home plate now at the southwest corner of the site. The location and configuration of Bennett Park is shown as a single-line diagram for comparison (© John Davids).

League Park, Comiskey Park, the Polo Grounds, and Griffith Stadium—rose grandly in two tiers or more.[83] In Boston, Fenway's location on filled marshland would not easily accommodate foundations that could support the extra weight of a second deck. In Detroit, economy most likely ruled the day, since the budget was spartan. Upper decks cost significantly more to build per seat than lower ones, and club president Frank Navin was famous for his thrift when not at the racetrack. This avoidance of height even extended to Navin's press facilities—reporters were originally located at field level behind the catcher for several years until they were finally moved upstairs.

Navin Field's Architecture and Engineering

The Roman architect Vitruvius famously wrote that a successful work of architecture must have firmness (structural strength), commodity (practicality and suitability to its purpose), and delight (style and visual beauty). Tiger Stadium clearly met the first two criteria, if not the third. It was the second ballpark ever to draw 100 million regular-season fans,[84] and ranked near the top in games played in the 20th century. Over most of its long life, it was subjected to change and accommodated it well. It evolved from a small venue to a large one in six stages without losing its exceptional intimacy, allowed large numbers of fans of various economic classes to see games, produced generous crops of home runs, and was receptive to remodeling and renovation, limited in that respect only in its later years by political intrigues and owners' egos.

Tiger Stadium was a solid example of pragmatism and ad-hoc evolution, rather than a textbook paradigm of architectural beauty and refinement. Except for a small Mediterranean revival-style office and ticketing building, it was devoid of decorative elements. Its guiding principles were function and economy rather than aesthetics.

Like about half of the other early fireproof baseball parks that opened between 1909 and 1916, its steel-framework design reflected an engineering approach more than an architectural one. There were four grand exceptions that were designed to high architectural standards, fully celebrating their status as the sport's first truly permanent venues. Cincinnati's short-lived Palace of the Fans (built largely of reinforced concrete) and Philadelphia's Shibe Park, Pittsburgh's Forbes Field, and Brooklyn's Ebbets Field (all combining a

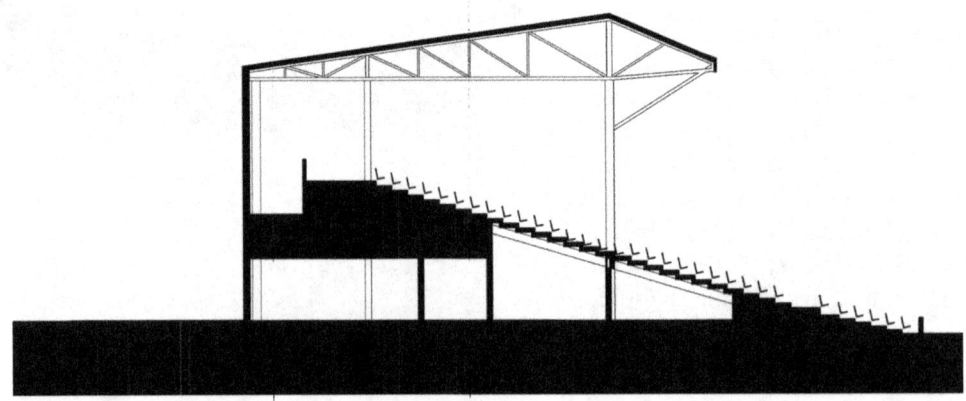

A section of Navin Field in 1912 showing the seating along the first base line. This construction would remain in place until the ballpark was demolished nearly a century later (© John Davids).

steel structural framework with double-or even triple-decked[85] concrete seating tiers in their main grandstands) exhibited refinement in their detailing and finish materials in architecturally ambitious exteriors embodying eclectic revival styles.

Three others—Cleveland's League Park, Chicago's Comiskey Park and New York's Polo Grounds—constituted an intermediate category. They offered some exterior stylistic display, usually in the form of interestingly detailed exposed brickwork, albeit far less extensively and more understatedly than the four exemplars mentioned above. The other seven classic fireproof parks of the 20th century's first decade and a half—Navin Field, Boston's Fenway Park and Braves Field, Cincinnati's Redland Field (later Crosley Field), St. Louis' Sportsman's Park, Washington's Griffith Stadium, and Chicago's Weeghman Park (later, Wrigley Field)—were almost purely pragmatic structures with few elevated architectural ambitions.

Five of the 13 jewel boxes were the work of the Osborn Company, a Cleveland engineering firm whose expertise in steel bridges and the relatively new material of reinforced concrete carried over nicely to the structural design of cantilevered grandstands and fireproofed seating decks. Navin Field was Osborn's fourth stadium, built two years after its 1910 debut at League Park in Cleveland. (It was also their first single-deck ballpark.) By 1934, the firm had been involved, wholly or in part, with some aspect of three of the eight National League parks, and eight of the nine[86] in the American League.[87] Until the late 1990s, Osborn boasted the most extensive portfolio of major league and significant minor league ballparks of any design firm; after that, it was overtaken and eclipsed by HOK Sport of Kansas City, now renamed Populous.

Not surprisingly for an engineering practice, Osborn's approach was straightforwardly functional. The firm's main grandstands were simple and unadorned. (The Polo Grounds originally had decorative friezes on the interior fascias of its roof and upper deck, but those were the work of an associated architect who specialized in theaters and were removed from view after about a decade.) The firm permitted itself some modest architectural expression in only three instances: small masonry ticketing and club office buildings, executed in Mediterranean or Mission revival styles, stood outside the right field corners of the parks in Detroit, Cleveland, and at Braves Field.

Osborn's company aesthetic prior to 1923 was primarily industrial. The symbolically important main entry portals of four of their first five designs verged on invisibility. Even the most dedicated ballpark aficionados, this author included, would be hard pressed to visualize, describe, or even find photos documenting the exterior appearance of the home plate ends of Navin Field, Braves Field, the Polo Grounds, or Griffith Stadium. The lack of a second deck rendered the first two entrance zones even less impressive.

Osborn's parks' exterior character varied over time, but in the early days it tended to be undistinguished, defined primarily by partially exposed steel frameworks, unglazed openings, simple cladding, and large banks of ventilation louvers. (By the 1920s and 1930s, however, they were designing unmatched baseball monuments such as Yankee Stadium and Cleveland Municipal Stadium.) Their ballparks' principal visual expression flourished on the inside, where capacious seating decks were, more often than not, their city's most impressively scaled public assembly space. Their internal character grew from the evocative geometry of their seating patterns and frankly articulated structural and circulation systems—the steel columns and intricate trusses supporting the roofs and seating decks (best seen from below), mysterious spaces underneath the stands, pedestrian ramps leading to the upper decks, and the short tunnels and suspended catwalks

Navin Field's offices and right field entrance on Trumbull Avenue (*Detroit News* from a print provided by Avanti Press).

giving final access to the lower and upper seating bowls. The patterns created by these elements were almost always complex and satisfying. Like so many bridges of the era, steel ballpark construction had an inherent complexity, character, and power that stood convincingly on its own without need for applied decoration. The main visual events were usually horticultural and dramatic rather than architectural: the lush green playing field at the center of each park, and the game action that was the ultimate reason for the parks in the first place.

Just before Navin Field opened, *Baseball Magazine* published an effusive unsigned article that perhaps inadvertently shed light on Osborn's emphasis on pragmatism over architectural ambition. It began: "The magnificent new stadium which is being built for the future home of the Detroit Tigers is one of the greatest amphitheaters yet dedicated to the national game. It is fitting that the city which boasts the greatest player in the game, Ty Cobb, and the liveliest, most spirited of managers, Hugh Jennings, should have a ballpark to compare with the best in the land.… Detroit may well be proud of this beautiful structure. It is a triumph of architectural skill, combining in its ample walls the newest of those modern improvements designed for the comfort of its patrons."[88]

This may be a good place to point out that, in my research experience, every article about a ballpark debut has been favorable, even when assessing venues such as Candlestick and New Comiskey parks. In actuality, Navin Field demonstrated no architectural skill one way or another, and was far from being beautiful, or one of the greatest amphitheaters, or worthy of comparison with the best in the land. In fairness, it was built economically (for $300,000, or perhaps a third as much as a showplace would have cost), and could not have realistically been expected to compete with such gems as Shibe Park, Forbes Field, Comiskey Park, and the Palace of the Fans, or even Osborn's own League Park, all of which had been completed earlier, and Ebbets Field, which was then under construction.

In writing about architecture, *Baseball Magazine* fanned on three pitches, but the publication acquitted itself better when dealing with practical details. The most startling of

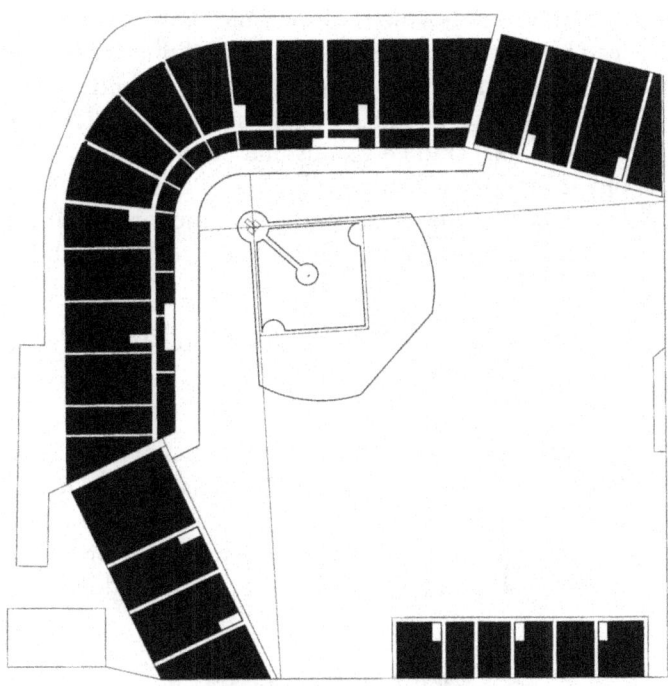

The lower deck plan of Navin Field in 1912 showing the grandstand and pavilions. The lower deck plan in 1923 was identical to this one (© John Davids).

these is that the "home players' bench is heated by steam in the cold days of spring and autumn." Obviously this arrangement did not last very long, otherwise it would have become legendary. Perhaps visiting teams complained about the Tigers' unfair advantage and had the unusual amenity removed. The most substantive part of the article deals with crowd-handling and circulation: "The seating capacity of the new park is about 23,000.... [It] has been constructed so as to permit easy access to the enormous crowds.... All entrances and exits are inclined ways [i.e., ramps] thus doing away entirely with stairways. In this manner the whole grandstand and pavilion may be emptied in a very short time compared to that required under the old system." (Paul Bruske was also impressed with the park's exiting system, writing that "the most remarkable demonstration of all ... occurred ... when 25,000 persons walked comfortably and without interruption out of the elaborately-planned series of exits, and the field was virtually emptied in ten minutes.")[89]

Baseball Magazine continued: "Every class of seats has its own special entrances." (How uncannily prophetic of the private entrances for suite and club seat holders in our own age.) "The boxes, of which there are 112, accommodating from six to eight persons each, may be entered from the grand level." (Surprisingly, only about three percent of the seats were boxes, with an even lower proportion at big games with overflow crowds.) "The 75-cent seats have their own special runway and are reached from the top of the structure." (Meaning that the occupants of those seating sections had to climb up to the last row of seats and then back down to their particular row, and repeat the process in reverse to leave the park.) "The grandstand [structure] is provided with seven exits. Four of these are exits from the boxes and the reserved seat section, while the remaining three lead from the upper portion of the building. There are in all seventeen exit gates situated at various advantageous points on the grounds." The complexity and differentiation of the class-based circulation systems at Navin Field is remarkable in that baseball's high-capacity steel-framed grandstand phenomenon was effectively only three or four years old at the time. Clearly, ballpark designers' skills were evolving quickly, and there was much more to the classic-park phenomenon than interesting playing field shapes, bridge-derived structural frameworks, and felicitous architectural details.

Navin Field's Upper Deck Addition and Viewing Proximity

Like three other classic fireproof ballparks—Fenway Park, Braves Field, and Wrigley Field—Tiger Stadium was first built as a single-deck grandstand. All four had columns in their seating areas, but their function was to support only a roof rather than a much heavier upper deck and roof combination. Braves Field remained low throughout its four-decade lifetime, and Fenway Park has added a small club section and some rooftop seats (but not a full-fledged upper deck) in recent decades. Spurred by the prosperity of the 1920s, Tiger (1923) and Wrigley (1927) expanded vertically with substantial upper decks, and Yankee Stadium (1923) was built as an immense and impressive triple-decked monument to Babe Ruth's colossal drawing power during that decade. By 1927, there were a dozen multideck major league parks, and, from then on to the present date, all new major league parks would fall into that category, except for a few temporary facilities used by expansion teams while awaiting permanent homes.[90]

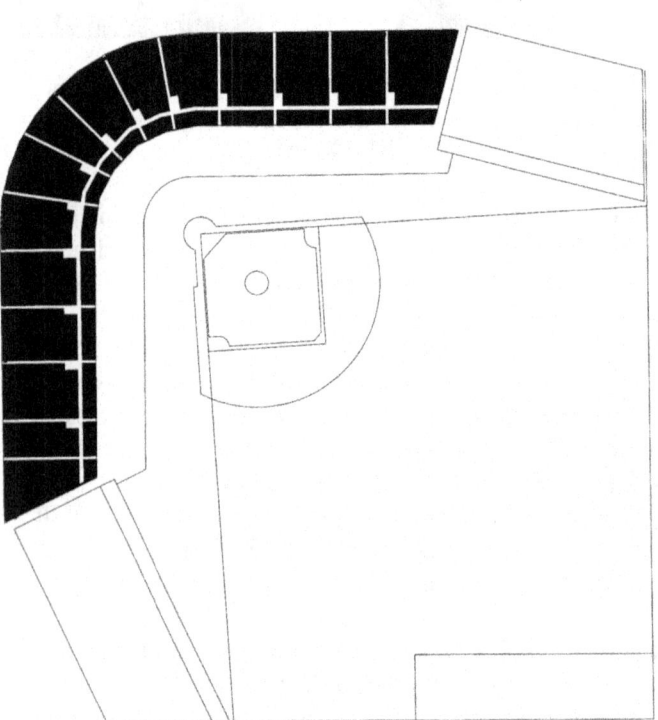

The upper deck plan of Navin Field in 1923. The new upper deck was placed directly above the existing lower deck, with a deep cantilevered overhang providing excellent proximity to the field. After 1962 and until 1999, this proximity was unmatched in the major leagues (© John Davids).

Upper decks are not just a way of adding to ballpark capacity in limited spaces. (The classic parks almost all had tight sites.) They are also an effective way of bringing seats closer to the action, compared to a single-deck layout, by enabling significant horizontal overlaps between seating tiers. In the most extreme case, when the monodeck Los Angeles Coliseum saw temporary duty as a baseball venue, some of its seats were as far as 710 feet from home plate.[91]

Arguably, upper decks provide the best seats in the house, allowing a more informative and comprehensive elevated perspective and the ability to see more of the field and high flies without blockage by other spectators' heads and overhead structural elements. The baseball world does not always understand or accept this contention and often assigns the highest seat prices to the first few dozen rows of the lower deck. Many fans value even the rearmost lower deck seats over an upper deck location, branding the higher ones as "nosebleed territory." But theaters, opera houses, and concert halls almost always ask for, and get, top dollar for seats in their first balconies and often designate those seats with such honorific names as founders' circle, grand tier, loge, and the like. Similarly, in the early days of ballpark design evolution more than a century ago, upper decks were sometimes referred to as balconies and some premium seats were called opera boxes.

By bringing seats closer to the action, upper decks produce viewing intimacy. But fostering intimacy is something of an art, and not all upper deck seats are created equal. The most intimate upper decks were all built in the first few years of the fireproof ballpark building boom prior to 1914, and, as time went on, viewing distances steadily grew, due partly to more generous space standards and sometimes growing from increasing capacity but largely due, after the mid–1960s, to premium-seating decks occupying the prime territory between the lower deck and the topmost main deck. Here is a chronological sampling of viewing distances, measured from home plate to the midpoint of the upper deck, and grouped into four historical periods:

The Tigers' dugout from the upper deck stands directly above, late summer 1999 (© Rebecca Cook).

Table 6a: Upper Deck Viewing Distances of Early Fireproof Parks of the Deadball Era, 1895–1919[92]

Distance	Ballpark, City and Year That the Upper Deck Opened
100'	Baker Bowl, Philadelphia, 1895[93]
118'	Shibe Park, Philadelphia, 1909[94]
128'	Sportsman's Park, St. Louis, 1909[95]
125'	Forbes Field, Pittsburgh, 1909[96]
105'	League Park, Cleveland, 1910
129'	Comiskey Park, Chicago, 1910
105'	Griffith Stadium, Washington, 1911[97]
123'	Polo Grounds, New York, 1911[98]
135'	Crosley Field, Cincinnati, 1912
113'	Ebbets Field, Brooklyn, 1913
118'	Average of early fireproof parks sample

Table 6b: Upper Deck Viewing Distances, Second Fireproof Generation, 1920–1960[99]

Distance	Ballpark, City and Year That the Upper Deck Was Built
121'	Navin Field, Detroit, 1923
148'	Yankee Stadium, New York, 1923
163'	Wrigley Field, Chicago, 1927
167'	Municipal Stadium, Cleveland, 1932
184'	County Stadium, Milwaukee, 1952
177'	Memorial Stadium, Baltimore, 1953
178'	Municipal Stadium, Kansas City, 1955[100]
199'	Candlestick Park, San Francisco, 1960
167'	Average of Second Fireproof Generation Sample

Table 6c: Upper Deck Viewing Distances, Fully Cantilevered Modern Parks, 1961–1991

Distance	Ballpark, City and Year That the Upper Deck Was Built
175'	Metropolitan Stadium, Bloomington, 1956/1961[101]
197'	Anaheim Stadium, 1966
208'	Jack Murphy Stadium, San Diego, 1969
204'	Veterans Stadium, Philadelphia, 1971[102]
215'	Royals Stadium, Kansas City, 1973[103]
220'	Stade Olympique, Montreal, 1976[104]
177'	Kingdome, Seattle, 1976[105]
209'	Yankee Stadium Reconstruction, New York, 1977[106]
191'	SkyDome, Toronto, 1989
210'	New Comiskey Park, Chicago, 1991
201'	Average of Fully Cantilevered Modern Parks Sample

Table 6d: Upper Deck Viewing Distances, the Retro Ballpark Era, 1992–2013

Distance	Ballpark, City and Year That the Upper Deck Was Built
209'	Jacobs Field, Cleveland, 1994
212'	The Ballpark in Arlington (Texas), 1994
210'	Coors Field, Denver, 1995[107]
208'	Safeco Field, Seattle, 1999[108]
197'	AT&T Park, San Francisco, 2001
212'	Miller Park, Milwaukee, 2001
196'	Petco Park, San Diego, 2004
204'	Citizens' Bank Park, Philadelphia, 2004[109]

Distance	Ballpark, City and Year That the Upper Deck Was Built
202'	Nationals Park, Washington, 2008
217'	New Yankee Stadium, New York, 2009
207'	Average of Retro Era Sample

As can be seen, average upper deck viewing distances have risen steadily and significantly between the late 19th and late 20th centuries, growing from 118 feet to 167 feet and then to 201 feet for the three major periods between 1895 and 1991. Since then, in the Retro ballpark era, the average increase has slowed but not fully abated, reaching 207 feet, and peaking with New Yankee Stadium's 217 feet.

Starting with the baseball debut of the Twin Cities' Metropolitan Stadium in 1961,[110] structural columns have been banished from within the seating sections to locations just behind their last rows,[111] meaning that intermediate and upper decks have been horizontally shifted away from the playing field. Also, new premium-seating tiers—club-seating decks and private suites—have taken over the space where older upper decks once were, thereby pushing the new top decks upwards and thus even further away from the field. (Conventional upper decks have multiplied within individual parks, too.) Wider seats and greater legroom have added to seating tier dimensions, increasing the number of rows for a given seat count and making those rows deeper. Finally, higher seating capacities also contributed to greater viewing distances until about 1990, especially in the case of multisport stadiums. Since then, the fashion has been to build baseball-only parks with lower seat counts in the name of intimacy.[112] Even so, despite this rhetoric, the smaller-capacity ballparks of the retro-design era are, on average, somewhat less intimate than their higher-capacity predecessors.

Tiger Stadium does exceptionally well in this historical comparison of upper deck intimacy. Lower deck intimacy is a simple design matter, since it merely involves keeping the foul area small, and there are no constraints, trade-offs, or conflicts involved. But designing a well-configured upper deck is a virtuoso exercise in balancing upper and lower deck seating slopes and sight lines and potential and real structural obstructions while providing a profitable level of seating capacity.

In this sample of 38 fireproof ballparks spanning 115 years, Tiger Stadium was the fifth-most intimate, with a viewing distance of 121 feet, compared to an average of 174 feet for the others. It had the closest upper deck built after 1913. The four with top deck seats closer to the field—Baker Bowl, League Park, Griffith Stadium, and Ebbets Field—had upper tiers that were built a decade or two earlier and had much lower seat counts than Detroit's, averaging less than half of Tiger Stadium's peak capacity. By late 1961, all four had been vacated, making Detroit's upper deck the most intimate in baseball. The Tigers' home maintained that distinction, by a comfortable margin, until the club moved out in 1999. As of the end of the 1974 season, when the Yankees began a radical reconstruction of their home park, Tiger's closest competitor for the intimacy title was a legendary Chicago ballyard whose friendly confines were actually very roomy in comparison.

It is interesting to compare Wrigley Field's and Tiger Stadium's viewing proximity. The Chicago park has undeniable charm, thanks to its ivy-clad outfield walls, prevalence of day games, quaint red marquee sign, nearby clattering el trains, quirky wind patterns, eccentric bleacher-fan culture, off-site rooftop seats (wildcat bleachers reincarnated), and location within a prosperous, intact, and trendy urban neighborhood. But none of those endearing assets change the fact that Chicago's upper deck midpoint is 163 feet from home plate, or 35 percent farther than Detroit's 121 feet. In the popular mind, Wrigley's abundant charm equates to intimacy, while a park that had much more of that elusive and precious quality never came close to matching Wrigley's status as the stuff of sentimental and cult-like legend.

Similarly, it is interesting to compare Tiger Stadium's upper deck intimacy with that of the present retro-era parks. These have been vigorously marketed as a return to the features and spirit of classic ballparks, but upper deck proximity cannot be counted as one of those virtues. The retro parks tabulated above have upper deck viewing distances ranging between 196 feet and 217 feet (despite some very determined design efforts to keep the upper decks compact in cities such as Baltimore, San Francisco, Philadelphia, and San Diego), compared to 121 for Tiger, or about 62 percent to 80 percent greater than at The Corner. And these new parks have, on average, significantly lower seating capacities than Tiger Stadium did.

Admittedly, the intimacy of the older upper decks came at a cost. The only practical way to achieve good field proximity was to have view-blocking columns throughout the seating areas, and, often, to have partial views of the playing field caused by the position and angle of the upper decks. Also, the deeply projecting upper decks could block the visibility of high flies from rear lower deck seats. The latter two problems can occur as well in contemporary ballparks, which also seem prone to a high frequency of guardrails and handrails blocking critical parts of the playing field—even, in the worst cases, home plate, the corner bases, and the pitching mound.

Beyond columns, the very existence of an upper deck could be taken by some fans as a step backward. Writing in *The Sporting News* in 1934, Sam Greene, a refreshingly restrained and level-headed Motor City scribe, reflected that "Bennett Park has a fond place in the memories of old-timers. The grandstand was so close to the playing field that fans could maintain personal relations with [Tiger players]. Many regret this loss of contact that came about when Bennett Park was dismantled and the concrete stands of Navin Field erected in its stead."[113]

When Tiger ownership was waging its win-at-any-cost campaign for a new stadium, it frequently cited as evils the very columns that gave the old park its intimacy, exaggerating their numbers and the severity of their effects. In reality, most column-obstructed seats usually went unsold and unoccupied, and, had it chosen to do so, the front office could have permanently cut the price of the seats in these problem locations or even taken them off the market altogether. Using the columns as a campaign tactic was made possible by an evolving set of fan expectations. From organized baseball's birth in 1871 until 1961, every permanent big league park had some seating-area columns, even the single-decked ones, where posts were needed to support the roof. Soon after the Twins' Metropolitan Stadium placed all of its columns behind each tier's last row of seats, that configuration became standard in new parks. The 1960s and 1970s saw a massive building boom in stadiums, most of which were concrete, circular (or nearly so), designed to host both football and baseball (neither of them all that well) and were eventually derided by nearly all baseball fans. By 1972, only a decade after Metropolitan Stadium's innovation, half of the 24 teams played in column-free homes. Ten years after that, 17 of 26 major league stadiums were essentially column-free. Less than a decade later, by the time the Tiger management and its political surrogates were in the thick of their campaign to replace the old ballpark, column-obstructed seats were found in only a fifth of contemporary parks and could thus be safely denounced as irritating relics, rather than being appreciated as the mechanism that produced baseball's most intimate seating. Today, Wrigley Field and Fenway Park are the only surviving ballparks making significant use of columns, and it is no coincidence that they are the two most cherished venues in baseball.

Depression-Era Expansions

Somewhat surprisingly, Navin Field grew enormously in size and capacity during the latter part of the Great Depression, expanding from about 29,000 seats to about 54,000 at a time when other private construction had generally slowed to a trickle in the United States.[114] The reasons were threefold and interconnected: greatly improved teams; dramatically rising attendance; and an ambitious, wealthy, and free-spending new owner. In the last year of the economic bubble of the Roaring Twenties, more than 869,000 fans turned out to watch a Detroit team that finished 14 games under .500 and 36 games out of first place. At the time, this was the third-best attendance in Tiger history. For the next four seasons, the teams continued to perform miserably on the field (averaging 32 games behind the first-place teams), and the turnstile count dropped each year until bottoming out at 321,000.

However, beginning in 1934, all that changed. A revitalized Tiger club won two consecutive pennants, drawing 919,000 and then 1,035,000 and setting local single-season and two-year records in the process. These two flags, and the enthusiastic fan interest they kindled, inspired baseball's most radical experiments in temporary bleacher construction. Detroit was then the nation's fourth most populous city, but its ballpark ranked only tenth in seating capacity. With an ambitious co-owner, Walter Briggs, and with pennant-winning teams, the stage was set for three anomalous temporary seating installations in two seasons.

The first consisted of three separate clusters of spindly bleacher seats located throughout the playing field during the regular season.[115] One was in the left field corner, and reduced the home run distance just to the right of the foul line to a bush-league but still legal 290 feet, according to an estimate by John Davids.[116] This substandard distance, combined with a low fence, seems to have prompted a special ground rule that treated balls hit into those bleachers (and into overflow crowds of fans on the field) as doubles rather than home runs, since Hank Greenberg hit 41 two-baggers at home in 1934, the only year that these bleachers existed. This was just one short of the single-season record set by Tris Speaker at Cleveland in 1921,[117] and neither number has been matched since.[118] The other two bleacher clusters encroached on the playing field in left-center field and in the right field corner and were not as close to home plate and thus would have had a less dramatic but still noticeable effect on game action.

The next two wooden bleacher installations were far more immense affairs hastily built in left field for the 1934 and then for the 1935 World Series. Meeting the classic definition of bleachers, the seats were cramped benches built of inexpensive pine planks, lacked backs, and were sheltered from neither sun nor rain. The first of them had the good manners to restore the old playing field shape and dimensions by removing the three intrusive temporary bleacher sections. It was built behind the left field wall and property line on Cherry Street, which had been speedily vacated in early September by mayor Frank Couzens and the City Council as the World Series approached. The designer

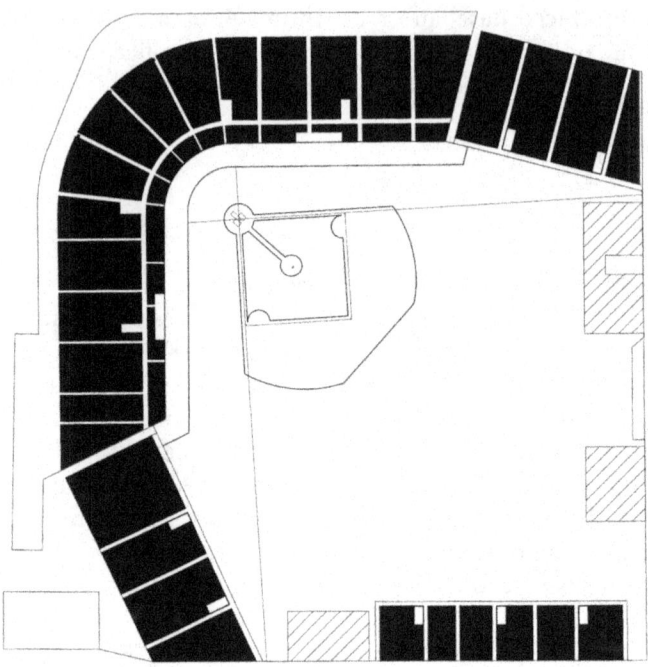

and builder was Jerome A. Utley, a prominent and well-connected Detroit engineer and building contractor[119] who had pitched and coached baseball for the University of Michigan[120] and three class-A minor league teams three decades earlier and who had "been for many years an enthusiastic supporter of the Tigers."[121]

Top: The lower deck plan of Navin Field in 1934 showing temporary bleachers built during the season to accommodate the larger crowds (© John Davids). *Bottom:* A diagram of field configurations and outfield dimensions in 1912, 1923, the 1934 regular season, and the 1934 World Series (© John Davids).

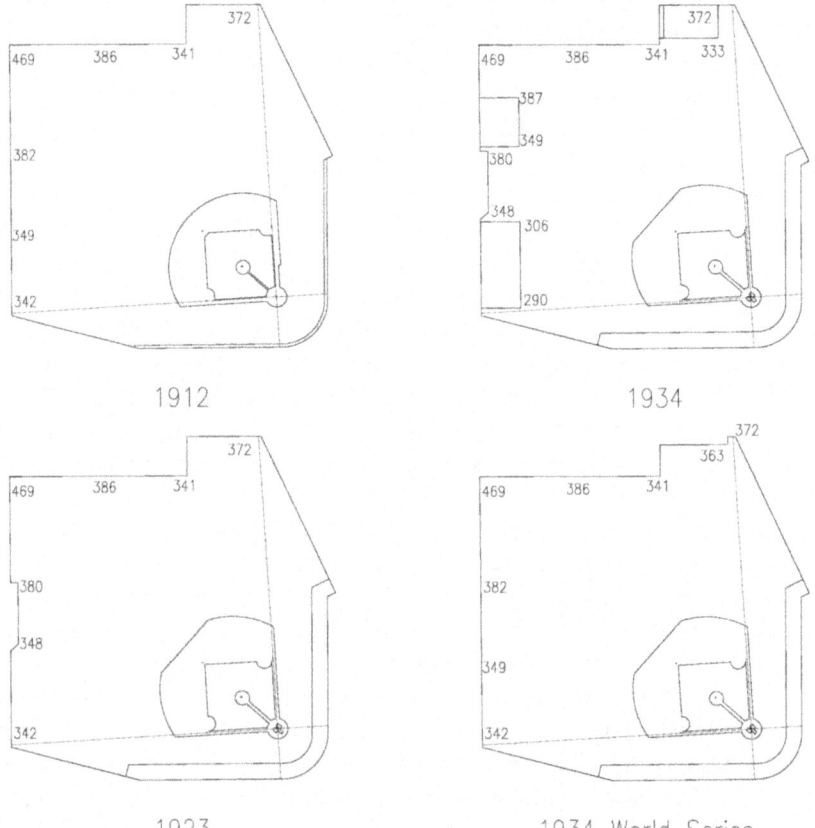

This colossal demonstration of Depression-era carpentry was roughly 70 rows deep and blocked the views of any remaining wildcat-bleacher freeloaders hoping to watch a ball game from Cherry Street without an official ticket. It stretched from the left field foul pole to center field and held about 17,000 spectators—the largest single bleacher structure in baseball up to that point. The permanent right-center field bleachers accommodated about 2,500 more. These two structures made up baseball's largest stock of bleacher seats by a wide margin, exceeding Yankee Stadium's by more than a third.[122]

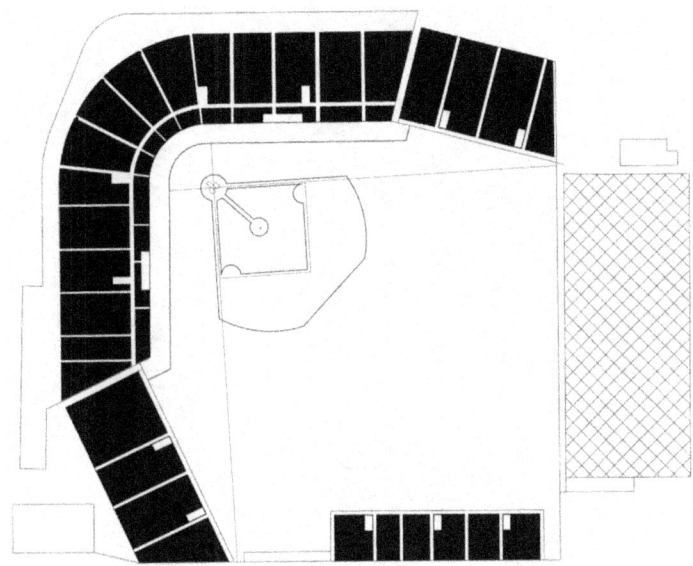

The lower deck plan for Navin Field during the 1934 World Series showing the temporary closing of Cherry Street for construction of a large section of temporary bleachers built for the Series. The positioning of these seats required removal of the left field wall that stood along the Cherry Street sidewalk (© John Davids).

In the last game of the 1934 Series, that new seating section gained infamy as a perch for unruly hometown fans protesting a hard slide by Cardinal left fielder Ducky Medwick into Tiger third baseman Marv Owen. With their team losing 9–0, frustrated occupants of the cheap seats pelted Medwick with food, bottles, seat cushions, and even shoes—so persistently that, after several cleanups, lulls, and new barrages, commissioner Kenesaw Mountain Landis ordered Medwick replaced so that the game could go on safely. It finally did, but the Tigers lost the game, 11–0, and with it the series.

These bleachers apparently remained in use during the 1935 regular season,[123] with Landis's proviso that a 10-foot-tall wire fence be installed in front of them to reduce the chances of future fan bombardments. With the Tigers once again winning the pennant and setting a club attendance record of 1,034,929, the left field bleachers were rapidly expanded for the World Series. Photographic evidence strongly suggests that these already immense bleachers were enlarged by being completely disassembled and rebuilt—not merely added onto. Now they purportedly held 19,000[124] and encroached 39 feet onto the left field playing area, except at the foul line, where the new structure left a thin wedge of fair territory to nominally preserve the old 340-foot distance to the left field corner. A few feet to the right of the foul line, the fence was just 301 feet from home. Overall, the addition reduced the distances to 305 feet in straightaway left, to an average of 314 feet for the leftmost third of the outfield, and to an average of 333 feet for the entire left half of the field between the left field foul pole and dead center.[125] This was effectively the second-shortest big-league left field since 1884 (the 1934 regular-season left field just described was shorter), even shallower than Fenway Park's or the Polo Grounds.'[126] To partly compensate for this travesty, the wire mesh fence was raised to 20 feet—a bit more

90   Part I: History and Background

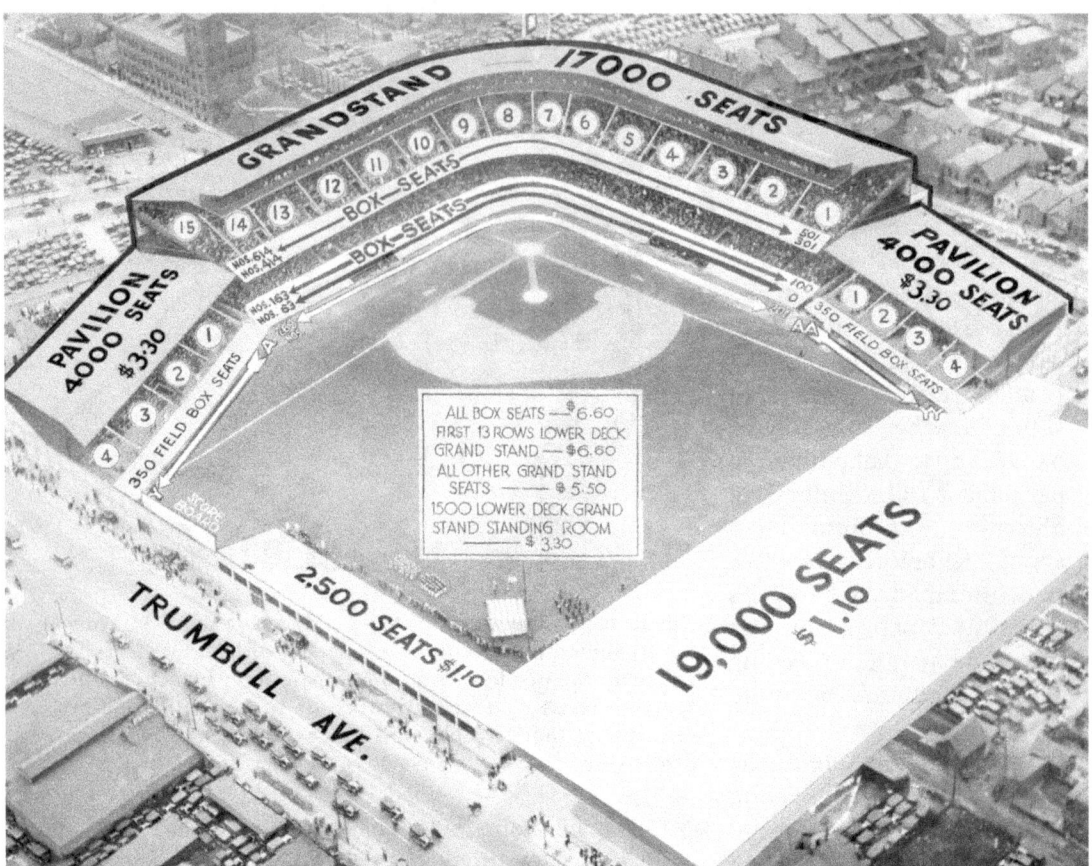

This ticket pricing diagram provided by the Tigers is superimposed on the 1930 aerial photo of Navin Field (page 21) and shows the expanded bleacher section in left field made possible by demolishing homes and closing Cherry Street (*Detroit News* from a print provided by Avanti Press).

than half the height of the Green Monster. Although the sample size is small, the official record of the 1935 World Series suggests the impact of this Lilliputian left pasture. At Navin Field, the Tigers and Cubs hit all three of their home runs to left in 198 at-bats. At the friendly confines of Wrigley Field, they hit none to left in 210 at-bats.

Altogether, the 1935 World Series configuration was about 89 rows deep at its maximum and produced about 21,500 bleacher seats (including the permanent ones in right-center), numbers never seen in a legitimate baseball park before or since. This figure was considerably greater than its closest rival, Yankee Stadium. It amounted to nearly 46 percent of Navin Field's total seating capacity, a proportion that was also without precedent. The bleachers actually exceeded the capacity of Navin Field's permanent double-decked grandstand by about 36 percent.[127]

A sold-out ballpark would hold about 48,700 people, including 1,500 standing-room places in the lower deck. At World Series prices, this would equate to about $160,800 per game, with the bleachers contributing about $23,600 of that number, or about 15 percent of the total. Stated somewhat differently, the series games at Wrigley Field generated $4.41 per ticket, while those at Navin Field produced only $3.30. While one might question the economic logic of building so many cheap seats contributing so little to the bottom line (a Tiger official even claimed that the club actually lost money on the World Series), one must applaud the provision of such plentiful, if spartan, accommodations for Motor City fans.

The following table provides some historic context for the magnitude of the Tigers' depression-era temporary bleachers. As a yardstick, Wrigley Field's iconic pyramidal bleachers of 1937 are about 75 feet deep at their greatest and extend about 38 rows back at their maximum, numbers that are too low to qualify for this list.

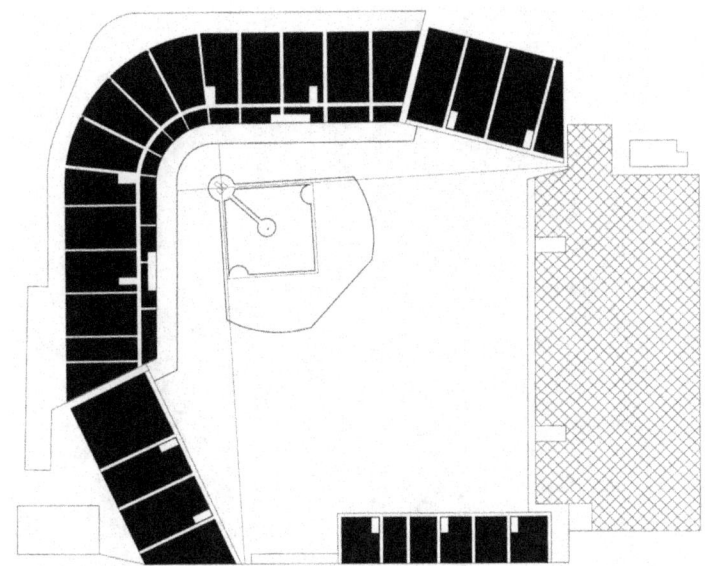

The lower deck plan of Navin Field during the 1935 World Series showing Cherry Street closed off once again to provide for construction of a new set of temporary bleachers for the Series, larger than that built for the 1934 Series. These bleachers extended onto left field approximately 42 feet (21 rows plus a front aisle). The left field wall, rebuilt after its removal for the 1934 World Series bleachers, remained intact this time, with the new bleachers built both in front of and behind this wall (© John Davids).

Table 7: A Chronology of Deep Bleacher Sections[128]

Year	City	Ballpark	Field	Depth[129]	Rows[130]	Status	Structure
1909	Pittsburgh	Forbes Field	Left (in foul territory)	88'[131]	47	Permanent	Concrete
1912	Cincinnati	Redland Field	Right	83'[132]	45	Permanent	Concrete
1912	Boston	Fenway Park	Center and Right	91'	49	Permanent	Unknown
1923	New York	Polo Grounds	Center	112'	60	Permanent	Concrete
1923	New York	Yankee Stadium	Left	99'[133]	52[134]	Interim	Wood
1923	New York	Yankee Stadium	Right	117'[135]	61[136]	Interim	Wood
1932	Cleveland	Municipal Stadium	Center	107'[137]	54[138]	Permanent	Concrete
1934	Boston	Fenway Park	Right	96'	50[139]	Permanent	Concrete
1934	Detroit	Navin Field	Left	126'[140]	68	Temporary	Wood
1935	Detroit	Navin Field	Left	163'[141]	89	Temporary	Wood
1938	New York	Yankee Stadium	Left-Center to Right-Center	92'[142]	43[143]	Permanent	Concrete
1969	Montreal	Parc Jarry	Left	129'	69	Temporary	Metal
1969	Seattle	Sick's Stadium	Right	119'	64	Temporary	Wood

Longevity and Adaptability (Pastier with J. Davids) 93

The stadium in transition in 1936, with the upper and lower deck bleachers stretching into deep centerfield, a configuration that would last only two years (*Detroit News* from a print provided by Avanti Press).

The colossal temporary bleachers of the 1935 postseason may have been a rabbit's foot, because, after four unsuccessful tries over the years, the Tigers won that season's World Series in six games. Shortly after this victory, club president Frank Navin announced that he would invest the season's $150,000 profit into expanding the ballpark. To this end, he again retained Jerome Utley to oversee the project. There is no good evidence that Osborn Engineering also had a role in this expansion phase, but credible sources make it clear that they were involved in the later expansion of 1937–1938.

Before Utley could complete his design, Navin fell off a horse and suffered a fatal heart attack in November. Co-owner and auto-body magnate Walter Briggs immediately bought out Navin's share of the club and, after a brief period of reflection, decided to implement the expansion. Utley's design called for an 8,307-seat[144] two-deck grandstand

Opposite, top: The much enlarged 1935 temporary bleachers. Observe the 20-foot-high fencing installed in order to prevent a repeat of the 1934 Ducky Medwick incident. *Bottom:* An aerial view of a 1935 World Series game showing the large temporary bleachers built across Cherry Street. Note the bumper-to-bumper parking behind the bleacher section (both photographs, *Detroit News* from a print provided by Avanti Press).

extension that replaced[145] the single-deck right field pavilion in foul territory beyond first base. The old pavilion section could not be saved and reused because it was steeper than the adjoining grandstand and thus would prevent proper alignment of the existing and new seating tiers.[146] This inexpandability suggests a possible lack of foresight in Osborn's original 1912 design.

In fair territory, the existing 200-foot-long and 47-foot-deep permanent concrete bleachers running from nearly dead center to straight right were retained to form the lower half of a double-decked stand. The columns of a new steel upper deck framework penetrated the old bleachers but remained structurally independent of their concrete frame. This was not the only nonstandard structural technique that Utley used. Because the old bleachers were only about 23 rows deep (equivalent to just 15 grandstand rows and a cross-aisle),[147] the Tigers front office sought to squeeze in as many rows as possible. Utley's response was to place the front steel columns at the line of the right field wall (rather than back within the bleachers) and cantilever the upper deck so that it overhung the lower by ten feet (four rows) toward home plate. Another cantilever behind the last row of seats projected out over Trumbull Avenue to provide space for a 430-foot-long[148] enclosed elevated passageway.

The old right field distance there was 372 feet, which was excessive as a modern foul line boundary (the average right field line dimension of the time, not counting Navin Field, was 320 feet)[149] yet would not allow room for both a decent grandstand depth and a credible home run dimension. Utley ameliorated this problem with a nice bit of pragmatic geometry. The fair territory portion of the new structure was a somewhat skimpy 47 feet deep (about 19 rows) at field level, allowing a respectable 325-foot foul line distance,

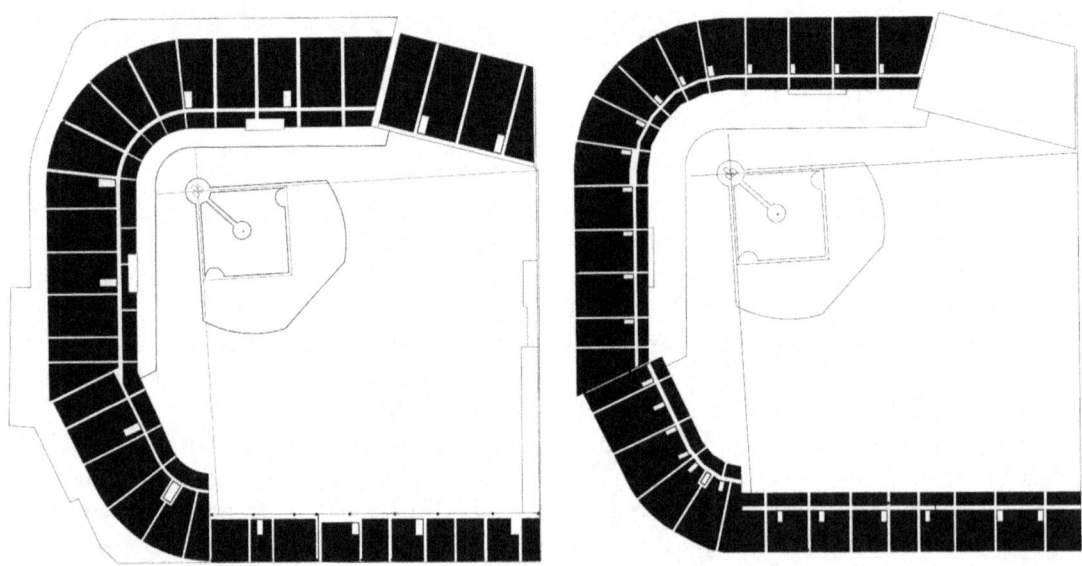

Left: The lower deck plan for Navin Field in 1936. The single-deck pavilion along the right field line has been demolished and replaced by new double-deck seating which also extends into center field. *Right:* The upper deck plan for Navin Field in 1936. Due to limited space along Trumbull Avenue, the upper deck in right field was built to overhang the playing field to maximize the seating capacity (both diagrams, © John Davids).

This shot of fans on Trumbull Avenue in 1945 provides a good view of the streetside projection (*Detroit News* from a print provided by Avanti Press).

while the upper deck was 67 feet deep, projecting ten feet (or four rows) toward home plate and ten feet out over the Trumbull Avenue sidewalk. The street-side projection was used for a covered concourse serving the upper deck seating.

The field-side overhang, dubbed the home run porch, would become one of the park's legendary features. The entire 10,000-seat addition, combined with the removal of the pavilion and the small permanent bleachers in right field and the immense temporary ones in left, reduced the park's overall seating capacity to about 36,000 but improved the sight lines of most right field patrons and gave the stadium a much higher proportion of comfortable, shaded chair seats than had existed for the two previous World Series.

Some structural anomalies (in addition to the right field street and field-side overhangs) marked this expansion phase, most of them in or near the right-field corner. There were subtle vertical and horizontal misalignments of the seating decks in that zone and what appeared to be redundant columns as close as two feet from one another. Also, the seats nearest dead center, located at the end of a 330-foot-long unyieldingly straight run of rows from the right field corner, wound up facing the left field corner rather than home plate and the infield.

Design and construction of this portion of the ballpark took place during the 1935–1936 offseason. After a year's hiatus (possibly caused by the need to acquire property beyond left field), Briggs concluded his ambitious ballpark expansion between the 1937 and 1938 seasons at a cost of about a million dollars, a tidy sum in those days, and about three times the cost of the original Navin Field construction. This time, the left side of the field was reconfigured, and the design team consisted of a Detroit firm bearing the cumbersome title of "Giffels & Vallet, Inc., L. Rossetti, Assoc. Engineers and Architects." Unlike the tight squeeze in right field caused by immovable Trumbull Avenue, left field was free of obstacles by then. Cherry Street had already been closed off for the temporary bleachers, and now the city permanently shifted it northward to give Briggs and Osborn plenty of room (about 129 feet)[150] for expansion. As a result, the new left field fair territory stands and the service spaces behind them were markedly deeper than the older main grandstands in foul territory—a very unusual configuration.

Like its counterpart in right field, the quarter-century-old left field pavilion in foul territory was torn down and replaced by a two-deck structure[151] which turned the foul corner and marched all the way to center field to meet the 1935–1936 extension, about 70 feet of which had just been demolished after less than two years' service in order to create a smoothly curved transition between the two phases of construction and better sight lines in center field. A large new scoreboard rose above that center-field bend, and a new press box sat atop the second-deck roof and extended through most of it, making it the largest such facility in the sport.

Here, too, there were structural and geometric quirks similar to those in right field, but none of them as obvious as the Trumbull Avenue and field overhangs. A utilitarian façade lent a unified exterior veneer to what was internally a definitive example of ad-hoc ballpark design. It was, to a casual observer, a reasonably integrated whole: one mammoth enclosed stadium with a seating capacity well over 50,000; a huge building almost completely taking up an oversized city block of nearly nine acres. But to a sharp-eyed ballpark devotee, this impressive and superficially well-behaved structure was also a monument to pragmatism and a mother lode of internal and external quirks. Adjacent seating sections did not always align perfectly, structural columns were often unevenly spaced, adjoining seating sections sometimes had different numbers of rows, and exterior ramps, concourses, and a spindly, largely freestanding elevator shaft projected from the main exterior walls, which occasionally hung over the property line. Here was an unapologetically idiosyncratic and inconsistent ballpark uncannily fitting baseball enthusiast Walt Whitman's famously unapologetic self-description: "Do I contradict myself? / Very well, then I contradict myself. / (I am large, I contain multitudes.)"[152]

The end result of Briggs's 1936–1938 demolitions and expansions was baseball's first ballpark completely ringed by two decks of seats and, similarly, the first with a 360-degree upper deck. (The Polo Grounds and Comiskey Park had earlier approached such a bi-level configuration through grandstand extensions designed by Osborn Engineering in the 1920s, but their upper decks had gaps of 120 feet or more in center field.) Because the expanded site had grown in the north-south direction, both the upper and lower left field decks were substantially deeper than their counterparts in right field.

This final expansion phase increased seating capacity for baseball to either an often-published but almost surely overstated 58,000[153] (which is very close to the stadium's football capacity of 58,210) or a less ubiquitous but more credible 54,000,[154] giving the park the third-greatest number of seats in the big leagues at the time.[155] It also made

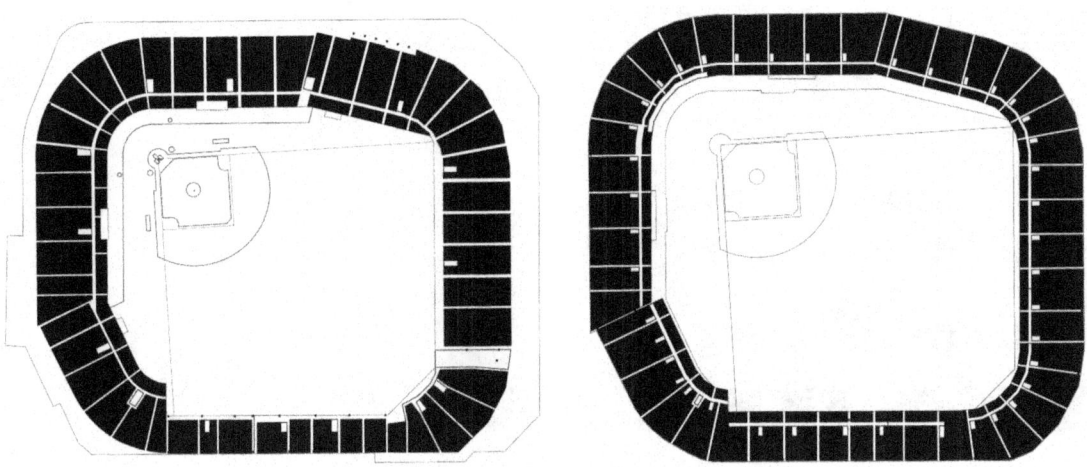

Left: The lower deck plan for Briggs Stadium in 1938. The northernmost sections of the right field seating, built just two years earlier, had to be demolished to connect it with the new seating built in center field and stretching all the way around left field and up to the original 1923 double-deck along the third base line. *Right:* The upper deck plan of Briggs Stadium in 1938. The complete double-decking of the stadium gave it a unique place in pre-expansion ballpark design and helped create the sense of intimacy that was a hallmark at Michigan and Trumbull (both diagrams, © John Davids).

Detroit's fledgling big-bleacher tradition permanent, providing 11,211[156] such seats on two levels (another unprecedented feature), with the lower deck benches in right and center under cover, sheltered by the upper deck, whose left and center field bleachers were exposed to the elements. With his unconventional, complicated and monumental reinvention of Navin Field complete, Walter Briggs deservedly renamed the stadium after himself, continuing a practice that had previously occurred in at least ten other classic ballparks.[157] Reshaped, improved, enlarged, and impressive, Briggs Stadium opened on April 22, 1938, to a then-record Detroit crowd of 54,500.

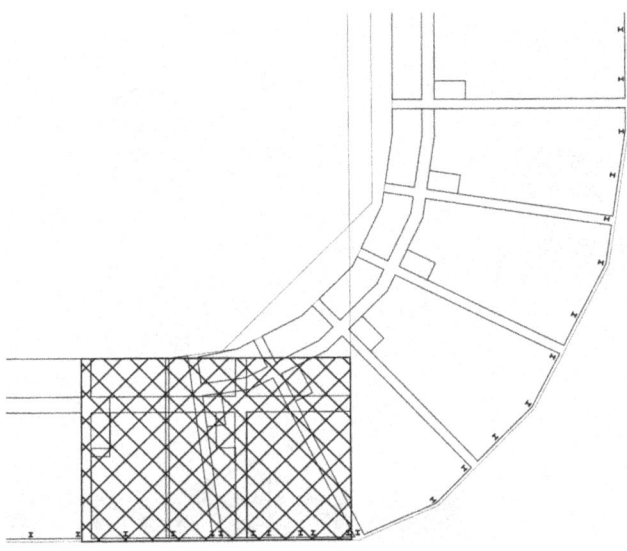

A diagram illustrating the bleachers (crosshatched) at both levels that had to be demolished in order to complete the final phase of construction in 1938. This area had been built just two years previously (© John Davids).

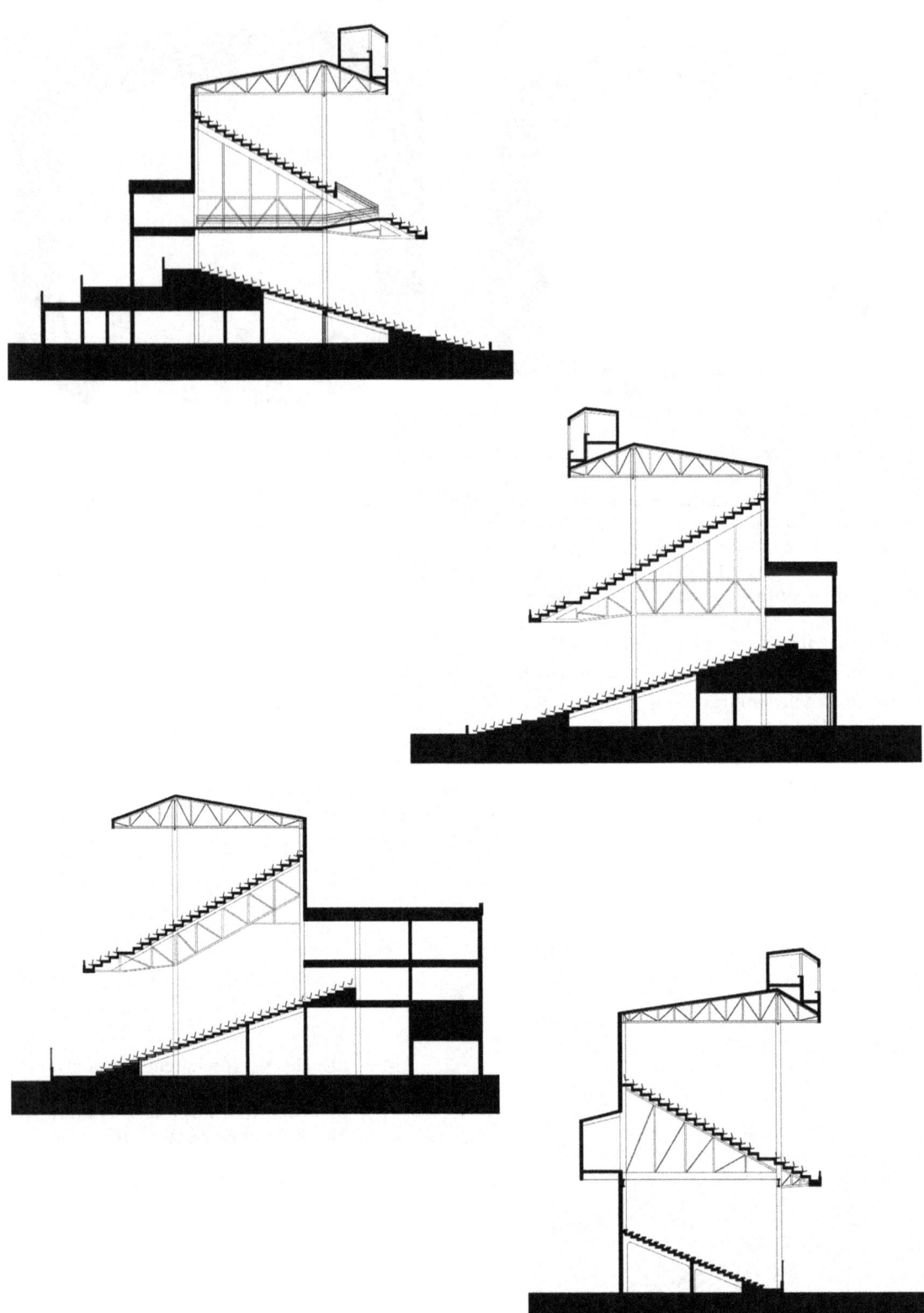

Longevity and Adaptability (Pastier with J. Davids) 99

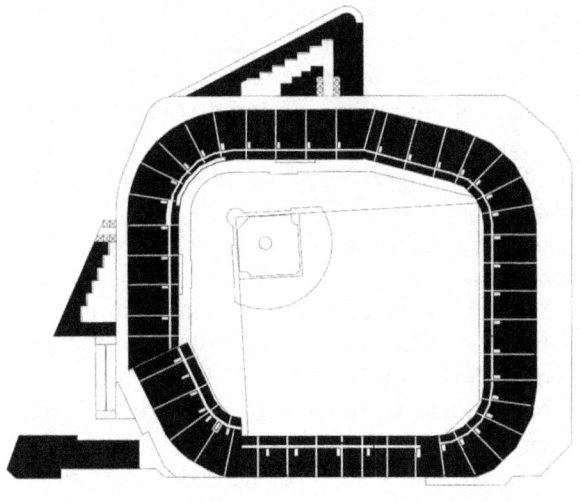

Football at the Corner

This comprehensive expansion was not only a boon for Motor City baseball fans, but it also made Briggs Stadium a very good professional football venue for its time. (In that era, the biggest and best football stadiums were built for college games, which were far more popular and held in higher regard than pro contests.) In 1938, the Detroit Lions of the National Football League began to play there, and it remained their home for 37 seasons (all but 1940) and 185 games, until the end of 1974. Like most contemporary pro football venues, its layout was designed and optimized for baseball and was therefore often less than ideal for gridiron action. In this case, the end zones were perilously close to the left field and first base stands,[158] while the sidelines were about 110 feet distant from the seats in right field and along the third base foul line.[159] But Briggs Stadium had one major advantage over almost all the other National Football League venues of the time: its 360-degree upper deck provided a

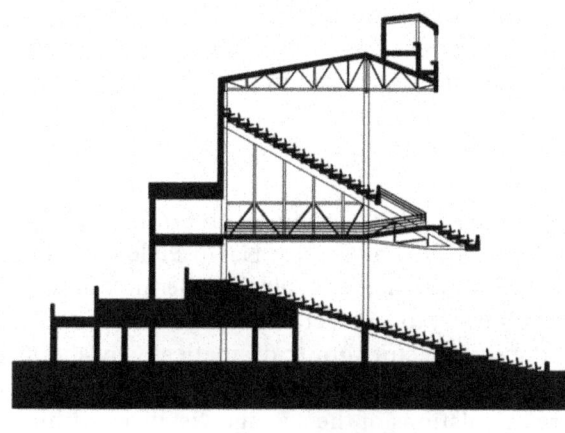

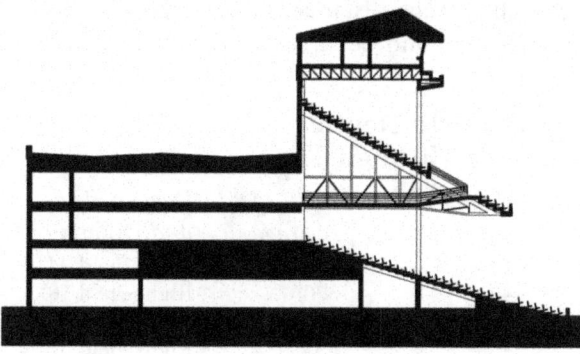

Top: The Cochrane Plan upper deck design showing similar amenities provided for fans. The two section drawings below it show a comparison of the existing Tiger Stadium (middle) and the proposed changes of the Cochrane Plan (bottom). The public seating at both levels remains unchanged (with the exception of the removal of columns), and the unused third deck is replaced by the new level of suites (both diagrams, © John Davids).

Opposite, top left: A section of Briggs Stadium in 1938 through the seating along the first base line. *Middle right:* A section of Briggs Stadium in 1938 through the seating along the third base line. *Middle left:* A section of Briggs Stadium in 1938 through the seating in left field. *Bottom right:* A section of Briggs Stadium in 1938 through the seating in right field that shows the overhangs both above the playing field and above Trumbull Avenue (all diagrams, © John Davids).

high proportion of elevated seats whose sight lines and viewing angles were especially desirable for football. (When the stadium opened for football, all its upper deck seats carried the maximum $2.20 ticket price.)[160] It also had a considerably greater than NFL-average seating capacity—58,210 in its football configuration—an important feature for a sport that, in those days, had to earn its keep in just a half-dozen official home games a season. (The Polo Grounds and Cleveland Stadium were other contemporary ballparks that provided similar advantages for football.)

Over the years, 11 million football fans attended professional games at Michigan and Trumbull, and college and high school games were common there as well. Professional gridiron games began at The Corner in 1921, when teams such as the Detroit Heralds, the Detroit Tigers, and the Detroit Panthers struggled unsuccessfully to establish a Motor City toehold for the NFL during a post–World War I recession. With its high seating capacity and elevated viewing angles, Navin Field's 1938 metamorphosis into Briggs Stadium arguably set the stage for the golden age of Detroit football. (In September 1964, 59,203 spectators, the largest sports crowd in stadium history, turned out for a Lions-Packers contest.)[161] At the end of the 1974 football season, the Lions moved from Michigan and Trumbull to an indoor venue in suburban Pontiac, where they played for 27 years. In 2002, things came full circle when they returned to central Detroit, occupying a new stadium at the northern edge of downtown, just across the street from Comerica Park and about a mile away from vacant but still-standing Tiger Stadium.

A Place for Homers

Briggs' permanent seating expansions of the late 1930s produced an outfield whose overall size averaged about 377 feet, roughly five feet shorter than Navin Field's during the first two decades of the latter's history, and about 12 feet shorter than Bennett Park's. The left sector of the outfield grew by about nine feet to 360 feet, the center field portion remained relatively stable at 420 feet, and the right sector shrank dramatically by about eight yards to 347 feet, as shown in the following table of evolving outfield dimensions at The Corner. (The dimensions shown are calculations of the average distances within each 30-degree outfield sector, and the overall average distance, rather than the more familiar but less informative single-point foul line and dead center distances usually listed in reference works.)

Table 8: Average Outfield Depths at Michigan and Trumbull Through Time[162]

Years	Full Field Average	Left Field Average	Center Field Average	Right Field Average	Deeper Field and Difference
1901–1911	389'	351'	441'	375'	Right Field 24'
1912–1922	382'	352'	422'	370'	Right Field 18'
1923–1933	381'	349'	421'	370'	Right Field 21'
1934	360'	316'	406'	353'	Right Field 37'
1934 WS-1935	381'	352'	422'	365'	Right Field 13'
1935 WS	359'	315'	393'	365'	Right Field 50'
1936–1937	369'	346'	411'	347'	Right Field 1'
1938–1954	377'	360'	420'	347'	Left Field 13'
1955–1999	376'	360'	418'	347'	Left Field 13'
Weighted Average 1912–1999	377'	357'	419'	353'	Left Field 4'

Temporary on-field bleachers in the 1934 regular season and the 1935 World Series created absurdly short home-run distances in left and left-center, but aside from those short-lived aberrations, the ballpark's roomier field shifted from right to left after its first 26 years. The 1955 dimensions reflect a shortening of the dead center distance from 440 feet to 425 feet, and they stayed constant for the remainder of the ballpark's existence, or just over half its lifetime. This is the configuration that virtually all living fans inevitably associate with the park.

Near the end of its existence, Tiger Stadium became the most productive home run park in major league history, thanks to a combination of extreme longevity and favorable dimensions. It took the better part of a century to achieve that status, as seen below:

Table 9: Baseball's Most Prolific Home Run Venues (Progressive Totals)

City	Park	HR Milestone	Year Reached
Philadelphia	Baker Bowl	500	1913
Philadelphia	Baker Bowl	1,000	1921
New York	Polo Grounds	1,000	1921
New York	Polo Grounds	1,500	1925
St. Louis	Sportsman's Park	2,000	1929
St. Louis	Sportsman's Park	3,000	1935
St. Louis	Sportsman's Park	4,000	1940
St. Louis	Sportsman's Park	5,000	1946
St. Louis	Sportsman's Park	6,000	1951
St. Louis	Sportsman's Park	7,000	1957
St. Louis	Sportsman's Park	8,000[163]	1964
Detroit	Tiger Stadium	9,000	1988
Detroit	Tiger Stadium	10,000	1994[164]
Detroit	Tiger Stadium	11,111[165]	1999

On July 23, 1993, baseball fans around the nation learned from their daily papers that, the night before, Tiger Stadium had become the first major league park to record 10,000 home runs, thanks to a Gary Gaetti four-bagger.[166] That interesting news proved to be highly premature. The actual event took place on June 5, 1994,[167] and the honor fell to Tiger left fielder Tony Phillips, who had two homers on an 84-degree Sunday afternoon when six balls flew into the seats.[168] (The 10,000 home run club was later joined by Wrigley Field in 1999, Yankee Stadium in 2002, and Fenway Park in 2003.)

Clearly, The Corner was receptive to four-baggers, but it was not an incubator of cheap home runs like several other ballparks were. The shortest possible over-the-fence home run during the stadium's final and longest-lived fence configuration, which would be a sharply descending high fly just nicking the overhanging upper deck exactly at the right field foul line, would have been about 325 feet. This is more than (and in some cases, much more than) the minimums in many parks that saw at least some service after 1936, including those tabulated below. (These minimums take fence height into account and are estimates of where a ball would theoretically strike ground level, rather than where it would land in the seats):

Table 10: Minimum Home Run Lengths in Selected Major League Parks[169]

Minimum	Location	Park and City
261'	Right Field	Polo Grounds, New York
262'	Left Field	Polo Grounds, New York

102   Part I: History and Background

Minimum	Location	Park and City
266'	Left Field	Memorial Coliseum, Los Angeles
286'	Right Field	Baker Bowl, Philadelphia
296'	Right Field	Yankee Stadium, New York
301'	Left Field	Yankee Stadium, New York
303'	Right Field	Fenway Park, Boston; League Park, Cleveland
306'	Left Field and Right Field	Memorial Stadium, Baltimore
307'	Left Field	Sick's Stadium, Seattle
308'	Right Field	Forbes Field, Pittsburgh
309'	Right Field	Ebbets Field, Brooklyn
312'	Right Field	Sportsman's Park, St. Louis
315'	Right Field	Kingdome, Seattle
316'	Right Field	AT&T Park, San Francisco
317'	Left Field	Kingdome, Seattle; County Stadium, Milwaukee; Tropicana Field, St. Petersburg
318'	Right Field	County Stadium, Milwaukee
320'	Left Field	Fenway Park, Boston
321'	Left Field and Right Field	Municipal Stadium, Cleveland
322'	Right Field	Sick's Stadium, Seattle
325'	Right Field	Tiger Stadium, Detroit

Altogether, there have been at least 34 post–1900 examples of parks permitting shorter home runs to right field than Tiger Stadium, not all of them listed here. At least 59 ballparks in that period had left field minimum distances shorter than Tiger Stadium's 342 feet.

What this means is that Tiger Stadium's friendliness to long-ball hitters was not due to substandard distances near the foul lines. It had an excellent batting background, a 600 foot altitude,[170] and 94-foot-tall outfield stands that would temper any wind blowing in towards the plate, but a more significant factor was its lack of any "Death Valley" dimensions in the power alleys. Granted, it did have a deep straightaway center field (either 425 feet or 440 feet, depending on the time period), like so many other rectilinear parks completed before World War II,[171] but that was a relatively narrow zone—nearly two-thirds of the outfield was shorter than 375 feet.[172] While there were no absurdly cheap four-baggers, a reasonably well-struck ball not hit to center had a fair chance of reaching the seats. This is borne out by the home-road splits of the most prolific Tiger sluggers from the 1930s until 1999. The top seven, measured by round-trippers hit in a Tiger uniform, were:

Table 11: Home-Road Home Run Splits of Leading Tiger Sluggers

Total as a Tiger	Home	Road	Difference	Player
399	226	173	53	Al Kaline
373	212	161	51	Norm Cash
306	187	119	68	Hank Greenberg
262	124	138	-14	Willie Horton
245	130	115	15	Cecil Fielder
244	146	98	48	Lou Whitaker
239	140	99	41	Rudy York
2,068	1,165	903	262	Total of Top Seven

Overall, these sluggers hit 29 percent more home runs at home than on the road. Normally, there is about a 10 percent "home cooking" advantage in home run rate, partly offset by about a five percent reduction because home teams get fewer at-bats since they do not always come to the plate in the last of the ninth.[173] Greenberg's splits are remarkable: he hit 57 percent more HRs at home than on the road, and during his spectacular 1938 season, he hit more than twice as many (39) in Detroit than on the road (19). No one, not even the unprecedentedly prolific record-breakers of the steroid era—Mark McGwire, Sammy Sosa, and Barry Bonds—has ever matched Hank's single-season home field home runs mark. Willie Horton's splits are also noteworthy: he is the only Tiger slugger on this list to be penalized by his home park, an ironic distinction for a Detroit native.

A wider-ranging analysis, which considers every player with 50 or more lifetime home runs as a Tiger between 1930 and 1999,[174] yields these figures:

Table 12: Aggregate Home Run Splits of Top 50 Tiger Sluggers Since 1930

Number and Type of Batters	Total	Home	Road	Surplus	Average Difference
28 Right Handed Batters	3,821	2,049	1,772	277	9.9
18 Left Handed Batters	2,415	1,349	1,066	283	15.7
4 Switch Hitters	363	194	169	25	6.3
50 Total Batters	6,599	3,592	3,007	585	11.7

These players, who accounted for the great majority of Tiger home runs in that period, hit 19.5 percent more round-trippers in Tiger Stadium than on the road. Lefties hit 26.5 percent more, righties 15.6 percent more, and switch hitters 14.8 percent more.

Lefty Ted Williams loved to hit in Briggs Stadium, saying that the excellent batting background enabled him to see the ball especially well. His lifetime home run figures bear this out. He hit 87 round-trippers against the Tigers, 55 in Detroit and 32 in Boston—about 72 percent more at Briggs than at Fenway.[175] Such a performance suggests that, had he played as a Tiger, he might have had about 400 home runs at Michigan and Trumbull and threatened Babe Ruth's lifetime record, despite all the playing time he lost to military service. Similarly, righty Joe DiMaggio, Williams' contemporary, hit 76 percent more homers in Detroit (30) than in Yankee Stadium (17) against the Tigers.[176] These numbers suggest that he might have had about 70 more had he spent his career as a Tiger. Righty Jimmie Foxx also thrived in Detroit, which was his most productive road park. He hit 52 there, a rate of 8.7 HR per 100 at-bats that bested Babe Ruth's 8.5 and Barry Bonds's 7.7 lifetime performances.[177] Had the Beast performed that well in all of his venues, he would have finished just short of 700 round-trippers in his career.

How does Tiger Stadium stack up as a long-ball hitting environment within the wider universe of all classic parks? The home run park factors for the most slugger-friendly pre–World War II ballparks in their final playing-field configuration are as follows:

Table 13: Park Factors for Home Run Friendly Classic-Era Ballparks

Home Run Factor[178]	City	Park	Year Built	Study Period	Home Home Runs	Road Home Runs
205	Los Angeles	Wrigley Field[179]	1925	1961	248	121
174	Philadelphia	Baker Bowl	1895	1920–1938	2,211	1,268
173	New York	Polo Grounds	1911	1920–1963	6,104	3,534

Home Run Factor	City	Park	Year Built	Study Period	Home Home Runs	Road Home Runs
145	Los Angeles	Memorial Coliseum[180]	1923	1958–1961	743	511
127	Detroit	Briggs/Tiger Stadium	1912	1938–1999[181]	9,151	7,201
122	Brooklyn	Ebbets Field	1913	1948–1957[182]	1,750	1,436
117	Chicago	Wrigley Field	1914	1920–1999	9,058	7,759
116	St. Louis	Sportsman's Park	1909	1920–1966	8,168	7,030
114	Cincinnati	Crosley Field	1912	1940–1970[183]	3,761	3,312
112	Boston	Fenway Park	1912	1940–1999[184]	7,725	6,885
125		Average	1913	1942–1971	4,892	3,906

As seen here, there were ten early fireproof parks (including a football and track stadium) that produced at least a 12 percent surplus of home runs hit on their premises compared to those hit on the road. The figures are totals for both teams in each contest, both at home and on the road, and the time spans studied are limited to the periods when the parks' evolving outfield sizes were at their smallest, or nearly so. Deadball Era seasons (those before 1920) are excluded. as were seasons when major league ball was no longer played at Michigan and Trumbull (i.e., after 1999).

Among these old parks conducive to the long ball, Tiger Stadium falls pretty much in the middle. Its home run factor of 127 is just above the overall weighted average of 125 and ranks fifth out of ten. It is clearly higher than the figures for Wrigley, Crosley, and Ebbets Fields, and Fenway and Sportsman's Parks but is well below the stratospheric levels attained by Baker Bowl and the Polo Grounds, not to mention the incredible 205 score put up by the one-year wonder, Los Angeles' Wrigley Field.

Tiger Stadium was a very good home run park, but not an excessively easy one, such as the four above it in the table. Nor, to use a contemporary comparison, was it as much of a home run heaven as Coors Field, which had a park factor of 165 in its first seven seasons. For the eighth, the Colorado Rockies' management installed a humidifier to deaden game balls. This tactic reduced the home run factor noticeably, and the experiment was generally pronounced a success. But even so, Coors' score during its first 11 humidor seasons was 131, higher than Tiger Stadium's and higher than the average of the homer-friendly classic parks analyzed above.

Some of the reasons for Tiger Stadium's home run friendliness, such as a very good batting background and moderate power alleys, have already been mentioned. They may not occupy as prominent a place in fans' perceptions as the idiosyncratic right field upper deck overhang that was one of the park's most legendary features. It was purportedly duplicated in the Texas Rangers' Ballpark in Arlington under the title of a "Home Run Porch," but that was a marketing device lacking any credibility or grasp of the meaning of the word "overhang." Arlington's design did place some columns in its right field seating sections, but the upper deck was further back from home plate than the lower deck, rather than being closer, and thus did nothing whatsoever to increase home runs or frustrate right fielders.

Detroit's right field was one of four upper deck projections in the major leagues in the 20th century, but despite its great fame as an interceptor of catchable fly balls, it had far less quantitative effect on home run totals than the power alleys and batting backdrop. Two of those four "home run porches" that protruded beyond the lower deck had relatively modest dimensions. Tiger Stadium's jutted forward ten feet at the foul line and about 13 feet near center field at a height of 34 feet; the Polo Grounds' right field overhang ranged from nine feet to 15 feet at a height of 38 feet.

Theoretically, these overhangs were capable of intercepting catchable high flies and turning them into home runs (Tiger Stadium's slightly more so than the Polo Grounds' right field), but this effect is hard to quantify. There is no doubt that it happened, but with what frequency? It should be remembered that not all first-row upper deck shots in these places would necessarily have been in play in the absence of the overhang. Bill Brown, who worked in the Tigers' front office from 1968 to 2013, says: "My guess is that no more than twice a year—and that is a generous estimate—would the porch turn an out into a homer. My best estimate would be 0.75 'porch shots' per season, or 3 every 4 seasons."[185] Based on this reckoning, about 24, or three-sevenths of one percent of the 5,705[186] home runs hit at Tiger Stadium during the 32 years that Brown worked there, were attributable to the overhang. During that same period, there were 26 roof shots,[187] so porch-enabled home runs seem to have been quite rare.

The third instance, Shibe Park's, is difficult to analyze because reliable geometric evidence is scarce. The overhang may have been as much as ten feet at the line and about 14 feet in center at a height of about 24 feet. This would have had a greater effect than the higher Tiger Stadium overhang. But the overhang may have been as little as four to six feet; thus, the resolution of the issue awaits better data.

The fourth case, however, was spectacularly unambiguous. The Polo Grounds' left field foul line distance was 279 feet at field level but was overshadowed by a 29-foot overhang, which increased to about 40 feet in straightaway left field. That extreme configuration was clearly one that could, and did, convert many normally in-play balls into upper deck home runs and was a significant component in that ballpark's abnormally high home run factor.

Roof shots were another mainstay of Tiger Stadium lore and are well documented. The park's dimensions were such that reaching the 94-foot-high grandstand roof was difficult (especially in left field) but doable. In the 62 seasons that the stadium had double-decked stands throughout fair territory, 26 players hit balls over the roof a total of 36 times. Every two years or so, someone would reach the right field roof, and every 16 years, on average, someone would conquer left field. Al Kaline, the all-time Tiger Stadium home run leader with 226, never managed the feat. The righties who did—Harmon Killebrew, Frank Howard, Cecil Fielder, and Mark McGwire—were notably beefy, averaging about 70 pounds more than the trim Kaline.[188] Lefties turned the trick 30 times, beginning with Ted Williams as a rookie in 1939, and led by Norm Cash with four; Mickey Mantle and Kirk Gibson with three each; and Jason Thompson, Mickey Tettleton, and Tony Clark, each with a pair. Willie Horton claims to have hit a light standard on the right field roof as a 16-year-old high schooler, but such a feat defies belief, since he was never able to reach the roof in 15 seasons as a Tiger and three more with other American League clubs. Only four right-handed batters have ever hit roof shots in roughly 5,000 major league games, and none were to the opposite field, like Horton's purported blow.[189]

Home runs were a key aspect of Tiger Stadium's character and functionality. Inherently exciting and entertaining, and highly valued by most fans, they were nurtured generously at Michigan and Trumbull. In contrast, its successor, Comerica Park, was somewhat inexplicably designed as an extreme pitcher's venue, so much so that the club had to bring in the left half of the outfield by a startling 25 feet, just three years after opening.[190] This was done not only to satisfy fans who preferred to see more scoring and home runs but also to attract and retain power hitters who understandably felt that their careers would be damaged by playing in a venue that would significantly undercut their strengths. It will be interesting to see whether Comerica Park is eventually able to generate a degree of fan loyalty and affection comparable to that earned by Tiger Stadium.

Postwar Rehabilitation and Proposed Reconfigurations

The massive Briggs Stadium expansions of the mid- and late 1930s produced a ballpark that, with one major exception, needed no significant further improvements, combining a convenient location, a fully double-decked enclosure, high capacity (its single-game attendance peak was 58,369 on July 20, 1947), honest no-nonsense character, unaffected eccentricities, remarkable viewing intimacy, ample opportunities for power hitting, and a bountiful supply of reasonably priced seats. In Al Kaline's words, "Tiger Stadium's strengths lie not in its dazzling architecture or creature comforts, but in its character and charm."[191]

There was a small tweak just after World War II: the ticketing and club office building at Michigan and Trumbull was stripped of its Mediterranean-revival façade, expanded vertically by one floor, and given a simplified utilitarian exterior. While this was more in keeping with the unadorned main structure, it was far less picturesque than its predecessor. Another minor adjustment was the removal of about 40[192] field-level seats in the right field foul corner in the mid–1950s. According to one account, after Kaline had collided with the stands at that location, Tiger management opened up the playing field a bit to spare their star right fielder further exposure to potential injury, creating what quickly became known as Kaline's Corner. Another version has it that the seats were removed to allow the wide-ranging Kaline to catch more foul balls.[193] According to at least one experienced researcher, both stories have merit.[194]

The major postwar change was the installation of lights, which was done in 1948. Briggs Stadium was the last American League park to achieve night game capability, leaving Wrigley Field as the final big league venue to install lights, which it did 40 years later. This belated illumination, said to be the best and the brightest in the majors, allowed Briggs Stadium to compete without handicap at the box office. The 1948 attendance of more than 1.7 million topped the previous season by 30 percent and set a new club record. There can be no doubt that this was attributable to night baseball: Games under the lights averaged more than 44,000, while those played in daylight drew less than 20,000 on average. By implication, the 13 night games added at least 342,000 paid admissions to the Tiger's coffers and almost certainly many more than that, since the choice weekend and holiday dates and doubleheaders were all scheduled as day games while night games were all booked for the less attractive midweek dates.

In 1961, broadcasting executive John Fetzer bought the club from the Briggs family and modestly renamed the ballpark after the Tigers rather than after himself. The rooftop BRIGGS STADIUM sign above Michigan and Cochrane was altered with a minimum of fuss at a cost of about $20,000 by removing the B, the S, and one of the Gs, acquiring a new E and T, and reshuffling the remaining I, G, and R.[195]

The next changes came two decades later, were more substantial, and cost $18 mil-

Above: The redesigned office building decked out for Detroit's 250th birthday celebration in 1951 (*The Detroit News*). *Left:* The removal of seating in the right field corner of Briggs Stadium in 1955 following Al Kaline's 1954 injury in a collision with the front rail of those seats (© John Davids).

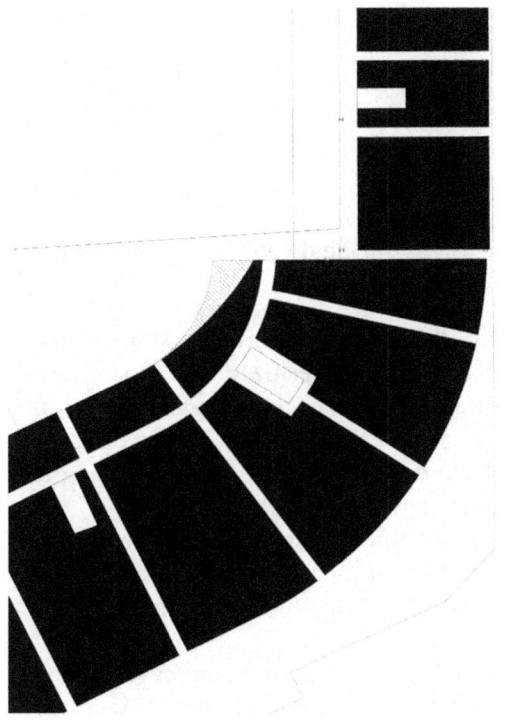

lion. Between 1977 and 1984, there were extensive renovations that kept aging Tiger Stadium intact and running. The Detroit area architectural practice of Rosetti Associates designed and oversaw the work in two phases. Although less sweeping than an ambitious $23 million renovation and expansion plan proposed by the firm in 1978, it still involved extensive changes, including major repairs to the stadium's deteriorating foundations, the replacement of the old wooden seats with larger orange and blue plastic ones (reducing seating capacity to 52,806), the installation of a new press box and a computerized scoreboard, the addition of new

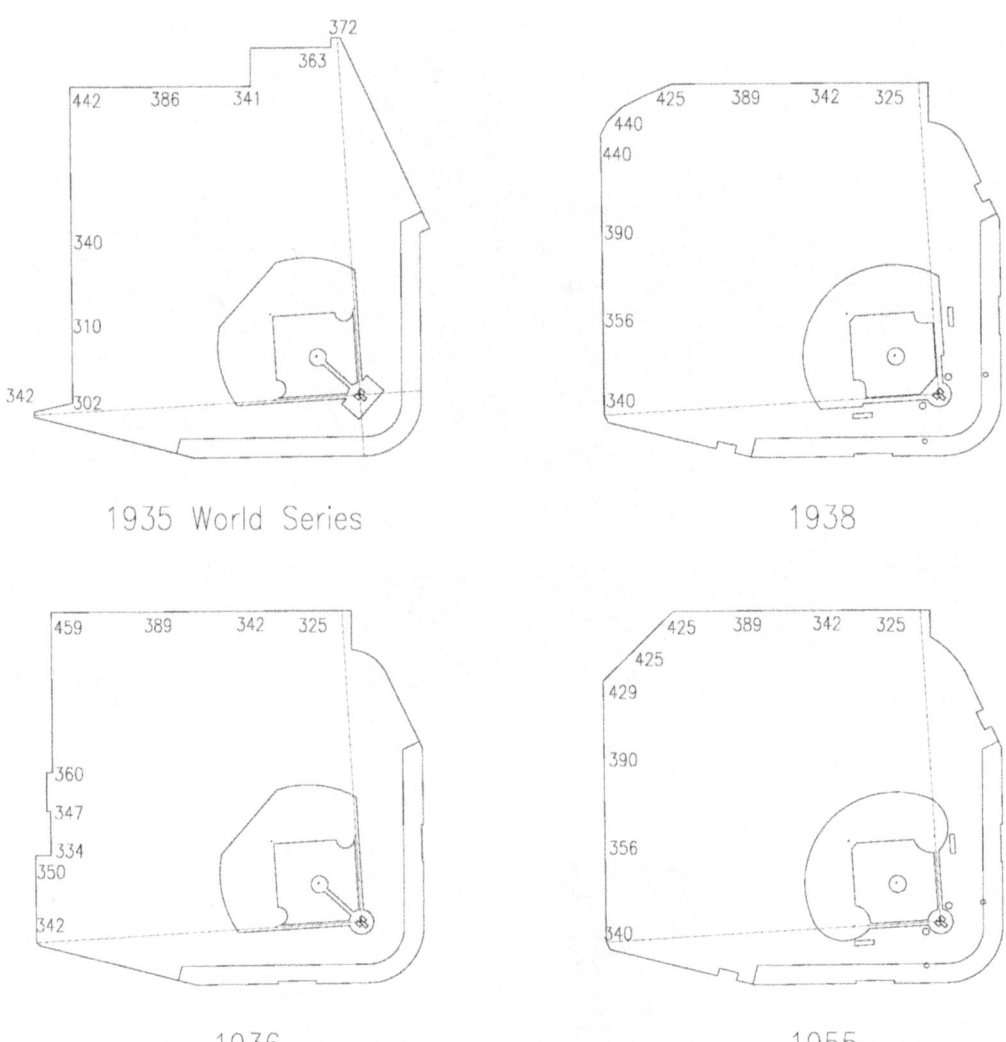

A diagram of field configurations and outfield dimensions during the 1935 World Series and in 1936, 1938, and 1955 (© John Davids).

white metal exterior cladding and blue glazed graffiti-proof masonry (both of which spared the club the cost of an expensive annual paint job), modernized clubhouses, and a pair of new public restrooms. In addition, there were roof and decking repairs, electrical upgrades, restroom refurbishing, and other plumbing work. Finally, there were two luxury suites suspended from the front of the upper deck, one for the press and one for the owner, unfortunately blocking the fly ball views of many lower deck patrons.

The new cladding gave Tiger Stadium a clean and unified exterior face that concealed the weathered appearance and cobbled-together nature of more than a half-century of various additions and expansions. It seems fair to say that the aging Queen of Diamonds had never looked this good before.

One might think that these visual and functional improvements would have insured the future of Tiger Stadium for at least another generation, especially since Fetzer had signed a 30-year lease on the property running through 2008, with an option for a 30-year extension, and since the park had achieved official landmark status by virtue of being declared a State of Michigan Historic Site in 1975 and being listed on the National Register of Historic Places since 1989. The National Trust for Historic Preservation included the stadium on its 1991 and 1992 lists of America's "11 Most Endangered Historic Places." Over the years, that listing has included 242 sites, of which only a handful have been lost. Unfortunately, Tiger Stadium was one of those rare exceptions.

Both before and after the renovation, steady drumbeats of discontent with the ballpark had been emanating from politicians and club owners. Both groups agitated for a new publicly funded stadium, either single-purpose or combined with facilities for other uses. Not all of them will be mentioned here. Just after the second renovation, in 1983, Domino's Pizza mogul and architecture enthusiast Tom Monaghan bought the Tigers and immediately vowed to preserve the ballpark and never construct a new one, saying "as long as I own this team, we will not build a new stadium." Later, however, his allegiance to the old landmark proved fickle, as he interviewed at least one European "starchitect"[196] unfamiliar with baseball to design a new home for the club. This may have been only a personal amusement, since he was not offering to pay for such a project, and no public funding was on the horizon at the time. In 1988, John McDevitt, his chief stadium aide, claimed to have overseen a feasibility study to re-renovate the ballpark and add an inflatable roof (something that had never been attempted with an existing baseball stadium at the time) at a cost of more than $100 million. Mayor Coleman Young promptly chimed in to say "it's obvious that the damned thing is falling down" but offered no evidence to support his dramatic accusation. The Tiger Stadium Fan Club,[197] a grassroots preservation group founded the year before, questioned McDevitt's figure and argued that the public was entitled to more information about the project. As it turned out, there was no such study; the figures were political misinformation concocted (or perhaps inflated) from thin air. This unplanned plan died on the vine, but the long-term threat to the stadium continued unabated.

In 1990, Monaghan hired retired University of Michigan football coach Bo Schembechler as his point person for a new stadium. Although no one seemed to notice it at the time, there was a colossal irony to this appointment—in his more than two decades at Michigan, Schembechler's teams played without complaint in an old, oft-expanded Osborn-designed stadium with mediocre field proximity. (Some premium seats were nearly 300 feet from the nearest edge of the gridiron.) Now, he was tasked with leading the charge to abandon an old, oft-expanded Osborn-designed ballpark with unmatched field proximity. A year into his new role, he contributed the most memorable piece of rhetoric in the battle over the ballpark's future, telling the Economic Club of Detroit: "It's unfair for you to think that you can shackle us to a rusted girder in Tiger Stadium and expect us to compete and win, because it's not going to happen." Young's and Schembechler's charges of severe structural inadequacy were as groundless as they were attention-getting. The real issues in the preservation battle were economics, amenities, and manufactured nostalgia rather than public safety. The baseball world was witnessing the beginnings of a ballpark design revolution whose principal elements were single-sport use; reduced seating capacities (but within relatively bulky building envelopes); super-premium seating sections (club seats and private suites); expanded food, drink, and merchandise sales points; kids' play areas; ubiquitous on-site advertising; and self-consciously quirky retro design meant to impersonate the classic old ballparks.

This thirst for nostalgia and neotraditionalism was understandable in cities such as Arlington, Atlanta, Cincinnati, Cleveland, Houston, Minneapolis, Montreal, Oakland, Philadelphia, Pittsburgh, St. Louis, San Francisco, and Seattle. There, the local nines previously played in multisport, circular (or nearly so), gray concrete venues, three of them indoors, having little warmth, individuality, or authentic baseball character. But Detroit had the real thing, a ballpark of immense character, unmatched intimacy, and rich history.

Plans for Preservation and Renovation

To preserve these qualities, two independent, pro bono plans for remodeling Tiger Stadium were produced locally[198] in 1990 and 1991. The latter was developed by Gunnar Birkerts, a Detroit area architect of national repute, working with contractor Joe O'Neal. They proposed a dramatic structural makeover that called for moving most of the upper deck trusses and lower deck columns outward and upward and fully cantilevering the roof, in order to make room for suites and to allow removal of three-fourths of the seating-area columns, thereby sharply reducing the number of obstructed-view seats. This arrangement would have met most of the Tigers' goals for premium seating and greatly expanded support spaces at an estimated cost of $75-$95 million, but the result would have been a radically different venue than the familiar one that had stood largely unchanged since 1938.

Upper deck viewing distances would have grown by about 34 feet, the ballpark would have been 25 feet higher, and the upper portions of the structure would have spread outward by more than 60,000 square feet. Parts of this expanded upper structure would have been larger than the site, overhanging the Michigan Avenue curb line by 40 feet.[199] The sharply slanted field-facing fronts of the three levels of suites would have given the main grandstand a zippy, futuristic look very much at odds with the ballpark's long-established character, which would have been preserved only in the unchanged outfield seating structure and in the retention of the playing surface.

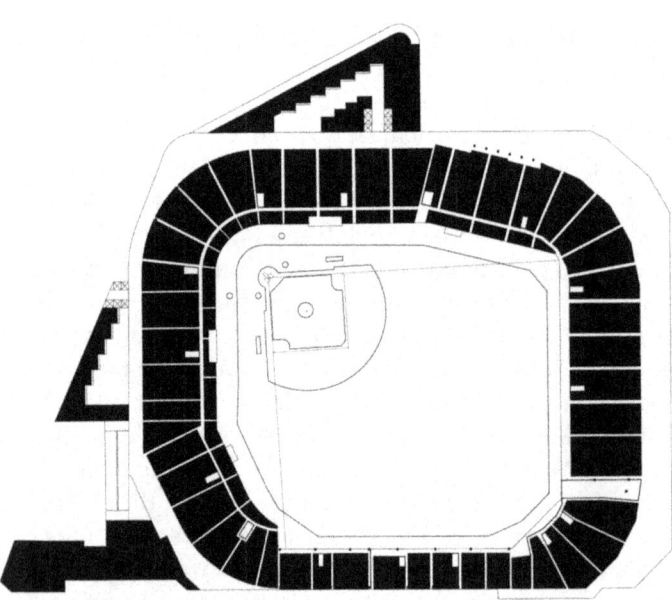

The Cochrane Plan lower deck design showing additional amenities built along both baselines, including new team facilities, concession stands, toilet rooms, and office space (© John Davids).

The prior year's preservation proposal, called the Cochrane Plan in honor of Detroit's Hall of Fame catcher and manager of the 1930s, was less radical and more thoroughly worked out. It was sponsored by the Tiger Stadium Fan Club and designed by architect John Davids (who designed Monaghan's private suite at Tiger Stadium in 1983–1984) and interior architect Judy Davids. It left the playing field and seating bowls intact, added rooftop loges, removed 42 percent of the upper deck columns, and substantially increased the public and support spaces beneath and beyond the stands. The Jeffsan Corp., construction cost estimating specialists located in suburban Southfield, calculated its price tag as $26 million, or about 15 percent of the cost of a new stadium and land.

The genius of this plan was that it preserved the best features of Tiger Stadium—its field geometry, traditional appearance, seating intimacy, and historic continuity—while improving viewing conditions in the upper deck and significantly enhancing the park's functionality and revenue potential. Most of the exterior would have been unchanged, while spacious new wings behind first and third bases would be designed in a mildly postmodern vein.

Upon its release, the plan was endorsed by architectural educators and many officers of the local chapter of the American Institute of Architects. Gino Rosetti, architect of the well-received Palace of Auburn Hills arena and of the Tiger Stadium renovations of 1978–1984, praised the fan club's efforts and affirmed, based on his hands-on knowledge of the stadium's structural conditions, that further renovation would be cost-effective and justified by preserving the virtues of "a great park." But Tiger management, consistent and vociferous foes of renovation, studiously ignored the Cochrane Plan. While it did not fully meet the club's criteria for their desired stadium, it came reasonably close at a small fraction of the cost. No sensitive adaptation of any classic park could have met those criteria, some of which were so inflated that they exceeded contemporary space standards for new stadiums on unrestricted sites. For example, at one point the Tigers were impractically seeking 150 luxury suites, whereas there are only 102 suites in Tiger Stadium's successor, Comerica Park.

In 1991, with relations between the Tigers and city government strained, Wayne County (which includes Detroit) took on the ballpark question. It received an evaluation of the Cochrane Plan from BEI Inc., a local engineering firm that did the work gratis in hopes of "continued participation in the County's effort to provide a state-of-the-art baseball stadium for the Detroit Tigers." Although seemingly disqualified by this apparent conflict of interest and a total lack of stadium experience and expertise, BEI was chosen for its "independence and reputation," according to county staffer Patricia Kukula. The firm claimed to have "invented and patented" a design providing ideal viewing distances and angles,[200] which was an "office secret" whose revelation awaited some future stadium client, according to BEI president Christopher Kittides.[201]

Working to provide a new state-of-the-art stadium necessarily precluded a favorable opinion on saving the old one and inevitably compromised BEI's objectivity in assessing renovation proposals. Predictably, the firm recommended against implementing either the Cochrane Plan (arbitrarily doubling its estimated cost) or the Birkerts-O'Neal proposal. Rosetti, the region's most qualified stadium architect at the time, and the one most professionally familiar with Tiger Stadium, opined that BEI "doesn't have the experience" for stadium cost estimating. Nothing came of BEI's transparent attempts to get further ballpark work, but its report served its short-term political purpose of shooting down the preservation proposals, especially the carefully crafted Cochrane Plan.

The Seven-Year Ilitch Occupancy and Beyond

In 1992, Tiger Stadium's penultimate chapter opened when Little Caesar's Pizza magnate and one-time minor league second baseman[202] Mike Ilitch bought the Tigers from Monaghan for $85 million, nearly a third of his personal worth. The involvement of this dedicated fan who named one of his sons after Ty Cobb[203] brought some hope to the old ballpark's supporters for several reasons: He had moved his corporate headquarters from the suburbs to Detroit—unlike Monaghan, who steadfastly centered his business and personal life in outlying Ann Arbor. He had meticulously renovated downtown architectural landmarks for his entertainment enterprises. And finally he had vowed to keep an open mind and study the stadium situation for a year before deciding on a course of action.

In the meantime, however, Ilitch increased the types and quantity of advertising at the park to saturation levels, introduced loud rock music to the premises, and converted the players' parking lot at Michigan and Trumbull to a gaudy food court called Tiger Plaza, which retired 43-year front office stalwart Jim Campbell felt "looked like an amusement park."[204]

In light of those first-year changes, Ilitch's decision about Tiger Stadium's fate was not really surprising: He seemed more focused on the sizzle than the steak and wanted a ballpark with plenty of room for attractions other than baseball, something that Tiger Stadium, for all its strengths, obviously could not supply. He proposed an ambitious development called Foxtown (after the ornate picture palace he owned and restored), a mixed-use project that included entertainment venues, retail stores, and a new 47,000-seat stadium on an 80-acre downtown site, just east of the theater district where he already owned several entertainment properties. He offered to pay $175 million toward stadium costs on the condition that the city, county, and state fund the more expensive but less glamorous portion of the plan—land acquisition, demolition, transportation upgrades, and other infrastructure improvements.[205]

When this offer met with public criticism, Ilitch withdrew it and, in 1994, declared that he wanted to lease a publicly built stadium. After two more years of political wrangling that included referenda and lawsuits, the way was finally cleared for a new stadium in 1996. Jim Campbell's amusement park assessment of 1992 proved prophetic when Comerica Park opened in 2000 boasting a merry-go-round, a Ferris wheel, a view of the downtown skyline, a menagerie of enormous white fiberglass tiger sculptures that roared whenever a Tiger hit a home run, and "a mammoth water feature in center field that can be choreographed to any music."[206] Whether these elements are attractions or distractions is a matter of personal taste. Until Ilitch's ownership, all the old parks at Michigan and Trumbull had a single focus, constant throughout their many changes in ownership and physical structure: the game itself.

When the club left The Corner in 1999, those recent distractions left with them, and the game became paramount once again, albeit on a lesser scale than in the heady major league days. Amateur ballgames, both organized and informal, were played frequently, first against the backdrop of the stadium's impressive structure,[207] then against a largely demolished facility where the two decks behind the bases and home plate still stood, and finally on an open field conscientiously maintained by volunteers—an urban "field of dreams" where men, women, and children could take inspiration from knowing that they were literally following in the footsteps of Cy Young, Ty Cobb, Babe Ruth, Ted Williams, Al Kaline, and nearly every other Hall of Famer who had ever played in the American League.

Postscript: Building Industry Professionals Active at The Corner

Some old ballparks were the work of a single design firm over several decades (notably Yankee Stadium and Milwaukee County Stadium), while others were the product of many hands over time. Tiger Stadium clearly fell into the second category and may have been the poster child for a client sampling various building professionals, cafeteria style, over eight decades.

Received wisdom has it that Osborn Engineering, the colossus of classic ballpark consultants, was the prime shaper of the Tigers' various homes. In actuality, things were not so simple. Osborn's records of their work at Michigan and Trumbull have largely vanished,[208] with apparently only a letter-sized site diagram from the late 1930s surviving, and it appears that they may have worked only on two phases of Navin's/Briggs'/Tiger's evolution. Another traditional belief was that the original Navin Field design was the product of company founder Frank C. Osborn and his son Ken, but the latter had not yet joined the firm in 1911–1912, when that work was done.[209]

The record of architects, engineers, and contractors who executed projects at The Corner is scattered and incomplete, but what is known today is interesting. Under the auspices of multiple owners, the Tigers have patronized local firms unless highly specialized expertise was needed, such as in the case of Osborn or General Electric, but have not seemed inclined to stick with any of the Detroit professionals for very long.

Prior to 1937, roles and responsibilities sometimes seem blurred, with builders, contractors, or even mechanical engineers also acting as building designers. The table below lists ten firms known to have worked on the Tiger Stadium site over an 88-year period:

Table 14: Building Industry Firms Active at Michigan and Trumbull

Period	Name & Location	Role	Scope of Work
1896	Walker & Co., Detroit	B	Construct Bennett Park's wooden boundary fence
1902	James A. Moynes, Detroit	B	Expand grandstand and bleachers
1911–1912	Osborn Engineering; Hunkin & Conkey: both Cleveland	E, B	Design and build Navin Field, new steel and concrete grandstand and pavilions seating 23,000
1922–1923	John Finn & Son, Detroit	E, B	New 6,500 seat second deck above original grandstand
1934	Jerome A. Utley & Co., Detroit	E, B	Temporary 17,000 seat bleachers for World Series
1935–1936	Jerome A. Utley & Co., Detroit	E, B	19,000 new temporary World Series left field bleacher seats. 12,000 gross new permanent seats. Removal of left field temporary bleachers and right field pavilion, double-decking of right field corner and right half of outfield.
1937–1938	Giffels & Vallet, Inc., Louis Rossetti, Assoc. Engineers & Architects, Detroit; Osborn Engineering, Cleveland	E, A E	18,000 net new seats. Removal of left field pavilion and part of right-center field stands, double-decking of left field corner and left half of outfield

114   Part I: History and Background

Period	Name & Location	Role	Scope of Work
1948	Robert Swackhamer, General Electric Co., Schenectady NY	E	Field lighting design and supervision
1977–1981; 1982–1983	Rosetti Assoc., Southfield MI	A, E	Major renovation/replacement of structural system, plumbing, electrical system, seating, and exterior cladding.

A = Architect; B = Builder/Contractor; E = Engineer

This view from the lower deck (c. 2001) shows the juncture of the original double-deck grandstand and the area that was initially a single-deck pavilion down the first base line. In the right foreground are some of the boxes hung at the front of the upper deck for camera crews (Lowell Boileau).

Notes

1. Derived from basic data contained in the standard ballpark reference books.
2. *Ibid.*
3. Dan Austin, "Tiger Stadium," http://historicdetroit.org/building/tiger-stadium/ (accessed on March 15, 2013).
4. According to the caption printed on a historic photograph, one political rally connected to a parochial schools issue in 1920 drew a purported 100,000 people, most of whom occupied the playing field. A more plausible estimate might be 60,000 to 70,000, which very likely still would have been a record for the site.
5. Calculated by author.
6. Sam Greene, "Visiting the Major Parks—Navin Field," *The Sporting News*, March 22, 1934, 6.
7. As the crow flies. In Detroit's case, this is also the walking/transit/driving figure since Michigan Avenue runs straight into the center of downtown. None of the other cities have a comparable directness of route; thus, this table actually understates Detroit's proximity advantage by perhaps 10 to 20 percent. Table data was generated by scaling Google maps and satellite views in July 2013.
8. Excluding Detroit.
9. He was widely disliked by his fellow owners, many of his players, and even some members of the press. One journalist broke his nose in a fistfight over unpaid services as his official scorer, and he eventually lost the team in 1900 as the result of an alimony dispute.
10. *Sporting Life*, December 7, 1895, 9.
11. *Ibid.*
12. *Ibid.*
13. *Sporting Life*, April 4, 1896, n.p.
14. Richard Bak, "The First Night Game at Michigan & Trumbull Was Played in 1896," *Detroit Athletic Company*, August 31, 2011, http://blog.detroitathletic.com/2011/08/31/the-first-night-game-at-michigan-trumbull-was-played-in-1896/; and Scott Ferkovich, "Bennett Park (Detroit)," SABR Baseball Biography Project, http://sabr.org/bioproject (both accessed on August 18, 2014).
15. *Sporting Life*, January 22, 1898, 11.
16. *Sporting Life*, December 7, 1895, 9, and April 4, 1896, n.p.
17. Average of all the other major league parks, determined by scaling and computing architects' diagrams and from estimates in Ron Selter, *Ballparks of the Deadball Era* (Jefferson, North Carolina: McFarland, 2008).
18. Calculated from an 1897 Sanborn Insurance map.
19. Philip J. Lowry, *Green Cathedrals: The Ultimate Celebration of Major League and Negro League Ballparks* (New York: Walker, 2006), 83; and Michael Betzold and Marc Okkonen, "Tiger's Lair Has a Corner on Lore," *Detroit Free Press*, September 13, 1987, all say 7,000. But both Lowell Reidenbaugh, *Take Me Out to the Ballpark* (St. Louis: The Sporting News, 1983), 114, and Selter, 95, give a conflicting figure of 8,500.
20. Selter, 95.
21. *Ibid.*
22. Scaled and calculated from Osborn and Clem diagrams.
23. Lowry, 83, and Selter, 102.
24. *The Sporting News*, October 20, 1937, 1.
25. Scaled and calculated from Osborn and Clem diagrams. Strictly speaking, the Tigers' property was not quite this large. The figure given includes public property occupied by Cherry Street, which was closed off and used to build immense temporary bleachers in 1934 and 1935.
26. Estimated as midway between the 1934 and 1938 site areas.
27. Calculated from an Osborn Engineering site diagram, ca. 1938, showing the Tigers' newly expanded property, bounded by a newly relocated Cherry Street.
28. Stated on an Osborn Engineering site diagram, ca. 1938. Also stated in Lowry, 84. Lowry's figure is for 1953. Both citations are more credible than the most commonly encountered number of 58,000.
29. The author's estimate based on the site's original construction, multiple seating expansions, partial demolitions in 1934, 1935, and 1937, and full demolitions in 1911 and 2008. This does not include "circus seats," which were sections of temporary bleachers placed in the outfield for big games and then removed until the next high-demand occasion.
30. Clearly not all of these fluctuating and conflicting figures can be correct, but all come from reputable sources.
31. Approximation; Richard Bak, *A Place for Summer: A Narrative History of Tiger Stadium* (Detroit: Wayne State University Press, 1998), 60, and Selter, 91.
32. Four sources differ; see note 9.
33. Selter, 95.
34. Reidenbaugh, 114; Selter, 91, 95.
35. Lowry, 83.
36. Reidenbaugh, 114; Lowry, 84; and Selter, 102.

116   Part I: History and Background

37. *The Sporting News*, October 20, 1937, 1. Multiple other sources say 29,000, still others say 30,000, and one says "between 29,000 and 30,000," so 29,500 seems a reasonable estimate. Reidenbaugh, 114; Lowry, 84.
38. Computed from a 1935 *Detroit News* hybrid drawing/aerial photo prepared for the 1935 World Series.
39. Reidenbaugh, 114; Lowry, 44.
40. Emory S. Roberts, *Engineering News-Record*, November 19, 1936, 711.
41. Lowry, 84.
42. Taken from an Osborn Engineering diagram, ca. 1938.
43. This figure appears in several places in the literature, including contemporary accounts such as the Bureau Service Dept. of the Heilbroner Baseball Bureau, Ft. Wayne, Indiana, August 1, 1938, 1, and an unsigned AP wire story dated August 7, 1938, and published a day later in the *Meriden* (CT) *Record* and no doubt many other newspapers. The latter mentions the 58,000 figure in passing in an article about the Tigers' firing of manager Mickey Cochrane. Later appearances include Reidenbaugh, 114; Lowry, 84; David G. Surdam, *How Baseball Outlasted the Great Depression* (Lincoln: University of Nebraska Press, 2011), 264 ("almost 60,000 seats"); several websites, and, most significantly, 14 consecutive annual editions of *The World Almanac and Book of Facts*, from 1940 to 1953. The figure is almost certainly exaggerated. If accurate, it would have made Briggs Stadium the third largest true baseball venue between 1938 and 1972 and larger than any National League park. (This excludes the Los Angeles Coliseum, which was a football stadium pressed into service as a temporary venue for the Dodgers in 1957.) The 58,000 number is included here because of its ubiquity and because it was not only reached but exceeded when a standing-room crowd of 58,369 paid their way into the park to see a doubleheader vs. the Yankees on July 20, 1947. See Bill Shannon and George Kalinsky, *The Ballparks* (New York: Hawthorn Books, 1975), 255.
44. Lowry, 84; *The World Almanac and Book of Facts*, 1954–61 editions.
45. Lowry, 84; *The World Almanac and Book of Facts*, 1962 edition.
46. *Tigers Media Guide*, 1962.
47. Lowry, 84; *Tigers Media Guide*, 1970.
48. Lowry, 84.
49. Bradford Wornle, *Crain's Detroit Business*, April 8, 1991, 1.
50. Lowry, 84. This drop in capacity is unexplained and is likely to be erroneous.
51. *Ibid.*
52. "Comerica Park: Detroit, Michigan," http://www.ballparks.com/baseball/american/detbpk.htm (accessed on March 8, 2013).
53. These comparisons are for populations within city limits. Metropolitan area population comparisons would yield somewhat different results.
54. Faster in percentage terms. New York and Chicago grew more when measured in absolute numbers.
55. Rounded off to the nearest thousand and calculated from individual city population figures in the decennial tables found at http://www.census.gov/population/ www/documentation/twps0027/tab01.txt (accessed in February 2013).
56. Calculated by dividing the total population of the ten major league cities by 16 teams.
57. For 1900, the average is for the 16 major league teams as of 1901, when the American League became a major league. This average reflects the 1901 presence of Milwaukee and Baltimore as major league teams.
58. Michael Betzold and Ethan Casey, *Queen of Diamonds: The Tiger Stadium Story* (West Bloomfield, Michigan: Altwerger and Mandel, 1992), 22.
59. *Sporting Life*, October 31, 1896, 7. Its expanded 1896 seating capacity was under 5,000 after bleachers were built along the left field foul line.
60. The 1897 Sanborn fire insurance map for Detroit documents this layout and orientation.
61. Marc Okkonen, *Baseball Memories 1900–1909* (New York: Sterling, 1992), map, 52; and Jack E. Schramm, Thomas D. Worman, and William H. Henning, *Detroit's Street Railways: City Lines, 1922–1956* (Chicago: Central Electric Railfans' Association, 1980).
62. Scaled off and calculated from an 1897 Sanborn insurance map. Selter gives the site area as 4.2 acres.
63. Data for other major league ballparks of the period are taken from Selter.
64. Betzold and Casey, 31–32.
65. Bak, *A Place for Summer*, 111.
66. *Ibid.*, 94–95.
67. The following drawings by John Davids document the succession of ballparks at Michigan and Trumbull. They derive from various graphic sources, including eight decades of historic photos, 19th- and 20th-century insurance maps, working drawings developed by Rossetti Architects as part of their 1978 renovation plan, and design drawings for the Cochrane Plan (1989–90).
68. Paul Bruske, "Detroit Doings," *Sporting Life*, May 1, 1909, 3.
69. *Sporting Life*, July 10, 1909, 2.
70. *Sporting Life*, November 13, 1909, 2.
71. Overflow crowds seated on the field cheapened the game and created uncomfortable experiences for most of their denizens but were beloved by owners because they were nearly pure profit. No structures

had to be built to accommodate them, and they required no maintenance other than a little additional groundskeeping.

72. Sportsman's Park also opened that year but lacked the architectural ambition and grandeur of its two iconic cohorts.

73. In the case of Forbes Field, the cost ranged somewhere between $750,000 and nearly $1,000,000. See David Cicotello and Angelo J. Louisa, *Forbes Field: Essays and Memories of the Pirates' Historic Ballpark, 1909–1971* (Jefferson, North Carolina: McFarland, 2007), 17, 227.

74. A convincing case could be made that Baker Bowl (1895) and the Palace of the Fans (1902), the two earliest fireproof parks, deserve to be on this list. On the other hand, they are extreme chronological outliers, dissimilar to the other parks, and their seating capacity was very low, even at their peak. There is no simple way out of this dilemma. My compromise is to exclude them from this list but bring them into various discussions of early fireproof parks where warranted.

75. Osborn Engineering is often credited with designing the 1909 version of Sportsman's Park, but this is an error. The firm did design the major 1921 expansion but did not claim credit for the earlier Sportsman's Park in a 1912 *Sporting Life* ad touting its ballpark experience. The 1909 work may have been done by St. Louis architects Beinke & Wees, who designed the nearby Robison Field, but this is just informed speculation.

76. Photographic evidence, supported by the writings of Marc Okkonen, shows that there were slender metal columns in the front seating rows of Bennett Park, even though most of the structure was wood.

77. *Sporting Life*, February 3, 1912, 10.

78. Jordan A. Deutsch, Richard M. Cohen, Roland T. Johnson, and David S. Neft, *The Scrapbook History of Baseball* (Indianapolis: Bobbs-Merrill, 1975), 78.

79. Estimated from U.S. government census data found at http://www.census.gov/population/www/documentation/twps0027/tab01.txt (accessed on August 13, 2014).

80. The non-parallel relationship between the outfield stands and the foul lines is apparent in seating diagrams and aerial photographs. This sort of disparity was common in classic parks, also occurring in Sportsman's Park, Ebbets Field, Griffith Stadium, Wrigley Field, League Park, and Crosley Field.

81. Measured by Pastier from the 1897 Sanborn insurance map.

82. Within four years, Boston's Braves Field and Chicago's Cubs Park (later renamed Wrigley Field) would also open as single-deck structures.

83. Forbes Field had a rudimentary third deck atop its main roof.

84. In 1992 Yankee Stadium became the first to reach that milestone. Tiger Stadium followed in early 1997. Fenway Park was the third, and Dodger Stadium was the fourth. (Pastier calculations from standard reference works and the SABR Home Run Log.)

85. Forbes Field had a shallow third deck devoted to roof boxes, later deepened for the 1925 World Series.

86. Cleveland had two active parks at the time.

87. In some cases (Cleveland League Park, Braves Field, Yankee Stadium, and Griffith Stadium), the firm had full design responsibility from the beginning; in others (Comiskey Park, Sportsman's Park, and Fenway Park), it was involved in expansions or renovations but not in the original design; and in yet others (Navin Field, the Polo Grounds, and Cleveland Municipal Stadium), it worked in collaboration with other design firms.

88. "Detroit Notes: The New Home of the Tigers," *Baseball Magazine*, March 1912, 96.

89. Paul Bruske, "Detroit's Day," *Sporting Life*, April 27, 1912, 2.

90. These included San Francisco's Seals Stadium, the Los Angeles Coliseum, Houston's Colt Stadium, Montreal's Jarry Park, Arlington (TX) Stadium, Seattle's Sick's Stadium, Toronto's Exhibition Stadium, and, arguably, Jersey City's Roosevelt Stadium.

91. Calculated from an Andrew Clem diagram.

92. The author compiled these distances over a period of about 12 years beginning in 1989. Data sources included direct measurements, scaling, and calculations from architects' working drawings; published cross-sections; interviews with stadium architects; and as-built surveyors' drawings.

93. Scaled and calculated from diagram on Andrew Clem's website, http://www.andrewclem.com (accessed on April 19, 2015).

94. *Ibid.*

95. *Ibid.*, with some modification based on architects' diagram.

96. Scaled from HOK cross-section.

97. Calculated from Osborn Engineering working drawing.

98. *Ibid.*

99. All these parks had their upper decks built after the Deadball Era (which concluded in 1919) and had columns in their seating areas. The period ended with the opening (for baseball) of the Minnesota Twins' Metropolitan Stadium in 1961, which had all its columns behind the last rows of seats, as did all later parks.

100. Scaled and calculated from diagram on Andrew Clem's website, http://www.andrewclem.com (accessed on April 19, 2015).

101. *Ibid.* The stadium was built in 1956 but didn't see major league use until 1961.

118   Part I: History and Background

102. Derived from the architects' drawings.
103. Philip Bess, *City Baseball Magic: Plain Talk and Uncommon Sense About Cities and Baseball Parks*, 2nd ed. (Madison: Minneapolis Review of Baseball, 1989), 13.
104. Scaled and calculated from diagram on Andrew Clem's website, http://www.andrewclem.com (accessed on April 19, 2015). The stadium was built for the 1976 Olympics but didn't see major league use until the next year.
105. Calculated from data contained in a professional as-built survey made circa 1990, adjusted to reflect the stadium's opening year configuration, which, due to a shift in the home plate location, had a viewing distance about four feet greater than the later figure. Completed in 1976 and used that year for professional football and soccer, it first saw baseball use a year later.
106. Scaled and calculated from diagram on Andrew Clem's website, http://www.andrewclem.com (accessed on April 19, 2015). The 1974–1976 reconstruction of Yankee Stadium produced an upper deck that bore almost no resemblance to the 1923 original. Its typical viewing distance of 209 feet was more than 42 percent greater than its predecessor's 148 feet.
107. Scaled from HOK cross-section.
108. Scaled and calculated from diagram on Andrew Clem's website, http://www.andrewclem.com (accessed on April 19, 2015).
109. Calculated by Ewing-Cole architects, Philadelphia.
110. Metropolitan Stadium opened five years earlier as a football venue.
111. The Texas Rangers' stadium is a slight exception to this practice. It has a small number of columns near the back of the lower deck seats behind home plate and some in the right field seats. None of these seem to have contributed to seating intimacy, however.
112. Some newer baseball-only parks, including those in Seattle and San Francisco, have been put to occasional use for soccer and football, but their playing field geometry is optimized for baseball, in contrast to the compromise geometries that shaped the design of older multiuse facilities between 1931 and the late 1960s.
113. Sam Greene, "Visiting the Major Parks—Navin Field," *The Sporting News*, March 22 1934, 6.
114. Other ballparks underwent reconfigurations during the 1930s, including Ebbets Field, Fenway Park, Wrigley Field, and Yankee Stadium, but in none of them were the changes as extensive as those at Navin Field.
115. Shown on John Davids' field plan.
116. In those days, the official major league minimum home run distance was just 250 feet.
117. League Park in Cleveland had a 290-foot right field foul line with a 45-foot-high fence, making it a doubles paradise for left-handed hitters.
118. Email correspondence with researcher Bill Deane, July 2014.
119. Roberts, 712.
120. Full information on Utley can be found at http://en.wikipedia.org/wiki/Jerome_Utley (accessed on April 19, 2015).
121. *The Sporting News*, September 13, 1934, 1, and October 17, 1935, 1.
122. Yankee Stadium's original wooden bleachers, still in use in 1934, held about 14,500 spectators based on the author's analysis of Osborn's engineering drawings.
123. The absence of regular season photos from 1935 precludes certainty on this subject.
124. According to text in a hybrid drawing/aerial photo in the *Detroit News*.
125. Calculated from a John Davids scale diagram.
126. The Polo Grounds had a shorter left field foul line dimension, but the wall fell away so sharply that straight left field was well over 400 feet from home plate.
127. This calculation excludes the two single-decked pavilions located down the lines in foul territory.
128. These are not necessarily the bleacher sections with the highest capacities. (Finding that information for all parks might be an impossible task at this date.) But these estimates give an overview of the bleachers with the most rows and greatest depths and also give an idea of how high these structures may have been.
129. Estimated, except where a source is cited.
130. Estimated, except where a source is cited.
131. Measured from large-scale plan in Len Martin, *Forbes Field: Build It Yourself* (Pittsburgh: Point Four, 1995).
132. Scaled from Sanborn insurance map.
133. The original Yankee Stadium wooden bleachers of 1923 were irregularly shaped. In left field, they were 99 feet deep on average and reached a maximum depth of 112 feet. These measurements are calculated from data contained in a 1921 Osborn Engineering Co. working drawing.
134. Calculated from the Osborn Engineering working drawing. The left field bleachers averaged 52 rows and reached a maximum of 58 rows.
135. The right field bleachers were 117 feet deep on average and had a maximum depth of 133 feet, according to Osborn Engineering plans of 1921.
136. *Ibid.* The right field bleachers had an average depth of 61 rows and reached a maximum of 70 rows.
137. Taken from a 1929 Osborn Engineering Co. working drawing.

138. *Ibid.*
139. http://www.preciseseating.com (accessed on July 17, 2014).
140. Data provided by John Davids, based on his original drawings.
141. *Ibid.*
142. The permanent steel-and-concrete Yankee Stadium bleachers installed in 1938 were irregularly shaped and ranged in depth from 68 feet to 128 feet. The average depth was 92 feet. Data taken from a 1936 Osborn Engineering Co. working drawing.
143. *Ibid.* The number of bleacher rows ranged from 31 to 61 and averaged 43.
144. Seat count taken from a 1937 Osborn diagram of Briggs Stadium Seating evolution.
145. According to Betzold and Casey, 56.
146. This is confirmed by photographic evidence.
147. Counted from a John Davids cross-sectional drawing.
148. Scaled from an Osborn Engineering field diagram.
149. Only three others were greater than 353 feet, and all were shortened in later years.
150. Scaled from John Davids's cross-sectional drawing.
151. Bak, *A Place for Summer*, 185; Betzold and Casey, 57.
152. Walt Whitman, part 51 of "Song of Myself," *Leaves of Grass*, available from Project Gutenberg, http://www.gutenberg.org/files/1322/1322-h/1322-h.htm.
153. See note 28 concerning the ubiquity of this figure, dating back to 1938.
154. This figure is from an Osborn Engineering seven-park site plan and field diagram titled "Layout of Baseball Parks," which carries this caveat "Note: Seating Capacities are only approximate."
155. Cleveland Municipal and Yankee Stadium unquestionably had higher capacities, but the Polo Grounds, usually listed as having 55,000 seats, may actually have seated just 52,000, according to the Osborn drawing cited just above. The three zeroes at the end of the number suggest that the standard figure is at best an approximation, and recorded single-game attendance highs at the New York park strongly suggest that it is an exaggeration.
156. Shannon and Kalinsky, 246. This number was second only to Yankee Stadium's bleacher capacity of 13,738.
157. These include Baker Bowl; Shibe, Weeghman, Wrigley, and Comiskey parks; Navin, Crosley, and Ebbets fields; and Griffith, Brush, and Briggs stadiums.
158. This tight fit was not unique among classic parks used for football. At Wrigley Field, one corner of the gridiron actually encroached into the first-base dugout, where the playing surface was extended with sheets of plywood supported by wood framing.
159. Dimensions scaled from an Andrew Clem park diagram.
160. Bak, *A Place for Summer*, 258.
161. Betzold and Casey, 292.
162. Calculated from field area measurements provided by John Davids.
163. This high number is due not so much to any abnormal ease of hitting home runs at Sportsman's Park than it is due to having two teams playing there simultaneously for more than four decades.
164. Data from David Vincent, manager of the SABR Home Run Log, via e-mail dated September 9, 2013.
165. *Ibid.*
166. Wire story in *Lakeland* (FL) *Ledger*, July 23, 1993, and in other newspapers.
167. David Vincent e-mail message, September 9, 2013.
168. www.baseball-reference.com game log.
169. Calculated by author.
170. The higher the park, the farther balls travel. Six hundred feet adds a bit more than one percent to a ball's flight, compared to sea level, or four or five feet in Tiger Stadium's case.
171. Center field was often listed as 440 feet after the 1938 expansion, but for most of the ballpark's last six decades an inner fence reduced the actual distance to 425 feet.
172. Scaled from Andrew Clem diagram.
173. Conversation with Cooperstown baseball researcher Bill Deane, ca. 1995.
174. The reason for choosing the 1930–1999 period is to confine the analysis to Detroit sluggers performance after the Dead Ball Era (when many home runs were inside the park and therefore the product of speed and distant fences rather than close ones) and before the team's move to Comerica Park. It also reflects the shorter right field dimensions instituted in the 1930s. This deliberately excluded someone like Ty Cobb, an outstanding slugger for his time, who hit 79 of his 111 Tiger home runs on the road and whose 46 inside-the-park home runs as a Tiger is a highly atypical proportion of this rare home run type.
175. Derived from data in the SABR Home Run Log, accessed through www.baseball-reference.com.
176. *Ibid.*
177. *Ibid.*
178. This is a basic park factor calculated by dividing total home home runs by total road home runs for both the Tigers and their opponents. Other methodologies are more complicated, and some require suc-

cessive iterations to attain their final results. The simplified method used here is sufficient for its purpose, namely to compare and rank parks that are home run friendly in a systematic and consistent manner.

179. One might question the inclusion of Los Angeles's Wrigley Field in this table, since it wasn't a true major league park and only saw one season's service in the big leagues. However, it was widely considered the finest and most substantial minor league park of the pre- and early expansion era. It was fully double decked, was the work of Zachary Taylor Davis (the same architect who designed Chicago's Wrigley Field and Comiskey Park), and had a seating capacity of about 22,000, roughly equal to some permanent major league venues of its time. (It was built in 1925.) Its extreme home/road ratio deserves to be listed here to show an extreme case of a home run friendly ballpark. Its outfield dimensions were respectable, ranging from 339 feet to 412 feet, but with one critical exception: its power alleys were only 345 feet.

180. This too may be seen as an arguable choice. The Coliseum clearly was not a true baseball park, but it set attendance records and hosted a World Series and an All-Star Game. Its home run totals exceeded Babe Ruth's, and it is an excellent (albeit deplorable) example of how a ballpark's configuration can influence home run output.

181. Briggs Stadium effectively assumed its final outfield configuration in 1938.

182. Ebbets Field began life as an extreme pitcher's park with outfield dimensions averaging about 405 feet. But several seating expansions eventually made it a slugger-friendly venue, especially in its final configuration, from 1948 onward.

183. Final outfield configuration was established in 1940 with the installation of a right field inner fence.

184. Final right field configuration created in 1940 with installation of right field bullpens.

185. Email correspondence with Bill Brown, July 2014.

186. The author's calculations.

187. *Detroit Tigers Media Guide*, 2000.

188. According to various internet reference sites, Kaline's playing weight was 175 or 180 pounds, while the four big bashers averaged 248 pounds.

189. For a contrary view and an account of Horton's home run, see "16-Year-Old Willie Horton Hits the Briggs Stadium Roof," by Bill Dow in "Tiger Stadium Souvenirs," later in this volume.

190. Clem dates the change as occurring before the 2002 season, while Lowry puts it at 2003.

191. Lowry, 85.

192. John Davids's estimate, confirmed by Marc Okkonen in *Baseball Memories 1950–1959: An Illustrated Scrapbook of Baseball's Fabulous 50's, All the Players, Managers, Cities & Ballparks* (New York: Sterling, 1993), 47.

193. Betzold and Casey, 69.

194. Okkonen, 47.

195. Reidenbaugh, 114.

196. Englishman James Stirling.

197. The other four authors and editors of this book were active members of the TSFC.

198. The eventual replacement for Tiger Stadium was designed in Kansas City.

199. In comparison, the 1936 Trumbull Avenue overhang was well within the curb line.

200. This is something that has eluded ballpark designers for nearly a century and a half.

201. John Pastier, "Operation Rescue," *Inland Architect,* September/October 1991, 47.

202. According to www.baseball-reference.com, Ilitch played 336 games for seven teams between 1952 and 1955, ranging from class D (292 at-bats) to class A (12 at-bats). His playing record is incomplete.

203. Ronald Tyrus Ilitch, cited in Ilitch's *Wikipedia* entry (accessed in July 2013).

204. Bak, *A Place for Summer*, 367.

205. *Ibid.*, 370.

206. Detroit Tigers website (accessed in June 2013).

207. The seating structure was 94 feet high and had a perimeter of more than 1750 feet, and the light towers were 155 feet high.

208. When the firm moved its offices from midtown Cleveland to downtown in 1967, many of its stadium-related drawings and other documents were discarded, including virtually all of those pertaining to Griffith Stadium, Sportsman's Park, the Polo Grounds, and Navin Field/Briggs Stadium.

209. *A Century of Progress* (Cleveland: Osborn Engineering, 1992), 15.

The Mallparking of America
Tiger Stadium and the Subsidy Game

Neil deMause

Back in 1987, when a baseball fan heard the word "ballpark," it conjured a very different image than it does today. In that year, as the Tigers made their late-season charge to the American League East pennant and the first rumblings began that would result in the decades-long battle over the fate of Tiger Stadium, most baseball parks were still divided between two basic models. There were the traditional structures from the first half of the century, their names redolent with whiffs of Cobb and Ruth: Yankee Stadium, Fenway Park, Comiskey Park, all holdovers from the first great era of steel-and-concrete stadium building. And there were the modern suburban facilities of the previous 25 years, starting with Dodger Stadium and leading up to the indistinguishable multipurpose buildings disparaged as "concrete donuts" that sprung up in multiple cities (Philadelphia, Pittsburgh, St. Louis, Cincinnati) in the 1960s and '70s. By the '80s, domes were the latest novelty; artificial turf, it seemed, was the wave of the future. Only one new stadium had opened in the previous ten years, and that one—the Minneapolis Metrodome—was so widely derided as a cartoon version of a baseball stadium, with trash-bag outfield walls and rubbery turf that turned every hit to the outfield into an adventure, that the very mention of a "modern" stadium seemed like tempting fate.

Behind the scenes, though, a seismic shift was coming—one that would affect not just baseball, but the sports industry as a whole. And by the time it was over, it would transform not just who attended sporting events and how, but the entire way that America's cities and towns thought about the meaning and purpose of "development."

The first salvo of the new stadium war is apparent only in retrospect. Toronto's Sky-Dome, built at tremendous public expense to replace the recycled football stadium that had temporarily housed the Blue Jays from 1977 through 1989, was in many ways aesthetically the last gasp of the previous age. Designed as a multipurpose facility, for both baseball and the Canadian Football League Argonauts, it offered one flashy new innovation—its steel-and-concrete roof could slide open to let in sunlight—but otherwise in many ways resembled the concrete donuts: symmetrical and generic, splitting the difference between the ideal baseball wedge and football's horseshoe.

Where SkyDome innovated, however, was beyond the seating bowl. The building featured the first-ever hotel embedded in a stadium wall (and one that would famously require a "no sex with the blinds open" covenant for all guests after one couple provided some unintentional in-game entertainment during a 1996 game against the Red Sox), as well as some of the most spacious restaurant and food courts that the sports world had ever witnessed.[1] "I'd seen the ultimate marriage between government, which builds these facilities, and the corporations and the people who tie into them," raved then–Seattle Mariners owner Jeff Smulyan upon visiting SkyDome soon after its opening. "You take the suites, the signage, throw the media on top, and you have an economic juggernaut."[2]

If SkyDome pioneered what sportswriter Rob Neyer would dub the baseball "mallpark," Baltimore's Camden Yards, opened three years later, would provide the other piece of the puzzle, introducing retro elements like exposed steel and brick that retained some of the aura of the classic parks that new stadiums would replace. Much of the "intimate" feel of the new crop of stadiums was more hype than reality—the front row of the upper deck at the Chicago White Sox's 44,000-seat modern version of Comiskey Park (later renamed U.S. Cellular Field in exchange for naming-rights cash) was farther from the field than the back row of the upper deck at the 52,000-seat 1910-era Comiskey that it replaced, and the figures for Camden Yards and other new stadiums were not much better.[3] Nonetheless, nostalgia became a selling point for stadium builders across the nation: *You can have the best of the past and modern amenities, too.*

SkyDome and Camden Yards transformed the baseball world in the best way imaginable to get club owners' attention: they sold tickets. In their new stadium's second full year of operation, the Blue Jays became the first team in history to sell more than four million tickets in a season. (It did not hurt that the team won the first of three straight division titles that year.)[4] Camden Yards cleared 3.5 million in its first season, besting the Orioles' old top mark by more than a million fans.[5] A year later, Cleveland's Jacobs Field opened, and bolstered by a resurgent Indian team on the field, soon ran off a streak of 455 consecutive sellouts.[6] Fans would turn out just to see new stadiums, it appeared, and visions of a ballpark-spawned honeymoon period began to dance in the eyes of club owners. If the INDIANS could draw fans to a new ballpark, surely anyone could.

It was, in retrospect, a perfect moment for a new stadium boom. The United States was in the midst of a dramatic rise in disposable income for the wealthy: While the median U.S. household gained $3,400 in after-tax income between 1979 and 1997, the average household in the top one percent was a whopping $414,000 richer by the end of that time period, thanks in part to the tax cuts launched by Ronald Reagan and his cohort.[7] This shift ensured that a small sector of sports fans (and corporations hoping to cater to clients who were sports fans) would have increasingly deep pockets from which to spend on sporting events—particularly on the club seats and luxury suites that were the hallmarks of new stadium design.

The new stadiums were providing club owners with an economic boost in another way, though, one that would last long after the attendance honeymoon was over. The revolution in food courts and luxury suites, it turned out, would be nothing compared to the revolution in stadium subsidies.

Baseball's original multitiered stadiums were built the old-fashioned way: A club owner would cobble together whatever cash and bank loans he could and build as much ballpark as he could afford. If tickets sold well—and as the Deadball Era and World War I gave way to Babe Ruth and the Roaring Twenties, most sold very well indeed—he would build another deck here, another there, slowly growing to meet demand. (Early photos of Yankee Stadium show that the House That Ruth Built was called that for good reason: cash from Bambino-spurred ticket sales was poured back into expanding the stadium from 58,000 to 82,000 seats over its first few seasons.[8]) Tiger Stadium was a perfect example: holding a mere 23,000 fans when it opened as Navin Field in 1912, it gradually grew through a series of expansions to a 52,000-seat structure by the time of Hank Greenberg and Charlie Gehringer.[9]

The second half of the 20th century brought a different funding scheme. Starting in the 1950s, as clubs began to decamp for new cities in the West, and throughout the expansion era that followed, they sparked a wave of new stadiums built not by club owners but by local governments either hoping to lure teams, or, just as often, fearful of losing them. (The donut shape, meanwhile, was a nod to the demands of another sport then growing in popularity: pro football.)

Still, even if taxpayers were fronting the money for these stadiums' construction costs, club owners still ended up paying much of it back, largely via rent payments. The much-reviled Minneapolis Metrodome, for example, though originally entirely paid for by Minnesota taxpayers, ended up turning a profit for the state in the end thanks to a lease that required high rent payments from the Twins and Vikings—something that helped spur those clubs' increasingly active attempts to flee to new buildings before the dome was even 15 years old.[10]

By the late 1970s, though, the conditions were being set for a new round of stadium deals that would offer a very different financing scheme. A sagging economy, especially in the Rust Belt cities that were home to many of baseball's oldest stadiums, had led to a new desperation among local elected officials eager to claim that they were helping to revitalize their cities. And no large city was more desperate than Detroit, which lost 44 percent of its population and over 80 percent of its manufacturing jobs between 1950 and 1990. Once the Reagan administration cut federal aid to local governments in the mid-'80s, many politicians, like Detroit mayors Coleman Young and Dennis Archer, decided that the only solution was to battle for private investment, doubling down by offering what little money remained in the municipal budget as incentives for companies to relocate to their cities.

The result was what Minneapolis Federal Reserve economist Arthur Rolnick would dub the "economic war among the states," with cities and states engaged in an escalating series of subsidy one-upmanship in hopes of warding off other municipalities desiring to steal their companies—or in hopes of stealing their neighbors' companies. "While states spend billions of dollars competing with one another to retain and attract businesses, they struggle to provide such public goods as schools and libraries, police and fire protection, and the roads, bridges, and parks that are critical to the success of any community," Rolnick told Congress in 2007.[11] Local businesses, sensing an opportunity, soon began threatening to leave town at the drop of a hat unless granted subsidies; even the New York Stock Exchange got into the act, receiving an offer from New York Mayor Rudy Giuliani of $1 billion toward a new Manhattan headquarters if it promised not to move to New Jersey.[12] Tax breaks or outright cash grants became standard operating procedure for "economic development": whereas in 1977, less than half of all states offered tax incentives or public bonds for private developments, by the early 1990s such local subsidies were almost universal.[13]

The new world of economic development incentives not only provided sports owners the rationale they were looking for to get stadium cash, but it also provided them with the leverage to extract even more favorable conditions in these deals. The rent payments and revenue sharing that had allowed stadiums such as the Metrodome to retire stadium bonds out of club profits evaporated after 1989. It did not help when a provision of the 1986 federal Tax Reform Act intended to limit the use of federally subsidized tax-exempt bonds for projects that generated private rent payments backfired, and instead cities simply stopped charging club owners rent in order to keep their stadiums eligible for the cheap bonds.[14]

This was important because as stadium demands grew more lavish—in particular, the desire for luxury suites with a view of the sky and for larger concessions areas—was massively expanding stadium footprints, exponentially compounding both land and materials costs, it would have been increasingly difficult for clubs to turn a profit if they would have built the structures themselves. Though club owners like to paint stadiums as cash cows that needed just a little help, the reality was that in most cases the tail was wagging the dog: the stadiums themselves were money losers after construction costs were factored in—but by socializing the costs and privatizing the profits, club owners could still cash in.

In all, cities, states, and counties spent $6.5 billion on sports stadiums and arenas in the 1990s, according to Harvard researcher Judith Grant Long, and $10.1 billion more the following decade[15]—with additional hidden costs like lease breaks, property tax exemptions, and tax-exempt government bonds likely hiking those figures by at least another 10 percent. And the economic bonanza that was supposed to result was often hard to find. Years after Comerica Park's opening, the scene in the surrounding blocks, with the Fox Theatre and a handful of other attractions, was typical of many big-city stadium districts, where you might find a handful of sports bars but little else. "The streets are often empty on nights when there are no sporting events or shows," the *Cleveland Plain Dealer* wrote six years after the opening of that city's taxpayer-constructed Gateway complex, which included both an Indians' baseball stadium and a Cavaliers' basketball arena. "Some popular restaurants and bars have not survived."[16] In St. Louis, a "ballpark village" that was supposed to rise near the Cardinals' new stadium lay fallow for years; sports venues from Washington, D.C., to Harrison, New Jersey, treated fans to year after year of "coming soon" billboards of developments that had not yet materialized. Other cities that did have success—San Francisco, San Diego, Denver—had had the foresight to place their new stadiums in districts that were already in the midst of building booms, making it hard to say if any of the activity should be credited to the sports team. To a lesser extent, this has been true of Detroit's Comerica Park, which was built near a long-planned housing development and an existing entertainment district largely controlled by the Tiger owner.

This "but-for" problem, as economists have dubbed it, is just one of the difficulties of determining what economic benefits, if any, stem from sports stadiums and arenas. Another is the substitution effect: increased spending in the immediate area of a new stadium is no net gain to a city if it is offset by those same residents decreasing their spending elsewhere. (This has been dramatically demonstrated by several studies of local economic activity during sports strikes and lockouts, during which overall spending invariably does not budge despite there being no game tickets to buy.[17]) Plus, all spending is not created equal: because such a disproportionate share of sports spending ends up going to pay the profits of club owners and the salaries of players, who likely as not live in other states much of the year, more of that money leaks out of the local economy than if residents spend it at, say, a local restaurant.

All this helps to explain how, even though fans clearly spend billions of dollars every year at sporting events, legions of economists have been unable to measure any significant impact on local economies. When Washington, D.C., was considering spending $440 million on a new stadium to lure the Expos from Montreal, 90 economists sent a public letter to Mayor Anthony Williams warning that "the vast body of economic research on the impact of baseball stadiums" suggests that one "will not generate notable economic or fiscal benefits for the city."[18]

Williams went ahead and built the stadium anyway. The final cost: $667 million, almost all of it falling on taxpayers.[19]

For Tom Monaghan and Mike Ilitch, the Tiger owners during the stadium drive, the boom in new stadium campaigns in the early '90s meant two things. First, the idea of replacing Tiger Stadium at public expense no longer sounded quite so outrageous now that cities like Baltimore had done the same. And second, they could now draw from a growing playbook of standard tactics that their fellow owners were using to extract their own stadium deals.

When Tigers president Bo Schembechler declared that "it's unfair for you to think that you can shackle us to a rusted girder," and Mayor Coleman Young predicted that Tiger Stadium would "fall down" within five years, they were following the same script that the White Sox owners had followed in Chicago, where an engineering study was unable to find any significant structural flaws in Comiskey Park—even after stacking 50-gallon water drums in concourses to see if the floor would give way—yet recommended razing the structure regardless.[20] Tiger Stadium and its early-20th-century contemporaries had not abruptly become obsolete—when a chunk of metal fell at Yankee Stadium in 1998, sparking worries that the House That Ruth Built was crumbling, the head of the city buildings department declared that "there's no reason why Yankee Stadium can't be around for another 75 years if it's maintained properly."[21]

Likewise, when Tiger board member Jay Bielfield threatened in 1994 that "we must explore all of our options," including moving the franchise to St. Petersburg, Florida, if a new stadium was not forthcoming, he was following in a grand tradition: at least five other club owners had threatened to move to the Tampa Bay area in the years since St. Petersburg broke ground on what would become Tropicana Field in 1986.[22] Chicago White Sox owner Jerry Reinsdorf had even hopped a last-minute flight to St. Pete to put pressure on Illinois legislators, later explaining, "A savvy negotiator creates leverage. People had to think we were going to leave Chicago."[23]

Tiger execs pushed the economic development angle, too. A new stadium, promised a brochure put out by the pro-stadium group Detroiters for Jobs & Development in 1996, "will pump new life into our community, will support 1,500 permanent jobs and 3,000 construction jobs, will encourage other businesses to locate in a rejuvenated downtown area." But perhaps the most important moment in the Tigers' stadium campaign came when pizza billionaire Tom Monaghan, who had only weak ties in the Detroit political community, sold the club to fellow pizza billionaire Mike Ilitch, who was much more well-connected. As Kevin Delaney and Rick Eckstein found in researching their 2003 book, *Public Dollars, Private Stadiums*, the most significant factor in whether club owners were successful in their stadium demands was whether there existed what they call a "growth coalition" of local political and business leaders willing to spearhead a campaign and twist arms where necessary.[24] In Detroit, Ilitch, the only prominent remaining white businessman who was still willing to keep his operations downtown, enjoyed nearly iconic status as a business leader, and his wishes were readily accommodated in most cases. (Eventually, this included a new hockey arena to replace one built in 1979; the growth coalition was by then a sports and entertainment empire sprawling across much of downtown.)

In the end, partly because of Monaghan's tone-deaf ownership stint and partly because of the persistence of Tiger Stadium supporters, it still took nearly a decade for the Tiger owners to get the public money for their stadium and four years longer to get it built. Years-long stadium battles were more the rule than the exception, though: the owners of the Marlins, Twins, and Yankees all spent even longer lobbying for their own stadium deals. But when there is a check for hundreds of millions of dollars waiting at the end, a little patience can prove a virtue.

John Marty, a Minnesota state senator who spent the better part of a decade fighting against various stadium demands by the Twins, only to see his colleagues finally approve nearly $400 million in sales tax hikes for the team in 2006, said that in the end, Twins' lobbyists were able to take advantage of "stadium fatigue" to push through a subsidy package: "We're all sick of the issue, so one of the lobbying efforts that's very effective is 'the only way this issue will ever go away is if we pass it.'"[25]

At the time that this essay was written in the summer of 2013, the sports industry was an entirely different world from what it was three decades ago. Twenty-four of 30 MLB franchises have stadiums opened since 1989. All but three—the Atlanta Braves, St. Louis Cardinals, and San Francisco Giants—had the bulk of their costs paid for with public money. For baseball fans wishing to see what a ballgame was like in the pre-luxury-suite era, only Fenway Park, Wrigley Field, and a handful of 1960s and '70s parks remain.

Yet the push for new stadiums has not abated, with signs that some club owners may be preparing to circle around and get back in the line that they themselves started 20 years ago. The Oakland A's (home stadium built in 1967) and Tampa Bay Rays (home stadium finished in 1990) are the two clubs currently at the top of the list of those seeking new homes, but other cities that could see new stadium demands include Toronto, where Blue Jays general manager J.P. Ricciardi declared SkyDome (now renamed Rogers Centre) "obsolete" in 2004, saying it "may have been state of the art fifteen years ago, but it's old now," and Los Angeles, where the Dodger owners are reportedly considering a land development deal that would put a new NFL stadium on the site of their ballpark, at unknown public cost.[26]

Other sports have already seen an ever-shortening shelf life for stadiums. After the Dallas Cowboys opened their new $1.2 billion stadium in 2009 (which received, depending on the source, somewhere between $325 million and $651 million in public subsidies), clubs like the Atlanta Falcons, St. Louis Rams, Carolina Panthers, and Miami Dolphins, all with stadiums less than 20 years old, began demanding—and in most cases getting—public money for either entirely new buildings or substantial renovations to their teenaged ones.[27] It is not hard to foresee a future baseball version of Cowboys Stadium—perhaps with the "holographic replay system" that the Cincinnati Bengal owners' new lease guaranteed they would get at public expense once other clubs had them, to keep their stadium "state of the art"—leading to yet another frenzy of stadium spending in the near future.[28]

Because that is what the sports business has become. Twenty-five years ago, the sports business was still largely about selling tickets to individual fans. Today, it is about maximizing profits and franchise values by any means possible, and one of the easiest routes is the public purse via stadium subsidies. It is a trend that has taken not just billions of dollars in public money but some irreplaceable public spaces: Yankee Stadium followed

Tiger Stadium to the wrecking ball in 2009—to be replaced by a model with fewer seats and poorer sight lines but more high-end dining options, at a cost of more than $2 billion, about $1.2 billion of which was paid for by the public. And while Boston's Fenway Park was saved at the last minute—thanks in part to a new owner with a fondness for the building, and in part to a group of Boston fans and preservationists who, inspired by the Tiger Stadium Fan Club, campaigned for years on behalf of a historic renovation of the facility—baseball's only other surviving pre–World War II ballpark, Wrigley Field, has continued to be a target of controversy, with Cubs owner Tom Ricketts threatening to "take a look at moving" if he was not granted the right to erect video boards inside and outside the ballpark and build a hotel and other developments on neighboring blocks.[29] (The huge video scoreboards were finally installed for the 2015 season.)

In the midst of all this, *Chicago Tribune* sports columnist Phil Rogers penned a column that began: "Quaint ballparks are cool, no question about it. But they don't win championships. That's why the Yankees did an ugly overhaul on the House That Ruth Built in the mid–1970s and scrapped the original Yankee Stadium altogether five seasons ago."[30]

The Yankees and Tigers, of course, did manage to win a few World Series in their original stadiums, just as the Red Sox have recently in venerable Fenway. But as with economic windfalls that never appeared and move threats that never came to pass, in the stadium game, no one ever lets a little reality stand in the way of a good "meet you there."

Notes

1. "Love in the Afternoon at Skydome," *Seattle Times*, May 13, 1996.
2. John Helyar, *Lords of the Realm: The Real History of Baseball* (New York: Ballantine Books, 1994).
3. Neil deMause and Joanna Cagan, *Field of Schemes: How the Great Stadium Swindle Turns Public Money into Private Profit* (Lincoln: Bison Books, 2008), 141.
4. "Blue Jays Win to Clinch American League East Title," *New York Times*, October 3, 1991.
5. "Baltimore Orioles Attendance, Stadiums, and Park Factors," http://www.baseball-reference.com/teams/BAL/attend.shtml (accessed on April 23, 2015).
6. "Indians' Record-Setting Sellout Streak Over," *USA Today*, April 5, 2001.
7. Neil deMause, "The $25 Million Man: The Real Reason Baseball Players Are So Rich," *Village Voice*, December 3, 2002.
8. "Yankee Stadium," http://www.baseball-reference.com/bullpen/Yankee_Stadium (accessed on November 4, 2012).
9. "Tiger Stadium," http://www.baseball-reference.com/bullpen/Tiger_Stadium (September 1, 2012).
10. Neil deMause, "How Much Is the Stadium in the Window? Determining the True Public Costs of Big League Ballparks," http://www.baseballprospectus.com/article.php?articleid=4591 (accessed on April 23, 2015).
11. Arthur J. Rolnick, "Congress Should End the Economic War between the States Testimony," http://www.minneapolisfed.org/publications_papers/studies/econwar/rolnick_testimony_2007.cfm? (accessed on April 23, 2015).
12. "New York Stock Exchange Subsidy Deal," http://fiscalpolicy.org/new-york-stock-exchange-subsidy-deal-2 (accessed on April 23, 2015).
13. Greg LeRoy, *The Great American Jobs Scam* (San Francisco: Berrett-Koehler, 2005), 84.
14. deMause and Cagan, 52.
15. Personal communication, as part of research for Neil deMause, "Why Do Mayors Love Sports Stadiums?" *The Nation*, August 15–22, 2011.
16. Alan Achkar and Bill Lubinger, "Gateway's Scorecard: Sports Complex Still Trying for Home Run," *Cleveland Plain Dealer*, September 10, 2000.
17. Neil deMause, "No Basketball, No Problem," *Slate*, October 5, 2011.
18. "An Open Letter to Mayor Anthony Williams and the DC City Council from 90 Economists on the Likely Impact of a Taxpayer Financed Baseball Stadium in the District of Columbia," http://www.dcfpi.org/ (accessed on April 23, 2015).
19. Neil deMause, "Why the *Wash Post* Killed My Nationals Stadium Op-Ed," http://www.fieldofschemes.com/2012/10/09/3914/why-the-washpost-killed-my-nationals-stadium-op-ed/ (accessed on April 23, 2015).
20. The statements from Schembechler and Young can be found in Michael Betzold and Ethan Casey,

Queen of Diamonds: The Tiger Stadium Story (West Bloomfield, Michigan: Altwerger and Mandel, 1992), 209–210, and 141.

21. David Seifman, "Ruth Built House to Last," *New York Post*, April 20, 1998.
22. "New Stadium, or, the St. Petersburg Tigers?" [Toledo] *Blade*, September 8, 1994.
23. Edward Kiersh, "Playing Hardball," *Cigar Aficionado*, Summer 1995.
24. Kevin Delaney and Rick Eckstein, *Public Dollars, Private Stadiums: The Battle Over Building Sports Stadiums* (New Brunswick: Rutgers University Press, 2003), 3.
25. deMause and Cagan, 227.
26. Dave Perkins, "Dome Is No Longer Home Sweet Home," *Toronto Star*, May 20, 2004; Sam Farmer, "Is Dodger Stadium a Possibility for the NFL to Return to L.A.?" *Los Angeles Times*, February 25, 2013.
27. Paul Munsey and Cory Suppes, "Cowboys Stadium," http://football.ballparks.com (accessed on April 23, 2015); Judith Grant Long, *Public/Private Partnerships, for Major League Sports Facilities* (New York: Routledge, 2013), 140.
28. deMause and Cagan, 240.
29. "Ricketts Threatens to Move Cubs Without OK for Wrigley Upgrades," *Chicago Tribune*, May 1, 2013.
30. Phil Rogers, "Key to Wrigley Renovation: Will It Lead to a Title? More Revenue Doesn't Guarantee Success, but Impossible to Sustain Success Without Lots of Money," *Chicago Tribune*, May 1, 2013.

Losing Tiger Stadium, 1987–1997

Frank Rashid

Cities other than Detroit have debated the issue of replacing their classic major league ballparks, and, as of this writing, all but two have succumbed to the pressure to tear down and replace. Four cities—Philadelphia, Pittsburgh, Cincinnati, St. Louis—have now replaced the original replacements, all, significantly, with retro-style ballparks that incorporate, at least superficially, some of the features of the original classic parks built in the 20th century's first decades and razed by the early 1970s. Nevertheless, many elements of the long Detroit stadium struggle result from the city's distinctive history, economics, and politics.

Detroit's civic leaders had few effective ways to respond to the devastation wreaked by unprecedented deindustrialization in the decades following World War II and the concurrent, government-subsidized abandonment of the city by most of its middle-class residents.[1] After the social programs of the 1960s failed to have the needed impact on urban America and after a succession of presidential administrations that were indifferent, sometimes even hostile, to cities and the societal challenges imposed upon them, big-city mayors and legislators were left to do the bidding of an uncommitted and opportunistic private sector. Detroit's leaders tried to persuade industrialists and retailers to keep at least some of their jobs here; they attempted to lure new employers; and they invested heavily in large projects intended to change the city's image and make something, anything, happen. In the process, they made promises and built up hopes that could never be fulfilled; they made deals with private corporations that handicapped the city and its residents; they changed long-standing practices and laws to benefit the corporate sector at the expense of individual citizens. The corporations had Detroit and other cities at a serious disadvantage. They played cities off against one another in hopes of getting the best deals; they made vague and unsubstantiated promises about how many jobs and other benefits they would bring; and they made demands with ruthless disregard for residents and small businesspeople. Major League Baseball was no better than any of these corporations; in some ways it was worse.

Redevelopment in Detroit: A Familiar Pattern

By the late 1980s, anyone familiar with Detroit's recent history recognized the pattern. The city's political leadership and corporate elite would collaborate on a grand project that would, said the hype, serve as an "economic engine," create "synergy" that would enliven the community, and act as a "game-changer" for Detroit. Promoters used similar arguments in the 1950s when the city's historic African American neighborhoods, Black Bottom and Paradise Valley, were razed to make way for freeways and middle-class housing and when the city rezoned its historic Irish neighborhood, Corktown, for light industry, tearing down most of its housing so that downtown businesses could relocate after being displaced by a new riverfront convention center and civic center. These arguments were heard again in the mid–1970s about the construction of the Renaissance Center, a massive isolated downtown complex of office buildings, retail space, and a hotel. Political and corporate leaders made the same promises in the early 1980s about the huge General Motors factory complex called the Detroit/Hamtramck Assembly Plant—or "the Poletown Plant"—that displaced over 4,000 eastside residents and demolished 1,300 homes, dozens of small businesses, a hospital, and six churches. They made these promises yet again in the late 1980s about construction in the center of the city of the world's largest trash-to-energy incinerator. In 1987, such arguments about proposed gambling casinos were already being put forth, and soon similar arguments were being put forth about stadiums.

By 1987, however, it was clear that none of the promises about the earlier projects had come true. The new district that replaced the old African American neighborhoods had brought some new middle-class residents to the city, but the freeway that replaced Hastings Street, the main artery of Paradise Valley, had facilitated the movement of many more people to the suburbs, and the ruthless treatment of the neighborhood's black residents and businesses had added to the resentments that erupted in the 1967 rebellion.[2] Rather than relocate to Corktown, most of the displaced downtown businesses had moved out of the city, leaving the Irish district a fraction of its previous size without most of the promised light industry.[3] The riverfront convention center, even after hosting the 1980 Republican convention, had done nothing to reverse Detroit's economic decline.[4] Most of the high-class retail shops in the Renaissance Center, the massive John Portman-designed glass fortress on Jefferson Avenue, had departed within years of its opening, and it was obvious that it had not turned the city around as its boosters had predicted; rather, by adding to the downtown's surplus office capacity and diluting its retail market, the huge project had arguably done more harm than good.[5] The Detroit/Hamtramck Assembly Plant never brought the number of jobs it promised, though it did contribute to the city's population loss.[6] The massive incinerator never produced the positive economic benefit that was to come from selling the electricity it generated.[7] Detroit's economic decline continued because none of these initiatives, despite the promises made about them, could reverse the process of disinvestment from the city by industrialists, retailers, and upper- and middle-class residents.

From the outside, Tiger Stadium was not the most ornate structure ever designed. It was, however, a distinctive building and a memorable place for most Detroiters. It held significance, not only in the history of sport but also in the city's history, as a place where Detroiters collectively enjoyed themselves. It eventually came to be a place that gave their city an identity different from that of the gritty, problem-ridden, post-industrial dystopia

This southward view c. 1950 illustrates the ballpark's proximity to the Detroit River and shows Corktown, still largely tree-covered all the way to Fort Street, prior to its rezoning for light industrial development and the subsequent demolition of much of its housing (Walter P. Reuther Library, Archives of Labor and Urban Affairs, Wayne State University).

exploited by fear-mongering media, mocked by television comedians, and disdained by suburbanites. For many of my generation, if there was a source of romance and hope in our troubled city, it was grounded in our experience at Tiger Stadium. Since pro baseball had been played at the corner of Michigan and Trumbull since 1896, it was among the oldest sites in American professional sports, noteworthy not only for the number of games played, runs scored, and home runs hit there, not only for its great games and great players, but also for its connection with our personal and collective histories. And, unless a fan sat behind a post or a big hat or hairdo, it was a great place to see a game. John Pastier determined that the average seat at Tiger Stadium was closer to the field than the average seat in any other major league ballpark: "No better spectator park exists," Pastier wrote. "By actual measurement, its seating proximity to the field surpasses all other parks, old or new.... As design, it is a rare specimen of the Golden Age of ballparks, full of complexity, and miraculously combining both monumentality and human scale."[8] There were plenty of reasons to save it. But the most important might have been our understanding that successful societies and, of course, successful cities, invest their resources wisely and prudently in their people and that by preserving older buildings those resources are not wasted on unnecessary new ones. Preserving Tiger Stadium as the home of the Detroit Tigers would prevent another mistake, another waste of Detroit's energy and resources.

The year 1987 was the year in which a group of longtime Detroit residents and baseball fans, myself included, started the Tiger Stadium Fan Club (TSFC). Over the decade of its formal existence and thereafter, we would come to understand the difficulties of fighting city hall and the corporate and political interests it represents.[9] Tiger Stadium's

A panoramic view of Tiger Stadium from behind home plate, September 22, 1999 (© Rebecca Cook).

replacement and ultimate destruction, the behavior of Major League Baseball and its local affiliate, the compliance of local and state political leadership and of the local media constitute only a recent instance of a familiar pattern of perverse development schemes that have deprived Detroiters of their scant resources, erased their shared history, and diminished their future prospects.[10] The story of Tiger Stadium's abandonment and ultimate destruction demonstrates how a city's corporate leaders repeat the pattern by exploiting the desperation resulting from it and how, despite the odds, groups of Detroiters persist in organizing to break the pattern, resist the exploitation, and overcome the desperation.[11]

Learning the Game

Familiar with the flawed development schemes of the city's past, our small group of Detroit residents and baseball fans formed the TSFC on September 2, 1987, as soon as we heard rumors that Tigers owner Thomas Monaghan and the City of Detroit were actively discussing a new stadium. As Detroiters, we took to heart the city's motto, composed in 1805 by a lonely French priest after the frontier town in which he had invested his hopes burned to the ground: "We hope for better things," wrote Gabriel Richard. "It will rise from the ashes." We never lost hope for better things or our love for the remnants of greatness amid our city's destruction. Sensitive to any threat to our beloved structures and spaces, we thought that appealing to the Tiger owner's reputed love of architecture and respect for tradition would persuade him to stay in Tiger Stadium. Later, we believed that if we could present a cost-effective way to renovate the stadium, Monaghan or his successor Mike Ilitch would see the wisdom of preserving it as the Tigers' home.

Five months later, on February 2, 1988, three TSFC leaders—Bob Buchta, Mike Gruber, and I—were meeting with Tiger officials at the stadium office annex on Michigan Avenue and Eighth Street. John McDevitt, the chief stadium aide for Monaghan, asked to meet with us so that he could respond to an open letter we sent to his boss asking that he "make full public disclosure of all engineering and feasibility studies" about Tiger Stadium's structural integrity and renovation costs. (The letter also asked Monaghan to "enlist the best talents" he could find to preserve the stadium "for the people of this community and for baseball fans everywhere" and to "repudiate threats to move the Tigers out of Detroit.")[12] As we began what would become a ten-year effort to keep the Tigers in Tiger Stadium, we really did not know much about the building's condition. We just knew that we did not want the stadium to be destroyed without a fight, without making sure that the Tigers and the City of Detroit, which owned the building, would do everything possible to preserve it as the home of the Detroit Tigers.

McDevitt told us that the big problem threatening Tiger Stadium was caused by salt. In the years (1938–1974) when the stadium hosted the Detroit Lions, salt had been thrown on the stadium decking to melt ice and snow, and, he said, the salt had caused the decking to corrode. He also told us that there was no written study to back up the $45–$100 million estimate he had recently told the *Detroit Free Press* would be needed for stadium repair and renovation. The dollar figure, he said, was based on an informal, in-house review, not a real study. "$45 million," the Fan Club's newsletter, *Unobstructed Views*, reported later that month, "would cover structural maintenance and ... the higher figure would include changes better described as remodeling."[13] But McDevitt's numbers were fuzzy, and his refusal to disavow any threat to move the Tigers out of the city made us suspicious. Moreover, we shortly received undeniable evidence that the stadium was not dangerous. In March 1988—at the request of Lowell Cauffiel, a reporter for *Monthly Detroit*—noted structural engineer Lev Zetlin performed a visual inspection of the stadium and called it "landmark construction—a classic." With proper maintenance, he said, it could last "indefinitely."[14]

Six months after our meeting with McDevitt, a *Detroit News* reporter named Scott Faust revealed that a Freedom of Information Act request proved a study actually did exist; it had been completed by Turner Construction in November 1987, less than three months before our meeting with McDevitt. The total estimate for repairs came to less than $6 million. It included replacing a section of the lower deck and resurfacing some of the aisles and concourses. The study noted that "the harsh means of cleaning the stadium, using high water pressure hoses, [would] continue to create leakage problems."[15] This is the only reference to the deterioration's cause. There is no mention, anywhere in the study, of even a grain of salt.

So our skepticism about pronouncements from the Tigers organization and the City of Detroit increased. We knew that they were distorting, oversimplifying, and exaggerating, and we recognized the similarity between their statements and those of the promoters of the earlier projects that had done little or nothing to improve our city and in some ways had made things worse. In the months and years that followed, we would study the work of the many economists and urban planners who have shown that stadiums are a poor public investment and a dubious use of prime real estate, but, when we started out, we knew best the lessons of local history. We knew how many of Detroit's landmarks and neighborhoods had already been sacrificed to spurious ideas about progress.[16]

We recognized the disingenuousness of the Tigers' pizza-baron owner Thomas Monaghan when he spoke of his reluctance to part with Tiger Stadium and said that Detroit's mayor, Coleman Young, was the one promoting the new facility. Young, we knew, was no friend of preservation, but Monaghan stood to gain the most from a new publicly subsidized stadium. Later actions proved that his January 14, 1988, response to a *Detroit Free Press* reporter's question about a new ballpark was as self-serving as it was insincere: "I stand back," Monaghan said. "I love the old stadium, but I'll let the mayor and the engineers figure out what to do. I'll let them build a new stadium. Then I'll cry." Young at least was straightforward, even if prone to hyperbole: "It's obvious," he told reporters on January 23, 1988, "the damn thing is falling down." Later he claimed, "Nobody in their wildest dreams expects that stadium to last beyond ten years. Most people say it will fall down in five." After Lev Zetlin pronounced the stadium structurally sound, Young was dismissive: "I gather this guy spent two hours in the stadium. He didn't go into any of the key rooms. He didn't look at any of the blueprints. So he doesn't know what the hell he's talking about."[17] This was our first experience of a politician belittling expert opinion. It would not be the last.

Club officials and politicians continued to argue that Tiger Stadium was structurally deficient, although they had to be careful not to suggest that it was dangerous. (They were still opening it up to millions of customers every year, after all.) And the TSFC continued to collect testimony that the structure was sound. In addition to the Turner study and Zetlin's assessment, Ann Arbor engineer Robert Darvas and Osborn Engineering's Dale Swearingen asserted that the stadium was sound enough to undergo renovation.

During the decade in which the TSFC fought to keep the Tigers in Tiger Stadium, no structural engineer came forward to dispute its structural integrity, although club officials and politicians still proclaimed the building structurally unsound. In 1990, one club official likened the stadium's condition to a patient with inoperable cancer.[18] In April 1991, Bo Schembechler, the legendary University of Michigan football coach hired by Monaghan as general manager, delivered a much publicized speech before the Detroit Economic Club in which he claimed that renovation would cost nearly four times the TSFC's estimate, once what was "in the bowels" of the stadium was uncovered.[19] As late as March 1996, Mayor Dennis Archer, who had been repeatedly presented with evidence of the stadium's structural soundness, referred to its "foundational problem," calling it a "tired old grandlady."[20]

In addition to pointing to the stadium's alleged weaknesses, club officials issued veiled threats to move the Tigers to the suburbs or to another city if Detroit did not cooperate in providing a new stadium, a strategy often successfully employed by sports franchises hoping to squeeze stadium subsidies from their hometowns. After decades of disinvestment by its industrial and retail base, Detroit was especially vulnerable to this kind of threat. Its auto companies and major retailers had moved out of the city or had significantly curtailed operations, and two of its major league clubs, the Lions and the Pistons, had already departed for the suburbs.[21] Members of the media were willing to carry this message forward, and it clearly made politicians and citizens nervous.[22]

Building a Team, Adopting a Game Plan

When we started the TSFC, we hoped to attract to the cause the kind of expertise we needed to wage a serious campaign. We knew that a small group of writers, teachers, and artists might be able to raise awareness of the issue but that we lacked the practical skills needed over the long haul. We needed attorneys, architects, urban planners, preservationists, and policymakers. And, along with dozens of other folks who volunteered, these people came forward. Three hundred people attended out first meeting on January 24, 1988; hundreds more attended our demonstrations and rallies, thousands took part in two demonstrations—"Hugs"—that circled the stadium in 1988 and 1990, and at its height, our mailing list consisted of names of over 11,000 people, many of whom contributed money or volunteered their time.[23] These were the volunteers who did the work to secure historic designation, argue our cause in court, develop renovation plans, and bring the stadium issue to the center of local attention; they passed out hundreds of thousands of leaflets; they published newsletters, position papers, and fact sheets; they sold merchandise and held fundraisers; they maintained an office, mailing list, and database; they gave interviews, put out news releases, held press conferences, sponsored information sessions, and engaged in debates on television and radio and in print; they lobbied city, county, state, and federal legislative bodies; they met with corporate and political leaders and members of the media; they filed suit to prevent the use of public money for a new stadium; they twice—in 1992 and 1996—collected signatures and brought the issue to the Detroit ballot, winning the first time by a large margin and losing the second time by an even larger margin. Among the group's active members were artists, architects, attorneys, writers, teachers, urban planners, preservationists, community organizers, neighborhood representatives, business owners, developers, ministers, nuns, priests, and a bishop.

Our membership was deficient in one important area. We were unable to attract to the cause significant numbers of African American Detroiters. Our most active African American member, Rosemary Hogan, lived in suburban Livonia. African American physician Edward Turner, who had a long but frustrating history of trying to get the Tigers to be more responsive to the African American community, joined our effort. As the issue heated up, we were fortunate to have the visible representation of longtime Detroit African American activists David Rambeau, Hodges Mason, and Ron Scott, who joined us because they recognized the injustice of public subsidies for major league sports. Although our leadership consisted largely of Detroit residents, we did not reflect the majority population of Detroit, and our overall membership reflected the racial makeup of baseball fans, who were overwhelmingly white, and of residents of the suburbs rather than of the residents of the city of Detroit. The reasons for this are complex and long-standing:

1. The legacy of racism in major league baseball in general and the Detroit Tigers in particular left many African Americans indifferent if not hostile to the sport, its history, and its landmarks.
2. Joining us meant opposing African American political leadership just as it was gaining control of the city.
3. African Americans have a healthy distrust of progressive whites who claim to be acting in their interests.
4. Many black Detroiters, though certainly not all, are conflicted about preservation of buildings that represent the long stretch of time when blacks were an oppressed, underrepresented, often excluded, and mostly powerless minority.

We argued that public support for stadiums would tax Detroiters of all colors to support the enterprises of wealthy white suburbanites. But we could not overcome the political power of those arrayed against us. Most of those arguing in favor of keeping Tiger Stadium were white, and most of the city officials arguing in favor of replacing it were black. This became our greatest vulnerability.

None of us were blind to the odds against us. We knew that few efforts to save ballparks had succeeded, and that the most recent group that had engaged in such an effort, Save Our Sox, had lost its battle to prevent the Chicago White Sox from replacing Comiskey Park.[24] Of the other existing historic ballparks, we knew that Fenway was threatened and that Wrigley, for the time being, seemed secure, having recently undergone the type of renovation the TSFC ultimately advocated for Tiger Stadium. The case of Yankee Stadium complicated our efforts. Although we never recommended the kind of drastic renovation undertaken by the Yankees in the mid-'70s, that scenario was often used as an example of the perils of renovation.

Despite our awareness of the challenges we faced, we took heart from the writings and activism of people like Jane Jacobs who had successfully confronted powerful interests in New York and prevented freeways from cutting through its dense and lively neighborhoods. We knew, too, that San Francisco activists had similarly stopped freeway development and consistently rejected new stadium subsidies at the ballot box. We also found encouragement in local examples. Detroit's Orchestra Hall, celebrated for its superb acoustics and saved by a band of concerned citizens at the last minute from the wrecking ball, had recently undergone renovation and was once again the home of the Detroit Symphony Orchestra. In addition, thanks largely to the efforts of developer Chuck Forbes, a number of Detroit's great downtown theaters were being restored. The grandest of these, the Fox Theatre, had been bought from Forbes by the city of Detroit, which then sold it to Mike Ilitch, who, with the help of a $12.2 million grant from the city, completed the Fox's restoration.[25] When Ilitch purchased the Detroit Tigers in 1992, he was still heralded as a friend of preservation. These successes gave us hope that Tiger Stadium could be restored and renewed.

The members of the TSFC embarked on an ambitious campaign to persuade the Tigers, the politicians, and the media that Tiger Stadium was too important to lose. We sought to raise public awareness of the issue, build support, and recruit volunteers by generating media coverage through our newsletter, *Unobstructed Views*, and through public meetings, rallies, demonstrations, and other events, the most noteworthy of which were the two hugs of the ballpark.[26] The TSFC historic designation committee researched and wrote a proposal that secured a spot for Tiger Stadium on the National Register of Historic Places.[27]

We even attended meetings of city councils of suburban communities mentioned as possible sites for a new stadium, successfully petitioning them to pass resolutions to reject any stadium deal and keep the Tigers in Detroit. Our legal committee researched the terms of the stadium lease, discovering that, in securing the bonds for the renovation of the stadium in 1978 and selling the ballpark to the city, the Tigers agreed to a 30-year enforceable lease binding them to Tiger Stadium until 2008 and, to some extent, undercutting the threat to move elsewhere.[28]

Perhaps most important was the work performed by volunteer architects. Once we learned what the Tigers wanted in a new stadium, we asked John and Judy Davids, two architects who joined our ranks in 1989, if the Tiger management's wishes could be fulfilled through renovation. They assembled a small team of architects and designers, put in hundreds of volunteer hours, and, over time, produced an elegant vision of a renovated stadium. The "Cochrane Plan"—named after the great Tiger catcher-manager Mickey Cochrane—addressed most of the Tigers' stated needs, provided modern amenities for fans, removed some of the view-obstructing upper-deck posts, and preserved the most important features of Tiger Stadium for $26.1 million, a small fraction of the cost of a new stadium. In fact, we argued, through the extra revenue generated by luxury suites and improved concessions, the plan would pay for itself. No public money would be necessary.

The Cochrane Plan was not the only renovation option available. The owner of an Ann Arbor construction firm, Joe O'Neal, proposed a more dramatic renovation plan, designed by noted architect Gunnar Birkerts, that would have removed all of the posts by cantilevering the upper deck from a new exterior structure outside the existing walls of the park. Luxury suites would then be hung from the upper deck, somewhat closer than the Cochrane Plan's third-deck suites. Although the Birkerts-O'Neal plan was much more expensive ($85 million) and went further than many TSFC members liked by lifting the stadium's distinctive upper deck and sacrificing its remarkable proximity to the field, this plan was extremely useful in the stadium debate, since the existence of two credible proposals showed that renovation was clearly a realistic option. Moreover, O'Neal added to the stadium discussions the views of engineer Robert Darvas, whose expert assessment of the stadium's structural strength and persuasive advocacy of renovation added authority to the cause of saving Tiger Stadium.

Along with the work on Tiger Stadium itself, the TSFC gained expertise in the economics of stadiums and stadium construction. We learned plenty about the actual costs and benefits of sports facilities and about issues connected with public subsidies for their construction. We learned, for example, why public investment in stadiums does not serve the public interest, why it is absurd to expect a part-time business to create the kind of "synergy" that stadium boosters promised. We studied the work of a diverse group of economists and urban planners who have examined the impact of sports.[29] No serious economist advocated stadium development as a way to bring economic vitality to a city or region. Stadiums for new professional franchises do not bring benefits commensurate with their expenses. Replacement stadiums for older franchises like the Tigers do not create permanent new jobs; they do not stimulate significant new economic spin-off; they do not strengthen the tax base. Stadiums inevitably cost more and do less than promised. The public costs of stadium development go beyond the dollars spent, and the peculiar nature of stadium financing often disguises the true public expenditure. Nevertheless, in the decades since the 1980s, professional sports clubs have raided public coffers for billions of dollars. What we found out about the economics of stadium construction buttressed our resolve. More even than when we started our campaign, we realized that a new stadium would fit the pattern established by previous development projects that wasted civic energy and resources, ultimately doing nothing to improve quality of life for the residents of the metropolitan region.

Winning and Losing by Forfeit

On Detroit's dusty sandlot softball fields, I have played on teams that won games when the opponent did not show up and, more often I am afraid, on teams that lost when not enough of our players showed up. But until playing the stadium game, I had never seen a team that won by not showing up. We operated under the assumption that club officials could be made to see the wisdom of keeping Tiger Stadium as the home of the Detroit Tigers. Tiger Stadium, we argued, was one of the most important historic sites in our city and state as well as in the game of baseball. Replacing it would cost much more than renovating it. Detroit, Wayne County, and the state of Michigan had hundreds of more pressing needs than building new sports facilities. Besides, there was that legacy of ill-conceived publicly supported projects that had never fulfilled their promises. Sooner or later, we hoped, either in response to their better angels or to public pressure, the Tigers owners would at least seriously consider renovation as an option.

But they never did. The Monaghan organization ignored every offer to have a presentation of the Cochrane Plan and gave only a cursory look at the Birkerts-O'Neal plan. Monaghan's successor Mike Ilitch met with TSFC representatives only once, in 1992, but, after creating a retail plaza at Tiger Stadium, set his sights on a new park. No matter how much attention our efforts received, the Tigers management acted as if we did not exist. We had assembled a respectable team and we wanted to play, but the Tigers simply did not show up.[30]

The case of the political leadership is more complicated. In the late 1980s and early 1990s, poll after poll in the local media indicated clear public preference for saving Tiger Stadium, and several members of the legislative branches of city and state government strongly supported renovation and rejected public subsidies for professional sports. Progressive Detroit City Council members Maryann Mahaffey and Mel Ravitz were outspoken on the issue, and state senators John Kelly, George Hart, Joe Conroy, and Philip Arthurhultz worked the capitol aisles in Lansing to defeat state funding initiatives. In a short-lived 1989 attempt to unseat Mayor Young, Detroit's longtime congressman John Conyers posted a billboard across from the ballpark proclaiming that "John Conyers will save Tiger Stadium," becoming the only African American politician to take such a position. Although deferring to the city's political leadership, Carl Levin, Michigan's senior senator, met twice with TSFC representatives; expressed strong, consistent interest in saving the stadium; and, after the Tigers left in 1999, found resources that could be used to preserve the building and then to maintain the site once the building was finally destroyed in 2009.[31]

The executive branches of the state, county, and city were another story. Whether or not they were sincerely concerned about preserving Tiger Stadium, the people in the offices of governor, county executive, and mayor were aware of the amount of attention given to the issue and sought at the very least to appear to weigh renovation seriously. In 1988, Governor James Blanchard, a Democrat, was involved in discussions with the city and the Tigers but backed away from state funding of any new facility that did not include seats the average citizen could afford. His surprise defeat by Republican John Engler in 1990 ended his involvement in the issue. Engler at first promised that no state money would go toward a stadium, but a few years later he changed course. In a meeting with TSFC representatives, Art Ellis, an official from his office, explained why: He acknowledged that the city of Detroit deserved much more support from the state of Michigan than it was receiving but that many outstate Republicans would not stand for doing what really needed to be done. Whether or not a stadium would be good for the city, supporting it was a way for the administration to placate critics with the appearance of responsiveness to the city's needs, and this was why Engler, who initially opposed stadium financing, changed his policy. As a state senator, he had criticized Governor Blanchard's 1984 establishment of the Michigan Strategic Fund, intended to promote economic development and increase employment, but as governor he decided to take advantage of the fund to support the building of a stadium that would generate little development and do nothing to address the city's declining employment rate.

Wayne County Executive Edward McNamara met with TSFC representatives in early 1991, and his deputy, Michael Duggan, had several interactions with us over a period of months. Duggan quickly sought ways to undercut the Cochrane Plan, but he was interested enough in the Birkerts-O'Neal proposal to arrange a meeting between Tiger GM Bo Schembechler, Mayor Young, and Gunnar Birkerts and Joe O'Neal.[32] Even Young was impressed and began investigating the possibility of renovation. But Schembechler would not budge. Thereafter, Young avoided visible involvement in the issue, while Duggan did all he could to aid and abet the Tigers. However, inner turmoil and financial troubles within Monaghan's organization; its ill-conceived firing of broadcasting great Ernie Harwell; our decisive victory, as the major force behind the Common Ground Coalition, in a March 1992 ballot initiative preventing the use of Detroit tax revenues for stadium construction; and the sale of the Tigers to Mike and Marian Ilitch later that year temporarily thwarted efforts to replace Tiger Stadium.

Two years later, Coleman Young decided to retire after Dennis Archer resigned from the Michigan Supreme Court to challenge him. After winning election and taking office in 1994, Archer waded cautiously into the stadium debate, meeting with all constituencies and, at least for a time, giving TSFC members an opportunity to make their case. He met on several occasions with TSFC representatives and even flew with us to Chicago for a tour of Wrigley Field. We were willing to believe that he was sincere in his effort to get from us the information he would need to make the case to the Ilitches and the Tigers. Whether or not this was true, the Ilitches continued to press for a new facility, and in 1994 powerful forces began to coalesce around securing public funds for a new stadium. In May, Archer made a presentation before Detroit's City Council during which he summarized his investigative process, presumably as he had done as a courtroom justice weighing the evidence before reaching a decision. All of the sources he mentioned came from us; it would be impossible to have read the works and consulted the experts he mentioned and come to the conclusion that a new stadium was the best option for Detroit. But he merely mentioned titles and names, not the substance of the work, giving the appearance that his decision was based on evidence. Then, to no one's surprise, he announced that he was supporting a new stadium. In December 1995, the Detroit City Council rescinded our 1992 ballot initiative.

The Tigers had stepped up their efforts to secure funding for a new stadium, hiring John McHale, Jr., away from Denver, where he had secured public funding for Coors Field. McHale, at least, spoke forthrightly about stadium subsidies: "We're one of the very few businesses in the world that at least has a case to make that the government ought to build our building for us and let us do our business in it." But his candor thinly disguised his failure to make that case. "You always have to remember," he said, "that you're down there swilling at the public trough like everybody else."[33]

The Same Old Game

Club officials clearly had an interest in debunking Tiger Stadium's historic significance, exaggerating its structural weaknesses, and dismissing renovation as an option. Local politicians had other reasons for doing so. Throughout the decade in which we battled to keep the Tigers in Tiger Stadium, two mayors of Detroit and their representatives attempted to sell a new stadium based on Tiger Stadium's alleged structural weaknesses, and the Wayne County executive and his deputy did everything possible to undercut our efforts so that they could take part in sponsoring a new stadium. At first, we assumed that the leaders of cash-strapped cities and counties would want to appear to be fiscally responsible and that proof of the stadium's structural soundness and the existence of realistic, cost-effective renovation options would create the political climate to keep the Tigers where they were. Although the Cochrane Plan was much praised by architecture critics, stadium experts, and baseball historians, state and local CEOs never took it seriously. A few years later, Louis Beer, a development consultant who began to work with us in 1991, told us the reason: The budget was too small, and it required no public money. We had to make it bigger if we expected it to go anywhere. How could we expect the mayor and county executive to be interested in anything that took them out of the project? We were not willing to increase the cost of the project in order to make it more attractive to politicians.

Although new stadiums contribute little or nothing to the quality of life of the taxpayers who fund them, and although their hidden costs amount to much more than the dollars specifically expended on them, building them has become a way for political leaders of desperate cities like Detroit to appear to do something for a community while ignoring its real needs. Detroit's leaders, who have limited funds available for redevelopment, focused on stadiums as one kind of project that could happen, not because they would do any good, but because of the vast array of powerful interests—the professional sports leagues, the club owners, real estate developers, construction firms, building and trade unions—that benefit from them and support campaigns to make them happen. Of course, such projects include a built-in incentive for mayors and county executives themselves, since the availability of public funds gives them power to satisfy the demands of wealthy campaign contributors and dispense lucrative contracts to them. Highly visible projects like stadiums also generate publicity for a politician, giving a false impression of progress.

This means that the job of the local political leader is to get the deal done, to trumpet the claims of major league sports about the benefits a stadium will bring, to exploit the desperation of residents by persuading them that stadiums are a quick fix to myriad social problems.[34] Rather than safeguard public resources and ensure that they are put to the best possible uses, mayors and county executives become the agents of powerful corporate interests. The municipal CEOs push the project through any approval process as quickly and with as little oversight from legislative bodies as possible, sell the stadium project to the public, and then dispense the funds to the powerful interests. In the early 1990s, the Detroit Tigers gave the City of Detroit and the County of Wayne six months to come up with a plan to finance a new baseball stadium, or else.... Later, Michael Duggan, the deputy county executive, bragged to the media that the deadline was his idea, that he had advised Bo Schembechler to announce a deadline for Wayne County to come up with a funding plan for a new ballpark; in other words, coaching Schembechler about how to blackmail the public body which Duggan himself represented.[35] Such collusion, though rarely so blatant, is common in stadium deals.

Major League Baseball plays off political leaders against one another and against the executives of other municipalities. Like auto company executives or major retailers, MLB executives and club owners know that no mayor wants to lose a major business, especially a highly visible one, and that, in order to spark action, they simply have to whisper in the presence of a gullible columnist about the possibility of moving to a suburban location or a Florida city. They know that the mayor of a city in crisis has few good options. In a televised debate with me, Mayor Archer asked me what I brought to the table. Although I responded that I had rights as a Detroit citizen and taxpayer to speak out on issues no matter how rich or poor I happened to be, it was clear that if I had a few million dollars to invest, he would have regarded me more seriously.[36] It would take an act of civic courage to stand up against the Tigers and Major League Baseball. Most leaders of cities in crisis cannot afford this kind of courage. Big projects seduce politicians into believing that what is good for them is also good for the city. This process is not necessarily corrupt (although as Archer's successor Kwame Kilpatrick demonstrated, it lends itself to corruption); it simply reflects the options that are limited by the large corporate and financial interests that create the desperation in the first place. Unfortunately, that is the way things get done in a troubled city.

In late 1995 and early 1996, after the Detroit City Council rescinded our 1992 ballot initiative, TSFC members again collected signatures to put the issue of stadium financing on the ballot. We knew that, unlike 1992, the forces pushing for a new stadium, led by Mayor Archer, now had the resources and the will to mount an all-out effort to defeat us, and, indeed, we were outmaneuvered and outspent at least 20 to one. The forces arrayed against us were overwhelming and included all-out TV, radio, and direct-mail campaigns featuring the mayor's bold promises of all the good things that a new stadium would mean for Detroit. Archer himself made the pitch in a $600,000 media blitz featuring TV and radio ads and direct-mail pieces. One flyer promised a "one year equivalent of 3,300 construction jobs" and "support [for] 1,514 direct and indirect permanent jobs with more to follow from the spin-off businesses." The flyer promised that half of the construction workers would be residents of the city. Archer repeated many of these claims in our televised debate. A new stadium, he promised, would "help rebuild Detroit" and help the city to "prosper"; it would generate taxes to bring improved city services, more police, better parks, and improved garbage pickup and street lighting, especially in the neighborhoods. He spoke of spinoff, synergy, and jobs. Archer's staffers introduced the issue of race into the campaign, emphasizing that the TSFC's leadership was largely white and included several suburbanites like Bill Dow, who had taken on a strong leadership role on the issue.[37]

Under the category of "promise them anything" fell a pro-stadium radio announcement by David L. Snead, then the superintendent of the Detroit Public Schools, who called a new stadium "a major economic development project that will affect everyone in Southeast Michigan, *especially our graduates and our students in the Detroit Public Schools*" (my italics). Snead said that the new stadium would "create thousands of new jobs for city residents and our graduates" and would "result in the cleanup of a blighted area through which many of our students pass on a daily basis." This last claim was ludicrous, since both sites under consideration were in downtown areas well removed from residential areas and school routes. This announcement was broadcast on WDTR-FM, a taxpayer-funded radio station run by the Detroit Public Schools.

Everything we had researched showed us that, like the promises made about earlier Detroit projects, most of the promised long-term benefits from a new stadium would be impossible to achieve. Of course, the project would generate short-term temporary construction jobs and maybe even meet some of the targets for hiring minority-owned contractors and Detroit businesses, but it fell dramatically short in the number of jobs that went to Detroiters: only 31 percent of these jobs—not the advertised 50 percent—went to city residents.[38] And little new construction followed in the wake of the stadium project. As urban policy critic Roberta Brandes Gratz demonstrates, cities would do better to engage in smaller-scale neighborhood development strategies that generate construction leading to permanent jobs, improving life for residents, and strengthening the tax base of the city. She points to Detroit as an example of a city that has followed a misguided development strategy.[39]

The pro-stadium literature's interestingly specific number of 1,514 supported jobs clearly refers to the employment generated by the Tigers themselves, either the club's payroll or those of its vendors, which included not only the high salaries of the players and executives but also low-wage seasonal service jobs belonging to ushers, food preparers, vendors, and janitors. The only source for this specific figure in 1996 could be the jobs that already existed with the Tigers in Tiger Stadium. Hence the distinction between new and supported jobs, and hence the lack of specificity about how many of these jobs would go to Detroit residents. Project boosters already knew that most of these jobs, especially those with the highest pay, would not go to city residents, black or white, female or male. The media drew little or no attention to these false promises.

Long-range promises were clearly impossible to fulfill. A stadium would not generate any more police or better city services in Detroit's neighborhoods than Tiger Stadium did. While the mayor asserted in the March 1996 debate with me that income taxes from employees would pay for the increased services to residents, no new tax revenue would be forthcoming from the project, since the Tigers would employ pretty much the same number of people at a new stadium as at the old one. Although Archer and the campaign materials used city ownership as a selling point, this simply disguised the lack of any property taxes to be generated from the project. In the cases in which ownership really might have added to the city's coffers, as in the collection of the revenues for stadium naming rights, city ownership was revealed for the ruse that it is: the Detroit Tigers, not the City of Detroit, have received the annual installments toward the $66 million paid by Comerica Bank for having its name attached to the stadium.

The promises made about the financing of the project are challenging to unravel. The 1996 campaign flyer asserted, "The Tigers will pay $140 Million in construction costs, plus pay the $6.5 Million per year in operating costs. The Tigers will cover the costs of any construction overruns." The public money consisted of $55 million from the Michigan Strategic Fund and $40 million from the City of Detroit. It appeared—and still appears to many observers—that this was a reasonably good deal for the city: the Tigers were putting up most of the money for the project. However, the private money would not be in place for two years. Ilitch had difficulty finding a bank to loan the money for the project. Even Comerica Bank refused to loan the money. Finally, in August of 1998, the Tigers completed an agreement with Sumitomo Bank of Japan, which fronted the money for the Tigers' share of the project.

Several quid pro quo arrangements ensure that the city compensates Mike Ilitch for much if not all of his part of the financing: As part of the deal, the city gave Ilitch "the exclusive option to purchase more than 20 blocks of property west of his Woodward Avenue entertainment complex after nine years" and handed over parking revenues, which Ilitch then was free to use as partial collateral for the loan he eventually secured to cover the Tigers' part of the stadium costs.[40] As mentioned above, the Tigers sold the naming rights, even though the stadium is nominally publicly owned and city ownership became a selling point when the project was promoted.[41] Moreover, a consortium in which Ilitch's wife, Marian Ilitch, onetime co-owner of the Tigers, now holds a majority interest, was given the rights to one of Detroit's three gambling casinos.[42] But Mike Ilitch received other benefits that ensured that he would generate much more in revenue. Comerica Park is located adjacent to the downtown theatre district in which Ilitch already owns restaurants and bars along with theatres and other entertainment venues. Moreover, the move from Tiger Stadium allowed Ilitch to terminate the Tigers' long-standing food-services contract with Sportservice and substitute his own company, Olympia Entertainment, which provided service for Joe Louis Arena. (Two years later, because Olympia Entertainment had not met the challenge of serving the larger crowds at baseball games, he did return to Sportservice.[43]) Moving to Comerica Park gave Ilitch control of almost all ancillary revenues while creating hardship for small business owners in the Tiger Stadium area. Bars and restaurants in the neighborhood either closed or now invest in buses to transport patrons to the stadium. Two well-established souvenir shops went out of business, as did the dozens of small parking lots, including one operated by a church and nonprofit organization that used parking to support charitable activities.

Back in 1992, the ballot initiative put forth by the Tiger Stadium Fan Club as part of the Common Ground Coalition had passed by a 63–37 percent margin, but on

144   Part I: History and Background

March 19, 1996, in a primary election with very low turnout, our proposal was defeated by an 84–16 percent margin. Meanwhile, however, the TSFC had taken the battle to the courts. On November 2, 1995, we filed suit in Ingham County Circuit Court to block the use of the $55 million from taxes paid by Native American gambling casinos and deposited in the Michigan Strategic Fund, which had been established in 1984 "to promote economic development and create jobs."[44] We based our lawsuit on Governor Engler's use of this money without formal appropriation by the state legislature, arguing that the gaming revenues, as state funds, could therefore not be placed into the Michigan Strategic Fund or spent by it without appropriation by the legislature and that doing so violated the Michigan constitution's separation of powers clause. Our lawsuit asserted that the Michigan Strategic Fund did not have "statutory authority to make a grant."[45] After Judge James Giddings ruled against us, we took the case to the Michigan Court of Appeals, which argued that the funds were "gratuitous payments," not subject to the appropriations clause.[46] So we appealed to the Michigan Supreme Court. A few weeks after the defeat of our ballot proposal, the Supreme Court issued its ruling, approving a one-time-only use of the Michigan Strategic Fund for stadium construction but refusing to establish a precedent for the governor's end run around the legislature.

Once voters had approved city funds for the stadium in 1996, Wayne County's political leaders wanted in on the stadium game and sought to provide funding for the new baseball stadium and for a newly proposed adjacent football stadium for the Detroit Lions. The county officials restored a previously established but long-dormant stadium authority that would be less subject to federal restrictions imposed in intervening years to close tax loopholes. In preparation for putting this proposal on the ballot, the Wayne County Commission held a public hearing which TSFC member Kim Stroud and I

Cartoon from a TSFC flyer distributed after the proposal for a new stadium (courtesy Jerome Lemenu).

attended after we had been assured that there would be opportunity for public comment.[47] Michael Duggan controlled the proceedings—pressuring the commissioners with an artificial, self-imposed deadline. When commissioners complained that he had given them no time to review the lengthy document outlining the proposal, Duggan told them that he was prepared to stay all night and answer any questions but that it was absolutely necessary to approve the proposal during that session. We asked the staff when public comments would be heard and were handed an agenda on which public comments were scheduled after the vote. The only member of the "public" allowed to speak prior to the vote was the daughter of the Detroit Tigers' owner.

Wayne County and the City of Detroit collaborated on another well-financed campaign to persuade voters to support Proposal S, which repackaged the earlier $240 million baseball-only stadium proposal into a $505 million proposal for two stadiums with additional financing coming from a tourist tax of one percent on hotel rooms and two percent on car rentals. This time a flyer produced by the Committee to Rebuild Detroit & Wayne County promised "new restaurants and shopping in a rebirth of the downtown," "5,000 construction and permanent jobs," "$200 million economic impact annually," and the "ability to attract Super Bowls, Final Four basketball games and national conventions." "Yes on Proposal S," the flyer boasted, "can change the way the world looks at us." The flyer reproduced a *Wall Street Journal* headline: "Lions and Tigers Help Detroit Roar Back to Life" and another from the *New York Times*: "After Years of Stagnation, Detroit is showing signs of resurgence." "Wayne County's ticket to the future," the flyer proclaimed, "won't cost you a dime." One evening, prior to the November 5, 1996, election, I was listening to Detroit's jazz broadcasting legend Ed Love on WDET-FM, Detroit's public radio station, when Mayor Archer showed up in the studio to promote Proposal S and the Lions' stadium. Archer was typically full of hype about all the great things the stadium would do for the city. Love was trying to go along but then realized that this public investment in a huge football stadium was doing nothing for Detroit's music scene. This was great, he said, but what about investing in a venue for Detroit's jazz audiences? The mayor replied that the 65,000-seat football stadium would be a great place to hear jazz.

As I write, 17 years later, this all seems sillier than it did then. Even though the tax presumably affected visitors more than it did residents, it still absorbed our taxing and bonding potential and added to the public's tax wariness. Money invested in stadiums could not be invested in any of the dozens of projects that *Detroit Free Press* readers had identified—in response to a request from Joe Stroud, the paper's editor—as worthier uses of public funding than a stadium. Rather than the advertised $505 million for both stadiums, Ford Field, by itself, ended up costing $430 million. (Some sources say $500 million.) Comerica Park cost between $300 and $360 million, rather than its advertised $240 million. The clubs were supposed to have covered the $225-$300 million in extra costs, but the blurred lines between county, city, and state and the changed funding formulas brought about by two stadium agreements along with the different versions of each proposal have made it difficult to determine how much ended up being nominally public and how much private.[48] Wilbur C. Rich mentions the difficulty of "calculating the hidden costs" of stadiums: "Teams will release data about initial agreed-upon construction cost sharing but little is revealed about the continuing cost of the stadiums to cities."[49] As of this writing, neither stadium has hosted a jazz concert.

As a result of these and other deals, Mike and Marian Ilitch, whose fortune rose to a reported $3.2 billion, became the fourth wealthiest owner in major league baseball.[50] On paper, it appears that Ilitch contributed more to this stadium project than have many other owners, but in reality the people of Detroit, the nation's largest American city to fall into bankruptcy, subsidized his contribution and ensured that he would take all profits from the stadium, while the city would incur all the risk. The Tigers pay no rent and, of course, no property taxes at Comerica Park.

But dollars constitute only part of the stadium damage. The stadium projects have also cost our city heavily in missed opportunities.[51] Detroit has limited funds to stimulate revitalization efforts, and the stadiums sucked up resources that could have been used for schools, police, libraries, parks, and development projects with potential to produce lasting benefits. Detroit needs to encourage downtown residential development. However, when interest in building lofts and condominiums was growing in other cities, the two new stadium projects used up the Downtown Detroit Development Authority funds that could have helped spur earlier creation of residential lofts in the central city.[52] More profound was the loss of $55 million from the Michigan Strategic Fund. Wise stewardship of this money could have helped to address the effects of the economic crisis in which Detroit and Michigan found themselves. Instead, we wasted much of it on a stadium that employs the same number of people as the stadium it replaced. Although the Michigan Strategic Fund's guidelines appear to ensure that no such expenditure will be repeated—the maximum amount that can be devoted to any project under the fund's current programs is $10 million[53]—the Ilitches secured nearly $300 million in funding for their new hockey arena.[54] In 2006, Taxpayers of Michigan against Casinos (TOMAC) argued before the Michigan Supreme Court that its decision in the 2002 case had implicitly overturned the Court of Appeals decision. Taxes paid on gaming revenues were not "gratuitous payments," as the appeals court had asserted, and were therefore subject to legislative appropriation.[55] This case and the state Supreme Court's 2004 reversal of its 1981 Poletown eminent domain decision mean that the legal arguments for extracting private land and taxpayer money for the new stadiums were overturned. Of course, by then, the $55 million had been spent, private land had been seized for stadium construction, Comerica Park had been built, and the Tigers, Lions, and their owners had been well subsidized by the people of Detroit, Wayne County, and Michigan.

The Tigers and the Town

After our losses in court and at the ballot box, Detroit built two professional sports stadiums, Comerica Park for the Tigers and Ford Field for the Detroit Lions, from which club owners, players, developers, and the owners of construction firms have benefited. At this writing, Comerica Park and Ford Field have been in operation for more than a decade, but the blessings of major league sports have yet to rain down upon the people of Detroit and Michigan. The club owners, on the other hand, have been blessed with dramatically increased franchise value.[56] They have also taken advantage of the opportunity afforded by the new stadiums to raise ticket prices.[57] In effect, we gave hundreds of millions of public dollars to two billionaires so that they could charge higher prices and become even wealthier. The project boosters told us that new stadiums were an important investment in our city. They might have been great investments for the club owners, but for the public they were a subsidy of the one percent by the 99 percent.

As *New York Times* reporter David Cay Johnston, summing up decades of published research, asserts, "Subsidies for commercial sports teams never produce a net gain for society. They are just a government-sponsored transfer of wealth from the many to the few."[58]

The projects led to a few thousand temporary construction jobs and kept some seasonal employment in the low-paying service sector. While the return of the Lions to Detroit after a quarter century in Pontiac may have brought some of these low-end jobs back to Detroiters, the metropolitan region has seen no net gain in employment from these two projects. In the years after the two stadiums were built, Detroit hosted the biggest events in American sports: Major League Baseball's All-Star Game, the Super Bowl, the World Series, and the NCAA's Final Four. Yet, despite the attention and activity these events generated, the Motor City continued to hemorrhage population, lose tax base, and cut city services, including police and fire protection. Thomas J. Sugrue, writing after Detroit hosted the 2006 Super Bowl, likened its attendant hype to that generated by the 1980 Republican Convention, also held in the city. He called the belief that downtown projects and big events will turn the city around "trickle-down urbanism," and, as he pointed out, "it won't work."[59]

But desperation makes Detroiters vulnerable to any scheme that holds any hope, no matter how far-fetched, to change things in our city. The proponents of big projects like stadiums, arenas, and casinos know how to manipulate this desperation, and the wealthy and powerful usually can buy enough media time to influence voters to support projects that will support them.

I often reflect upon our interactions with representatives of government—especially the meeting with Art Ellis, the debate with Mayor Archer, the hearing run by Michael Duggan, and the rulings by the Michigan Court of Appeals and the Michigan Supreme Court—as episodes that reveal why a small citizen group had very little chance to save an old ballpark or block a new one and why Detroit and Detroiters continue to live with the legacy of wrongheaded projects. In such moments, too, we see the mechanisms employed by society's wealthiest people to increase their distance from the rest of us. Despite the promises made by its boosters, a new stadium was never what was best for the city and its citizens. It was just a project that could get done because of the power and influence behind it. To do something that would seek to ameliorate the impact of decades of disinvestment in the city was more than any politician was willing and able to take on. Instead, politicians here and elsewhere have backed projects of high visibility and negligible impact. They lack the imagination and courage to use our resources to support strategies—some bold and innovative, others tried and proven—that might have reversed or slowed decades of decline and actually benefited the citizens of this city and region.[60]

Major League Baseball might appear to be no worse than the other corporations that have exploited our troubled city for their own ends. But professional sports are different: The automobile companies try to extract tax abatements, land, and infrastructure from the cities they play off against one another, but at least they produce some real jobs. Major League Baseball produces little employment, and most of it consists of low-paying, seasonal work in the service sector. As John McHale acknowledged, most corporations at least build their own facilities, but professional sports leagues demand a significant public investment in the actual physical plants of their franchisees. Finally, most corporations offer few illusions about the nature of their relationship with the places where they are located. They are there to make money and sell products. But illusion is the business of major league sports, the illusion of identity with a community, of a distinctive experience in that community. It is the Ford Motor Company, but the *Detroit* Tigers. The illusion that this is our team is the basis of the business. Fans willingly accept this illusion and the bargain at its center: the club owner goes to the expense of fielding a team, and fans support it by buying tickets and merchandise, by following it in the media and, in the process, subjecting themselves to the messages of advertisers. This has always been a matter of individual choice, and it was a choice we members of the TSFC had willingly and happily made for most of our lives. But public financing of stadiums destabilizes the relationship between the professional franchises and their communities because the franchises are taking more, much more from the home cities and their citizens than they can ever give back. Whether or not they like baseball, the people of Detroit and Michigan, most of whom do not attend professional baseball games, are subsidizing the Detroit Tigers and their owner. Once we acknowledged this injustice, it became impossible for many TSFC members, including me, to support the Tigers as we had. The illusion, for me at least, has been destroyed. Major league sports is at best a distraction from the real injustices affecting the people of my ravaged city; at worst, it contributes to these injustices.

The Tigers began to play in Comerica Park in 2000, the Lions in Ford Field in 2002. In the intervening years, the City of Detroit has closed more than 120 schools, five branch libraries, 17 community recreation centers, and five police precinct stations along with nearly 50 community mini-stations. We have hundreds fewer police officers and firefighters. The remaining police stations have cut business hours. We have two stadiums for millionaire athletes, but our parks and playgrounds go untended, and the city sponsors few organized youth sports leagues. In 2012, after cutting the Detroit Recreation Department's budget 43 percent, then–Mayor Dave Bing announced the formation of a trust, funded by foundations and nonprofits, to try to keep the remaining recreation centers open.[61] Finally, in July 2013, after the appointment of an emergency manager by Governor Rick Snyder, the City of Detroit declared bankruptcy. In the meantime, the Detroit Tigers' franchise value increased to $680 million, and Mike and Marian Ilitches' net worth of $3.2 billion put them 157th on *Forbes'* annual list of the wealthiest people in America.[62]

So the long-established pattern of abandonment and exploitation by the corporate and political elite continues. The new stadiums could never have improved life for our city's residents, but they were sold as if they would, and they prevented our city from using its limited resources in ways that held more promise. Most of those who sold us on a new baseball stadium have moved on.[63] The people of Detroit are left to pay for one more set of broken promises and with a reminder of past glory and lost opportunity at the corner of Michigan and Trumbull.

When we began our long campaign to save Tiger Stadium, we knew that the opposing forces would be formidable and that the odds against our success were steep. As over the years, we understood more profoundly the issues involved in losing our ballpark and the implications of building a new one, we came to believe ever more fervently in the importance of our cause. Nothing that has happened since our loss has changed our minds, not the World Series, the Super Bowl, the All-Star game, or the Final Four.

NOTES

This essay relies in part on previous pieces I have written about the battle to save Tiger Stadium: "Against the Empire: The Lost Struggle to Save Tiger Stadium," *The Elysian Fields Quarterly* 16.1 (1999): 6–8; "Baseball, Scholarship, and the 'Duty to Justice,'" *Baseball/Literature/Culture 2002–2003: Selected Papers*, ed. Peter Carino (Jefferson, NC: McFarland, 2004): 93–105; and "Testimony Prepared for the Subcommittee on Domestic Policy, Committee on Oversight and Government Reform," *Build It and They Will Come: Do Taxpayer-Financed Sports Stadiums, Convention Centers and Hotels Deliver as Promised for America's Cities?* Hearing before the Subcommittee on Domestic Policy of the Committee on Oversight and Government Reform, House of Representatives, 110th Congress (Washington, D.C.: U.S. Government Printing Office, March 29, 2007).

1. For analysis of the way deindustrialization, suburbanization, and federal housing and highway programs combined to devastate Detroit, see Thomas J. Sugrue's *The Origins of the Urban Crisis: Race and Inequality in Postwar Detroit* (Princeton: Princeton University Press, 1996) and David M.P. Freund's *Colored Property: State Policy and White Racial Politics in Suburban America* (Chicago: University of Chicago Press, 2009).
2. For a full examination of the clearance of the African American neighborhoods and businesses, see June Manning Thomas's *Redevelopment and Race: Planning a Finer City in Postwar Detroit* (Baltimore: Johns Hopkins University Press, 1997), 45–50, 55–65.
3. *Ibid.*, 75–80.
4. In the Brookings Institution study *Space Available: The Realities of Convention Centers as Economic Development Strategy* (2005), Heywood Sanders shows why convention centers are a dubious way to revitalize cities. Sugrue's post–Super Bowl op-ed in the *Detroit Free Press* ("Still a Poor City," February 6, 2006), incisively demonstrates how big sporting events and conventions have been disappointing as redevelopment strategies for Detroit.
5. Thomas, 154–155.
6. For analysis of the Poletown plant's short and long-term effects, see Jeanie Wylie [Kellerman]'s *Poletown: Community Betrayed* (Urbana: University of Illinois Press, 1990), which describes the loss of the neighborhood and the construction of the GM factory. See also Thomas, 161–166; the documentary film *Poletown Lives!*, George L. Corsetti, producer (Detroit: Information Factory, 1983); and John Bukowczyk's "The Poletown Case and the Future of Detroit's Neighborhoods," *Michigan Quarterly Review* 25, no. 2 (1986): 449–458. In addition to destroying a neighborhood, the project necessitated a change in eminent domain laws, allowing private property to be taken for another private use, setting a new precedent that was used in several other projects, including Comerica Park. In 2006, the Michigan Supreme Court reversed some of the worst aspects of the earlier decision.
7. In order to produce sufficient electricity to be profitable, the incinerator must devour more trash than the city can produce, and it often has relied on refuse from other communities, undercutting attempts at comprehensive recycling programs and, depending on the wind's direction, fouling the air of different neighborhoods while threatening the health of its residents. Curt Guyette gives a useful examination of the incinerator's history in "The Big Burn: America's Largest Garbage Incinerator and the Movement to Shut It Down," *Metro Times* (April 2, 2008).
8. Michael Betzold and Ethan Casey, *Queen of Diamonds: The Tiger Stadium Story* (West Bloomfield, MI: Altwerger and Mandel, 1992): 179.
9. The TSFC formally existed for just over ten years, but many of its members continued to fight in support of the Old Tiger Stadium Conservancy, to save all or part of the building until its 2009 demolition. Some, led by the intrepid Tom Derry, continued working to maintain and preserve the field.
10. Lynn W. Bachelor's "Stadiums as Solution Sets: Baseball, Football, and Downtown Development" (*Review of Policy Research* 15, no. 1 [1998]: 89–102) examines the connections between Detroit's 1980s industrial redevelopment and its more recent sports development strategies. Her essay is reprinted in Wilbur C. Rich, ed., *The Economics and Politics of Sports Facilities* (Westport, Connecticut: Quorum Books, 2001), 126–140.
11. Political scientists, as Wilbur C. Rich observes, describe Detroit politics as a "corporate-dominating governing regime," controlled by a "classic pro-growth machine elite," now focusing on "downtown development," especially stadiums, as central to urban vitality. As Rich points out, such regimes exaggerate the benefits of publicly subsidized stadiums, which are then promoted by politicians and an uncritical press. See "Introduction: Professional Sports, Economic Development, and Public Policy" in *The Economics and Politics of Sports Facilities* mentioned above, 1–10. Rich includes several essays that illuminate the relationship between cities and stadium development.
12. "An Open Letter to Tom Monaghan: Renovation or Preservation," *Unobstructed Views: A Tiger Stadium Fan Club Publication*, February 1988.
13. "Meeting with McDevitt," *Unobstructed Views*, February 1988.
14. Lowell Cauffiel, "Squeeze Play," *Detroit Monthly*, May 1988.
15. City of Detroit Building Authority, Turner Construction, and Charles S. Davis and Associates, Inc., *Tiger Stadium Renovation—Phase III Study* (Detroit, November 1987): II-4.
16. In addition to the neighborhoods mentioned earlier, the landmark buildings that had been lost

included all but a few of its 18th-century homes; the old city hall, a distinctive French Revival building built in 1871 and torn down to build an underground parking lot covered by the aesthetically bland Cadillac (later Kennedy) Square; several of its downtown office buildings and hotels; and dozens of ornate theaters and movie palaces designed in the first two decades of the twentieth century. Destruction and abandonment have of course intensified since the 1980s. Scores of amazing Romanesque and Gothic churches have been razed or stand empty, testifying to the loss of Detroit's middle-class and largely Catholic population, and the city is home to many long-abandoned landmark factories, which transformed (for better or worse) the course of industrial production in America.

17. The statements by Monaghan and Young can be found in Betzold and Casey, 132–134 and 141.

18. Tigers Vice President Bill Haase quoted by *Detroit Free Press* columnist Bob Talbert, June 3, 1990. See Betzold and Casey, 142–143.

19. Betzold and Casey, 143.

20. Debate between Dennis Archer and Frank Rashid, WXYZ-TV, March 1996.

21. As Thomas illustrates, Mayor Young had used his considerable political gifts to keep the Detroit Red Wings in the city by publicly financing Joe Louis Arena on the riverfront (157–158). This led to the abandonment and subsequent destruction of Olympia Stadium in an inner-city Detroit neighborhood. An attempt in the late 1960s and early 1970s to replace Tiger Stadium with a domed, multipurpose facility on the riverfront went down in flames when the Michigan Supreme Court recognized that the project had been sold to the public as being financed by revenue bonds that would ultimately become general obligation bonds when the project inevitably could not finance itself. See Betzold and Casey, 85–100.

22. I had one brief exchange with Mayor Young as he was leaving the stadium after a game. I asked him to keep the Tigers in Tiger Stadium, and he replied, "I'm just trying to keep them in the damn city!"

23. Noteworthy among the many who guided, maintained, and promoted the TSFC are
- Catherine Darin, a retired Detroit Public School teacher's aide who fell in love with the Tigers after arriving in the U.S. from Ireland after World War II;
- Eva Navarro, a legal secretary whose love affair with Tiger Stadium began when attending games with her father;
- Patty and Doug Warner, two residents of Flint, who helped carry the battle to outstate Michigan;
- Tom Derry, who continued fighting to preserve the ballpark's field;
- Corktown residents Pat and Brian Muldoon, Mark and Carmen Crowley, Tom and Maureen Allenson, John and Barbara Prusak, and Brian Tremain;
- Carl Allison, Nancy Burke, Kathy Burke, Kim Stroud, Rosemary Hogan, Mary Moroz, Betty Moroz, Tom Piluras, and founding members Jerry Lemenu and Kevin Rashid;
- Father John Meyer, for many years the pastor of St. Peter's Episcopal Church, also located at Michigan and Trumbull, and Bishop Thomas Gumbleton, longtime pastor of St. Leo's Catholic Church.

24. As we began our effort, I contacted Mary O'Connell of Save Our Sox, who advised me about what we were up against. As a gesture of solidarity, Save Our Sox donated a significant portion of what remained of its treasury to the TSFC. Ten years later, as our struggle wore down, we made it a point to offer similar advice and support to Save Fenway Park.

25. Frank Provenzano, "The Big Stories: Little Caesar Entered into a New Theater of Operations." *Crain's Detroit Business*, February 27, 1995, Special Section, A85. See also Curt Guyette, "Render unto Caesar: The Devil's in the Details and Pizza Man Mike Ilitch Got One Hell of a Deal," *Metro Times*, April 23, 1997.

26. Our initial strategy was to keep the movement light by focusing on the stadium's attributes and its history. To the extent possible, our first demonstrations and activities were non-confrontational. In addition to the two Hugs, we held a march in which participants carried small placards with the names of all Hall of Famers who had played at Tiger Stadium. When it appeared that the mayor was promoting a retractable dome, we invited the press to our presentation at City Hall of our more cost-effective strategy for protecting fans from the elements (an umbrella). Signed petitions promoting the stadium's preservation were presented at the stadium by children pulling their wagons. Later our efforts became more substantive and our actions more direct.

27. Other members of this committee included Gordon Bugbee, Tom Derry, Marianne Maher, Michael Samojeden, Donald Voelker, and Susan Zielinski. The listing on the National Register could not prevent Tiger Stadium's destruction; it just ensured that federal dollars could not be used in the process, but the listing did generate attention and led to the stadium's placement on the National Trust for Historic Preservation's list of 11 most endangered sites in 1991–1992.

28. Among the many lawyers who advised the TSFC, researched the law, and/or argued our cases in courtrooms were Louis Beer, Alex Bensky, Bill Dow, Stuart Dowty, Steven Finegood, John Kelly, Charles Moon, Michael Pitt, and Susan Zielinski.

29. A wide range of academic economists have critiqued the rationale for stadium development and argued the economic benefit of stadiums and sports is overstated. These included Lake Forest College's Robert A. Baade, Pepperdine University's Dean Baim, Smith College's Andrew Zimbalist, Stanford University's Roger G. Noll, Baruch College's Neil J. Sullivan, the University of Chicago's Allen R. Sanderson, Washington State University's Rodney Fort, Cal Tech University's James Quirk, Indiana University's Mark Rosentraub, and Brad

Humphreys of the University of Illinois Urbana-Champaign. Many of these economists are contributors to *Sports, Jobs & Taxes: The Economic Impact of Sports Teams and Stadiums*, edited by Noll and Zimbalist (Washington, D.C.: Brookings Institution Press, 1997), and most have published extensively on stadium financing since then.

30. Often the media were exploited in this strategy. Addicted to the need for "balance," television and radio producers would schedule a debate or a discussion on the stadium issue only to cancel when the Tigers or their political allies refused to send a representative. Detroit's public radio station, WDET-FM, recognized this as a form of censorship and would continue with the program as scheduled, but many commercial broadcasters would not.

31. These funds were apparently used in the PAL project (see p. 161).

32. Betzold and Casey, 173–174.

33. "Owners Still Begging Despite Baseball's Mess," *Unobstructed Views*, May 1995, 2–3.

34. Pro-stadium campaign literature from the 1996 referendum proclaimed that the stadium would bring "New Jobs," "New Business," "More Police and City Services," and "Restored Spirit & Pride." "Blight" would be "eliminated" in the area of the new stadium.

35. Betzold and Casey, 227–228.

36. We had not been blind to this. Over a period of years in the early 1990s we met privately with corporate and political leaders hoping to build support among those with money and power. Although we had some success in influencing individuals, none was willing to take a public stand against public stadium subsidies.

37. A front-page story with the bold headline, "Stadium Critic Lives in Suburbs," appeared in the Detroit area's African American newspaper, the *Michigan Chronicle*, February 21–27, 1996: 1A, 4-A.

38. Despite this, the project's construction management team received accolades for its hiring of firms owned by minorities and women. See Senator Spencer Abraham's remarks in the *Congressional Record* 146.48, April 25, 2000, which also reveal the percentage of Detroit workers hired.

39. Roberta Brandes Gratz and Norman Mintz, *Cities Back from the Edge: New Life for Downtown* (New York: Wiley, 1998), 336–337.

40. Curt Guyette, "Render unto Caesar: The Devil's in the Details and Pizza Man Mike Ilitch Got One Hell of a Deal," *Metro Times*, April 23, 1997, 12–18. I was present at the Detroit City Council hearing in which, under questioning, C. Beth Duncombe, the cochair of the Detroit–Wayne County Stadium Authority, acknowledged that "a portion" of these revenues could be used for collateral for this loan.

41. Campaign literature promoted public ownership of the stadium as one of the benefits of the financing package. In fact, the people of Detroit get very little out of "ownership" of the stadium, which is primarily a way to ensure that the Tigers take all of the profits while the public absorbs most of the risks. The description of the naming rights deal on the "Community Involvement" page of Comerica's website (now removed) described this private deal done with this nominally public property:

In the fall of 1998, [former Comerica Chairman Gene] Miller began discussions with Tigers Owner Mike Ilitch [sic] about naming the new park. Miller, who retired as Comerica's chairman Oct. 1, 2002, saw a naming-rights agreement with the Tigers as a "once-in-a-30-year opportunity." That an agreement was reached quickly attests to the strong, enduring relationship the two business leaders continue to have with one another as well as their sharing of a positive vision for Detroit's future.

"We are pleased by Comerica's confidence in the Tigers and continued support of the Detroit community," said Ilitch [sic].

In 2007, Comerica announced that it was moving its headquarters out of Detroit. The bank continues to pay $2.2 million annually to the Tigers for naming rights on a stadium belonging to the City of Detroit.

42. When the Ilitches bought the Tigers in 1992, Mike and Marian Ilitch were listed as co-owners, but when the opportunity arose to gain an interest in a casino, Ms. Ilitch cut her formal ties to the team. Major League Baseball, which has long sought to avoid any connection with the gambling world, is looking the other way about this and about the very likely use of casino revenues to service the debt.

43. Daniel G. Fricker, "Vendor Returns to Detroit Baseball Stadium," *Detroit Free Press*, April 2, 2002.

44. *Michigan Strategic Fund, Michigan Economic Growth Corporation*, http://www.michiganadvantage.org/Michigan-Strategic-Fund-MSF.

45. *TIGER STADIUM FAN CLUB, INC., a Michigan non-profit corporation, Plaintiff-Appellant, v. Hon. John Engler, GOVERNOR of the State of Michigan*, Defendants-Appellees, Docket No. 194133, Court of Appeals of Michigan, submitted June 6, 1996, at Lansing.

46. *Ibid.*

47. We learned about this hearing the day before it was to be held. When we called to find out the details, we were told it would begin at noon. Once we arrived, after spending hours preparing our statement, we found out that it had begun at 9 a.m. See Neil deMause and Joanna Cagan's *Field of Schemes: How the Great Stadium Swindle Turns Public Money into Private Profit*, rev. ed. (Monroe, Maine: Common Courage Press, 2008), 118.

48. For example, while Comerica Park's cost is usually given as $300 million and the public contribution as 38 percent, sports economist Judith Grant Long gives the cost as $364.8 million and the public contribution

at 31 percent. See "Table C.11 Detroit MI Comerica Park," *Public Funding for Major League Sports Facilities, Data Series (1): Major League Baseball*, Rutgers University, 2001, MLB File 2: 52–54 (accessed on September 29, 2012). Similar discrepancies exist in reporting that provides estimates for Ford Field and for both stadiums together. As I mention in the text, these figures do not account for other ways in which the public supported Comerica Park.

49. "Introduction: Professional Sports, Economic Development, and Public Policy," in *The Economics and Politics of Sports Facilities*, 3.

50. Tom Van Riper, "Baseball's Billionaire Owners," *Forbes*, March 27, 2013. See also Brian Reed, "How the Five Wealthiest MLB Owners Got Rich," *Yahoo Sports: The Sports Game*, March 5, 2012, http://www.thepostgame.com/blog/list/201203/how-5-wealthiest-mlb-owners-got-rich#4 (accessed on July 11, 2012). Reed's short piece attributes Ilitch's fortune to his successful pizza business but mentions the Detroit Tigers' dramatically increased franchise value: $82 million when he bought the team in 1992 and roughly $680 million at the time of the writing. Most of this increase happened after Comerica Park was built.

51. See the analyses of stadium financing and impact in Noll and Zimbalist's *Sports, Jobs, and Taxes: The Economic Impact of Sports Teams and Stadiums*, James Quirk and Rodney Fort's *Hard Ball: The Abuse of Power in Pro Team Sports* (Princeton: Princeton University Press, 1999), and DeMause and Cagan's *Field of Schemes: How the Great Stadium Swindle Turns Public Money into Private Profit*.

52. Kristin Palm, "Lofty Words: Bringing Residents Downtown the Slow Way," *Metro Times*, February 17, 1999.

53. See the approval guidelines for grants and loans under the Michigan Business Development Program and the Michigan Community Revitalization Program and for the use of Private Activity Revenue Bonds at the Michigan Strategic Fund's website, http://www.michiganadvantage.org/Michigan-Strategic-Fund-MSF.

54. For a thorough analysis of the Red Wings' arena funding, see Bill Bradley, "Red Wings Stadium Upset," http://nextcity.org/forefront/view/red-wings-stadium-upset-subsidies-arena-taxpayers(accessed on April 26, 2015); and Bradley's follow-up piece, "Infographic: How the Red Wings Scored in Detroit," http://nextcity.org/daily/entry/infographic-how-the-red-wings-scored-in-detroit (accessed on April 26, 2015).

55. See the appeal filed in 2006 based on the Supreme Court's decision in the 2002 case *Taxpayers of Michigan against Casinos v. the State of Michigan and others*, Supreme Court Case # 129816, which quotes then-Chief Justice Maura Corrigan's statement: "I am starting to think that the Tiger Stadium Fan Club case was wrong, and I am really bothered by that." Lawyers for TOMAC argued that the "Court's implicit repudiation of Tiger Stadium is decisive, because if revenue sharing payments from the tribes are not a mere gratuity … they must either flow to the state treasury alone, or enjoy the support of a corresponding legislative appropriation."

56. The value of the Detroit Tigers rose from $83 million in 1995, the year before their victory in the election insured that a new stadium would be built, to $200 million in 2000. At this writing the franchise is valued at $680 million. The Lions' increase in value is even more dramatic, rising from $150 million in 1996 to $917 million in 2008; in 2013, the team was valued at $855 million. These figures come from *Forbes* and Rodney Fort's *Sports Business Data Pages*.

57. Average ticket price increases are also dramatic: The Tigers' average ticket prices more than doubled between 1999, Tiger Stadium's final year, and 2000, Comerica Park's first year, from $12.23 to $24.83, before the team's mediocre record forced management to lower prices to an average of $17.90 in 2003. In 2011, the average ticket cost $29.32, and in 2012 the average ticket was $31.00; in 2013, it declined to $26.36. The average price of a Lions ticket in the last year of the Pontiac Silverdome (2001) was $39.05; this increased to $50.21 in 2003 and has since increased periodically. After several years of price freezes (because of the team's poor performance), the Lions raised prices 8 percent in 2012, to an average of $67.60. See Rodney Fort's *Sports Business Data Pages* and DetroitLions.com.

58. David Cay Johnston, *Free Lunch: How the Wealthiest Americans Enrich Themselves at Government Expense (and Stick You with the Bill)* (New York: Penguin, 2007), 81.

59. "Still a Poor City," *Detroit Free Press*, February 6, 2006.

60. Such strategies have been promoted successfully by Jane Jacobs in *The Death and Life of Great American Cities* (New York: Modern Library, 1993) and Gratz and Mintz.

61. Cecil Angel, "Bing Announces Plan to Keep Detroit's Recreation Centers Open," *Detroit Free Press*, August 22, 2012.

62. "The *Forbes* 400: The Richest People in America," *Forbes*, September 16, 2013.

63. John McHale, Jr., became the chief operating officer of the Tampa Bay Devil Rays in 2001 and moved on to Major League Baseball's central office where he is executive vice president for administration and chief information officer. Dennis Archer and John Engler have left office. Coleman Young, Ed McNamara, Art Ellis and Mike Ilitch are deceased. After leaving county government, Michael Duggan became chief executive officer of the Detroit Medical Center and in 2012 established residence in the city of Detroit so that he could run for mayor. He was elected Mayor of Detroit on November 5, 2013.

The Battle for Sacred Ground, 1998–2011

Rebecca Long

With a 2016 Postscript by
Michael Betzold

On a cold, snowy day in late December, I sit in a booth in a restaurant at the corner of Michigan and Trumbull. I watch as car after car stops, passengers emerge, and they walk around the empty field across the street from the restaurant. Some people linger for only a few minutes; others stay for hours, snapping endless photographs and walking. Every so often they stop and glance at their surroundings, taking in the emptiness, the void, the field, and the lone flagpole flying the stars and stripes—the flag that proudly waves as if to say with each cold gust of wind, "I remember. I will not forget."

What battlefield is across the street? Who was killed at this site that so many would stop and pay homage to an empty field devoid of any objects save the flagpole and a fence? But I am not across the street from a battlefield, and no one has died at this site. In fact, I am sitting in a Coney Island restaurant, in one of the grittiest urban settings in America: Detroit. And the empty field that so many make pilgrimages to is the former home of major league baseball's Detroit Tigers, the site of the now demolished Tiger Stadium. The stadium may be gone, the victim of greed and vindictiveness, but its field, where so many legends stood, remains.

Just as at a battlefield, these people come to mingle with ghosts, the ghosts of their heroes: To run the same baselines as Ty Cobb and Babe Ruth, to stand on the same pitcher's mound as Mark Fidrych and Hal Newhouser, to man the same bases as Hank Greenberg and Charlie Gehringer, to patrol the outfield of Al Kaline, and to stand in the same place that the "Iron Horse" Lou Gehrig stood when he decided to end his consecutive games streak.

These legendary individuals are just a few of the baseball greats who prowled this field, to say nothing of all the others who once called this field home and the countless moments in history that have taken place on this patch of grass and dirt. But to many, this field and the stadium than once surrounded it are more than just a place for sport: it is a place where memories were made, where fathers and sons shared a common bond, where husbands and wives had first dates, and where a city rife with racial strife went to find healing. For almost 100 years it was a landmark for an entire state. In fact, it was a national landmark. What happens when a structure of this magnitude disappears? Does its function as a landmark also cease? In most cases, the answer would be yes. For without those stands, it can no longer provide safe haven; without those lights, it is no longer a beacon; and without those walls, we are no longer in its shadows. But this is not the case here. This field has instead become a place for congregation and remembrance, a place to celebrate the past, and a symbol of possibilities for the future—a future that still offers the hope of preservation made possible by a group of individuals who have decided to say, "Enough!"

Preservation Efforts, 1998–2011

The Proposals

While the beginning of the new millennium marked the end of major league baseball at Tiger Stadium, it did not signal the end of the movements bent on preserving the ballpark. Although Detroit officials preferred to back a new publicly funded stadium, they did recognize the site's economic development potential. Prior to the stadium's abandonment, the Corktown Citizens District Council (CCDC) in early 1998 expressed concern about the hole the Tigers' departure would leave in their community. Many would not miss the crowded streets and rowdy fans, but they would miss the economic benefits that the Tigers' presence had provided area residents and businesses.[1] The CCDC, with the support of the City of Detroit, put forth a proposal to retain the historic field while renovating the stadium into a multiuse residential, commercial, and sporting facility.

This proposal included plans for 200 lofts, ice rinks, basketball courts, rock-climbing walls, jogging mezzanines, and street-level commercial shopping. All told, the renovation was projected to cost $150 million to $200 million.[2] As Curt Guyette of the *Detroit Metro Times* reported, this strategy, while uplifting for the preservationist cause, was a little unrealistic, considering developers were given only six weeks to reply to the city's nationally distributed July 1999 request for proposals. Consequently, it was no surprise when newspapers reported that the city had received only three partial responses.[3] Understanding that perhaps the abbreviated submission period had limited enthusiastic replies, the city eliminated the deadline. But by October 2000, more than a year after the stadium's closure, the city's plan had still failed to garner any feasible ideas. According to Sylvia Crawford, spokeswoman for Detroit's Department of Planning and Development, "Fewer than five developers have submitted plans to redevelop the stadium since the city publicly asked for proposals in July 1999.... None of the developers has had the experience the city wants in historic preservation as well as residential and commercial work."[4]

Finally, in December 2001, the *Detroit Free Press*'s Daniel G. Fricker reported that the City of Detroit had issued a holding letter to Nonrahs-Sinacola Stadium Redevelopment LLC of Livonia, effectively agreeing not to consider any other development offers for a period of six months.[5] Based on the city and CCDC's original plan, Nonrahs-Sinacola's mixed-use proposal included condos, shops, offices, and underground parking, as well as a 226,000-square-foot sports club constructed in a space created by the proposed demolition of the north section of the stadium. Fundamental to the plan, Fricker noted, was Nonrahs-Sinacola's desire to "preserve the playing field and 8,000 stadium seats for such uses as Little League and high school baseball playoffs, a minor league baseball franchise, concerts, and perhaps a outdoor ice rink."[6] Unfortunately, the project was never realized. In order to complete studies to determine the feasibility of their proposal, Nonrahs-Sinacola had requested access to the city's $2 million ticket surcharge fund.[7] While previous mayor Dennis Archer would have supported this request, newly elected mayor Kwame Kilpatrick was not so accommodating.[8] Mired in the city bureaucracy, Nonrahs-Sinacola's repeated letters to the city went unanswered.[9] On May 30, 2002, Nonrahs-Sinacola's holding letter expired. By November, Kilpatrick's administration issued a new request for proposals. According to Guyette, this RFP was "virtually identical to the one issued in 1999. Despite Kilpatrick's announcement that he had a different vision for the site, his Planning Department apparently still thought the original concept was worth pursuing."[10] Due to Tiger Stadium's location and access to freeways, Kilpatrick's "different vision" included plans for big-box retailers, a development option that did not please the residents of Corktown. Guyette reports:

> In a March 2002 letter to Kilpatrick, Corktown CDC administrator [Kelli B.] Kavanaugh wrote: "The RFP (request for proposal) issued by the City was the result of years of community planning—a true Community-Based Initiative ... we were afforded the rare opportunity to chart our own future and decide what we actually wanted to happen in our neighborhood." Kavanaugh then quoted Kilpatrick, reminding him of what he said in his State of the City speech: "CDC's, neighborhood associations, and communities ... are at the table at the front end of the planning process and not the back end." Kavanaugh says Kilpatrick should practice what he preaches and listen to the people of Corktown when they say they want to see Tiger Stadium reused the way they envisioned it, and not torn down to make way for a big-box retailer.[11]

Kilpatrick's new RFP received three responses, one of which was a resubmission by Nonrahs-Sinacola; all three included the park's use as a site for minor league baseball. None of them was accepted.[12]

Nonrah-Sinacola's proposed use of Tiger Stadium for minor league baseball was not the first time that idea had been put forward. In late 2000, Peter Comstock Riley, former Tiger employee and founder of Michigan and Trumbull, LLC, approached the city regarding the possibility of bringing minor league baseball to "The Corner." However, Riley's dealings with the city would prove to be just as frustrating as Nonrah-Sinacola's. Riley's proposals never included renovation but rather just continued use, a purpose that concerned the Tigers more than the city. Since the Tigers' 1999 abandonment, the city had paid the ball club $420,000 a year to maintain the city-owned park. For some unexplained reason, this payment gave the Tigers the right to decide how the stadium should be utilized.[13] Frustrated and confused about the Tigers' involvement in the decision, Riley approached the Detroit City Council, where he was told by councilwoman Sheila Cockrel, "It's up to Mr. Comstock Riley to decide if he wants to go to the Tigers to see if he wants to negotiate a deal."[14] Although he ultimately succeeded in getting two college games at the stadium, this result was not quite what Riley was hoping for. In 2001, Michigan and Trumbull LLC approached the city yet again. This time Riley's offer involved utilizing Tiger Stadium as a venue for a Frontier League team which would also manage the site and pay the city for its operating expenses.[15] The fully funded plan he presented did not restrict the city from developing the site but rather stated his club would leave should the city find prospective developers whose strategy did not accommodate minor league baseball. Although this proposal enabled the city to eliminate its monthly maintenance payment to the Tigers, Detroit officials ultimately declined Riley's offer. Guyette reported, "Riley contends that the Ilitches have used their political influence to kill any attempts

One of the games Peter Riley brought to Tiger Stadium in 2001 (courtesy Lowell Boileau).

at reusing Tiger Stadium. It's in their interest to collect the $420,000 in yearly management fees as long as possible, then let the stadium be demolished so that there is no threat of any sort of competition from The Corner."[16] Riley's opinion was echoed by others, most notably Detroit City Council president Maryann Mahaffey, who stated, "I think what the Ilitches want is to see Tiger Stadium torn down."[17] The city denied ever receiving any messages from the Tigers' organization regarding Riley's offer.[18]

While it certainly seemed that the Tigers' organization was opposed to anyone else prospering from the stadium's use, it was perfectly acceptable for them to utilize its memory to generate their own revenue. Shortly after the Tigers abandoned the site, they began to sell bottles of dirt from Tiger Stadium at Comerica Park. Referred to as "Ground from the Mound," these sealed bottles sold for $9.99. Although the bottled dirt was actually the brainchild of local start-up company A Piece of the Field, LLC, the Tigers had no qualms about partnering with it to profit from the excavations.[19] How city officials felt about it is unknown.

For the next several years, various proposals for the stadium's renovation were submitted to the city. All of them were denied. Steve Thomas, president of a Corktown business, the Detroit Athletic Company, and a member of one of the renovation groups, the Navin Field Consortium, explains:

> We actually proposed to the Detroit Tigers that [they] move one of their minor league affiliates to the corner of Michigan and Trumbull. The biggest obstacle is the city of Detroit and the Detroit Tigers don't want that to happen. The meetings that we had, the reaction that we had, was typical of meetings that were over with before they started. There was absolutely no interest in the concepts from either the Detroit Tigers or the City of Detroit. And we knew probably within the first fifteen minutes of meeting with the Detroit Tigers that the plan wasn't going to go forward with the current ownership.[20]

In order to circumvent the obstacle the proposed minor league use created, Riley decided to try a different tactic. According to Guyette, in 2005 he approached the city and offered to maintain Tiger Stadium for free. He even offered to help the city find interested developers. The city refused. In an emailed reply to Riley's proposal dated February 1, 2005, chief development officer for the City of Detroit Walter Watkins stated, "After careful consideration, we have decided that we cannot accept your offer. Several prospective developments are under consideration, and we feel we can provide the necessary maintenance and security in the interim. We continue to appreciate your interest in the Stadium and wish you all the very best."[21] Riley viewed this latest rejection as yet another example of the Ilitches' influence. Why would the city rather pay the Tigers for maintenance unless it was to keep one of its richest citizens happy?[22] While many rejected developers empathized with Peter Comstock Riley, the majority of the Detroit metropolitan area was unaware that viable offers even existed.

One of the issues that always plagues stadium preservation movements is the lack of objective reporting. Although several respected developers with more than adequate financial backing had approached the city with proposals, most of these proposals were not reported. With the exception of the Nonrahs-Sinacola proposal, the two newspapers with the highest circulation in the region, the *Detroit News* and the *Detroit Free Press*, did not report on the multitude of viable proposals. Instead they ran stories stating that the city had failed to receive realistic proposals, statements that seemed to be written at the desks of city officials.[23] While small independent newspapers such as the *Metro Times* featured stories relaying potential developers' frustrations, this perspective was suspiciously absent from the stories featured in the *News* or *Free Press*, if stories regarding the stadium were published at all.[24] Like the advertising blitz that targeted the Tiger Stadium Fan Club in 1996, this absence of fair and balanced reporting from the major news sources helped doom Tiger Stadium.

In June 2006, the *Detroit Free Press* reported that, after almost seven years spent "entertaining" renovation proposals, "Detroit Mayor Kwame Kilpatrick has decided to raze Tiger Stadium, the historic but decaying home of Ty Cobb, Hank Greenberg and the 1984 World Series champion Tigers. In its place, Kilpatrick envisions a ring of retail shops and residential housing surrounding the historic playing field, which will be preserved as a nonprofit park and ball diamond."[25] The plan involved the demolition of approximately 90 percent of the stadium, with the possible retention of the area immediately surrounding home plate, including the dugouts.[26] Not unlike the Tigers' earlier scheme to make money from the sale of Tiger Stadium dirt, this new proposal created an opportunity for city revenue through the piecemeal auction of Tiger Stadium seats and other structural memorabilia. Immediately the city began to talk with officials at the Detroit Economic Growth Corporation (DEGC), the nonprofit organization in charge of development that would assume control of the site upon the Detroit City Council's positive vote for demolition. Eerily reminiscent of earlier proposed uses, the plan differed by excluding any minor league affiliation. As DEGC staffer Peter Zeiler explained, "by honoring the history of the site, it provides an outstanding opportunity for young ballplayers to learn the history of baseball."[27] Perhaps this new use would not attract the disapproval of Mike Ilitch.

The Old Tiger Stadium Conservancy

From 2006 to 2007 various individuals, including members of the defunct Tiger Stadium Fan Club, pressed for the preservation of Tiger Stadium. About this time a new player appeared on the preservation front: the Old Tiger Stadium Conservancy (OTSC), a nonprofit organization composed of various Detroit area professionals. The Conservancy hoped to preserve the original Navin Field configuration by cooperating with the city. Many preservationists still held out hope that the Detroit City Council would vote against demolition. In July 2007, their efforts received an influential boost when Hall of Fame sportscaster Ernie Harwell announced his support for preserving a portion of the stadium. Through attorney Gary Spicer, Harwell had an ally on the council in Spicer friend Martha Reeves. Reeves, former lead singer of the Motown recording group Martha and the Vandellas, invited Harwell and Spicer to the June 27, 2007, City Council meeting.[28] At the meeting Harwell urged the council to postpone a decision.[29] Believing they had the support of Reeves, preservationists were shocked when Reeves voted with the 5–4 majority to hand over control of the stadium to the Detroit Economic Growth Corporation.[30] According to onetime Tiger Stadium Fan Club spokesman Bill Dow, who was present at the meeting:

> There was a guy who worked with George Jackson [president and CEO of the DEGC]; I remember him grabbing her arm when the session was in recess and saying, "We have you, right? We have you?" And she looked scared, and it was embarrassing for her because she was standing in front of Gary Spicer and Ernie Harwell, who she invited. She turned on us, and it was the swing vote to switch the other way which led to the eventual demolition of Tiger Stadium.[31]

By handing control of the site to the DEGC, instead of the Economic Development Corporation, which would have worked towards the stadium's partial preservation, the council had essentially voted for complete demolition. Undeterred by the council's decision, Harwell and Spicer joined the board of the Old Tiger Stadium Conservancy in September, hoping to assist the conservancy in its mixed-use plan, which retained the original Navin Field configuration of the stadium.[32]

While the conservancy was still pursuing its plans to save a portion of the stadium, the city approved a contract for the stadium's demolition in June 2008.[33] Four days later, on June 30, demolition crews began ripping holes in the exterior.[34] Undeterred, the conservancy continued to push its redevelopment plans, and at the end of July it reached an agreement with the DEGC. The conservancy had until March 1, 2009, to raise an estimated $15.6 million for its proposal.[35] Their plan had the guaranteed backing of architectural firm Hamilton Anderson Associates and programming firm Ripken and Associates (owned by former Baltimore Oriole Cal Ripken) and the financial backing of development firm Zachary and Associates. The plans were viable and had a realistic chance of gaining funding. By December, *Ballpark Digest* reported that the conservancy had raised $12 million towards its goal, but just a month later the overall price tag was pushed up to $27 million after the conservancy met with a contractor to receive an updated restoration estimate.[36] In late February 2009, with the deadline looming, the conservancy received an influential boost when Michigan Democratic senator Carl Levin presented it with a $3.8 million federal grant dedicated for development within the neighborhood of Corktown.[37] By this time, demolition crews had finished removing all but the contested dugout-to-dugout Navin Field configuration of Tiger Stadium. Finally, in June, the board of the DEGC voted 7–1 to tear down the remainder of the historic park, even though the conservancy had been able to raise $22 million of the now $33.4 million goal.[38] The conservancy was not notified of the meeting until after it had occurred.[39] National TV commentator Keith Olbermann labeled DEGC president and CEO George Jackson one of his "worst people in the world."[40] On June 9, 2009, demolition of the stadium resumed, and by September 20 the last remnants of the structure were gone.[41]

Navin Field

The demolition crews at Tiger Stadium tore down the structure but left the field untouched. Its infield never appeared to have been driven over by heavy demolition machinery or scarred in any way. Consequently, the field that had witnessed so much greatness still existed; the chance to walk in the footsteps of legends was still available.

Demolition of the left center field wall begins on June 30, 2008 (© Rebecca Cook).

Now it was more easily accessible. In 2010, several months after demolition crews had cleared away the last remnants of Tiger Stadium, Tom Derry, a Redford Township mailman and onetime member of the Tiger Stadium Fan Club, drove by the corner of Michigan and Trumbull and became upset. What he saw was not just another unkempt empty lot in the city of Detroit dominated by four-foot-tall grass and weeds but the field of his sporting heroes. He decided to do something about it. He returned armed with landscape equipment, bent on restoring the still recognizable field to its former state, going through several lawn mower blades in the process. Soon Derry's efforts attracted others, and one by one more and more people appeared at Michigan and Trumbull to assist with field maintenance. The Navin Field Grounds Crew was born.

Eventually chalk lines were drawn along the base paths, and bases were placed in their rightful spots; an old home plate was even unearthed from the ground where it had been buried, preserved. Soon people were not just showing up to help with the maintenance but were arriving to play pick-up games.[42] Facebook posts helped the Grounds Crew attract new supporters and pilgrimages to the site. Perhaps inspired by Derry's efforts, the Old Tiger Stadium Conservancy and Peter Comstock Riley both renewed their efforts to preserve history. While the conservancy began to create new development proposals, Riley's efforts took a different path. When the stadium had been demolished, the demolition crews spared the historic flagpole that dated to 1896—the only structure of its kind to ever exist in fair territory in a major league baseball park. Riley decided it was time for the American flag to once again fly at the corner of Michigan and Trumbull. Although soon afterwards someone removed not only the flag and its hoisting wire, but also the cleats that secured the flag, Riley was not deterred.[43] Along with local businessman Claude Greiner, he just erected another flag and attached two cleats at varying heights to ensure its security.[44] Since the flag's installation, the owner of Brooks Lumber across the street on Trumbull Avenue agreed to pay for and install a spotlight that continually highlights the flagpole.

Meanwhile, the Old Tiger Stadium Conservancy put forth another proposal for the Tiger Stadium site. This $65.3 million redevelopment plan recommended that the historic field be surrounded with a structure that would house two local nonprofits, a charter school, retail shops, and residential housing. The plan had already received the commitment of the nonprofits, The Greening of Detroit and WARM Training Center, and Cornerstone Charter Schools, when the DEGC decided to reject it in March 2011.[45] Its continuous rejections of viable well-funded proposals stood in stark contrast to its website's claim that the "DEGC has been designed to make business success in Detroit possible."[46] If this is its "mission," why was it so averse to any proposal that included preservation of the field, regardless of its economic potential? In September 2011, the DEGC rejected Chevrolet's offer to maintain the field for free and refurbish it for possible use as a site for youth baseball, feeling that would make it unattractive to prospective developers.[47] In an interview with Stephen Henderson on his Detroit Public Television show *American Black Journal*, the DEGC's George Jackson explained, "In New York, when they tore down Yankee Stadium, did they put up a Little League field or are they going to develop the land? The term is 'highest and best use.' That is what's best for the city, not for a group that has a special interest."[48] Evidently Jackson was unaware that a Little League field along with a softball field and a re-creation of Yankee Stadium's original field existed at the former site of Yankee Stadium.[49]

In February 2012, with the deadline for its $3.8 million federal earmark approaching, the Old Tiger Stadium Conservancy once again proposed a new plan for the corner of Michigan and Trumbull, this time accompanied by the political backing of Senator Levin and state senator Morris Hood III and 15 of his colleagues.[50] The plan included the full restoration of the historic field and potentially a small museum, while leftover funds would be used for improvements along Michigan Avenue. Echoing Peter Comstock Riley's proposal from 2005, the proposal also included an offer to lease the land, giving a bankrupt city a much needed revenue source.[51] According to Hood, "We're talking mainly about making sure kids have the opportunity to experience baseball.... Baseball has done great for us in the past, getting inner city kids the chance to experience baseball, to learn baseball, to play baseball on a baseball field."[52]

Postscript 2016 (Michael Betzold)[53]

The Old Tiger Stadium Conservancy's 2012 proposal went nowhere as city officials remained unresponsive. But, as Hood hoped, kids would have opportunities to play baseball at Michigan and Trumbull.

Members of Tom Derry's Navin Field Grounds Crew maintained the area with their own volunteer labor and at their own expense each summer from 2010 through 2015. The city ignored the site and their work, and the gates to the field remained open. Baseball was once again played there, but without official supervision or admission fees. The field where so many great professionals had performed in front of massive crowds now hosted amateur adult hardball teams, vintage 19th-century baseball squads, Little Leaguers, and countless impromptu pickup games. People from all over the world stopped by to play catch, run the basepaths, or just walk on the field. The throwback Navin Field was a pleasant neighborhood park for Corktown residents. It hosted birthday parties and other celebrations, including weddings. In 2014, Derry himself got married at home plate.

Michigan and Trumbull also became a memorial grounds. Derry estimated that more than 100 parties came to spread the ashes of loved ones on the field during his years as volunteer chief caretaker. Among those so honored were Tiger Stadium Fan Club members Eva Navarro and Catherine Darin, mentioned elsewhere in this volume. Peter Comstock Riley noted that all the activity "stemmed just from opening the gates. That's what always started the day at Tiger Stadium: when the gates opened, people started coming in, and the memories started. It was all about people."[54]

For six summers, opening this free public space was a unique use of an abandoned major league baseball site—and to some citizens and fans, the best possible outcome, after the demolition of the stadium. Stripped of all trappings, the baseball played there was gloriously unprofessional. But in an area of the city in which patterns of gentrification and redevelopment are leading to increased privatized space and resources, this free public access to a valuable piece of property could not possibly last.

While all the proposals for redevelopment of the site that included any significant preservation component fell on deaf ears, city officials entertained many plans for uses inconsistent with the site's history, including retail shopping and a warehouse for Detroit's Thanksgiving Day parade floats. This state of affairs reflected the official ambivalence and disinterest toward the site. That changed when a new player arrived at the Corner: the Detroit Police Athletic League. A longtime nonprofit organization hosting youth sports on playing fields and gyms throughout the city, Detroit PAL had a worthwhile mission, a solid reputation, and, most importantly, valuable connections to city government—including the ear of new mayor Mike Duggan, who as a deputy county executive in the 1990s had played a role in the Tigers' move to Comerica Park.

Civic powers quickly lined up behind a new PAL proposal to build a 2,500-seat youth stadium along with a new PAL headquarters at Michigan and Trumbull. Crucial to the project was the federal grant obtained by Carl Levin. Although about $800,000 of his grant had already been spent on various economic development projects in Corktown, $3 million remained. The Old Tiger Stadium Conservancy controlled this grant money and voted, though not unanimously, to award it to the PAL project.

The plan for the field itself was paired with a project by developer Gary Larson to build housing along Trumbull and small retail along Michigan. This economic development component knit together a scheme for the entire parcel, making the deal attractive to civic and business leaders engineering a much-ballyhooed revival of portions of the city center.

However, there proved to be one hitch. In the fall of 2015, in a community meeting in Corktown and again at City Council hearings, PAL's CEO, Tim Richey, whose favorite sport is soccer, insisted that the youth field must have an artificial surface. Publicly, Thom Linn and other conservancy leaders maintained they were surprised by this and regretted not having made their support for the project contingent on maintaining natural grass. Whether that was true or not, the OTSC was now committed to the project, and Linn said it was too late to back out.

The Navin Field Grounds Crew, the very people who had kept the site clean and thriving since demolition of the stadium was completed, never had a seat at the table as PAL, the OTSC, and city officials developed the plan. When grounds crew members and other citizens at public hearings raised objections to the artificial turf, Richey insisted grass would not hold up under the intensive programming PAL planned for the site, including football, soccer, and lacrosse, as well as baseball. This debatable position was buttressed by some outright deception. In printed "talking points" distributed at the Corktown meeting and in public remarks, Richey cited leading turf management expert John N. "Trey" Rogers of Michigan State University as agreeing that turf was necessary at the site.

But when I contacted him, Rogers made it clear he strongly opposed artificial playing surfaces and had only reluctantly endorsed PAL's plan when presented with a proposed budget that was woefully insufficient to maintain a grass field and represented a total disinterest and lack of expertise in such maintenance. With a sufficient organizational commitment, Rogers told me, a natural surface could indeed hold up to a reasonably intense schedule of sporting activity, just as grass fields anywhere do.

It was not a question of money. In fact, a synthetic surface would cost about $1 million to install and would need to be replaced about every ten years. By all available calculations, installing and properly maintaining a grass field would work out to a very similar total outlay. Though Richey agreed with this financial assessment, he continued to insist a grass field would not support PAL's intentions to program the site to the hilt. He repeatedly invoked the threat of football games in the rain tearing up the field.

City Council and its economic growth arm unanimously approved the project. One council member, Andre Spivey, even stated publicly that the racism of Walter Briggs, the Tigers' owner of more than a half-century earlier, made him opposed to preserving the field. The history of Michigan and Trumbull remained troubling for some in the city— a legacy that seemed to them more appropriate to be carpeted over than remembered for all its glories and flaws.

PAL launched a "Kids at the Corner" campaign to raise at least $12 million for the project. In February 2016, the organization held a media event to hype the campaign. At that point, contributions depended heavily on five foundations and included no major local businesses. At least one donor, the Lear Corp., pulled its support for PAL because of the artificial turf controversy.

Though there was plenty of vacant land in Detroit that would have been suitable for the PAL stadium and headquarters, at no other site was $3 million in federal grant money available. It did not seem to matter that PAL had no plans for transporting its young athletes to Michigan and Trumbull from neighborhoods around the city.[55] On April 13, 2016, a public groundbreaking ceremony was held with Senator Levin, the mayor, civic officials, and former Tiger star and Detroit native Willie Horton in attendance. At the event, PAL announced its youth stadium would be named for Horton. Just days before, it had been revealed that the city had modified its plan to lease PAL the property. Instead, the city sold the field to PAL for $1 in order to avoid a zoning snafu that could have delayed the project awhile.

Thus, 104 years after the opening game at Navin Field and 120 years after the first professional game at Bennett Park, the corner of Michigan and Trumbull was reborn as "The Willie Horton Field of Dreams," a Detroit Police Athletic League multisport facility flanked by a private housing and retail development. PAL headquarters would occupy what was the old left-field corner of Tiger Stadium.

PAL has made no commitment to any preservation activities or programs at the Corner nor to any free public access to the site. Richey occasionally spoke vaguely about a possible "Hall of Heroes" on the second floor of the PAL headquarters to teach children about various sports figures—not specifically those who played at the Corner. The new owners of the property have no experience in preservation or historical commemoration. They will enable Detroit kids in years to come to play supervised sports at Michigan and Trumbull—on an artificial surface.

NOTES

1. Among the unique aspects of Tiger Stadium's neighborhood location were the resident-owned parking lots. When the Tigers moved to Comerica Park, this revenue was taken by Ilitch-owned parking lots. The move caused a loss of revenue for some Corktown residents and gave Mike Ilitch another revenue stream unavailable at Tiger Stadium.

2. Jennifer Dixon, "A Big-League Plan Renovating Tiger Stadium the Proposal Would Add Shops, Residences and Recreation to the Structure, but Will Anyone Step Up to Pay for It?" *Detroit Free Press*, June 9, 1999.

3. Curt Guyette, "A Hole in the Heart: Corktown's Lost Field of Dreams," *Metro Times*, August 6, 2003.

4. Daniel G. Fricker, "Still No Builder for Tiger Stadium: City Hopes New Study Will Lure Seasoned Developers," *Detroit Free Press*, October 3, 2000.

5. Daniel G. Fricker, "Development Partners Offer Tiger Stadium Plan: City of Detroit Allows Firm 6 Months to Reach an Agreement on a Proposal," *Detroit Free Press*, December 1, 2001.

6. Ibid.

7. Guyette, "A Hole in the Heart."

8. Guyette reports that a similar request had been made during an earlier RFP response. At that time Senator Carl Levin offered to raise federal funds for the feasibility study, which the city declined. According to Guyette, Levin staffer Cassandra Woods stated, "We were advised that the city had a pot of money that could be used for that purpose."

9. Guyette, "A Hole in the Heart." According to records Guyette acquired through the Freedom of Information Act, although Kilpatrick's administration was alleged to have responded to Nonrahs-Sinacola's correspondence, no evidence of responses was ever found.

10. Ibid.

11. Ibid.

12. The rejected proposals included a plan by the Navin Field Consortium that suggested a return to the stadium's original Navin Field configuration. This plan would later be echoed by the Old Tiger Stadium Conservancy in its efforts to stave off the eventual 2009 final demolition of the stadium.

13. Guyette, "A Hole in the Heart." Some of the uses of the park that the Tigers sanctioned over the years included the filming of Billy Crystal's *61** in 2001 and the 2006 Bud Bowl during Super Bowl XL festivities in Detroit.

14. Ibid.

15. Ibid.

16. Ibid. Interestingly, the money the city paid the Tigers for maintenance was coming at the expense of other city landmarks. In an unrelated article in the *Metro Times* from March 9, 2005, titled, "The Tragedy of the Aquarium," Jack Lessenberry reported that Detroit's Belle Isle aquarium was in danger of closing. According to Lessenberry, the $420,000 the city annually paid to the Tigers could have kept the aquarium open and operating. It has since reopened.

17. Guyette, "A Hole in the Heart."

18. Ibid.

19. A televised report about "Ground from the Mound" and the relationship between the Tigers and A Piece of the Field, LLC, is available at http://www.youtube.com/watch?v=KRM743fyAy8.

20. Thomas is interviewed in the documentary film *Stranded at the Corner,* directed by Gary Glaser, Michigan & Trumbull, LLC, 2006.

21. Curt Guyette, "Striking Out: City Rejects Offer of Free Security, Maintenance at Tiger Stadium," *Metro Times*, March 16, 2005.

22. Ibid.

23. "Tiger Tale," *Metro Times*, March 29, 2006. As this article points out, one noteworthy exception to the two major dailies' poor coverage of proposals to reuse Tiger Stadium was *Detroit News* columnist Neil Rubin, who consistently asked probing questions about the process leading to the stadium's demolition.

24. Except for Neil Rubin, the *Detroit News* did little reporting on the issue. Although the *Detroit Free Press*, and especially business writer John Gallagher, did feature the stadium more often, most of this reporting pertained to its imminent demolition rather than the viable proposals submitted to preserve it. Almost all the stories that reported on the proposals appeared in smaller publications such as the *Metro Times* or from cities outside the Detroit area, including the *Toledo Blade* and the *Windsor Star*. Mlive.com, a statewide reporting conglomerate, also regularly featured stories regarding submitted proposals in the years prior to the stadium's demolition in 2009.

25. John Gallagher, "Demolition Set for Fall: Tiger Stadium, It's History," *Detroit Free Press*, June 16, 2006.
26. *Ibid.*
27. *Ibid.*
28. Bill Dow, interview by the author, Birmingham, Michigan, December 16, 2011.
29. "Detroit City Council Gives Group OK to Demolish Tiger Stadium," *Toledo Blade* July 27, 2007, toledoblade.com/Pro/2007/07/27/Detroit-City-Council-gives-group-OK-to-demolish-Tiger-Stadium.print (accessed on October 26, 2011).
30. *Ibid.*, and Dow, interview.
31. Dow, interview.
32. "Ernie Harwell Drops Plan to Save Large Piece of Tiger Stadium," *Toledo Blade*, September 10, 2007, toledoblade.com/Pro/2007/09/10/Ernie-Harwell-drops-plan-to-save-large-piece-of-Tiger-Stadium.print (accessed on October 26, 2011).
33. Joe Vardon, "Bottom of 9th for Detroit's Tiger Stadium, but Fans Hoping for a Rally," *Toledo Blade*, June 26, 2008, toledoblade.com/Michigan/2008/06/26/Bottom-of-9th-for-Detroit-s-Tiger-Stadium-but-fans-hoping-for-rally.print (accessed on October 26, 2011).
34. "Crews Begin Leveling Tiger Stadium," *Toledo Blade*, July 1, 2008, toledoblade.com/Pro/2008/07/01/Crews-begin-leveling-Tiger-Stadium.print (accessed on October 26, 2011).
35. "Deal Keeps Part of Tiger Stadium up," *Toledo Blade*, July 30, 2008, toledoblade.com/Pro/2008/07/30/Deal-keeps-part-of-Tiger-Stadium-up.print (accessed on October 26, 2011).
36. A $12 million figure appears in *Ballpark Digest*, December 1, 2008, ballparkdigest.com/200812011046/major-league-baseball/news/tiger-stadium; preservationists-we-have-the-money (accessed on September 26, 2011). A $27 million estimate appears in *Ballpark Digest*, "Tiger Stadium Preservation Takes Another Step Forward," January 20, 2009, ballparkdigest.com/200901201309/minor-league-baseball/news/tiger-stadium-preservation-takes-another-step-forward (accessed on September 26, 2011).
37. "Federal Money for Tiger Stadium Receives Initial Approval," *Ballpark Digest*, February 26, 2009, ballparkdigest.com/200902261475/at-the-ballpark/endangered-ballparks/federal-money-for-tiger-stadium-receives-initial-approval (accessed on September 26, 2011).
38. "Detroit Commission Votes to Tear Down Tiger Stadium," *Ballpark Digest*, June 2, 2009, ballparkdigest.com/200906021934/at-the-ballpark/endangered-ballparks/detroit-commission-votes-to-tear-down-Tiger-Stadium (accessed on September 26, 2011). It is unclear how or why the $27 million goal was increased to $33.4 million.
39. Travis R. Wright, "Save That Tiger (Stadium)," *Metro Times*, June 5, 2009. This blog entry, not available online, consists mostly of an email message to the *Metro Times* from Conservancy president Thomas Linn expressing shock that the DEGC held a meeting to vote on the demolition of Tiger Stadium without notifying him. He adds that even more troubling is DEGC's willingness to ignore the desires of college and youth teams "eager to play baseball on the restored field" and to lose $22 million the Conservancy had "secured … in federal earmarks, grants, and tax credits."
40. Nancy Kaffer, "Olbermann vs. George Jackson—Round Two!" *Crain's Detroit Business*, June 5, 2009, crainsdetroit.com/section/c?template=profile&uid=157308&plckPersonalPage=BlogViewPostplckUserId=157308&plckPostId=Blog%3a157308Post%3a93f0b138-0c58-4c01-b101-82d3b829ecb8&plckController=PersonalBlog&plckScript=personaScript&plckElementId=perso (accessed on January 1, 2012). George Jackson never responded to the author's requests for an interview.
41. Great Lakes Aerial Photos documents each stage of the Tiger Stadium demolition. See http://www.aerialpics.com/G/TigerStadiumDemo.html.
42. "Volunteers Maintaining Tiger Stadium field," *Ballpark Digest*, April 4, 2011, ballparkdigestf.com/201104043707/major-league-baseball/news/volunteer-maintaining-tiger-stadium-field (accessed on September 26, 2011).
43. Peter Comstock Riley, interview by the author, Detroit, Michigan, December 27, 2011.
44. Greiner and Tom Derry continued to purchase new flags and maintain the flagpole. In an email communication (November 22, 2014), Derry credited Greiner as being "the main man behind the flag pole."
45. "Detroit Rejects Redevelopment Plan for Tiger Stadium Site," *Ballpark Digest*, March 28, 2011, ballparkdigest.com/201103283681/at-the-ballpark/endangered-ballparks/detroit-rejects-redevelopment-for-tiger-stadium-site (accessed on September 26, 2011.
46. Detroit Economic Development Corporation, degc.org/ (accessed on April 19, 2011).
47. See Jonathan Oosting, "Detroit Balks at Chevrolet Offer to Rehab Baseball Field at Old Tiger Stadium Site," September 14, 2011, blog.mlive.com/new/detroitimpact/print.html?entry=/2011/09/Detroit_balks_at_chevrolet_off.html (accessed on September 30, 2011). See also "Detroit Rejects Tiger Stadium Fix-Up Offer," MYFoxDetroit.com, September 15, 2011, myfoxdetroit.com/dpp/news/local/detroit-rejects-tiger-stadium-field-fix-up-offer-20110915-mr (accessed on October 1, 2011).
48. George Jackson, interviewed by Stephen Henderson on *American Black Journal*, Detroit Public Television, September 25, 2011.
49. City of New York Parks and Recreation, "The Yankee Stadium Park Redevelopment Project," nycgovparks.org/park-features/future-parks/yankee-stadium-redevelopment (accessed on March 16, 2012).

50. Jonathan Oosting, "New Hopes for Old Tiger Stadium Site: Detroit Delegation Backs Proposal for Youth Facility," February 3, 2012, mlive.com/news/detroit/index.ssf/2012/02/new_hopes_for_old_tiger_stadiu.html (accessed on March 15, 2012).

51. *Ibid.*

52. *Ibid.*

53. This postscript is based on reporting I did that is reflected in the following articles: "The Plan for Detroit's Former Tiger Stadium Ignores History and Potentially Safety," *The Nation*, February 11, 2016, http://www.thenation.com/article/the-plan-for-detroits-former-tiger-stadium-ignores-history-and-potentially-safety/; "Detroit City Council Questions Plan to Put Artificial Turf at Old Tiger Stadium Site," *Deadline Detroit*, November 13, 2015, http://www.deadlinedetroit.com/articles/13655; "The Turf War at the Corner of Michigan and Trumbull," *Deadline Detroit*, November 21, 2015, http://www.deadlinedetroit.com/articles/13714; "The Irony Behind the Push for Artificial Turf at Old Tiger Stadium," *Deadline Detroit*, November 24, 2015, http://www.deadlinedetroit.com/articles/13724; "'Phony' Case Made for Artificial Turf at Old Tiger Stadium Field," *Motor City Muckraker*, December 7, 2015, "Reporter Removed for Asking, 'Why Artificial Turf at Tiger Stadium Site?'" *Motor City Muckraker*, February 15, 2016; "How to Prevent 'Bullheaded Plan' to Carpet Tiger Stadium Site with Artificial Turf," *Motor City Muckraker*, February 20, 2016; "PAL Lobbyist: Some Cops Want to Padlock Tiger Stadium Field Over Rumors of a Protest," *Motor City Muckraker*, April 1, 2016; "With No Public Input, City Sells Historic Tiger Stadium Field for Just $1," *Motor City Muckraker*, April 13, 2016; all at http://motorcitymuckraker.com/author/mibetzold/.

54. Peter Comstock Riley, interviewed by Rebecca Long, Detroit, Michigan, December 27, 2011.

55. In a March 31, 2016, email to me, Richey wrote:

We understand transportation can be challenging and, therefore, PAL works hard to program in every neighborhood. That being said, PAL has not historically provided any transportation for any programs yet hundreds of kids and families are able to get to PAL practices and games throughout the City every day much like sports programs in other communities—by carpooling and looking out for each other. Still PAL, along with many service providers in Detroit, continues to think of affordable ways to offer transportation for after-school programming.

Part II. Memories

Tiger Stadium Souvenirs

Bill Dow

These pieces are based on interviews I conducted between 2000 and 2011. Stories featuring these interviews were published in the Detroit Free Press *and the* Detroit Athletic Company's *sports blog between 2009 and 2013. Also, I have included some of my personal reminiscences.*

Rip Collins and Hank Greenberg

Standing outside of the player's parking lot at Navin Field in the spring of 1934, 14-year-old Charlie Collins held out an official American League ball that he wanted autographed by his hero, the Tigers' slugging first baseman Hank Greenberg. His heart pounding, the fair-haired Collins politely asked Greenberg to autograph the ball as the slugger walked out of the park with teammate Eldon Auker. A few years ago, Charles "Rip" Collins remembered Greenberg's reaction.

"Hank took that sucker and threw it straight down Plum Street," Collins recalled. "God, it just broke my heart. I thought Greenberg was supposed to be a nice guy. I chased the ball down, and it was all scuffed up. When I walked back, he said, 'Hey Whitey, I'm really sorry, things haven't been going so well. Come back here tomorrow, and I'll get you another ball and autograph it.'"

Although for one horrific moment his hero had clay feet, the incident soon led to a unique opportunity and a budding friendship. When Collins returned the next day, Greenberg gave him an autographed ball and an offer he couldn't refuse. "How would you like to shag balls for me in batting practice?" he asked the wide-eyed youngster.

"As you can imagine, it was quite a thrill," Collins said. "Hank paid me and some other neighborhood kids a dollar to shag balls. Every home stand, Hank would be out there by himself for a couple of hours taking his own batting practice. He would hit those balls a mile high. I also found out the hard way how a line drive can really curve at the last minute. Sometimes I would also get him a sandwich or take his suits to Sam the Tailor on Trumbull Avenue."

Collins grew up with his grandmother Genevieve Baker at 2834 National (now Cochrane). From the front lawn, he could see flags flying high atop the roof of Navin Field's left field pavilion.

"My grandmother was a huge Tiger fan who was always glued to the radio listening to Ty Tyson's play-by-play. Sometimes Hank would drop me off at the house in his Silver Hudson Terraplane and talk with her. Believe me, it was her moment in the sun," Collins said. "For years, he would send us a Christmas card."

Greenberg's kindness and interest in the neighborhood kid never wavered. He soon found other employment at the ballpark for Collins, who recalls, "He took me in to see the clubhouse manager, and said, 'Take care of Whitey for me, OK?'"

In the summer of 1934, and for part of the 1935 season, as Mickey Cochrane's Bengals were capturing two American League titles, Collins served as a batboy and clubhouse assistant for Tiger opponents.

"It was really something to be around players like Lou Gehrig and Jimmie Foxx," Collins said. "But I'll never forget once trying to avoid being hit with a foul ball shot at the dugout. Right in front of Connie Mack and the A's, I stepped into the water bucket and took quite a ribbing from the bench jockeys."

To top off his magical summer, Collins served as the batboy in the 1934 World Series for the St. Louis Cardinals, the "Gas House Gang." When St. Louis won the seventh game at Navin Field, the 14-year-old ran for cover. "I got out of that locker room as quick as I could when they started celebrating. They were a wild bunch," he says.

In the middle of the '35 season, Collins lost his position when the Tigers hired another kid to take his place. "I told Hank what happened, and he still went to bat for me. But he later said, 'The chief [Cochrane] has a friend that wants his kid in there. If it was anybody but Mickey I could straighten this out.'" As a consolation, Greenberg would often give Collins a ticket in section 17 behind home plate, a program, a soda, and a box of popcorn.

Years later, Collins once again found himself in the locker rooms at Tiger Stadium. After serving in the Marine Corps in World War II and Korea, Collins returned to Detroit as a fireman and soon found a part-time job at Michigan and Trumbull. From 1952 to 1972, Collins served as the assistant equipment manager for the Detroit Lions. In 1975, he became the clubhouse manager in the visitor's locker room at Tiger Stadium, the same spot where he had worked 40 years earlier as a young batboy. He held the job until 1992.

Virgil Trucks Recalls His 1952 No-Hitter at Briggs Stadium

In 1952, Tiger fireballer Virgil Trucks threw two no-hitters for the Tigers. On May 15, the team was mired in the basement, and a crowd of only 2,215 showed up at Briggs Stadium to see 33-year-old Trucks face the Senators.

"It seems like hundreds of people have told me they were there, but I know better, because the park was nearly empty," Trucks said. "We were playing so badly that nobody wanted to see us play." But the lucky diehard fans in attendance were treated to one of the most dramatic no-hit games in history as Trucks was locked in a pitcher's duel with Washington's Bob Porterfield.

"Virgil was throwing absolute bullets," recalled George Kell, the Hall of Fame third baseman. "He may have been as fast as Bob Feller. But as a fielder, protecting a no-hitter was absolutely nerve-racking. You make up your mind that you're going to get a glove on any ball if you can. And of course it's an unspoken rule that you never talk about it."

With two outs in the bottom of the ninth, and no score, Tiger slugger Vic Wertz stepped up to the plate. On the first pitch, Wertz belted the ball into the far reaches of Briggs Stadium's right field upper deck to win the game.

"I immediately jumped up in that small dugout and bumped my head on the ceiling," Trucks said. "I didn't draw blood, but I sure saw some stars." The dazed pitcher ran onto the field and was the first to greet Wertz at home plate.

"Believe me, it was a great relief to see Victor hit that one out," Kell said. "After the way Virgil pitched, you just wanted to get it over with." Trucks had someone else to thank. Prior to the game, Trucks noticed that his spikes had shrunk and were pinching his feet. Art Houtteman told Trucks he could borrow a pair of his, the same ones Houtteman wore earlier that year when his own no-hitter was lost with two out in the ninth. "They fit perfectly for me the rest of the year," Trucks said. "Art kept trying to get 'em back, but I wouldn't do it."

Three months later, on August 25 in Yankee Stadium, Trucks repeated his magic. Despite his two no-hitters, Trucks ended his season with a 5–19 record, thanks in large part to the team's anemic hitting. Remarkably, in his five victories, Trucks yielded only nine hits. The Tigers finished in last place for their first time in their history with a 50–104 record.

16-Year-Old Willie Horton Hits the Briggs Stadium Roof

There have been a number of historic homers hit at Michigan and Trumbull: Babe Ruth's 700th homer, Ted Williams' shot that won the 1941 All-Star Game in the bottom of the ninth, Reggie Jackson's 1971 All-Star Game homer off a light standard, and Kirk Gibson's 1984 World Series blast off Goose Gossage. Yet one of the most remarkable occurred on June 9, 1959, in the Detroit public high school championship game between Cass Tech and Northwestern at Briggs Stadium.

In the first inning, Northwestern catcher William Horton, a stocky 16-year-old sophomore from the Jeffries Projects, drove a ball that landed on the stadium's right center field roof before it struck a light standard and fell into the stands. It was estimated to have traveled 450 feet.

Years later, Horton recalled the home run in his 2004 autobiography, *The People's Champion, Willie Horton*: "The ball exploded off my bat and it kind of shocked me. I had never hit a ball quite that hard before. I just stood there and the umpire had to tell me to run. To be honest, not many people in the stands applauded my blast because it was primarily Cass Tech supporters in the early innings. The principal at Northwestern wouldn't let students out of school early to see the game and our fans didn't show up until the middle innings."

Northwestern ended up winning the championship that day, 13–10, as Horton also had a double, three runs scored, and three RBI. However, the 16-year-old's moon shot became the talk of the town.

Two years later Horton signed with the Tigers. However, he was disappointed when the team decided to convert him from a catcher to an outfielder. The reason? The club had signed a catcher named Bill Freehan out of the University of Michigan. Freehan's signing caused another catcher, Gates Brown, to be converted to the outfield as well.

Willie Horton's Northwestern teammates included future American League batting champion Alex Johnson and Matt Snorton, who would later play football at Michigan State and for the Denver Broncos.

Editors' Note: See John Pastier's comments on Horton's home run in "Longevity and Adaptability: Tiger Stadium's Evolution, Architecture, Functionality, Structure, and Urban Context" earlier in this volume.

Rocky Colavito and Willie Horton

In the 1960s, the Tigers were blessed with two slugging left fielders who brought fans to their feet when they blasted home runs into the left field stands at Tiger Stadium. Yet many are unaware of the close connection between Rocky Colavito and Willie Horton.

In one of baseball's most famous trades, just prior to the 1960 season, 1959 AL home run champion Rocky Colavito was traded from Cleveland to Detroit for fan favorite Harvey Kuenn, the 1959 AL batting champion. From 1960 through 1963, Colavito smacked 139 home runs for the Tigers before being traded to Kansas City in a multiplayer deal prior to the '64 campaign. Colavito's best season was 1961, when he hit 45 home runs and had 140 RBIs as the Tigers, led also by AL batting champion Norm Cash and perennial All-Star Al Kaline, battled the Yankees for the pennant until September. (Colavito and Cash had more total RBIs in 1961 than Roger Maris and Mickey Mantle, even though Maris hit his 61 home runs that year and Mantle slugged 54).

The man who replaced Colavito in left field was Horton, a Detroit sandlot star who, as one of the American League's premier power hitters, became a permanent fixture in the Tiger lineup for more than a decade. From 1965 through 1968, Horton hit 111 homers, 36 of them in the Tigers' World Series championship season of 1968. Willie Horton shared this story about his first encounter with Rocky Colavito.

"He probably doesn't remember this, but when I was in junior high, a buddy and me were stopped by security at Briggs Stadium after we had once again snuck in the ballpark. Rocky had just walked off Cleveland's bus and saw what happened. He took us over to the Tigers' clubhouse manager, John Hand, and asked him if he would give us a job working in the clubhouse, and sure enough we got the job. From that day on, Rocky was my hero. I would imitate his batting stance in a mirror, pointing my bat like he did, trying to get his stroke. Later, when he came to the Tigers, he took me under his wing when I joined the team and helped me become a major leaguer. He also told me that I would one day take over from him in left field. I will never forget what he did for me."

Collecting Player Autographs at Tiger Stadium

I fondly recall getting autographs as a kid at Tiger Stadium. I would occasionally get them from Tiger players as they walked from the locker room to the player parking lot or from opposing players as they stepped onto their bus on Michigan Avenue. This is, of course, when players were much more accessible and before they charged money for autographs at memorabilia shows.

What the allure was I still am not sure, but perhaps it was just an excuse to get closer to the players, even if it was for all of 15 seconds. Some, of course, were bothered by it and would blow you off, while others were gracious and friendly. I remember Tiger pitcher Joe Sparma saying to me, "Now why would you want my autograph?" and then walking right past me. But then there was George Kell, who I saw walking in the concourse, who could not have been nicer, just as you would expect.

Rocky Colavito had a reputation for signing for the kids after every game, home or away, and I asked him about it in a recent interview. "As a kid I would try to get autographs outside of Yankee Stadium, and I remembered not only how bad I felt when a player wouldn't sign for me but also the time I didn't want to wash my hair after Charlie Keller patted me on the head," he says. "My wife knew I wouldn't be home until a couple of hours after the game, because I would tell the kids to line up in a straight line, not to take cuts or push, and that I would sign for all of them."

I remember a story of a kid who asked Alan Trammell to sign an autograph outside of the ballpark, but the pen had run out of ink. Trammell told the upset fan to hold on as he went back inside the stadium to find a pen.

Jose Feliciano's Rendition of the National Anthem

Before the '68 World Series began, Tiger management asked announcer Ernie Harwell, a songwriter himself, to pick the singers to do the national anthem before games

First baseman Tony Clark signs autographs, 1999 (© Rebecca Cook).

three, four, and five. Harwell picked Margaret Whiting and Marvin Gaye for the first two Tiger series home games and for Game Five chose Jose Feliciano, a Latin guitarist/singer who that year scored a hit with his version of the Doors' "Light My Fire."

Standing in deep center field in front of the Merle Alvey Band (which did not play during the anthem), Feliciano performed his highly stylized version of "The Star Spangled Banner." When he was done, there was polite applause accentuated by loud booing. Meanwhile, the switchboard at NBC lit up like a Christmas tree as people called in and complained that they were offended by Feliciano's version.

Feliciano recently shared his thoughts about that World Series performance at Tiger Stadium: "It did surprise me, but I didn't give it any thought until Tony Kubek [the NBC announcer] asked me if I had known what I had just done. He said a lot of complaints had been coming in from war veterans and the like, and people wanted to deport me. But how do you do that? I am a citizen of the United States. I certainly didn't mean any harm. It was an innocent thing for me. I didn't do it for the desire of making noise. I was just interpreting the anthem for the ball game."

Although Feliciano would later release the actual recording of his Tiger Stadium effort, radio stations stopped playing his music, at least until 1970, when his Christmas hit "Feliz Navidad" was released. But his interpretation of the national anthem opened the doors for interpretations by other artists. When we listen to Feliciano's beautiful version today, we wonder why people got so upset.

Favorite 1960s Tiger Stadium Souvenirs

One of the all-time great Tiger Stadium souvenirs from the 1960s was the cardboard megaphone popcorn holder with a handle on it. When you were done stuffing yourself with the popcorn and nearly cracking your teeth munching on the kernels, you could scream into that cardboard megaphone and raise some hell. And I did: "Come on Willie, hit a homer! Pepitone, you're a bum!"

But that simple popcorn holder had still another use. After the ball game, when you were done eating your popcorn and tired of yelling into the megaphone, you could stand outside the Tiger locker room (until security said, "Time to go home, kid") or stand on the sidewalk at Michigan and Trumbull as the players pulled out of their parking lot and ask them to sign the popcorn holder. On the back of the holder was a small white box that said "autographs."

Another favorite souvenir in the 1960s was the "Detroit Tigers Picture Pack of 12 Star Players." It cost 25¢. If you didn't buy it at the ballpark, you could send the 25¢ to Detroit Sportservice Inc. at Tiger Stadium. The black-and-white five-by-seven photos fit into a nice window envelope and typically the displayed image would be either Al Kaline or Norm Cash. I still have a photo pack that contains the somewhat wrinkled images of Kaline, Cash, Rocky Colavito, Billy Bruton, Jake Wood, Frank Lary, Don Mossi, Eddie Yost, Steve Boros, Chico Fernandez, Charlie Maxwell, and manager Bob Scheffing.

Some kids would tack them to their bedroom bulletin board. But I liked to keep them in the envelope. When I would listen to Ernie Harwell on the radio, I would sometimes pull out the photo of the player who was at bat, stare at it, and pray he would hit a home run.

Al Kaline Day

When Al Kaline signed his 1970 contract for $90,000, the club announced that August 2 would be "Al Kaline Day." It was the first commemoration for an active Tiger player in three decades, since a day in 1940 for Charlie Gehringer. Kaline, still four seasons from retiring in his 18th season, had been idolized by Tiger fans ever since in 1955 he became the youngest American League batting champion in history at age 20.

On his day in the sun, 44,112 fans came to see my hero honored. I remember looking down and seeing Kaline and his family circle the field in a chauffeur-driven luxury convertible as the fans gave Al a standing ovation. Among those honoring Kaline that day were baseball commissioner Bowie Kuhn, American League president Joe Cronin, Governor William Milliken, Detroit mayor Roman Gribbs, hockey legend Gordie Howe, and the other half of the "KK Boys" of the 1950s, Harvey Kuenn. Harmon Killebrew from the visiting Minnesota Twins paid tribute, and singer Mel Torme sang "Thanks for the Memories" with adapted lyrics. Tiger owner John Fetzer announced that Cherry Street was being officially renamed "Kaline Drive."

Kaline wept as he thanked the fans: "I can still remember back to June 1953, and I can honestly say I thank God I chose to play for the team here in Detroit.... I will always remember this day, and I will always remember you, the fans, and the support you have given me, and I say that from the bottom of my heart."

Ten years later, Kaline was once again honored at Tiger Stadium. Just a few days following his induction into the National Baseball Hall of Fame, during pregame ceremonies, Kaline's number six became the first Detroit Tiger number ever retired.

Reggie Jackson and the 1971 All-Star Game Home Run Barrage

The last All-Star Game played at Tiger Stadium will always be remembered for the incredible home run hit by Oakland's Reggie Jackson, along with dingers slammed by five other Hall of Famers: Johnny Bench, Frank Robinson, Roberto Clemente, Harmon Killebrew, and Hank Aaron. Some consider it the greatest All-Star game ever.

The rosters had 21 future Hall of Famers, but hometown heroes Al Kaline, Norm Cash, Bill Freehan, and Mickey Lolich drew the loudest ovations from the sold-out crowd of 53,559 on July 13, 1971.

And although Detroit baseball fans were especially excited about seeing legendary National League superstars Willie Mays, Hank Aaron, and Roberto Clemente swing for the inviting fences at Tiger Stadium, they were also anxious to see the American League end its streak of nine consecutive losses.

With a game-time temperature of 85 degrees and a wind to right field that gusted up to 35 MPH, Tiger catcher Bill Freehan, appearing in the eighth of his eventual 11 All-Star Games, anticipated a slugfest.

"During batting practice you knew Tiger Stadium was going to take a beating," Freehan told me in a 2001 interview. "With the conditions and those big hitters, the balls were just flying to the far reaches of the upper deck. You did not want to be a pitcher that night." As a youngster from Royal Oak, Freehan had attended the 1951 All-Star Game.

The National League fireworks started in the second inning when Johnny Bench drilled a Vida Blue serving into the right-center field bleachers to take a 2–0 lead. In the third inning, Hank Aaron hit an opposite-field homer to right, giving pitcher Dock Ellis a 3–0 cushion.

But in the bottom of the stanza, the American League struck back as 25-year-old Oakland slugger Reggie Jackson hit the game's signature blast, a two-run blow that is still talked about today reverentially by those who personally witnessed it along with the 60 million NBC-TV viewers.

With a 1–2 count, Jackson choked up on his Adirondack and rocketed the ball into the light transformer on the roof in right center before it bounced back onto the field. It was estimated to have traveled 520 feet when its flight was interrupted. "All I can say is that ball had places to go," said Jackson.

Al Kaline and Sparky Anderson, the National League's manager, were awestruck by Jackson's blast. "It was one of the most amazing home runs," Kaline said years later. "It wasn't even at its peak when it hit the transformer." Added Anderson, "For me that's the hardest [hit] home run I've ever seen."

In a 2008 *Detroit News* article, Lynn Henning reported that a Wayne State University study conducted in the 1970s concluded that Jackson's ball would have traveled an estimated 650 feet had it not hit the light tower.

The Death of Chuck Hughes

It remains the greatest tragedy to have ever occurred during an NFL game. On October 24, 1971, at Tiger Stadium, Detroit Lions wide receiver Chuck Hughes died on the field of a fatal heart attack with just over a minute to play in a game that would be won by the Bears, 28–23.

The score was meaningless.

Life suddenly seemed more precious, especially to the stunned crowd of 54,418 fans, the players, and a press corps that would struggle to find the right words to describe what had happened. The 28-year-old Texan had just run a pass route on a play that turned into an incomplete pass intended for Lions tight end Charlie Sanders. As he jogged back to the huddle, Hughes suddenly fell face first on the Bears' 15-yard line. Everyone knew something was wrong when the Bears' vicious middle linebacker Dick Butkus started frantically waving his hands to the Detroit sideline signaling for help. Trainer Kent Falb and team physicians Edward Guise and Richard Thompson ran onto the field and were soon joined by a Lions fan who jumped out of the stands, Dr. Eugene Boyle, an anesthesiologist from Grosse Pointe.

A stadium had never been silenced so quickly. Witnesses said you could hear a pin drop, and at least one has said he is still haunted by the sound of the ambulance siren as it pulled away from the eerily quiet ballpark. Numerous attempts to resuscitate Hughes were made for up to an hour on the field, in the ambulance, and at Henry Ford Hospital. Hughes was officially pronounced dead at 5:41 p.m., but reports circulated that he had actually died when he hit the turf.

An autopsy revealed that Hughes, the father of a 23-month-old son, had arteriosclerosis, an abnormal thickening of the artery walls. Just a few weeks earlier at an exhibition game, he had complained of chest pains but was cleared to play. (His widow subsequently filed a $21.5 million malpractice lawsuit against Henry Ford Hospital for failing to diagnose the problem six weeks earlier. The case settled in 1974 for an undisclosed amount.)

Following the funeral attended by the entire team in San Antonio, Texas, the Lions wore a black armband on their left sleeves for the remainder of the season. At the next game, an ABC Monday night contest at Green Bay's Lambeau Field, a moment of silence was held in his memory. In his honor, the Lions retired Hughes's number 85, and annually they give an award in his name to the team's most improved player.

The Lions' Last Game at Tiger Stadium

On Thanksgiving Day 1974, the era of Lions football outdoors ended when the team lost to Denver, 31–27, at Tiger Stadium. It was the last Detroit Lions game ever played at the ballpark. The following year the club moved to the Pontiac Silverdome.

In front of a crowd of 51,157, with temperatures in the low 30s and snow flurries, the Lions were fighting for a wild-card playoff spot. In the game, Steve Owens, the 1969 Heisman Trophy winner, suffered a career-ending injury when his cleats got stuck in the turf and he was hit just before crossing the goal line. "It was frustrating," recalled Owens, "because as it turns out, we didn't get any points from that run."

"I left a big part of me at Tiger Stadium," said Owens. "I really enjoyed playing there. The Detroit fans were always great to me." It was an unhappy conclusion to the Lions' 34 years at the stadium, which included the glory days in the 1950s when the club won three National Football League championships. Despite the rich history, there was little fanfare about the last pro football game at Tiger Stadium.

"There wasn't a great deal of emotion about it being the last game there, because we were focused on winning and making the playoffs," said Lions Hall of Famer Lem Barney years later. "I really enjoyed the Tiger Stadium era. You can't replace the spirit of the great players who played there. From time to time I used to drive by Tiger Stadium to just look at it. I preferred playing outdoors with the natural aesthetics. Nothing can replace natural grass, a much more forgiving surface. With the Silverdome, it was more of a corporate scenario, and we kind of lost the family mystique of Tiger Stadium."

Kirk Gibson's 1984 World Series Heroics at Tiger Stadium

At 7:41 p.m. on October 14, 1984, San Diego's Tony Gwynn hit a shallow fly ball down the left field line at Tiger Stadium as Detroit left fielder Larry Herndon raced in with his wide eyes focused on the prize. Beloved Tiger announcer Ernie Harwell barked into his WJR microphone: "Here comes Herndon. He's got it! And the Tigers are the champions of 1984!"

As a light rain started to fall, delirious fans stormed the field to celebrate an 8–4 victory, thanks to hometown hero Kirk Gibson's aggressive baserunning and dramatic eighth-inning three-run bomb, his second homer of the game. While capturing the franchise's fourth World Series championship, the Tigers joined the famous 1927 New York Yankees to become only the second team to be in first place wire-to-wire through the regular season and win a fall classic. In addition, manager Sparky Anderson became the first manager to win World Series championships in both leagues.

After finishing the regular season 15 games ahead of second-place Toronto and with a 104–58 record, the most victories in Tiger history, Detroit swept the Kansas City Royals in three games in the ALCS to capture the American League title.

In recognition of his .417 playoff batting average and defensive plays, Kirk Gibson was named the ALCS MVP. He also could have been named the most pleasant surprise of 1984. In what became his breakout year, Gibson batted .282 with 91 RBI, 27 home runs, and 29 stolen bases. The Detroit area native and former Michigan State All-American receiver, who bypassed an NFL career for baseball, had graced the cover of *Sports Illustrated* in 1980 as a promising rookie. But Gibson had largely been a disappointment defensively and at the plate except for occasionally coming through with clutch hits. In 1983 he batted a mere .227, was an inhabitant of Sparky's "doghouse," and was at the lowest point of his young career.

In the off season, Gibson attended Seattle's Pacific Institute, where, over a four-day period, he learned the technique of "affirmation and visualization," a skill that he would later utilize in hitting two of the most famous home runs in World Series history.

Only once had the Tigers won a World Series at the corner of Michigan and Trumbull, and that had occurred 49 years earlier when, in the bottom of the ninth inning, Tiger manager and catcher Mickey Cochrane raced across home plate on Goose Goslin's single as the Tigers captured their first title.

With 51,901 lucky fans on hand and millions of viewers watching the NBC telecast by Vin Scully and Joe Garagiola, in the bottom of the first inning Gibson launched a rocket into the right field upper deck. Gibson said, "At Tiger Stadium as a left-handed hitter you're trying to pull the ball early in the count and find something in your happy zone in the inner part of the plate. It was a breaking ball, and I just got on it."

In the top of the eighth, the Padres battled back when Kurt Bevacqua hit a solo homer off Willie Hernandez to make it a narrow 5–4 Detroit lead. In the bottom of the eighth, Gossage walked Marty Castillo, who advanced to second on Lou Whitaker's bunt when Gary Templeton failed to cover second base. Trammell's sacrifice bunt then sent the runners to second and third with one out and Kirk Gibson stepping to the plate.

What followed was the signature moment of the '84 World Series and the biggest blunder of the Hall of Fame careers of Goose Gossage and Dick Williams. With first base open, conventional baseball wisdom called for an intentional walk to set up a double play or at least a possible force-out at the plate.

Sparky Anderson recalled what happened next. "I always watched the other manager because I wanted to see what he was going to do. I saw Dick [Williams] say 'four,' meaning walk him. But Gossage was such a competitor and had struck out Gibson so many times, Goose thought he could just get him again."

When Gossage shook off his manager's sign, Williams walked to the mound to confer with his pitcher. Television viewers could read the pitcher's lips, "Let's go after him." "When Dick walked back to the dugout, I screamed to Gibby, 'He don't want to walk you,'" said Anderson. "Let me tell you, Gibby will not allow you to embarrass him. That ain't going to happen. You're going to have problems on your hands."

For Kirk Gibson, standing on baseball's biggest stage with all the surrounding drama was the only place he wanted to be on that foggy, cool night: "Gossage had owned me, and he struck me out in my first major league at bat," said Gibson. "He threw hard, I swung hard, and he was just one of those guys who gave me trouble. I knew he thought he could strike me out again. I flashed ten fingers and yelled back to Sparky, 'Ten bucks they pitch to me, and I crank it.'"

"I couldn't stand there in the box when they were talking and think he's going to strike me out. I had to reverse that thought, so I visualized upper deck. It was right there. Come on, I was thinkin,' you've had your success against me and you've had your last laugh. The fact that he wouldn't walk me was even more challenging. I'm thinking I'm going to get you when it counts, and it counts right now. That was my thought process."

As Gossage stared in at Gibson, the game's ace reliever reared back and threw an outside fastball for ball one as the electrified crowd buzzed. On his second delivery, Gibson's eyes lit up on another fastball that he sent deep into the night and the right field upper deck, just as he pictured it.

In the ninth, Willie Hernandez shut down the Padres for good to secure an 8–4 victory, the Tigers' fourth World Series, and the end of a magical season. *Detroit Free Press* writer Bill McGraw said of Gibson's heroics, "He can always look back on what he did in the final game to win the World Series for his hometown team. He fulfilled the fantasy of every baseball playing 12-year-old kid in the world."

Fans seek autographs from shortstop Deivi Cruz, 1999 (© Rebecca Cook).

Tiger Stadium in Literature

Michael P. Gruber

From 1896 until 1999, the site at Michigan and Trumbull hosted professional baseball games, serving as home field for the Detroit Tigers. For some writers, the classic ballpark built on the site stood as an enduring symbol of stability, one of the most identifiable landmarks in a city profoundly affected by the major social, political, and economic upheavals of 20th-century life, and its loss would have been inconceivable. For others, the stadium's tie to the past and precarious hold on the present intensified its significance. In these works of fiction, creative nonfiction, and poetry, Tiger Stadium is a place of ritual and return, history and memory, a space with almost sacramental associations.

In its cameo appearances in fiction by Loren D. Estleman and Harold Livingston, the ballpark often receives the fleeting attention appropriate to an indelible feature of the cityscape, something taken as so fundamentally part of Detroit that the mere mention of it locks the setting in place.[1] Tiger Stadium is viewed as such a fact of life in Detroit that an arson conspiracy to destroy it comes to represent all that is evil in the fictional world of Duffy House, hard-boiled narrator of Crabbe Evers' *Tigers Burning*.[2]

For poet Philip Levine, too, Tiger Stadium is a Detroit fixture. In "A Walk with Tom Jefferson," the "gray conning towers / of the ballpark" evoke the same strength and durability his speaker remembers seeing during World War II

>   at a railroad crossing
>   near Joy Road
>   as the Sherman tanks passed
>   two to a flat-bed car,
>   on their way to a war

in Europe or the Pacific, shipped from a city that mass-produced tanks, if not submarines, as part of an American arsenal for democracy. Forty years later, presumably in the Tigers' championship season of 1984, urban survivors like Tom Jefferson, with a tenuous hold on the precarious streets of the city, seem to anchor a portion of their lives fast to the stadium. After all

>   During baseball season
>   the neighborhood's a thriving
>   business for anyone
>   who can make change
>   and a cardboard sign
>   that reads "Parking $3."

This was especially true in 1984 when 2.7 million fans attended games; the speaker muses about watching "the light rise / from the great bowl / of the stadium" with "50,000 / pulling at the night / air for one last scream."³

The ballpark's exterior is so familiar—and in some ways so unremarkable—that most native Detroit writers do not bother to describe it. But to Donald Hall, who lived in Ann Arbor from 1957 to 1975, the "old green and gray, iron and concrete fort" is worthy of note. In "Fathers Playing Catch with Sons," he compares the stadium to "an old grocer who wears a straw hat and a blue necktie and is frail but don't you ever mention it." Then he takes us inside:

Philip Levine at Marygrove College in 2001 (Marygrove College).

> As we approach at night, the sky lights up like a cool dawn. We enter the awkward, homemade-looking, cubist structure, wind through the heavy weaving of its nest, and swing up a dark corridor to the splendid green summer of the field.
>
> Balls arch softly from the fungoes, and the fly-shaggers arch them back toward home plate. Batting practice. Infield practice. Pepper. The pitchers loosening up between the dugout and the bullpen. We always get there early. We settle in, breathe quietly the air of baseball, and let the night begin the old rituals again.

For Hall, Tiger Stadium is "the old world ... like baseball is. It's Hygrade Ball-Park Franks, the smell of fat and mustard, popcorn and spilled beer."⁴

In "Like Colavito," Jan Mordenski writes of the stability an eight-year-old girl instinctively felt while with her father at Tiger Stadium in the early 1960s, when so many city neighborhoods underwent unusually rapid racial changeovers. In less pernicious changes, Briggs Stadium became Tiger Stadium and home run champ Rocky Colavito was acquired in a blockbuster trade from the Cleveland Indians for batting champ Harvey Kuenn. Mordenski writes, "Change was in the air in a city that negotiated its way into and through the Sixties. / 'Tiger' Stadium just made sense" then, for many reasons. Chalk lines marking foul territory from fair were permanent and non-negotiable, overseen by umpires. Ballplayers like Colavito digging in at home plate, even when transplanted from a place like Cleveland, seemed to put

> down roots, all the more important when
> things were changing, and nobody knew that better
> that year than an eight-year-old poised on the
> right-field line, bundled up against the winds
> in an Am. League jacket who, dusting the salt
> from the wounds of her hands, waited, crouched forward,
> stretching her glove to catch whatever time
> was going to toss her.⁵

The ballpark informs perhaps no poet's work more than that of Jim Daniels. Tiger Stadium remains for him every bit as stolid, and solid, a fixture in Detroit life as the one fan in "The Fat Man at the Ballgame" who always "stands behind the last row of general admission": "Every game ... back there / keeping score"—its abundant reasonably priced seating also affords common ground of sorts. People of all ages, sizes, and sexes—all colors, incomes, and persuasions—rub up against each other in democratic proximity, even intimacy. Where else, Daniels seems to ask in the same poem (even if his speaker never takes up his wife's suggestion to "just talk to him sometime"), can the so-called "fattest man in the world" inspire another "general admission man" like the speaker to claim him as "my pal" and to remind himself that

> What takes him here each night
> is what takes me here—we've all got
> a little weight to lose.
> I haven't been keeping score,
> But I know I should.
>
> We're both fans of the game.[6]

This grass diamond open to the skies both day and night has occasionally provided everybody with a green and welcome respite from the city's summertime heat and its sometimes hotter streets. In "Time, Temperature," a poem that explores the racial divide between Detroit and its suburbs, another Daniels speaker can find shared relief in an "open fire hydrant in hot August / after an afternoon game at Tiger Stadium" with a "young black kid, maybe six, ... dancing / in his underwear in the cool spray." Such relief, he knows, must sound "naïve," coming as it does after the roar of white voices, raw and racist and rage-filled, that he has remembered hearing in the searing decades of antagonism following the 1967 riots. Still, the common grounds of the stadium and its immediate surrounding streetscape do emphasize for this Daniels speaker that "we dance under the same sun / and there is room enough for both of us / in the spray on Rosa Parks Boulevard." After all, the "one big sun" will take us all, not out to but out of the (ball)game, will "take us all / in its own good time."[7]

Tiger Stadium itself has even done its own share to help close the gap between black and white, an ironic twist of history in light of the Tigers' own long refusal to sign black ballplayers after Jackie Robinson first broke the major-league color barrier in 1947. Not until 1958, when Ozzie Virgil joined the club, did any African American take the field wearing the Old English D and have a chance at hearing the cheers of the crowds. For many white Detroit fans in the late 1950s and early 1960s, the ballpark might have been the *only* place where they actively pulled for the success of a black man like Willie Horton, a graduate of Northwestern High School and soon a mainstay in left field. The speaker in "Willie the Wonder" still marvels at the moment in 1968 "after the Tigers won the Series": he "stood with Willie Horton ... / shaking his hand" and posed for a picture. What Horton had done on the field at Tiger Stadium that championship year, "his best"— "36 homers, 85 RBIs, .285 average"—led the speaker to try matching Willie's powerful grip when he "tried to squeeze as hard / as I could, twelve years old." Years later the memory persists just as "Willie's muscles still stand out": "I remember him as calm, passive, / my hand in his, just another sweaty palm, / another white kid in the long line." For how many of those white kids in 1968 was Willie Horton's the first black hand they shook, the hand of a man so strong "they say he once broke a bat / just by checking his swing"?[8] Such gestures should not be downplayed so soon after the 1967 riots that left much of the city burned out and left two races wary of Detroit's future as their mutual hometown.

To be sure, not all encounters have necessarily been pleasant in this place with more than 10,000 cheap seats in the double-decked bleachers. In "Stormin' Norman," the older voice speaking recalls how as a youngster he "never sat in the bleachers / with my father again" after one particularly raucous "Sunday doubleheader against the Yanks." He remembers "a man who called himself Old Red" who "wore / his shirt on his head like a swami" and grew more foul-mouthed with every two beers "(limit two to a customer)" guzzled under a sun that "blazed away." Even though Old Red had to be escorted from the bleachers by a security guard and "disappeared in the darkness / under the stands," the speaker who eventually has grown "old enough to venture alone / to the bleachers" has also acquired with the passing of years enough perspective and wisdom to understand Old Red. At least he can now interpret the drunkard's vulgar tirade against future Hall of Famer Al Kaline as the bellow of a lifetime "singles hitter himself, / ... who'd trade it all / for one over the roof," aspiring to follow the popular example of his hero, longtime first baseman Norm Cash.[9] The common grounds of the stadium have yielded an experience commensurate with the speaker's eventual capacity for sensitivity and insight.

Jim Daniels, probably Tiger Stadium's most attentive poet (Andrea Stephany).

The "drunk, angry, male crowd" at Detroit Lions games at Tiger Stadium elicits less sympathy from Donald Hall. In his essay on football, Hall explores the connections between the violence of the game and the behavior of the fans: a man in "a zombie mask ... toking a joint"; others, stoned or drunk, abusing each other; the players, ushers, referees joining in a "masculine fraternity" partaking in the "hobby of violence." Eventually, despite the beauty of the athleticism on display on the field, Hall stops attending Lions games.[10]

Of course Tiger Stadium can always reprise its century-old role as the "queen of diamonds" in any baseball-grounded fiction, as it does for Patrick Creevy and Troy Soos.[11] But for Daniels, the games played at Tiger Stadium and the players starring in those games provide the bases for enduring emotional connections. These connections often embrace friends and family across generations. In "Baseball Cards #1," Jake Wood seems to be calling to the speaker "across hundreds of miles" from a 1964 Series 2 baseball card, one among the "10,342 ... in my parents' attic." Only someone attached to the games played at the stadium, to the family members who took him there, could be so affected years later by one of the cards he collected as a boy.[12] Charlie "Paw Paw" Maxwell's pinch-hit home run in "Nightmare" resounds in the memory of another Daniels speaker every bit as clearly as it did that one late August night he spent outdoors in his sleeping bag, when the original play-by-play "voice of Ernie Harwell" from the stadium came through "on my father's old transistor / ... close to my ear."[13] That same Harwell voice is what a grandmother in "Play by Play" holds onto like "gospel.... / Even at the ballpark, she squeezes her transistor." The games of summer still shape the old woman's days: "*Instant runs*, she says / in the middle of making tea, / wiping the table." Though she once stayed home on a cold and rainy September afternoon and was not one of the "small crowd on Ernie Harwell Day," she still "applauded her radio." According to her dutiful grandson, whenever she cannot pick up the broadcast signal "she laughs nervously," as if losing touch with life itself—life being now like "the red glow of a burner she's left on" but forgotten.[14] Certainly the golden moments and passions of youth can get revisited with every trip down "the Lodge Freeway / toward the stadium," as happens in "31–6," dedicated to Denny McLain, baseball's last 30-game winner. The grown-up speaker has no desire to let go of his personal highlight from the season of 1968, "the year after the riots." It occurred at "Tiger Stadium: ... / Grass so green it seemed like a mirage / in the raging heat of an angry city." He recounts his 12-year-old's gut-level identification with McLain who "grooved one to Mantle, / put him third on the all-time list / his last year, your 31st win, best moment." Even years later, this speaker insists on his kinship with Dennis Dale McLain, since

> I was twelve, sitting in the bleachers,
> saying *goddamn* and *shit*, spitting,
> fighting dirty for home run balls.
> I cheered you because you were bad—
> dumping water on reporters ...
> gambling, mouthing off.

No matter that McLain later landed in prison after "another bankrupt deal." His less-than-heroic setbacks mirror the speaker's own measured fall from grace and the graceless pranks of youth:

> I'm in general admission now—my back
> can't take the bleachers
> and I can't afford the boxes.
> I'm not such a bad boy
> myself anymore.[15]

Of all performers at Tiger Stadium, Hall of Fame right fielder Al Kaline has probably drawn the most attention of the postwar generation of Detroit fans. In "Getting Al Kaline's Autograph," by Richard Behm, the prized signature may be won by requesting it "'for my Dad' / ... the lie like a hard earned double," but it would never be worth the trouble if somewhere in a dream the speaker had not seen Al Kaline in action at the stadium "delicately plucking a screamer from the wall / in deep right center field." The speaker has screening on a continuous loop in his mind the slow-motion sequence of how Kaline

> ... loped toward the dugout,
> saw me in the stands, flipped
> that pure, sweet sphere into my lap
> and the crowd roared.

Such ballpark dreams explain the speaker's avid pursuit years later of an autograph stretched "across the page / like a smoker down the left field line."[16]

Along with dreams, the ballpark hosting the Tigers has led to its share of disappointments, built as it was for a game where hitters consider themselves successful if they do not fail more than seven times every ten at-bats. Those sporting disappointments hurt at the time, but they are manageable pains, nothing compared to what life will dish out later; the stadium is a place to practice coping. So, in Daniels' "New Words," a man is reminded of how, as a boy on the cusp of adolescence, he lost his temper after "the

A typical daytime crowd in the upper deck bleachers in 1968 (Walter P. Reuther Library, Archives of Labor and Urban Affairs, Wayne State University).

Tigers lose another game. / Don Wert let a ball roll through / his legs and down the line in left." This young man then cried, "*You pimp* ... as the winning run scored" and promptly received from his mother a stern lecture on the more brutal life awaiting him in a world where "men sell women's bodies. / Don Wert was not a good third baseman. / Don Wert was not a pimp."[17] Even when the heartache of a 12-year-old was intense, as it must have been in Daniels' "World Series, 1968," watching the hometown Tigers lose 10–1 from "left field box seats, upper deck," the grown-up speaker can still recollect his refusal to leave early: "I wouldn't budge. I kept whispering *The World Series, The World Series* ... / but I was still cold." Hurts are more bearable at Tiger Stadium.[18] In "Polish-American Night, Tiger Stadium," a boys' night out with "girlfriends / in general admission" at first makes the speaker and his buddies feel "like old guys / taking our wives to the ballgame." But then everything goes wrong, on the field and in the relationships. Relief pitcher John Hiller's bum knee and, later on, his heart attack stand in for missteps in love—betrayals and infidelities and changes of heart. If Hiller himself came to realize "There's a risk any time you pitch," it is also true that the speaker and his friends are "just beginning to learn that night, / that it can all come on so suddenly / just by bending your leg the wrong way."[19]

Whatever the disappointments of life, Tiger Stadium seems to work to heal the wounds or at least to provide space for such healing to occur. In "The Bookkeepers Talk Baseball," a CPA sits trapped at a desk, bombarded from all sides by coworkers who put down the sport itself as "*boring*" and "*can hardly stand one game / much less two*." Casual fans question, "*Why go to the ballpark, / ... and deal with the traffic / and the crowds?*"

184   Part II: Memories

The speaker clearly feels bruised by the numbers-crunching office environment, pelted by audit-level abuse as he's "flipping through accounts, pulling overdrafts. / My ass squirms in padded comfort / longing for the bleacher's hard bench." To one of his colleagues' claims to like baseball "better / on tv" the would-be fan hears the echoes of Tiger Stadium vendors in his mind's ear and revives for his own sanity the sights and sounds, the taste and feel, of being at the ballpark. He feels utterly transported: "I bang my seat / to start a rally" right in the middle of the workplace, just to survive the tedium of the day's grinding labor, the numbing routine.[20] "Extra Innings, Tiger Stadium, 1982" suggests how an extended time at the ballpark might constitute, however temporarily, soothing balm for the scars of a failed marriage. This speaker remembers going to Tiger Stadium with a divorcee friend after he and his own wife "had split—the first time / we were both free in the ten years / we'd known each other." Their date unfolds on a "clear spring night / when we're flush with possibility, / the fresh upper-deck breeze blowing out." After all their respective heartache, and after a game filled with two "bench-clearing fights" which saw even the venerable manager Sparky Anderson "out there wrestling around," life starts to feel good again when Kirk Gibson

> wins it with an upper-deck blast in the twelfth
> and everybody's so happy no one wants to leave
> and we're hugging each other, a little hoarse,
> a little drunk, a little in love.

Later on, a bit of lovemaking behind them, these two new fans of each other even "joke about getting married, / how anything's possible in extra innings." The speaker does not really need to point out how "Marvin Gaye's 'Sexual Healing' comes on the radio," since the healing had clearly started already at Tiger Stadium. No intervening years can erase the speaker's sensation of feeling once more his patched-up "heart full / with the swell of that huge crowd / as the ball rose."[21]

That Tiger Stadium has curative properties is not a notion restricted to baseball faithful like Jim Daniels. In "Stadia," a short story by Alyson Carol Hagy, a bookstore clerk named Laura buys for herself and Dan, her boyfriend of six months, several pairs of tickets to Tiger ball games in the hope of helping him cope with the impending anniversary of his father's sudden death, a trauma she thinks he has yet to recover from.[22] That Dan's father had never taken his son to a game at Tiger Stadium is beside the point. Dan himself had gone with his friends many times, and Laura surmises that time there will bring a deeper solace than any other activity she might devise. Unfortunately, she cannot foresee how Dan's careless act of delinquency—trying to sneak a pint bottle of whiskey in his boot past the turnstiles—will sabotage her efforts at getting him to face life as his father might have wished him to. As Dan is forcibly escorted to the street outside by the stadium security guards, Laura catches a last glimpse of him "trapped as the cold metal fence that cut her sight of him into colorless pieces." If only he had been able to make it inside to his seat next to her, perhaps he could have been made whole again.

Those without such "issues" still carry therapeutic expectations through Tiger Stadium's turnstiles. *The Final Season* records author Tom Stanton's attendance at every home game in 1999, the stadium's last year as the home of the Detroit Tigers. Stanton articulates a key question for other Detroiters of his generation: "Why would a man my age with family, a respectable job, and a stable psychological history obsess over an aging ballpark?"[23] Stanton's experience of baseball at Tiger Stadium is predominantly masculine.

He records his meetings with parking attendants, stadium ushers, fans, players, and broadcasters, often getting people like Ernie Harwell and Al Kaline to reflect on their fathers. Stanton uses his visits to the stadium to strengthen his relationship with his own father and sons, to reunite his father and uncle after a long separation, to resurrect his grandfather in the stands watching Ty Cobb. Tiger Stadium is a place, Stanton suggests, for connecting, reconnecting, and healing. As the final game approaches, he offers this reflection:

> [No] matter how my life has evolved and how many years have passed and how far my hairline has shifted, I feel like a kid when I come here. This place awakens those spirits and allows me to reclaim those parts of myself that otherwise might be lost. Here my life echoes with those of the men and boys who have meant the most to me.
> We all need places like this.[24]

But how "many places like this" are there? Nothing ever has come close to Tiger Stadium as the diamond jewel of this city. With the building demolished and the field (though valiantly defended by the Navin Field Grounds Crew) threatened, we rely on poems and stories to awaken the spirits of the past and reclaim the otherwise lost parts of ourselves. Like a pendant, Tiger Stadium lies close to the very heart of Detroit and its literature.

The young boys of summer chasing their dreams at Tiger Stadium, 1999 (© Rebecca Cook).

Notes

Originally published as "Tiger Stadium" in the online *Literary Map of Detroit*, ed. Frank D. Rashid (Detroit: Institute for Detroit Studies, Marygrove College, 2003), http://www.marygrove.edu/academics/institutes/institute-for-detroit-studies/literary-map-of-detroit/, reprinted with permission of Marygrove College, updated in 2013 by Rashid.

Part II: Memories

1. Loren D. Estleman, *Jitterbug* (New York: Forge, 1998) and *King of the Corner* (New York: Bantam Press, 1992). Harold Livingston, *The Detroiters* (Boston: Houghton Mifflin, 1958).
2. Crabbe Evers [William Brashler and Reinder Van Til], *Tigers Burning: A Duffy House Mystery* (New York: William Morrow, 1994).
3. Philip Levine, "A Walk with Tom Jefferson," *New Selected Poems* (New York: Alfred A. Knopf, 1993), 277–292.
4. Donald Hall," Fathers Playing Catch with Sons," *Fathers Playing Catch with Sons: Essays on Sport [Mostly Baseball]* (San Francisco: North Point Press, 1985), 11.
5. Jan Mordenski, "Like Colavito," *Abandon Automobile: Detroit City Poetry 2001*, eds. Melba Boyd and M.L. Liebler (Detroit: Wayne State University Press, 2001), 261–262.
6. Jim Daniels, "The Fat Man at the Ballgame," *The Long Ball* (Pittsburgh: Pig in a Poke Press, 1988), 18.
7. Jim Daniels, "Time/Temperature," *M-80* (Pittsburgh: University of Pittsburgh Press, 1993), 29–43.
8. Jim Daniels, "Willie the Wonder," *The Long Ball* (Pittsburgh: Pig in a Poke Press, 1988), 14.
9. Jim Daniels, "Stormin' Norman," *The Long Ball* (Pittsburgh: Pig in a Poke Press, 1988), 6–7.
10. Donald Hall, "Football: The Goalposts of Life," *Fathers Playing Catch with Sons*, 188–193.
11. Patrick Creevy, *Tyrus: An American Legend* (New York: Forge, 2002). Troy Soos, *Hunting a Detroit Tiger* (New York: Kensington, 1997).
12. Jim Daniels, "Baseball Cards #1," *The Long Ball* (Pittsburgh: Pig in a Poke Press, 1988), 4.
13. Jim Daniels, "Nightmare," *The Long Ball* (Pittsburgh: Pig in a Poke Press, 1988), 5.
14. Jim Daniels, "Play by Play," *The Long Ball* (Pittsburgh: Pig in a Poke Press, 1988), 22.
15. Jim Daniels, "31-6," *The Long Ball* (Pittsburgh: Pig in a Poke Press, 1988), 10–11.
16. Richard Behm, "Getting Al Kaline's Autograph," *Michigan Quarterly Review* 25 no. 2 (1986): 350.
17. Jim Daniels, "New Words," *The Long Ball* (Pittsburgh: Pig in a Poke Press, 1988), 9.
18. Jim Daniels, "World Series, 1968," *The Long Ball* (Pittsburgh: Pig in a Poke Press, 1988), 13.
19. Jim Daniels, "Polish-American Night, Tiger Stadium," *The Long Ball* (Pittsburgh: Pig in a Poke Press, 1988), 15.
20. Jim Daniels, "The Bookkeepers Talk Baseball," *The Long Ball* (Pittsburgh: Pig in a Poke Press, 1988), 20.
21. Jim Daniels, "Extra Innings, Tiger Stadium, 1982," *The Long Ball* (Pittsburgh: Pig in a Poke Press, 1988), 16–17.
22. Alyson Carol Hagy, "Stadia." *Michigan Quarterly Review* 25, no. 2 (1986), 351–362.
23. Tom Stanton, *The Final Season: Fathers, Sons, and One Last Season in a Classic American Ballpark* (New York: St. Martin's Press, 2001), 11.
24. Stanton, *The Final Season*, 232–233.

Tiger Stadium Memories and Stories

Interviews were conducted and edited by Bill Dow.

From the Stands

A lifelong Detroit Tiger fan, Max Lapides was a successful businessman, who, with former Detroit sports columnist Joe Falls, cofounded the Eddie Lake Society, an organization of Tiger enthusiasts.

My very first recollection of going to Navin Field was, I believe, in 1934 when I was almost seven, and I went there with my father. It was a cold, overcast day against Cleveland, and they had an outfielder named Sammy Hale. [*Editors' Note: There was a Sammy Hale, but he played from 1920 through 1930, and never for Cleveland.*] I remember seeing him running towards the left field foul line and making a catch. It's the only thing I remember about that game, and I fell in love with the ballpark at that moment.

A favorite memory for me is, of course, seeing my hero Hank Greenberg hitting home runs onto Cherry Street when the left field stands were just bleachers. I also recall that on sellouts at Navin Field there was standing room only [on the field] along the wall in left field where the authorities would rope it off and stand there maybe six people deep. They stood out there in the middle of the summer and watched the game from that perspective, which was, of course, very unusual. If the ball was hit into that standing-room crowd on the field, it was ruled a ground rule double.

But one memory that really stands out was that on Labor Day, at the end of the game, the men who wore the straw hats would sail them onto the middle of the field. By that time of the year, the hats couldn't be cleaned because they had been worn all summer. If a home run happened in the middle of the game, they would start throwing them out onto the field.

I remember going to Briggs Stadium in 1938 when the renovation of the ballpark was completed with the upper deck completely enclosing the ballpark. It was overwhelming as a kid to see that after having gone to games when it was a smaller ballpark as Navin Field. It was like 'What was this place I was walking into?' after I had been in Navin Field. Everything is on a different scale when you're young. It was just gorgeous with all those green seats.

My father and I knew the guy in the advanced ticket window, and we always got good seats, and we went nearly every weekend.

My dad actually saw Ty Cobb in his very first game in 1905. While training to be a clothing cutter, my father went on a trip to Detroit at 16 to model for Bond Clothes. A salesman took him to Bennett Park. My dad liked to say he didn't realize that he was looking at the man who would become the greatest player of all time.

I probably went to 50 games a year with my father, but he would never let me keep score. He said if you did that you'll never remember what happened. I was very fortunate to have seen so much baseball at that wonderful ballpark.

The best night ever at Briggs Stadium was when they first used lights on June 15, 1948, and I was at that game. The game was supposed to start at 8:00 p.m. but it was delayed because it was still so light out. Everyone was so antsy to get it started, but we figured the Tiger authorities wanted the fans to get the full effect of experiencing the lights coming on. A little after nine, all of sudden, it was boom, the lights came on, and everybody just looked. For a few seconds there was absolute silence, and then a roar went up. The field and the ballpark were beautiful when illuminated.

One of the things about Briggs Stadium that was so exciting was the streetcar lines that came down Michigan Avenue and Trumbull Avenue. On game day when there was a big crowd, these streetcars would be lined up in each direction with people getting off, and it was so exciting to see that even before you got into the park.

Ernie Harwell became a good friend of mine, and one time he had me up in the radio booth. It was mesmerizing sitting up there. It was a very hot day, and Ernie was sitting in his undershorts. As any announcer will tell you, they were so close to the field you could actually hear the players talking.

Panoramic view from behind home plate, late 1990s (© Rebecca Cook).

I was there for the 1968 and 1984 World Series, the '71 All Star Game when Reggie Jackson hit the tremendous home run off the light transformer, the 22-inning game in 1962, and that 1950 slugfest against the Yankees, when the teams combined for a record 11 home runs and Hoot Evers won the game with a homer in the bottom of the ninth.

I was also at the last game at Tiger Stadium, and I cried, especially when the old players came out onto the field in the closing ceremony. A few days later, [sportswriter] Joe Falls called and asked me if I would join him and [former Tiger pitcher] Elden Auker for lunch. Afterwards he said, let's go to the stadium. A guard let us in, and the three of us sat down for an hour and a half and just talked about the place. That was really emotional reminiscing.

A Detroit area native, Dale Petroskey was the president of the National Baseball Hall of Fame (1999–2008), a senior vice president for the National Geographic Society (1988–1999), and the assistant press secretary for President Ronald Reagan (1985–1987).

My dad took me to my first game in 1961, when I was five years old and the Tigers played that great Yankee team. I remember that wonderful moment that you can only experience once: when you first walked into Tiger Stadium, and you see that green grass, and you smell the popcorn, hot dogs, and the cigar smoke. The great pageantry of it all was so appealing.

Rocky Colavito was my favorite Tiger. He was such a colorful player. I loved the way he stretched with the bat behind his back and pointed the bat at the pitcher. I looked in a book of saints and found Saint Rocco, so I took that as my confirmation name.

My dad would take us to Tiger Stadium about five or six games a year. We had nine kids in our family. We would bug him to death every weekend. But he found it within himself to take us all down there.

My greatest memory of Tiger Stadium occurred on June 22, 1962. It was Father's Day, and my dad took my brothers and sisters to the ball game, and we sat right behind the Tiger dugout. That was the game that went 22 innings, a seven-hour game, and it ended when the Yankees' Jack Reed won it on what turned out to be the only home run of his major league career.

I had a friend at school, Emery Fasano, whose father was an usher at Tiger Stadium. Emery used to go down to help his dad as a junior usher, and he asked me if I wanted to do that and work only for tips. For a couple of years I worked as a junior usher for Tiger and Lion games. Emery and I went down Michigan Avenue on the bus from Inkster. Our section was Section 29 and 30 down the right-field line. We would help Mr. Fasano fold all the box seat covers, and he took people to the box seats. We took people to the reserve seats. Most of the tips were a quarter, and most nights I would walk out with two or three dollars.

I'll never forget for the All Star Game in 1971 I walked out with $25, and I thought I was the richest guy in the world. Everybody talks about Reggie Jackson's famous home run that night, but my most enduring memory of that game was seeing Vida Blue throwing the ball in the first inning, because I was close to home plate. He must have thrown a hundred-mile-an-hour pitch.

My first Lions game was the famous Thanksgiving Day game in 1962 when the Lions devoured the Packers. We sat in the third-deck press box, and I remember it was freezing and I was drinking hot chocolate. It was the day the Fearsome Foursome was named, with Alex Karras, Roger Brown, Darris McCord, and Sam Williams.

I remember at the Lion games how cold it was and that smell of the hot dogs on the grills. With that stadium and all that cement, it held all the cold, and I would freeze like crazy.

I was working there the day that Chuck Hughes died on the field. Greg Landry was warming up with Hughes right at our section near the corner of the end zones at the beginning of the game, and towards the end of the game he died right there on the field. I can remember how quiet the stadium was when that happened, and it was so strange because, just before that, the crowd was very loud as the Lions were staging a rally.

The only time I was on the field for a Tiger game was the last game at Tiger Stadium in 1999 when I had first become the president of the National Baseball Hall of Fame. After the game, the flag was lowered and passed down the line of former Tiger players, and I was in that line. It was a fun moment, but at the same time it was very sad.

Donald Hall was named Poet Laureate of the United States in 2006 and four years later was awarded the National Medal of Arts by President Barack Obama. Donald Hall has also written books on baseball, children's stories, reviews, essays and plays. His sports books include *Fathers Playing Catch with Sons: Essays on Sport (Mostly Baseball)* (1985) and, with Dock Ellis, *Dock Ellis: In the Country of Baseball* (1974). He was a Tiger fan from 1957 to 1975, while a professor at the University of Michigan.

I grew up as a Brooklyn Dodger fan, and I was very mad at baseball when the Dodgers went to the West Coast. I spent some time pissed off, but Ernie Harwell brought me back to baseball and the Tigers. I used to listen to Ernie all the time. When I lived in Ann Arbor, I loved to take my son to Tiger Stadium, and sometimes one of his friends came with us.

In my book *Fathers Playing Catch with Sons*, I wrote about the time I was sitting with my son in the upper deck and I dropped a home run ball. I had a cigar in one hand, and I didn't drop the cigar as I tried to catch it with one hand. I ended up with a red thick bruise on it. There was of course a big jeer from the crowd who saw me drop it. That was my high point in my baseball history. It was all right. I thought it was funny. My son was old enough to think it was funny, too.

I also remember seeing Denny McLain come out of the bullpen before he became a starter. Before Denny got in trouble, he had a radio show, and I had it on one day, and he told a story of someone having a boa constrictor in Bloomfield Hills and buying rats for their snake. That fact inspired me to write my poem "Poem with One Fact."

I also took my son to Lion games and I noticed the difference in the football and baseball crowds. Crowds in baseball were more racially diverse and better behaved. The football crowd was almost entirely white, full of drunks, with a lot of nasties showing off. I remember a row of football fans in front of us and one in particular standing up, wavering his body with a big voice. I did enjoy going with my son anyway.

I loved Tiger Stadium. When I realized the Tigers were making a new stadium I wasn't surprised, but of course I regretted it because I had so much fun there. It was old and companionable.

❖ ❖ ❖

Mary Moroz of Warren, Michigan, has been a Detroit Tiger fan for more than 50 years and was a member of the Tiger Stadium Fan Club.

My first game at Tiger Stadium was in 1968. I was 12 years old, and it was a day that I will never forget. I went to the game with my dad, sister, and brother. Dad had gotten box seats along the first base line, a few rows above the aisle. We parked a ways from the ballpark, and I was amazed at the crowd as we all made our way to the gates. So many people! I don't know who was more excited, me or my dad.

As we walked up the ramp to our seats, I remember just stopping and staring at the field. Dad let us take in the view and didn't rush us. The field was smaller than I thought it would be, after seeing all the views on TV, and the stadium much larger! It was great. I could actually see the players up close!

I had already picked a favorite: Bill Freehan. I don't remember why. We made our way to our seats, and it seemed like we could reach out and touch the players. Dad bought all of us pennants and stuffed Tigers, as well as hot dogs and popcorn. We learned early that hot dogs were better from the grill at the concession stand, though popcorn should be bought in the stands. During the game, the vendors would sell the popcorn in containers that, when empty, could be used as megaphones to cheer louder! I still have many of those containers, some with autographs.

The day ended too soon, but I was hooked on baseball, and, more importantly to me, Tiger Stadium. The game would never be the same on TV!

Games at the stadium became an integral part of my life through high school, 1970–1974, and beyond. In the early '70s, we "lived" at the stadium. My sister, Betty, and I would take the Gratiot bus downtown to the games, arriving three hours before the game to wave to the players as they arrived, buying $2.50 general admission tickets, and staying at least two hours after the game to meet with the players.

Fan club presidents were allowed to wait for the players in the commissary at the entrance to the players' parking lot and down the hall from the lounge where the families waited. Betty and I were fan club presidents for Jim Perry, Chris Zachary, Tom Veryzer, Frank Howard, and Bill Slayback.

The commissary also held a huge bin where the canvas seat covers were thrown, to be washed after the game. After one game we thought it would be cool to have a couple of those, so we reached in and took one each, putting them in our bags. Immediately Norm Cash came sauntering into the commissary, with a cup of beer in his hand. We were giggling because we were feeling so guilty. Norm just looked at us and said, "I don't know what y'all did, but you look guilty," and he started laughing.

During those trips downtown on the bus, it was not unusual for us to bring a full sheet cake if it was a special birthday; we brought one once for Billy Martin.

Every Opening Day we'd ask the grounds crew for the sash that was draped across the "good luck" horseshoe presented by the fire department, and we still have a couple of those sashes too!

We were known as the Tigers' "cookie girls," a name given to us by Bill Freehan. We'd make their favorite oatmeal chocolate chip cookies, fill up a container, and send it to the clubhouse, using the security guard as a courier. The security guards knew we didn't bother the players and would ask one or the other to come to the door to visit before the game. We got to know them all very well, and many of them supported us when we walked in the March of Dimes walkathon and remembered us with cards at graduation.

More often than not, we'd have to walk from Michigan and Washington Boulevard down to the stadium, and, during that time, many players from the visiting teams would be walking to the ballpark from their downtown hotels. We would walk and visit with players like Brooks Robinson or Carl Yastrzemski. They were always interested in us as fans, and it made the walk to The Corner go by in seconds.

In addition to making the cookies, we would also make homemade *kruschiki* (angel wings) for the guys on Polish American Night. Joe Niekro loved them, as did Bill Freehan, who would come out of the dugout and do an exaggerated brush of the powdered sugar off his uniform. More often than not, we'd be playing Boston on that night, so we also brought some for Yastrzemski, who would come to the visitors' clubhouse door and visit with us. He was always a gentleman and a very kind man.

Only one of those walks back from the stadium to the bus stop was a problem. No doubt the kids that chased us just wanted our bats because it had been bat day, but we rushed into Howard Johnson's out of breath. Who's standing there, but Woody Fryman! At that time, a lot of the Tigers also stayed in hotels downtown if they lived out of town. He took one look at us, asked us what was going on, and stood with us at the bus stop until our bus came.

Before the All-Star Game, we'd pass out ballots, going from row to row, wearing "All-Star Game" silk sashes, like beauty contestants. The fans were always great, and we got in for free for volunteering! We still have those sashes! We would take hundreds of ballots home and manually punch them for all of our Tigers.

We had a great champion in Vince Doyle, who took up our cause when we wanted to be "base sweepers" for the Tigers. We had outfits of blue shorts and a white T-shirt with an Old English D on the front and red sleeves. We each had a broom and painted the handle orange and black. Vince featured us many times on his radio show and even had a suggestion for us to "sweep" the umpires in the butt as we dusted the bases. We were devastated when we received a letter from the Tigers organization stating they would not allow us on the field.

The players treated us like big brothers would. Jim Northrup came to our high school father-daughter breakfast as a guest speaker, no charge, and stayed until everyone spent time with him.

Bill Freehan came over to our house after a Tiger basketball game at Notre Dame High and spent time with us and our family. He also came as a friend of the family when Mom was honored at a Lou Gehrig's disease charity luncheon. We still keep in contact with him and his family. Because we collected SO MUCH Bill Freehan memorabilia, we were able to send many boxes to his daughters and grandchildren to enjoy.

Not only did we "live" at the ballyard during the season, but we would often go in winter during our lunch hours to walk onto the field through the snow and take pictures by the goalposts as well as in the dugout and bullpen. We just couldn't stay away. We were fortunate enough to have met many kind folks in the Burns security company, who knew we wouldn't bother anyone.

We went to a Lions game once with our dad and some of his friends, and we had seats in the third deck. We had gotten there early and were on the field with the Lions as they warmed up, just standing around behind the bench. Betty actually asked Errol Mann if she could hold the football while he was practicing his kick! Before the kickoff and sometimes right after, we'd need to get off the field in a hurry and run through the snow to the box seats before making our way to the seats.

Opening Days were always a treat, whether skipping school or playing hooky from work. Opening Day wasn't complete without a hug from Ernie Harwell. He was always walking through the stands as we came in as soon as the gates opened. He would open his arms and welcome us to another season! He was an awesome individual and inspiration. The only Opening Day we missed was the year they fired Ernie and we sat in defiance in a "bleacher" section with our tickets, across from the park. It killed us not to go in that day, but we stood our ground.

One of our saddest days at the ballyard actually started as the happiest as the Tigers won the World Series in 1984. Betty and I were up on the walkway by the third deck with Ernie Harwell as we watched a car burn on the street. We asked Ernie "why?" He just shook his head sadly.

When our beloved home became endangered, we signed on with the Tiger Stadium Fan Club to try and save it. Whether it was addressing flyers, marching down Michigan Avenue with our banner in the St. Patrick's Day parade, or being a "corner captain" for the famous Tiger Stadium hug, we were there. On the last day, again we were the first ones through the gate. Mary Conway from Channel 7 interviewed us with tears streaming down our faces. Later I learned at work that many people unknown to us were crying while they listened to us explain how much Tiger Stadium means to us. We were fortunate to have my company's box seats four rows from the field near the Tiger's on-deck circle. The night flew by. We cried as they pried home plate out, pleading for them to get their own and leaves ours alone.

Years went by, and I took some time to go down to The Corner when the filming of

Mary Moroz joins other Tiger Stadium Fan Club members at the St, Patrick's Day Parade on Michigan Avenue c. 1989. From left: Peggy Swift, Anne Rashid, Eva Navarro, Frank Rashid, and Moroz (courtesy Patricia Muldoon).

61* was taking place. I got to be in the movie for a second, but that wasn't nearly as important as being in my ballpark again. Hearing the lights go on during a night filming brought me to tears. I played every memory over in my mind, being so grateful that for some seasons in the '70s we missed only 12 home games a year. (We never had season tickets, always general admission.)

I said the wrecking ball would have to go through me first before I would let it destroy the park … not very well thought out, but I meant it.

It took us a decade to go to a game at Comerica, and we've been to only about five in all. It's really not worth the money, time, and effort. I'll always be a Tiger fan, but from afar. Being at a game in Comerica is like going to an away game.

We've been back to The Corner recently to play catch, run the bases, wander out to the flagpole in center field, and throw a few pitches from the mound. We can only hope that The Corner remains as a field for a game of catch and some great memories. Thank goodness for the Navin Field Grounds Crew, who have done such as awesome job in bringing dignity back to The Corner.

A native of Dearborn, Thom Sharp is an actor and comedian well known for his voiceover work and national commercials. He was a member of the Tiger Stadium Fan Club and wrote and recorded the song "Don't Tear It Down," a tribute to Tiger Stadium.

I went to my first ballgame at Tiger Stadium, then Briggs Stadium, with my dad in 1956, when I was eight years old. It was the first time I'd even been to any kind of ballpark with lights. The lights were so bright, and the grass and seats were so green. That feeling never really changed during my future visits to Tiger Stadium. Even when I was older and drove east on Michigan Avenue from Dearborn to Tiger Stadium, the minute that I spied those light standards and the club flags flying on top of the park, it turned me into an eight-year-old.

At my first game, I saw Ted Williams hit a home run in the upper deck. There are some home runs that I can still see in my mind. That was one of them, and I can never forget seeing Lance Parrish's line drive home run in the seventh inning of the fifth game of the '84 World Series and of course Kirk Gibson's homer the next inning.

I always tried to get to batting practice, and if somebody who I was going to go with said "I don't want to go to batting practice," I said, "Well, I'll meet you down there." It's because it gave me another hour and a half in the park. I loved it so much that I would hope for a non-game-ending rain delay. The longest game would be too short for me.

Especially the last four or five years at Tiger Stadium, I would come in from California at least four times a season to catch a weekend series. Often someone would recognize me from a commercial or something, and they would ask, "What are you doing in town?" And I'd say "Seeing the Tigers at Tiger Stadium." And they'd say, "No, really, are you shooting a commercial?" And I'd say "No, I am here just to see the Tigers play at Tiger Stadium." On late Sunday afternoon, I sometimes had to leave the game early, and it was so hard to leave the place. It was because of the stadium, because the Tigers stunk during that time.

I was an upper deck guy down the first base line. It was a perfect spot, like sitting in the balcony to see a play and watching everything unfold in front of you. I used to look out at the field and thought: "Babe Ruth played here, and Joe Jackson, and Roberto Clemente in the 1971 All Star Game." I also liked to look out at the different seats and sections where I had sat with my dad or Wally Lis, my neighbor, baseball coach, friend, and mentor.

The only time I was on the field was when the Mayo Smith Society hosted a benefit for the clubhouse boys. When I was standing there looking up at the upper deck, I thought I was at the bottom of the Grand Canyon looking up. I remember standing at Kaline's Corner on the warning track and thought about how he caught a fly ball and throwing a one-hopper to home plate from that far it was like, home plate is over there and I am in Mount Clemens. I would need three cut-off guys to get it there. And then standing in left field and thinking this is where Willie Horton threw the ball to get Lou Brock out at home plate in the '68 Series.

The thing that I remember most about the last game at Tiger Stadium was during the very beginning of the closing ceremonies when Mark Fidrych in full uniform came in from center field, knelt, and took some dirt from the mound. When all those former players came walking in from the center field stands, it was like seeing the Black Sox walking out of the cornfield in *Field of Dreams*.

I have a lot of favorite Tigers, like Charlie Maxwell, Harvey Kuenn, Al Kaline, Willie Horton, and Norm Cash, but if I have to pick one guy, it would be Fidrych. The 1976 season was my last full year in Detroit before moving to California. I went to three or four games when Fidrych pitched, and the World Series wasn't as exciting compared to one of his games. There would be 10,000 people the game before, and the next day it was standing-room-only to see this rookie pitch.

I got involved with the Tiger Stadium Fan Club in 1990, when I was asked to perform at Mark Ridley's Comedy Castle with Tim Allen at a fundraiser for the effort to save the ballpark. I wrote a song, "Don't Tear It Down," on the flight from Los Angeles and per-

Mark Fidrych grooms the mound to begin the postgame ceremonies after the final out on September 27, 1999 (© Rebecca Cook).

Thom Sharp stands between the State of Michigan Historic Site plaque and the Ty Cobb plaque outside the Detroit Tiger offices on Trumbull Avenue (courtesy Patricia Muldoon).

formed it at the benefit. I think the effort of the fan club probably added at least five years to the life of Tiger Stadium, and I loved it because I was able to see more games at the ballpark.

It's difficult to go by the site now and just see the diamond and the flagpole standing. If I could wave a magic wand, they would still be playing at Tiger Stadium. They could be the New York Knights before Roy Hobbs arrived. It wouldn't matter if they lost every game as long as I could still go to the park.

Kerrie Ferrell of Ann Arbor, Michigan, is the daughter of baseball Hall of Famer Rick Ferrell, a major league catcher for 18 seasons and a longtime executive and former general manager of the Detroit Tigers. With William Anderson, she is the author of *Rick Ferrell, Knuckleball Catcher: A Hall-of-Famer's Life behind the Plate and in the Front Office.*

We were living in Greensboro, North Carolina, and I had never been to Michigan until we moved in 1959. My father would leave in March, and we would basically not see him until the end of September, but every morning we would check the Detroit Tigers' box scores.

I was 11 years old when we moved to Michigan in June of 1959, and I had never seen a major league park before.

In those days people dressed up to go to the ballpark, and I remember we dressed like we were going to church. The policeman outside of the players' parking lot waved us in and ushered us in. We went through the commissary, which was like a tunnel from the parking lot, and it opened up into the concourse, with all the people and vendors walking by. I'll always remember the smell of hot dogs.

We had seven seats in the front row right next to the Tiger dugout directly behind third base. The back of the dugout actually stretched behind us, and there were two rows in that box. I remember the ushers wearing those green uniforms and escorting us to our seats, and they wiped down the seats with the rags. They were originally wooden removable seats, and later they padded them. They would then put on these light brown covers. The row behind us had Jim Campbell's seats, and often famous or VIP people would sit in them like Ted Kennedy, Wayne Gretzky, Roy Scheider, or Billy Crystal. We had those seven seats from 1959 to 1992. My dad knew how lucky we were to have those seats, because they were a gift from Jim Campbell based on his esteem for my father.

Opening Day was like a sacred holiday, and we were always there no matter where we were living.

We were so close to the players, sitting in those great seats, but the irony is my dad would not let us converse with the Tigers because he said they were working and that we were spectators. He always wanted us to dress nicely and not act silly. He never wanted the television cameras to show our box because he was concerned about what we might be doing.

One time I did meet Mark Fidrych. I had gone to see my dad in his office at Tiger Stadium, and Mark was there. He was such a bundle of energy with that hair all over his face, and he had those intense eyes. He was just so nice.

Our dad always came by our seats before the game to say hello. He worked really hard to keep people in those seven seats: he would give tickets away or to charities. We realized how lucky we were to have those seats, and he wanted to share them.

We used to go to almost every game, and even when I was older, even if I didn't have anyone to go with, I would drive down there by myself. I grew up at Tiger Stadium, and it meant a lot to me. Do you remember that Madonna song called "It Used to Be My Playground" from the movie *A League of Their Own*? That is exactly what I felt about Tiger Stadium because I had a real emotional connection to it. No matter how I felt in any period of my life, I could just go in the ballpark, and everything else would just fade away because it was pure baseball.

Everyone, of course, was struck by the green of Tiger Stadium. Now a lot of people like stadiums that are open where you can look out and see the city, but for my part I liked the insularity of Tiger Stadium. It was like an opera house where it was only baseball.

What I really remember is the sense of history at Tiger Stadium when I was there, and the fact my father played there in the '30s and '40s. You could almost hear the old voices coming up from the field, like those of Ty Cobb and Hank Greenberg. The bridge with my father was baseball, and I loved to listen to his stories: it was just wonderful. So I was very aware of the history of the ballpark.

In the early days when I went there, my father and Jim Campbell were such purists that they didn't want any gimmicks and none of the pop music or giveaways. They wanted just organ music and baseball. I've not been to Comerica Park. I'm kind of old school.

Of course, at Fenway Park, where my dad played for five years, they had a wonderful 100th anniversary. I wrote to my friends in Boston and said that if anyone tried to do anything to Fenway, you people would be rioting in the streets, and here in Detroit, we just tear it down.

I rarely go into the city, and one time I got lost when I was in the city, and I ended up on Trumbull, and I didn't even know which way I was going, and somehow I ended up near the ballpark, when they had nearly completed tearing it down. I wasn't prepared for that, and I just started crying. It was very sad. I'm not going back there.

Architect and baseball stadium expert John Pastier is one of this book's editors.

I've been to Tiger Stadium four times, and each visit produced something personally remarkable.

The first time I was ever in Detroit was in 1971 to cover a national architects' convention for the *Los Angeles Times*. I stayed downtown near the convention center and was delighted to be able to explore a new city on foot. My one regret was that there was no chance to see a ball game, since the Tigers were out of town.

On June 24, the last full day of my trip, at about 6:00 p.m. I was walking west along Michigan Avenue to my hotel when I noticed a cluster of bright lights about a mile down the street. Could the Tigers be back from their road trip? I bought a paper, which confirmed that they were. I hopped on a bus and, in about five minutes, was in heaven.

Five years earlier, I had moved from New York to Los Angeles, and in that time hadn't been able to see a game in an older ballpark. Now I was in one again. It was only my sixth big-league stadium, and my first classic park outside of New York. I sat in the upper deck bleachers in left center and can't remember who the visitors were or who won the game. That wasn't important. I was a National League fan and was at Michigan and Trumbull for the atmosphere. But thanks to *Retrosheet*, I am able to look up the game 42 years later. Mickey Lolich shut out the Indians 3–0, striking out 11 and bringing his record to 11–6 on the way to a 25-win, 308-strikeout season. For some reason, Al Kaline didn't play.

It was an archetypal old-park experience. The late-June night was warm, and the stands were about a third full. Seasoned fans who had been coming to games for decades chatted about several eras of players, comparing the old-timers with the current crop. Three-generation families sat contentedly, soaking up the experience. Several strapping blond youths dressed in bright two-tone jerseys looked as though they had come from playing softball; the stereotyper in me was sure that they were Polish American. Several couples were there, too.

Usually, people go to a ballgame for excitement, but what I found instead was a sense of peace and relaxation, of time nearly standing still. I was sitting in a well-seasoned container of baseball history, a huge oak cask of sherry where the contents, changing gradually every year, were slowly mellowing. After the game, I walked back to the hotel. This was the first time that I ever was able to travel to or from a ballpark entirely on foot.

My other three visits came about 20 years later, in the early 1990s. One was a personal off-season tour of the park, arranged by Brian Tremain, Sparky Anderson's stockbroker and an active member of the Tiger Stadium Fan Club. The club official who led me around was hoping to convince me that the old park desperately needed to be replaced. He proudly showed me "the worst seat in baseball," a lower-deck left field chair whose view was blocked by two columns standing less than a foot from each other. "So don't sell that seat" was my silent rebuttal.

The most memorable thing about that visit was that the entire field was covered with fresh snow. I had never seen anything like it in the major leagues and still haven't. There was a four-foot-high marker at home plate so that prospective season-ticket holders could tell how good their seats would be (in spite of the park's fatal obsolescence).

Visit number three was on an overcast Saturday afternoon. Outside on the Michigan Avenue sidewalk, a man with two young kids offered to sell me the fourth seat in his box, and I jumped at the chance. His season tickets were at the front of the upper deck, between third and home. I sat in the second row, and that vantage point was remarkable, high enough to see everything perfectly and yet closer to the field than any other upper-deck location I've ever experienced in the course of seeing hundreds of games from the upper deck at scores of parks. To this day, that privileged perch has been the unattainable benchmark against which I've measured seating quality. Red Barber might have called it "the catbird's seat," giving new meaning to one of his immortal catchphrases.

The next day, crisp and sunny, saw my last visit to the grand old ballpark. I sat in the upper deck bleachers in straightaway center along with about a dozen Tiger Stadium Fan Club members. The company was great, and there were enough empty seats so that we could move around and socialize freely. That was the day when I first saw in person a curveball break. I'm not a particularly good student of pitching, but almost 500 feet from the plate, the depth dimension was compressed so dramatically that I was easily able to see the pitch bending away from the batter—partly despite the great distance involved, and partly because of it. The height of our seats also contributed to this effect.

Although none of these experiences can ever again be duplicated, I nevertheless have a seat-of-the-pants sense that I'm back at the corner of Michigan and Trumbull. As I type this, I'm sitting on a battered and peeling green wood-and-metal folding chair with torn vinyl-covered padding that used to be a Tiger Stadium box seat many decades ago. For all I know, someone may have watched Hank Greenberg or Al Kaline while sitting in this very chair.

Tiger fan Joe Baker of Warren, Michigan, may hold the record for getting the most batting practice balls at Tiger Stadium.

I have a very fond memory of my first game at Tiger Stadium. It was in 1971. I was ten years old, and my mom took me and two of my friends. I remember walking up a little ramp into the upper deck and then looking out at that beautiful green stadium. We sat in the grandstand in the upper deck down the third-base line. I started wandering in the stadium, going down a few sections, when my buddies were checking out the souvenir stands. Next thing I knew I'm way out in left field standing in an aisle. All of a sudden a ball starts coming my way. It went over my head, bounced off someone's hands, and fell down to the box seat area where I was standing, and I ran down and grabbed it. It was a home run that Bill Freehan hit off Wilbur Wood. I was so pumped I couldn't believe it; it was my prized possession. From then on, I was hooked on getting baseballs.

After that, my mom would drop me off at the ballpark, or I would take the Van Dyke–Lafayette bus and then catch the Michigan Avenue bus. I went to as many games as I could, and I used to catch batting practice baseballs all the time in the lower deck and then sell them for a dollar or two and try to get some hot dog money. One time I caught nine batting practice balls in one day and later retrieved home runs hit by Brooks

The center field bleachers, August 1999 (© Rebecca Cook).

Robinson and Thurman Munson. Over the years, I caught several hundred batting practice balls. My favorite spot was in the left-center-field grandstands in the first aisle because I could run either way and chase them down.

One time during practice, a ball that was hit was coming right at me, and I was camping under it, when Mickey Stanley jumped about a foot and a half over the fence, and his mitt went inside of mine, and he caught the ball. He saw that I was bummed out, but then he had this grin on his face, and he flipped it back to me. It was incredible that Mickey could leap that high and get it.

Another time Jose Canseco hit this ball, and it was heading right at an 80- or 90-year-old lady, and I reached out and caught it before it hit her in the face. I gave her the ball, and her daughter bought me a beer. That was a grab I will never forget.

I also got to know Mario Muscat, a Tiger batboy, and he used to give cracked bats to me all the time.

One day the upper deck in right field was closed off, and during batting practice, a bunch of balls were hit up there, but I never saw an usher go get them. I told my buddy: "Let's try to get those baseballs after the game." The only way to get them was to go across the beams on top of the seats, so I scooted across the beam and went around the gate and started fishing up all the balls. We ended up with a bunch of them. I had a bat the Tigers had given me. All the lights were turned off at the ballpark except for the ones around home plate. We went onto the field and pitched to each other. All of a sudden Mario came out of the dugout in his batboy uniform, and he took his turn. He ended up hitting three of my balls into the upper deck in right field. A guard then saw us and told us it was time to leave. That was a pretty cool experience.

I really liked Tiger Stadium because I got to know a lot of the people there, all the ushers, and before the play on the field got better, I could sit in a lot of sections. It was like I owned the stadium. When they were winning in 1984, it was hard to get a seat.

One time after a game, my friend and I went up the elevator at the press box, and there was a catwalk that went up to the roof. We looked around for baseballs up there where the blue neon Tiger Stadium sign was located. There were gutters, and there were probably some balls in them, but that was a little freaky.

One time I participated in a fantasy camp at Tiger Stadium, and that's a special memory. Jim Northrup was my coach. My sister took a video of me making a nice backhanded running catch on a ball hit in the left-center-field gap. We met Ernie, and I sat with Willie Horton for the dinner at the Tiger Plaza.

Youngsters watching and waiting with gloves in hand, 1999 (© Rebecca Cook).

Tiger Stadium was like a second home to me. It kind of put you in a different world, and you could get away from things. It was hard to leave the ballpark. I was at the last game at Tiger Stadium, and it was very emotional for me. I was with my wife, and I cried like a baby.

I watched them start tearing it down. It was an emotional thing because they started in the left field area. I was standing on the overpass that I used to always cross over when I went to the ballpark. They were tearing my left field stands out, and it was real hard for me.

Comerica Park is a big disappointment compared to Tiger Stadium. At Tiger Stadium, there was the aisle to run up and down in lower left field to get baseballs, but they don't have that at Comerica Park. It's more of a circus atmosphere and more commercial. The seats are so far away in the upper deck that the players look like peanuts. At Comerica Park, there's the Ferris wheel, and people are just strolling under the stands, whereas at Tiger Stadium you didn't want to miss an inning. Now the ball game is like the sideshow.

Tom Derry is a U.S. postal worker who was a member of the Tiger Stadium Fan Club. He is the founder of the Navin Field Grounds Crew, a group of dedicated volunteers who cut the grass and maintained the historic diamond.

The first time I went to Tiger Stadium was in 1971 when I was eight years old and attended a Fireman's Field Day event. My first game occurred soon after that, and I was thrilled to see Mickey Lolich pitch and my favorite player, Norm Cash. I participated in the Big Brothers/Big Sisters program and my Big Brother was Dennis Bufford, who took me to a lot of games.

The game that really stands out for me was on July 15, 1973. We sat behind home plate and saw Nolan Ryan throw a no-hitter. That was the game when Norm Cash came up as the last batter and brought a table leg to the plate. I remember seeing him go back to the dugout to get a real bat. Everyone was cheering, and I didn't understand it because we were losing.

Besides the Ryan no-hitter, my other favorite game that I saw was when the Tigers beat the Blue Jays 1–0 on the last day of the '87 season. That was a great day with Larry Herndon's home run and Frank Tanana's fabulous pitching performance. Earlier that day, my friends and I visited Harry Heilmann's grave because we thought maybe that would help the Tigers.

From 1971 to 1999 I saw a lot of games, and it didn't matter whether the Tigers were good or not. I just loved going to the games at Tiger Stadium. In 1989, they lost over 100 games, of which I saw in person over 80 of them, including almost all of their home games and some on the road. My favorite spot was upper deck bleachers underneath the scoreboard. I could be out of the sun and, if it rained, everybody ran up, and I had my spot.

I joined the Tiger Stadium Fan Club in January of 1988, attended the first general meeting, and immediately signed up to be part of the historic designation committee. I wrote the history of Tiger Stadium that was presented for the historic board in Lansing.

I didn't go to the last game at Tiger Stadium. Going to games is about having fun, and I didn't see anything enjoyable about going to that. I never went down when they were demolishing the stadium because I didn't want to see that. It would be like seeing a good friend being axed to death.

Once it was torn down, I had heard that people were playing catch on the field after Ernie Harwell died. That was their way of remembering Ernie when other people were going to Comerica Park to pay their respects in May of 2010. I went down to the field on Mother's Day 2010 with a few friends to pay catch. When I saw how tall the grass was and how bad the field was, I wasn't excited about playing baseball anymore. I thought to myself, I've got a riding mower, I can cut the grass and friends would help me fix up the field. I called Frank Rashid, and he thought it was a great idea. Our first cleanup was May 12, 2010, and we got a big turnout of about 30 people. Someone from the city came out on the field and asked if we had permission, and we said no. The police came and asked if anyone complained, and we said no, and they left.

There were so many weeds it was difficult to make out the infield, the pitcher's mound, and baselines. We had to dig up the baselines. We basically brought back a baseball diamond from the dead. About two weeks later, we were chased off the field, and I was told that if I came back, I'd be arrested. I came back 12 days later on a Sunday with my riding mower. We've now done it on Sundays to keep a low profile. Over the last couple of years, we haven't had any problems. The city leaves us alone.

We've paid for everything ourselves, and we are a true, no pun intended, grassroots organization. It's been a labor of love. What makes it worthwhile is everyday people show up from around the country and come out to the field, and they thank us and tell us how much it means to them. That's what keeps us going.

I have to say that without our Navin Field Grounds Crew, there would be nine and a half acres of giant weeds, trees growing wild, and garbage everywhere. It would have been a major eyesore. I really enjoy riding my mower out there. When I am in left field, I'm thinking of Willie Horton, in center, Tris Speaker and Mickey Mantle, and in right field, I think of Ty Cobb and Al Kaline. It is an overwhelming experience just being on that hallowed ground.

We've been featured in *ESPN Magazine*, the *Detroit Free Press*, the *Detroit News*, the *New York Times*, *Preservation Magazine*, National Public Radio, and local television and radio. Several former Tigers have been back to walk the field, including Denny McLain, Dave Rozema, Lou Whitaker, and John Wockenfuss. Wockenfuss even played a pickup game with us.

There are many instances where people have placed the ashes of their loved ones, including two dear people from the Tiger Stadium Fan Club, Catherine Darin and Eva Navarro. I think about how hard they fought to save Tiger Stadium. I have seen people spread the ashes of their loved ones on at least five different occasions. Several other times I've been out there and have seen ashes that were left there. It truly is sacred ground to so many people, and there's so much history there.

It's amazing to stand at home plate where Babe Ruth and Ty Cobb stood. There's still a reason why that field should be saved for future generations. I'd like to see the whole field preserved in its entirety, and I'd like it to remain accessible for everyone to be able to use and have it as a park so people in Corktown and the rest of the city can enjoy it.

I don't think there is another instance where a major league ball club has moved from a ballpark and a group of volunteers came in to restore the old field and save it. People have a unique opportunity to go on this field and play, and they should take advantage of it while they can.

Tom Derry and his mower at the field, 2011 (Sarah Derry).

From the Workers

Jim McGinnis of Douglasville, Georgia, worked on the grounds crew at Tiger Stadium from 1958 to 1963.

I was always a baseball fan, and I wanted to work on the grounds crew at the ballpark. I worked with the greatest bunch of guys, and, believe me, they liked to drink and raise hell. The first job I did was to clean off the box seats before Opening Day in 1958. One guy I worked with there was Gil Clay, who had been around the ballpark since the days of Ty Cobb. He worked on the batter's box and pitching mound. Cobb got him to invest in Coca Cola and he was worth quite a bit, but he liked to work on the field.

I remember one time when Eddie Yost made an error that cost the ball game. He went to my boss Tony Kochevar, and he complained that the ball hit a pebble and he wanted something done about that. The next day we had to get on our hands and knees to pick up pebbles around shortstop and third base.

Tony wanted us to be the best grounds crew with the best diamond in the big leagues, and he had an ego. He had a thing about the tarp and wanted the tarp down in one minute or less in a rainstorm, and he made us practice. We would practice with that tarp when the team was out of town. Most of us were in our 20s and were in pretty good shape, and we could do it.

On day games, we started at 7:00 a.m. and had lunch at 11:30 a.m. at the Bengal Bar, and our lunch was in liquid form. We would often go in on payday and at checkout time, and usually we walked out broke. We were all probably about half stiff when we got back to the ballpark for the game. I often changed the bases, and the ball players got a bang out of laughing at us at the batting cage saying "Here come the drunks." They had a lot of nerve, because most of them were in the bag after the ball games. When the game was over, we would go to the saloon and then come back to put the cover on the field. Lots of people would buy drinks for us because we were still in our ground crew uniforms.

Opening Day in 1958 we heard a guy in the upper deck in left field had a heart attack, and Tony made me and another guy go up into the stands to take that guy down in a stretcher. We did, but it wasn't easy.

We gambled on everything. For instance, we would gamble about when the sun would shine in the morning. For a guy named Tom Keating, we bet whether he could spell *Cincinnati*. We would pick two players off the team and bet who would get the most hits that day. I picked Jimmy Piersall one day, and I went up to the batting cage and I said, "Jimmy, you gotta get some hits today." And he looked at me with those wild eyes. He said, "Who the fuck are you?" I told him I had placed a bet on him, and he kind of snickered and said, "OK, kid, I'll take care of you." I think he got three hits.

You talk about a live wire. He was a helluva ball player. He would take bug spray and spray around center field, because there were a lot of bugs out there in center field. It was funny. He would carry on a big conversation with the crowd and give them the bird. He was a little weird.

One time we were on coffee break, and we wagered who could throw the ball the farthest. We threw from the pitchers' mound to left field. I threw the ball into the second deck in left field. I did it twice in a row. Word got around to the Tiger team that Tony had a guy on the crew who could throw the ball into the second deck. Kaline went to

Tony and said, "There's nobody who can do that." The next week [when] I came to work, Rocky Colavito threw a ball from the left field foul line out of the ballpark in right field. He had a rocket of an arm.

In 1961 during batting practice, Kansas City's Marv Throneberry hit the third deck in right field. I told [Kansas City player] Norm Siebern I'd wager $5 that he'd never hit a ball there again [that season]. So we made the bet. And he never did, and I won the bet. Siebern came up to me during the last series [between Detroit and Kansas City] and gave me a $5 bill, and I still have it.

After a big crowd, we often had to sweep out the stands and, believe me, we found a lot of money. When they had those kids' days and they were all out in left field in those stands, they would get all excited and make a mess. One time, I found a very expensive watch, a Patek Philippe. I took it to Tony, and he said "If nobody claims it, you can have it."

One time Tiger catcher Lou Berberet came up to me and said, "Hey why don't you take a dip of this chewing tobacco?" I never tried the stuff. He said, "You might like it." I got a big chunk of it and spit about three times, but in a short period of time I was gagging and throwing up, and he got a big kick out of that. It tickled the hell out of Lou but made me sicker than a dog.

I loved seeing the Yankees in 1961. They were a lot of fun, too, laughing and joking. They would let us in the batting cage sometimes. Mantle, Maris, Boyer, and Skowron got a kick out of watching us trying to hit.

I had one incident with Ted Williams. He had the deepest, deepest blue eyes, and he was the best hitter I ever saw. We used to like to gather around him a little bit. All he wanted to talk about was hitting. I said, "Mr. Williams, there is a good-looking blonde over there looking at you. She has eyes for you." He said, "Do you think she could hit .300?"

Marvin Wells of Detroit was a souvenir vendor at Tiger Stadium from 1970 to 1999.

Most of the vendors worked two jobs, and many of us were postal workers. I retired from the postal service in 1983.

In 1970, a friend at work had a souvenir board and said, "Why don't you come down and give me a hand?" I thought I would work for maybe a month, but then I never left. He then said, "Why don't you work in the seats? You will make more money than I can pay you." I used to work at the Lion games also. That was a different crowd. They didn't always want that paraphernalia in front of them.

When I was selling novelties, it was as a walk-around man. I sold pennants, baseballs, small bats, anything you could carry. We would then go back and reload with things that were moving. You didn't want to keep lugging stuff around that people weren't buying. It was nice going around in the stands. I loved meeting the people; they were jovial. It was really great looking at a child's smiling face when a parent bought them a souvenir. Before the game, I enjoyed meeting the ballplayers and getting to know the people who worked at the ballpark. Ernie Harwell always came by to say hello.

I did that until a booth opened up under the stands. Everybody in my family worked with me at one time to help with the credit card machine. The last place I was located was at Gate 6 at Michigan and Trumbull. I used to kid the customers who occasionally said something was too expensive. I would say, "There's an ATM machine right behind you."

Marvin Wells (courtesy *Detroit Free Press*).

You always had to have helpers in case someone tried to take something while you were talking to a customer. If there was a shortage, it was your shortage. We worked on commission. When I first started working, it was a 20 percent commission, and later towards the end at Tiger Stadium, it was 12 percent on some items. The key to success was just being friendly with people.

I also liked working the concerts at Tiger Stadium because we sold a lot of concert shirts.

At the last game, I saw people with pliers and screwdrivers trying to take things. That was crazy.

Bill Fundaro was a fixture at Tiger Stadium, where he served as the ball man in front of the screen behind home plate from 1971 to the closing of the ballpark. The retired teacher and counselor now works as an usher at Comerica Park and is a freelance sports photographer.

As a kid, I went with my dad and uncle to Briggs Stadium three or four times a summer in the early '50s, and we especially liked the doubleheaders. When I was a sixth grader in 1954, I worked as a junior usher and did that until I went away to college in 1960. Some of my other friends had paper routes and here I was, going to select ballgames to work. I started out at sections 22 and 23 right at the edge of the screen on the first base side, which was a great area, and I later worked near the Tiger dugout. Before the game, we would sweep out the box seat area and fold the canvass box seat covers for the senior ushers. We would then go to our section and watch batting practice until the customers came in. In those days, I was making sometimes up to six dollars a game. By the second inning, I would find a seat and enjoy the ball game. I also worked the Lion games, including the 1957 championship game. I'll never forget running out onto the field and celebrating with all the other fans.

Later, when I started teaching in the mid–1960s, I began ushering again, and by 1971 I was given the opportunity to relieve the ball man behind home plate, a position I finally assumed and held full time from 1976 until the ballpark closed in 1999. I had so much fun working as the ball man, and I felt like I had the best seat in the house. I would pick up or catch the foul balls that fell off the screen and also bring new baseballs out to the umpires during the game. Before the game, the umpires gave me a bag of 60 baseballs all rubbed up with the special Delaware mud. Sometimes I had to do it during the game if I started running out of baseballs. If the mud was too dry, I had a fan pour some beer in the container I used.

People used to cheer for me when I ran up to the screen to catch the ball as it rolled off. Sometimes I would tell the fans near me: "I get a lot of applause, if you want to hear some boos, wait until the next one rolls off." I would then miss it on purpose and the boos showered down. Several times I got hit by baseballs because I would have to dive, and it typically hit me in the ass. It hurt like hell.

When I first started as the ball man, Billy Martin was managing the Tigers, and Gaylord Perry, the spitballer, was pitching [for Cleveland]. Billy asked me to let the balls roll off the screen and pick them up with two fingers and take them to him. I never noticed any stuff on those balls. The umpire finally stopped it.

Tiger Stadium ushers, 1999 (© Rebecca Cook).

One of the funniest things that happened was the time home-plate umpire Nestor Chylak asked me to get some water for him in between innings. I went to the visitors' dugout, and as I was getting the water Rod Carew said: "Hey boy, that's for the ballplayers. Get your ass out of here." I kept filling [the cup], and Carew pushed me and said, "Tell [Chylak] to get fucked." I told Chylak what happened. The next inning Carew walks to the plate to bat, Chylak turns in front of home plate, bends over with his butt to the scoreboard, and as he is sweeping the plate off he says to Carew without looking up: "Fuck me? Fuck me? Fuck you! You got three pitches to look at." The first pitch is outside. "Strike!" Chylak calls out, and Carew just looks at him. On the next pitch, I watched one of the game's greatest hitters reach out for another outside pitch and hit an easy grounder to Trammell.

Probably my biggest thrill on the job was Game Five of the 1984 World Series when Kirk Gibson hit his second home run of the game to seal the championship. In the tunnel of the dugout before the game and during the anthem, Gibson stood by himself staring at the wall at the urinal, and we heard him yelling, "It's going downtown! The fucker's going downtown. If I touch it, it's going downtown!" He was psyching himself like a football player. Tom Brookens said to me, "I think if he touches the fucker, it's going downtown," and we all laughed.

The electricity in that ballpark that night was flowing, and I still get chills thinking of it. I made damn sure I was up near the plate when Gibson came home after that second home run so I got into the photos. At the top of the ninth, I knew the fans were going to unload and come after me to get the balls, so I went to the dugout. Just before the game ended, the players jumped me and were taking balls as souvenirs. The only one who was proper was Johnny Grubb, who asked, "May I have a ball?"

Tiger Stadium was like a second home to me. I used to first go to Casey's for a quick beer, then walk up to the ballpark with the sun setting and the flags on top blowing in the breeze, and I was just as excited as a kid: What am I going to see tonight? A no-hitter? A colossal home run?

When my son was in grade school, sometimes I would take him to the stadium when the Tigers were away, and the guard would let us in. We would take in a plastic cooler, a radio, and a blanket and sit in center field, listen to the ballgame, and tell stories.

At the last game played at Tiger Stadium when nearly everyone had left, I stuck around. All of a sudden I heard a voice say, "I'm looking for Bill Fundaro," and a guard said, "It's time to go, everyone's gone." I said to the guard, "Excuse me, I want to speak to this man." He was crippled, and he said to me: "You don't know me, but I pray for you every day. I always remember you. When I was a little kid I sat behind you and you caught a ball off the screen. You then put it into my lap and told me not to raise it up and let anyone see it. I still have it in a cube on my dresser. It was the first time I received something as a kid, and not as a handicapped kid." It shows how you treat people comes back to you.

Art Witkosky was a popular hot dog vendor at Tiger Stadium from 1972 to 1999.

I first started going to the ballpark in the 1930s when I was a kid, and saw Hank Greenberg, Charlie Gehringer, and Mickey Cochrane.

It was a fun job all the way through because I loved talking to people and talking about the Tigers. I worked hard, but we always had our eyes open on the game. I got my exercise in and still got paid.

I used to throw a bag of buns way up in the air and catch it, and the crowd enjoyed it. I used to yell, "Hot doggies, hot diggedy dogs!" My favorite spot was in the lower deck between home plate and third base. But I enjoyed working the whole ballpark.

The hot-dog boxes weighed close to 75 to 80 pounds, so it was a good workout. I had no problem. I would get a percentage of the sales of around nine percent and then got the tips, so I made around $15 per hour.

I used to enjoy speaking with Ernie Harwell before the games started and knew him pretty well. I got to know a lot of the season ticketholders, and they used to call for me by name.

We had a great time in the '84 World Series, and that was always a special memory. That last game at Tiger Stadium was sad. I realized it was my last game. I was 74 years old, and I wanted to do it at Comerica Park, but they wouldn't hire me down there. I received a letter that said I was overqualified. I guess that's the way they do things, you know—corporate.

I've been to Comerica Park a couple of times, but I couldn't get into it like Tiger Stadium. You're too far away from wherever you're sitting. Even in the box seats, it seems you're far away.

I especially liked Tiger Stadium because of its history. To think Babe Ruth played there. It's sad there's nothing there anymore. It's holy ground. They had to tear it down? That's progress? Hey, you go overseas, and old buildings are still standing.

Raised in Corktown across the street from Tiger Stadium, Dennis Clotworthy in 1972 at the age of 16 started as a visitor's clubhouse attendant before becoming the visitor's batboy the next year. In 1974 and '75, he was the Tiger batboy and the last to serve former '68 champs Al Kaline, Norm Cash, Jim Northrup, and Gates Brown. Clotworthy then worked in the Tiger ticket office until 1985.

I was a stadium rat from across the street and a huge baseball fan. As kids, my friends and I would stand outside Tiger Stadium waiting for foul balls to be hit out of the ballpark. We used to all race to grab the baseballs.

One day, I asked clubhouse manager Jack Hand if I could help unload the trucks that brought in the visiting team's equipment. I did it for free several times and was thrilled to just get into the locker room. Finally he said, "Hey kid, would you like to work here?" I called my mom from the locker room and promised I would do my schoolwork. I was in the right place at the right time.

A few days before Al Kaline's last game he was honored for his 3,000th hit, and I rolled out a wheelbarrow with three heavy canvas bags. At the ceremony, I dumped the bags into the wheelbarrow and out poured 3,000 silver dollars for him. It was a highlight for me to participate because Kaline and Gordie Howe were my heroes growing up. At the end of his last game, I was cleaning out the dugout, and Kaline sat on the bench by himself, staring out at the field and taking it all in. You could tell he just wanted to be alone. I will never forget that.

One of the nicest players to be around was Norm Cash. I was shocked when the Tigers released him. He came up to me and asked if I would clean out his locker and call a taxicab while he said goodbye to his teammates. Norm was everybody's favorite in the locker room because he always had a smile and a joke. I walked out of the stadium with him and carried his equipment bag to a taxicab. He had tears in his eyes, and I wished him good luck. He thanked me for being a friend and a great batboy, and I watched him leave. It was very sad.

Being on the field at Tiger Stadium for those games was unbelievable, and I often heard kids saying they wished they could be a batboy. But the best part took place in the clubhouse with the friendships I made and the constant joking around. It was such a great atmosphere, especially after a victory. I was paid only $12 a game and worked often from 11 a.m. until 1 a.m., but I'll admit something now: I would have done it for nothing.

Joe Michnuk is a former Tiger Stadium home locker room security guard who is a member of the Navin Field Grounds Crew, a volunteer group that maintained the diamond at Michigan and Trumbull.

My first game at Tiger Stadium was, I think, in 1965, when I was seven. My dad took me to see the Tigers play the Red Sox because his favorite player was Carl Yastrzemski. When I walked from that dark concourse, the emerald green field was almost blinding. The whole feeling, the smells of popcorn, cigars, and hot dogs—it didn't get any better than that.

I grew up in west Dearborn, and I used to ride my bike to the corner of Princeton and Syracuse, where Norm Cash lived. He was my favorite player. One day I finally got the courage to ask him for his autograph. He was just a character, always having fun, and I liked that.

I used to skip school and go to Opening Day, and I went to a ton of baseball games. My favorite spot was the lower-deck bleachers in right field, where the tickets were a buck. I used to go early for batting practice. One year I caught about 46 baseballs. It was so much fun.

Probably my favorite memory as a fan before I worked there was the day Dave Winfield hit his first home run in the American League in 1981. The ball bounced from the seats and back to the field. Ricky Peters retrieved it and tossed it into the stands right to me. The ushers came over to me, and I agreed to give the ball to Winfield. I met him and Billy Martin after the game, and I got a couple of autographed baseballs and the Yankee lineup card.

Two years later, I saw an ad for security guards at Tiger Stadium in the *Dearborn Press and Guide*, and about five of my friends and I applied, and we all got jobs there.

On opening day of 1983, I was placed at a beer stand in the upper deck, and then the authorities found out I was a decent guy, so they moved me to be the Tigers' dugout guard. During any stoppage of play and between innings, I would stand on top of the dugout with two ushers. I would also give breaks to the guard inside the Tiger clubhouse and stay in there for 20 or 30 minutes.

In 1984, during a rain delay early in the season, I'm head of the crew, and we're on the field. The tarp is out, and some idiot runs out and slides on the tarp. One of the guys got him and brought him over to me. He comes with a roundhouse right that I don't even see, and it hits me in the nose. I threw his ass down in front of 45,000 people to the screaming cheers of the crowd. I grabbed his Members Only jacket and blew my bloody nose into it and dragged him off the field. I then testified against him in court the next day. I told my boss, "I've been punched in the face in front of 45,000 people. I've had people in the bleachers hit me with beer bottles. Give me an easy job." So, he gave me a radio and binoculars and told me to sit in the photo deck and call in problems. A few days after that, the guy in the clubhouse quit, and he gave me his job.

On my first day, Jack Morris comes in and says, "I gotta shake your fucking hand. For a guy to go from a bleacher bum to sitting in an easy chair in the clubhouse, I gotta hand it to you."

After one road trip, Morris said, "We've been gone for two weeks. What do you do when we're not here?" And I said, "I just go have fun. I went up to Traverse City and hung around with some friends." He said, "Oh, you're one of those fudgies?" From then on, everyone called me "Fudgie."

One time [Kirk] Gibson struck out for like the third time, and all I can hear are lights busting in the dugout tunnel and the bat thrashing against the walls and

The bleacher ticket booth at Tiger Stadium, 1999 (© Rebecca Cook).

him cussing at the top of his lungs, "Motherfucker, I fucking suck," and, boom, another light goes out. Another time Dan Petry is pitching, and he got pulled early and came in. He kicked the trash can like a field goal kicker, and everything went flying. I couldn't help it and I started chuckling, and a [pair of] spike[s] came flying across the room and hit right above my head. I got the hell out of there and went into the hallway where it was safe.

I used to listen to Ernie [Harwell's broadcast] in the hallway and also watch the game in the locker room.

When we won the World Series in 1984, the crowd noise from inside the locker room was deafening. When Gibson hit that second home run, you would not believe the electricity that was in that place. It was crazy. It was like being in the back of the Roman Coliseum.

It was a free-for-all when the players ran into the locker room. I got in trouble when they won the division because I ended up on *This Week in Baseball* pouring champagne on Al Kaline's head. So I was trying to stay out of the camera view. But I drank champagne with a towel around my neck, because that shit stings when it gets in your eyes.

The next day I was off, but I came back in because I wanted to get a home plate signed by the team, which, as it turns out, I ended up giving to Jack Morris. Jim Schmakel, the clubhouse manager, asked if I would ask the media to leave the clubhouse. This one man I asked to leave said he was the director of the victory parade in downtown Detroit that day, and I said "Sure, you can stay." I told him "good luck with the parade" because I was going to ride on the bus with the rest of the employees to Kennedy Square. He said, "I've got a spot in one of the cars for you." But then he said, "Wait, no one is riding with Sparky." I went up to him, and Sparky stood up, grabbed my hand, and said, "Joseph, my boy, you are riding with me." Our picture ended up on the front page of USA Today.

On Opening Day of 2010, I saw the news that people were running around the Tiger Stadium field. I thought, "That looks cool. I want to do that." A few weeks later, I was driving by on my motorcycle, and I walked onto the field and met Tom Derry and his girlfriend, Sarah. He told me they were cutting the grass and maintaining the field, and I said, "Look, you can count me in." Ever since, I have been down there hundreds of times to help groom the field. I do it because I love that site. It's The Corner. It's the most famous corner of Michigan. I have a connection to that piece of property that goes back to my earliest memories. No matter what's there, I'll never stop loving the site where I've had the best times of my life. It's in me; I cannot get it out of there. My connection to that land is in my soul.

One time Jim Navin, a direct descendent of Frank Navin, came down to the site and shook my hand and said, "Thank you for what you are doing," and he purchased two of our Navin Field Grounds Crew T-shirts. That was a highlight.

Steve Thomas began selling peanuts and souvenirs outside Tiger Stadium at age 13 in the early 1980s. His business evolved into the Detroit Athletic Co., a multimillion dollar Internet and retail store enterprise that specializes in sports products and memorabilia celebrating Detroit sports history and that is located one block west of the Tiger Stadium site.

My father owned the Devil Restaurant and a lot of the parking lots west and north of the ballpark, and my brother and I used to go down there with him to help out. We noticed during the ballgames that people were selling things outside of the stadium, and we wanted to give it a try. In April 1982, my brother Dave was 13 and I was 11, and we started selling peanuts and soon souvenirs at the corner of Cochrane and Kaline Drive near left field. It was a little frightening to me with some of the drunken people I saw, but what kept me coming back was the ballpark. I remember the sounds of the ballpark when the crowd would cheer. It sounded like the ocean, and it was the sound I would hear from my grandparents' porch in the Corktown neighborhood across from the stadium.

Dave and I had our transistor radio on to hear Ernie Harwell and Paul Carey do the play-by-play, but within about a year, I could tell what happened without the radio on. For instance, sometimes there would be an initial cheer, then there was a hush, then the cheer got really loud, and I knew it was a home run.

Occasionally, we would get foul balls that came over the roof. It seemed we got one foul ball every homestand.

I really never saw that many innings inside the ballpark, and I like to say I learned the game of baseball from Ernie Harwell. We knew the stadium guard "Tiger Joe" at Gate 13. When the game was going on, if I needed to use the restroom or get a hot dog, we just walked in the stadium. On a homestand, I would probably go in twice and catch an inning or two. But even today there is something really charming about listening to the ball game on the radio because that was what I was used to.

We both felt we were part of the show. You couldn't help but get caught up in the excitement. I stopped playing Little League baseball because I had a summer job by the ballpark. My friends were all jealous because I got to hang out at Tiger Stadium. We knew all the grounds crew, so on an off day we used to go onto the field. Looking back, I think any other kid would have died to have had that experience.

The level of excitement right out of the gate in 1984 is almost indescribable. The crowds were huge, and we did very well. We had a custom souvenir trailer built and called it the Designated Hatter. I remember a doubleheader in July when we made something like $4,000. Sometimes you're in the right place at the right time. We benefitted from two waves: the licensing of major league products and the Tigers being phenomenal. After that, we opened our store and called it the Designated Hatter before changing it to the Detroit Athletic Company.

When the Tigers decided they wanted to leave Tiger Stadium, our family was supportive of the Tiger Stadium Fan Club. Tiger Stadium and Fenway Park were in the same situation, with the clubs considering abandoning their classic ballparks. But in Boston, the ownership listened to the fans and renovated the ballpark, and they ended up winning two World Series championships.

Even though the stadium is gone, the field is still historic. This isn't a movie set in Dyersville, Iowa. It's the field where Ty Cobb and Babe Ruth played, and our store is 250 feet west of the field. It's amazing that, despite this history, the city and the Ilitches have treated it with loathing. It seems that we have to preserve it ourselves and explain to people that this is where for 104 years we watched professional baseball in the city. Every day there are people who come down and walk on the field, even with snow on the ground. That's a small sampling. If there was ever a true "Field of Dreams," it is at the corner of Michigan and Trumbull.

From the Booth

Paul Carey shared play-by-play duties with the legendary Ernie Harwell on Detroit Tiger radio broadcasts from 1973 through 1991, and for 16 of those years, he also handled the engineering for the broadcasts. Previously, he had produced the Detroit Tigers radio network from 1964 through 1971. Carey joined the announcing staff at WJR in 1956, became the assistant sports director in 1958, produced the shows on the Tiger radio network from 1964 through 1971, and worked there until his retirement in 1992.

I became a fan of the Tigers in 1935, but the first time I went to a ball game with my family was in 1937 at Navin Field as a nine-year-old. I saw the Yankees beat the Tigers,

7–4. Red Ruffing got the win, and my hero, Tommy Bridges, took the loss. One thing about it that I remember is the scoreboard part of the wall in left field. I was very frightened of all the traffic when we left the ballpark and I lay down on the floor in the backseat....

I also remember sitting in the right field lower deck in 1939 and watching the Tigers play the Red Sox. There was a young, skinny player for Boston shagging fly balls in the pregame practice, and my dad looked it up in the scorebook and said "That's Ted Williams." (It was his rookie season.) "The Splendid Splinter" was a great nickname for him. I remember Dom DiMaggio was the center fielder, and he covered all of Williams' territory, too, probably because Ted was thinking of his next turn at bat rather than what was coming at him.

I grew up listening to Harry Heilmann on the radio, and I remember looking up to see where he sat in his booth hanging down from the second deck just to the first base side of the screen. Of course, I never dreamed that one day I would be sitting in his seat broadcasting games.

I have thought of Heilmann over the years many, many times. I can even remember going down with my friend Ron Brookings when the Tigers were out of town to the Telenews Theater just off Grand Circus Park to watch Heilmann do the re-creation of the Tiger games, because he didn't do broadcasts on the road and reported the game off the ticker. Harry had such wonderful stories, and I loved the sound of his voice. He had a little drawl. He was fun and easy to listen to. He didn't put on airs or scream and shout.

My first experience as a broadcaster at the ballpark was in 1958, when I did the pregame shows at the corner of Cochrane and Michigan prior to the Van Patrick and Mel Ott broadcast. I would go into the Tiger [locker] room and try to find someone to interview. At that time, WJR only carried the night games, [and] there were a small number.

"The Corner" as seen after the addition of "Tiger Plaza" in 1993 (© Rebecca Cook).

I did the interviews inside the WJR mobile unit parked outside on the street. Mel Ott was so kind to me, as I was inexperienced, and he would introduce me to people.

When we broadcast from Tiger Stadium, our booth was closer to the field than any other ballpark. It was probably half the distance to the field compared to any other place. In that original booth, there was a sink to wash your hands initially, but it became a latrine. There was a ladder that went up to a trapdoor, but it was later sealed; originally it was Harry's entrance into that booth.

Our first booth looked right down the third base line, and then later our booth was a little more behind home plate. When the stadium was being renovated, we had to broadcast half a season from the third deck down the left field line beyond third base where Van Patrick used to broadcast the Lion games. Every ball hit looked like a line drive to us. That was not a good place to broadcast a ball game.

Every kid should have had the experience of seeing Tiger Stadium for a night game for the first time. To walk through one of those tunnels and see that green field: there was just nothing like it, especially before the seats were [blue and] orange.

The original booth had a heavy chain-link fence in front of us. We had a shutter that I would close up at night when I would leave. It was like a cathedral, and I felt very lonely doing the scoreboard show after the game, because everybody had left. My footsteps echoed on the old cement ramps when I walked out of the booth. I would go down that back ramp near the parking lot, and I was the only one left.

To say the least, being a kid from Michigan who grew up a Tiger fan and became a broadcaster for the club was very, very special. When you get old like me, all you have are your memories, and I like mine.

After playing nine years with St. Louis, Pittsburgh, Chicago, and the New York Giants, Joe Garagiola became a baseball broadcaster best known for his nearly 30-year association with NBC as an announcer on the popular NBC *Game of the Week* broadcasts. In 1991, the Baseball Hall of Fame honored him with the Ford Frick Award for outstanding broadcasting accomplishments.

I always enjoyed announcing at Tiger Stadium because it was a real fan-friendly ballpark. Heck, the fans were right on top of the players. The broadcast booth was behind home and then also down third base. The one behind home plate was really great except for the foul balls that came at you: that was always a challenge as they came whizzing by. I never got hit though. The booth behind home plate was nice because you could go to the bathroom, but you couldn't go at the one on the third base side. That was like broadcasting from a submarine. It was so close. Between innings I could holler at the umpires from the booth. The people were really great. It was always a delight to go into the clubhouse and speak to people like Sparky Anderson.

I did a pregame show once on the best place to catch foul balls, and it was along third base at Tiger Stadium. I remember there were three guys who had a system. One guy would get the ball, another blocked the aisle, and the biggest guy blocked the aisle coming down to the aisle where the seats were.

I remember in those dugouts you had to be careful because when you got out of your seat you could get a concussion.

Going to Tiger Stadium was like going to see an old friend. It really was.

Best known as the play-by-play announcer for the Los Angeles Dodgers, Vin Scully broadcast Dodger games since 1950 and held the longest tenure of any broadcaster with a single club in professional sports. The recipient of numerous awards, including the Ford Frick Award from the National Baseball Hall of Fame, in 2000 he was elected the top sportscaster of the 20th century by the American Sportscasters Association. He was NBC-TV's lead baseball broadcaster from 1983 to 1989. In 1984, he did the television broadcast of the World Series between Detroit and San Diego.

One of my first memories of Tiger Stadium was when I started doing the NBC *Game of the Week* in the early 1980s. I went in to see Sparky Anderson in his little office, and he said, "Come here, close the door. I'm going to give you all my signs. You are going to be the smartest guy who ever did a ball game." I laughed and said, "No way. I wouldn't remember your signs, and I'd mess them all up."

Of course the 1984 World Series stands out for me. I love calling a dramatic home run like Kirk Gibson's in the final game. I like to call it as quickly and as accurately as I can and then just shut up. Listening to the roar of the crowd in Detroit was just marvelous. It was so precious that I never thought that I could have words that were better than the roar. I remember just before that the exchange between Sparky and Gibson and the confrontation between Gossage and Gibby. It was wonderful, especially being in the World Series, I mean, holy mackerel. That was terrific.

After the Tigers won the championship, fans were throwing clumps of sod up towards the broadcast booth, and one of them fell on top of Joe Garagiola's head, and he got angry and left the booth. I actually read the closing of the broadcast for two minutes while I was on my back under the counter in the booth during the time that all the stuff came out. I was wondering why everyone was throwing clumps of dirt up our way. I found out afterwards that Jack Buck, God rest his soul, was in the next booth, and he was holding a baseball glove and asking the people to throw sod up to him. They threw it towards him and then up in our booth.

Tiger Stadium reminded me a bit of Ebbets Field the way the broadcast booth hung from the upper deck behind home plate. I was amazed how close you were at Tiger Stadium. I mean, I could hear the hitter grunt. When the balls came back to us, it was like they were shot out of a bazooka. It was really frightening. You couldn't take your eyes off the plate for a split second.

I did enjoy hearing the chanting from the center field bleachers. They would holler back and forth to each other. They were fun.

From the Gridiron

A member of the Pro Football Hall of Fame, Joe Schmidt is considered "Mr. Detroit Lion," having starred as one of the game's greatest middle linebackers while playing for the Detroit Lions from 1953 to 1965. The two-time National Football League champion and former team captain was the head coach of the club from 1967 to 1972.

When there were only 12 clubs in the league, Tiger Stadium was the most comfortable stadium to practice and play. It was always very friendly there and beautiful. There was nothing like being there on a beautiful autumn day with the sun out, the grass freshly cut, the smell of the grass, and the people sitting so close it felt like you could touch them.

When I started in 1953, I was only 21, and I didn't think I would even make the team. To then make the team and be on a national hook-up broadcast on Thanksgiving Day and the NFL championship game was a wonderful opportunity and a delight for me and people back home. I had just purchased a new car, and I thought if we win it would take me out of the hole. I remember standing on the sidelines when, with about 1:40 left, Bobby Layne hit Jim Doran with the winning touchdown to beat Cleveland for the championship. Our winning payoff was $2,400, and the loser got $1,800. The $600 difference was a lot of money back then. I was tickled we won so I could pay off that two-door Chevy.

Nineteen fifty-seven was a wonderful season. Tobin Rote did a magnificent job filling in for Bobby when he hurt his ankle. In the championship game, we were paying off a debt to the Browns for the '54 championship game in which they knocked the daylights out of us. Cleveland made five turnovers, and we got on them real fast. They never recovered from the first half. When the game ended, I went to the official to retrieve the game ball. Fans came onto the field and tried to get the ball. I ended up getting lifted up and carried, which helped get me and the ball out off the field. There are still a lot of people floating around the city who remember and cherish those days at Tiger Stadium.

Even though the only thing left at Michigan and Trumbull is the baseball diamond and the flagpole, I can go over there and show you exactly on the field where Jim Doran made that catch to win in the '53 championship game and where Chuck Hughes died. It's very sad to see the ballpark gone.

Pat Studstill was a popular wide receiver and punter for the Detroit Lions from 1961 to 1967 and later played for the Los Angeles Rams and New England Patriots before retiring in 1972.

I remember first walking into the ballpark my rookie season for an exhibition game during training camp, and I just thought, "My God, Ty Cobb played here, and Babe Ruth, and Mickey Mantle." I was in awe.

I also have fond memories of going down to the Lindell AC bar downtown and not too far from the stadium to meet other athletes like Norm Cash. We both wore number 25, and Norm used to always say, "Number 25 in your program, but number 1 in your heart." It was quite a crew up there.

Even though the ballpark was always packed, I never heard the noise when I was playing, but I heard it on the sidelines. I remember being able to see my wife in the stands in the upper deck along the third base line. I remember how nice and how loyal the fans were at Tiger Stadium. Before the game, when we walked out of the dugout, a fan always gave Bruce Maher a hot dog. I would tell him, "Bruce, that's going to screw you up," and he said, "Nah, it doesn't bother me, it doesn't bother me."

It always pissed me off when we ended up playing into the baseball diamond because, boy, that dust would just eat you up when you're running a pass pattern. The footing was tough when you went from the grass into the dirt infield, but it was just as tough for the defensive back because he didn't have any footing either.

But I loved that old stadium, I did.

I remember the fans who used to come out after every game and stand there waiting for us. I can picture that today. Right now I think back and realize what a great life it was playing there. I didn't appreciate it then like I do now. To think I was playing professional football for the Detroit Lions at Tiger Stadium.

Wayne Walker was a linebacker and placekicker for the Detroit Lions from 1958 to 1972. He ranks second behind Lion kicker Jason Hanson on the club's all-time list for games played (200) and seasons played (15). In 2009, he was selected to the Detroit Lions all-time team.

I didn't see Tiger Stadium until I played in it as a rookie in 1958. It was a Saturday night exhibition game against the Giants. Growing up, I was a big baseball fan, and I knew about the park. I remember getting off the bus and going through the tunnel and out onto the field. I never even bothered to look at the locker room. As a kid from Boise, it was like seeing the Seventh Wonder of the World. It was just what a ballpark was supposed to look like. I thought, if this is not from central casting, then what is?

I did find out pretty quickly how small the locker rooms were, especially the visitors'. The few times I was in the visitors' locker room, I thought this must be worth three points because those other guys must be so depressed.

I later saw a lot of games there as a baseball fan, but I really liked the stadium for football, too. Both teams were on the same side of the field, and that really led to some back-and-forth insults, something you didn't get at a lot of other places. My real breakthrough game occurred in the 1961 Thanksgiving game against the Packers. I had something like four sacks and a couple of quarterback hurries before they were counted. Don Shula was our defensive coach, and he told me after the game that that was the way he expected me to play and that I had a great future ahead of me. It really meant a lot to me. When I retired at age 36, I was still a starter, and I felt I could still play a couple of more years. Then I thought, wait, my kids are allowed to stay up later than I could when I was in training camp.

Named 1967's defensive rookie of the year, seven-time Pro Bowl selection Lem Barney starred for the Detroit Lions from 1967 to 1977 and was inducted into the Pro Football Hall of Fame in 1992. In 1999, Barney was ranked number 97 on *The Sporting News* list of the 100 Greatest Football Players.

My first time walking into Tiger Stadium was at an exhibition game my rookie year in 1967. I was in awe of the place because I had watched a lot of baseball on TV and seen the Thanksgiving Day game that was broadcast there every year. It was a joy to have the opportunity to walk onto that field.

The locker room was pretty cramped for football with all our equipment. I lockered next to Mel Farr and Alex Karras. Alex didn't really like rookies, but he embraced me because he said I was a good player. I had two interceptions in my first game at Green Bay.

When I walked down the steps into the tunnel from the locker room and then walked into the dugout and up the four dugout steps onto the field, my heart was palpitating. It was like that every game until I made the first hit.

When I made a good play at the stadium, the crowd was sort of deafening. Once you've got the ball in your hands and you've got the potential to go into the end zone or make a big yardage play, the crowd noise was there, and when you went into the end zone it was deafening. Sometimes it was so deafening you couldn't pay attention to it. I never tried to pay attention to the vibration of the crowd. I wanted to see how my teammates were affected by a play I made. I enjoyed my teammates' reaction more than the roar from the crowd.

I loved playing on grass as opposed to Astroturf, but there was a section of Tiger Stadium's infield between first base and second base on the diamond that had new sod for football and that made it difficult. Dick LeBeau and I used to remind each other to watch our footing over there, because if you slipped the wrong way, the receiver was by you. A lot of guys got twisted knees and ankles from that, and that is how Steve Owens' career ended. The bad weather games really stood out. I got beat on two touchdowns on Thanksgiving Day 1970 by Oakland's Fred Biletnikoff right in that sod area. I slipped on both of them. Opposing teams took advantage of that part of the field, and I don't know why we didn't.

I had a lot of good games at Tiger Stadium, but one favorite that fans remind me of was against Cincinnati, when I ran back an interception for a touchdown and ran a punt return back. It was a wounded-duck-like punt and was slowly rolling, and about five Bengals were running slowly in front of me surrounding the ball. I said to myself, "If this takes a hop and I can field it cleanly, I am going to try." Sure enough, the ball popped up chest high, I grabbed it and broke right through the middle of the five, moved to the left, and then ran right down the sideline for an 86-yard touchdown.

It was a joy for me to have played at Tiger Stadium for seven years. There were such great athletes who played on that field in both baseball and football. The Central Division all played outside on grass. I didn't want to go to the Silverdome. The Astroturf is so deadly on you.

After I was done playing, sometimes I would pull off the Lodge Freeway and look at Tiger Stadium and reminisce and think what could have been if they had refurbished it and never gone out to the Silverdome. I can tell you I have never gone back to the Silverdome.

From the Diamond

Jake Wood was a second baseman for the Tigers from 1961 to 1967 and the first African American player to come up through the Tiger organization and become a regular starter.

The first major league ballpark I ever saw was Ebbets Field, and I got to see my hero Jackie Robinson, too. That was a thrill for me.

But walking into Tiger Stadium as a rookie was something else. To see the vastness of it and how manicured it was—all that green was a joy. Just to stand out in that field in a Tiger uniform—here I was being on that field and playing with and against players that I admired growing up.

Just pulling into the players' parking lot and entering the stadium and interacting with the fans and the employees—that's something I won't forget.

In my very first game, when I came to bat, I heard something knocking, and it was my knees. Your heart and mind are just vibrating. Later in the game, I hit my first home run into the left centerfield stands. It wasn't much of an effort, but I must have caught it on the sweet spot, and there it went. Sometimes because you made that achievement, you think it would be easy after that, but was I mistaken. Then they start to go to school on you.

When I used to get on first base, I remember the crowd chanting "Go, go, go." One of my best assets was that I could run, so it was crowd pleasing to steal a base.

For hitters, Tiger Stadium was perfect because of the green background, and the dimensions weren't so astronomical. If Ted Williams had played his career at Tiger Stadium, he probably would have hit 1,000 home runs.

The environment was so nice at the ballpark, and so were the people you came into contact with, like the grounds crew. It had a calming effect for me. In those days it just seemed like you were an average person, and people were more connected with one another. You could be in a barber shop and you were just "Jake."

But the most difficult thing was playing there when the fans expressed certain negative feelings about their home team. That's the team you should be encouraging no matter what you do. Depending on your makeup, booing can be devastating, especially when you are playing at home. You expect that on the road but not at home. People expect perfection, but you're human and things happen.

I guess we were so successful in 1961 that the fans expected us to sustain that.

I certainly heard some racist remarks when I was playing, but it was not just limited to any one city. However, when I was in the minors, Florida was a culture shock for me. When you look at the bottom line, we're all human beings. When I came up in Detroit and I looked back at African Americans I had played with in the minor leagues, they were excellent ballplayers, but they never had the opportunity. I thank God for the opportunity that was presented to me. I just happened to be in the right place at the right time.

Jake Wood at Tiger Stadium, about 1961.

I'm reminded almost daily of my time playing at Tiger Stadium. I was at the last game and participated in the closing ceremonies. When a girl called me from the Tigers, she asked me my uniform size and then asked me if I needed a wheelchair. Then it dawned on me on how all the years had passed. I don't need a wheelchair because I play racquetball and I'm in a senior softball league, even though I'm 75 years old.

Tiger Stadium will always be part of my heart.

Rocky Colavito was one of the most powerful sluggers in major league baseball during his 14-year career from 1955 through 1968. While spending four years in a Tiger uniform as the clean-up hitter sandwiched between Al Kaline and Norm Cash, Colavito slugged 139 home runs and drove in 430 runs.

I understand why Ted Williams said Briggs Stadium was his favorite park, because it was a bandbox in right field. I remember the upper deck in right field hanging over the field because I was under a ball one time, and I thought I was going to catch it, and it dropped in the upper deck for a home run.

Believe it or not, Tiger Stadium was not one of my favorite ballparks. What bothered me was that the vendors and people wearing white in the centerfield lower-deck bleachers would walk around, and it was distracting as hell. For me, it was not the best ballpark for seeing the ball. I didn't hit real bad there, but I didn't think it was my best ballpark. Fenway was one of my favorites because you could see so well, and the other was Griffith Stadium in Washington, D.C.

My first real opportunity to play as a rookie in 1955 was at Briggs Stadium. I went four-for-four and hit two doubles off Ned Garver that should have been home runs because they hit the angled two-foot extension at the top of the left field fence. They got rid of that extension either the next year or the year after that.

When I was on a visiting team, if I was in a slump sometimes, I would walk from Tiger Stadium to the Book Cadillac Hotel, where we were staying. That stretch up Michigan Avenue used to be called Skid Row. I looked at those people sometimes and thought "I don't have it so bad," even I went 0-for-30. It would pick me up.

One time I got so mad at myself after an at-bat that when I took my position in left field, I threw the warm-up ball over the right field roof at Tiger Stadium.

One of the highlights of my career happened at Tiger Stadium in that 22-inning game, because I went 7 for 10. The sad thing is we lost when Jackie Reed hit that home run, the only one of his career. It was really disappointing because I had led off the bottom of the 10th inning with a triple and didn't score. I thought our manager, Bob Scheffing, made a major mistake because the best bunter on our team was Chico Fernandez. He let him hit, and he hit a line drive right to the right fielder. He should have bunted for a suicide squeeze.

I often felt the fans at Tiger Stadium were worse to the Tigers than the visiting team. I had one of the best years of my life in 1961. I hit 45 homers and had 140 RBI, but the next year I didn't have a home run in my first 100 at-bats. One time my brother was visiting from New York, and the fans booed the hell out of me and totally forgot the year before. My brother said afterward, "I never heard such crap." They were on me like you wouldn't believe.

As a kid, I would try to get autographs outside of Yankee Stadium, and I remembered not only how bad I felt when a player wouldn't sign for me but also the time I didn't want to wash my hair after Charlie Keller patted me on the head. I remember at Tiger Stadium standing in the parking lot or outside the lot, and I would tell the kids to line up in a straight line, not to take cuts or push, and I would sign for all of them.

Jimmy Piersall played from 1950 to 1967 in the majors, most notably with the Boston Red Sox and Cleveland Indians when he was one of the game's premier center fielders

as well as one of its most colorful characters. Piersall is famous for his early struggle with mental illness that became the subject of the book and movie *Fear Strikes Out*.

Detroit was the best town for me to play in because I always hit well there and made good plays. Briggs Stadium was such a great ballpark and the Tigers drew a lot of people.

The big thing about me was that my antics made the fans mad. I loved to rile up the crowd. I remember one time during a tied ball game, Fred Hatfield was on second and Harvey Kuenn hit a ball to right center and I made a nice catch. When I came up to bat, the fans were really booing me, and I hit a home run off of Frank Lary. Frank liked to screw around, too. He had a great curveball and this one time I stuck my bat butt out, and I threw the bat to his left at the ground. I walked out to get it, and he picked it up and just before he handed it to me he dropped it to the ground. He was a clown, too, just like Norm Cash.

The fans at Briggs Stadium threw a lot of stuff at me. One time a hammer was thrown and on it was written "Fuck You." Another guy threw a beer on me and he was taken to the police station. The judge made him send me an apology letter and it was a nice one. They used to call out to me, "Coo-coo. Coo-coo." Most of the time it didn't bother me because I thought I must be a pretty good player. When I ran around third base, I gave them the finger. I always played well against the Tigers. I prided myself on my defense, and I was always moving, so it didn't bother me.

When you were in a slump, it was great to go into Tiger Stadium to straighten yourself out because it was such a great hitter's ballpark. One time I went 5-for-5 against Jim Bunning, and they were all bloops. Boy was he mad. Bunning used to throw at you, too. Great pitcher. Back then, if the guy ahead of you hit a home run and you were the next batter, you were going down whether it was Bunning or whoever.

Many times I would walk from the ballpark to the Sheraton Cadillac Hotel, especially if I had a bad day. Fans would hang out outside the ballpark asking for autographs, and I hated that. They were very cruel to me, and they thought it was funny. I used to walk by and kick them in the shins. I would go past this area called "Skid Row," and the bums would say "Hi, Jim, how ya doin'? Got any baseballs?" They probably wanted to give them to the bartenders to get some booze.

Baseball's last pitcher to win 30 games, Denny McLain pitched for the Tigers from 1963 through 1970. The three-time all-star won the American League Cy Young Award in 1968 and 1969, and in 1968 he was the American League MVP, leading the Tigers to their third World Series championship.

When I first was called up to the Tigers in September of 1963, I was in awe of Tiger Stadium. There are no other ways to describe it. I had been to Wrigley Field as a kid, but it was not as enclosed as Tiger Stadium, and it was nothing like I had seen before.

In my first start, I pitched a complete game seven-hitter at the ballpark, and I hit a home run, the only one I ever hit.

It was a terrific place. When I walked in there from the players' parking lot, it felt like I was walking into a dungeon; there wasn't anything friendly about the entrance. You really thought you were big shit, parking inside the stadium.

I used to love to hit balls into the stands for the fans when I hit fungo fly balls to the outfielders before the game. Jim Campbell fined me once for doing that. I did it almost every day when I wasn't pitching. I wanted to give the ball to a fan as a souvenir.

In addition to winning the pennant at the ballpark in '68, my favorite personal memory was winning my 30th game. It was a typical game for us. I gave up a couple of home runs, and we came from behind and won another one. We really knew how to play. When we won it with Horton's hit, I was sitting next to Kaline on the bench, and when I jumped up, I hit my head really good on the low dugout ceiling.

It's a sad commentary when the man who is supposed to be entrusted with the responsibility to protect the history of the past, Mike Ilitch (the Tiger owner), didn't do it. He didn't have to allow the stadium to be torn down. I believe when you own a baseball franchise, you not only have a responsibility for the present and the future, but you also have to maintain and honor the past.

A couple of times, I drove by the stadium when they were knocking it down. It was really regrettable. There should have been more respect to that site. It was a disgrace what happened. They could have kept at least a section of the ballpark.

Bill "Spaceman" Lee was a left-handed pitcher for the Boston Red Sox from 1969 to 1978 and the Montreal Expos from 1979 to 1982. The author of several popular baseball books including *The Wrong Stuff*, Lee was inducted into the Red Sox Hall of Fame as the club's record-holder for most games pitched by a Boston left-hander (321) and the third-highest win total (94) by a Red Sox southpaw.

The first win of my career was at Tiger Stadium in September of 1969 when I came in for relief. It was great. I liked the ballpark because it was in a neighborhood, all the locals were parking the cars, and the Lindell AC bar was down the road. It was an old, old baseball venue, and I just loved it. It was a jewel, and it's too bad they closed it down. They could have fixed it up like Fenway Park and Wrigley Field, and it would be a jewel today.

Fenway and Tiger Stadium were just the opposite for a pitcher. Tiger Stadium was big to left field. The funny thing is, though, that when the wind blew out it was like a suction device. The ball just seemed to fly out of there. It was weird; it was totally encased in there. The ball carried and carried in there. Reggie Jackson's homer in the All-Star Game was the longest one I have ever seen.

In 1972 we lost the division to the Tigers at Tiger Stadium in the second-to-the-last game of the season. I'll never forget Luis Aparicio being waved around third, slipping and falling, and we lost by half a game. I was so upset over how we lost, and everybody was crying in the locker room. The manager really didn't care for me, and he didn't use me enough, and I was pitching well. I was walking to our bus, and I saw the Tiger fans were so exuberant. I said, I'm not being depressed. As we were walking to our bus some Detroit fans asked me to come party with them, and I did. I ended up in Birmingham on some pool table, shit-faced at four in the morning. I don't know how I got back to the hotel, but I was lit up like a Christmas tree.

The bullpen at Tiger Stadium was a little pillbox and the smallest in the league. You'd tell a rookie to get up in the late innings, and he'd stand up and bang his head. Anyone who was six-foot-two was going to bang his head.

From '69 to '72, I would sit out in the bullpen and just read. I would stick my books under my warmup jacket, sit down in the corner, and wait for the phone to ring. I would watch a little of the game, look up, and if nothing happened, I would just read. I was reading a lot of Vonnegut back then and textbooks. I remember Alvin Toffler's *Future Shock*. I read a lot of economics and a lot of history.

I didn't like pitching at Tiger Stadium. I didn't do well there. I had a rough time with them; they had good ball clubs. Tiger fans were very knowledgeable and very fair, and then you had a lot of Canadians come over, and they were very polite.

I felt bad when they tore it down. It was just the best.

A native of Grand Rapids, Dave Rozema made his debut with the Detroit Tigers at age 20 in 1977 and was selected by *The Sporting News* as the American League Rookie Pitcher of the Year. A member of the 1984 World Series championship Tiger team, Rozema played for Detroit from 1977 to 1984.

Our dad used to take us down to Tiger Stadium when I was kid growing up in Grand Rapids, and we'd go at least twice a year and sit in the center field bleachers. I loved going to the twi-night doubleheaders on Friday night and having hot dogs, cotton candy, getting a souvenir, and watching five hours of baseball, which was great. I remember getting a baseball with all the players' signatures stamped on it and the souvenir guy going through the stands with Tiger pennants, pencils, bats, and a great big cluster of things. I thought that was pretty cool. I also remember the Merle Alvey Dixieland Band walking through different areas of the ballpark.

I remember in seventh grade taking the bus with my schoolmates and sitting in the left field stands and yelling out to Mickey Stanley, who was also from Grand Rapids, and we would yell asking him to throw us a ball… "Hey, we're from Grand Rapids…." I think John Hiller threw us a ball, and we all went scrambling for it. And then, when I was playing, I liked throwing a ball or two to the fans.

When you are born and raised in Michigan and the Tigers are your team like Gibby and me, it was extra special to put on the Old English D for the very first time. It was quite an honor. My number in spring training when I first put a professional uniform on was 68, which was pretty cool.

I'll never forget when I first made it to Tiger Stadium as a player and looking up into the stands to see my grandparents, parents, my brothers and sisters, friends, and thinking "I made it." It was great that every time I pitched I got to use tickets for my family and friends that I obtained from my teammates who didn't need them, and I'd get 20 to 25 tickets.

It was strange that, just a few years after I was sitting in the stands as a teenager, all of a sudden I'm pitching to Carl Yastrzemski, and you're thinking, "Oh, shit." I walked him the first time I faced him, but then I remember Jim Rice hitting into a double play.

Being on the '84 championship team was obviously the ultimate, especially being from Michigan.

The last game at Tiger Stadium was very sad for me. I had so many memories there. It was nice being on the field with all those players at the closing ceremony. It reminded me of all the great players who played on that diamond like Babe Ruth, Joe DiMaggio, Bob Feller, Charlie Gehringer, Hank Greenberg, and Ted Williams, and I'm thinking,

"God … pretty cool." Made me think of the movie *Field of Dreams*: "If you build it, they will come." It gave me more goose bumps.

I remember when they asked Ernie Harwell if there was one thing you would like out of Tiger Stadium and he said "the urinal in the visitors' dugout tunnel because of all the greats who would have used it." That was pretty funny.

It's sad that the stadium is gone. It would have been nice if they had kept the dugouts and some of the stands, kept a thousand seats, and let the fans, who were such great fans, have the opportunity to play on that field. I mean the Lions played there; they could have had a tag football league there. A lot of different things could have happened.

Born in Detroit in 1948, Ron LeFlore played center field six years for the Tigers (1974–1979), after being paroled from the Jackson State Penitentiary, where his baseball skill drew the attention of Tiger manager Billy Martin. LeFlore was a fine hitter and an excellent base stealer and became the subject of *One in a Million: The Ron LeFlore Story*, a made-for-television movie starring LeVar Burton.

The first time I saw a game at Tiger Stadium, I was probably nine years old, and I sat with my dad in the upper deck bleachers, when the seats were like 50 cents. I wasn't really into baseball, but my dad wanted to take me there, and we went one or two times a year to see the Yankees because that was his favorite team.

I just remember the green seats, the green grass, everything just seemed so bright in there, and the way it was enclosed all the way around. I remember when the color barrier final started breaking in Detroit with Ozzie Virgil, Jake Wood, and Chico Fernandez.

I was more of a football fan. When the Colts came to town, my dad took me because he was a fan of Johnny Unitas and Lenny Moore and Jim Parker. I also enjoyed watching Night Train Lane, Lem Barney, Alex Karras, Joe Schmidt, and Darris McCord. We were at that famous Thanksgiving Day game in 1962 when the Lions beat the Packers.

For my tryout at Tiger Stadium, my dad picked me up at Jackson Prison, and on the way there, his car broke down, and we hitchhiked to the ballpark. A security guard at Massey Ferguson picked us up and dropped us off at Tiger Stadium.

When I walked into the locker room, Norm Cash was the first guy who came up to me, and he took me in to see Billy Martin.

It was an all-white locker room with bright fluorescent lights. It wasn't that bright in prison; it was like still being outside.

They gave me a uniform, and I went onto the field, and Mickey Stanley helped me out with throwing. I had a good arm, but Mickey Stanley really showed me how to keep the ball down and get it to the cutoff man. Al Kaline helped me out, too.

Going out onto the field gave me visions of the Lions playing out there, and the Tigers. I was kind of in a fog.

I had a great batting practice, and they let me bat for 30 minutes. I was hitting balls in the upper deck in left field, right field, and everywhere. I was very pumped up. I ripped the skin off both of my hands, and I thought it was sweat, but it was blood. I just threw some dirt on it and kept swinging. I didn't have the capacity to be nervous, having come from Jackson prison. That was easy. It was great being free for 48 hours. It was the first time in three-and-a-half years, and it was great not having any guards around me.

A couple of weeks later, I had a tryout at Butzel Field. I had on a pair of jeans and baseball spikes, and I outran everybody. Bill LaJoie said I was the fastest guy he had ever seen.

It wasn't long after that when I signed with the Tigers, and I was released early. I was assigned to Clinton, and Jim Leyland was my manager.

Center field at Tiger Stadium was one of the biggest in baseball, and I did enjoy playing out there because I was fast. But at the same time, there was so much you had to do because you got exhausted backing up the other fielders. It was a tough task to play center field at Tiger Stadium. The wall also wasn't padded as well as the walls are today.

I went back to Tiger Stadium for the last game played there, and for me it was a nightmare. It was amazing to go back onto the field in my uniform in front of that crowd and to see all the guys. But I was arrested right after the ceremony for back child support.

John Wockenfuss was used primarily as a backup catcher in his ten seasons for the Tigers from 1974 to 1983 and was a fan favorite for his unique batting stance and uncanny ability to execute the hit-and-run.

Tiger Stadium was kept up extremely well, and it was like a cathedral. There was nothing like it. It was home, and it was the greatest nine years of my life playing on that field. When you were sitting in the bullpen, it was dirt level. There were two sisters who were always right there. I'd give them baseballs, and they often ran up and got me a hot dog and soda. No one ever saw it because we were so pinched in down there. If I was tired, I'd bring a pillow and lay down on the bottom step and go to sleep until I knew Sparky was going to use me as a pinch hitter or something. One time I got this new camera and took close-up photos of guys hitting and playing in the outfield. I sure wish I still had those photos.

One of the funniest things that happened was when I was warming up reliever Steve Grilli in the bullpen, and some guy three rows up yells, "Hey Wockenfuss, what does it feel like to be a toilet bowl having to catch that shit?" Steve and I just starting laughing. Steve had hardly thrown ten pitches because we're still laughing, and Ralph Houk calls him into the game.

My favorite year had to be 1976 because of what Mark Fidrych did that season. It was the greatest thing ever in the history of baseball. I talked to older guys that knew the Babe Ruth era, and they said there was more excitement that summer than ever. Every place he went he packed the stadiums. Fid brought fun back to the game. I was fortunate to be on that team.

This summer on the Internet I found out about the Navin Field Grounds Crew. The last time I was at the field was at the closing ceremonies of the last game at Tiger Stadium. Dave Mesrey from the group called me and invited me to visit the field. I said "I have some time off. How about if I bring a bucket of balls, and you get some guys together, and let's have a game?"

I got there early and some kids were taking batting practice. I broke out some new balls and threw to them, and they were all jazzed up. Everybody else showed up, and we had a fantastic time playing a pickup game. It brought back great memories. They even had a sign for me that said "Welcome Back Fuss." That was really cool. I always wanted to come back and look at where the stadium used to be. A couple days before that I went

John Wockenfuss (seated and holding catcher's mitt) with members of the Navin Field Grounds Crew in 2013 (courtesy Navin Field Grounds Crew).

over to the field and sat on the bench and visualized where everything used to be, where Jason Thompson and Kirk Gibson had hit them over the roof. I could picture where everything was: the clubhouse was over there, down the left field corner was my favorite spot, which was the bullpen. I spent about an hour walking around and just remembering the good days. Tiger Stadium was such a wonderful ballpark, and it brought back many great memories for me.

Mike Reilly is a former major league baseball umpire who worked from 1977 to 2010 and umpired in four World Series, including 1984. He was raised in Battle Creek, Michigan, home of Kellogg's, so Ernie Harwell nicknamed him "Corn Flakes Reilly."

I came from a family of five boys, and my parents were diehard baseball fans, and some of my favorite memories as a kid were going to games at Tiger Stadium with my dad and brothers. In 1968, as a senior in high school, I went to quite a few games that summer with my friends.

What I cherished most about Tiger Stadium is that it was a place that our family shared. I remember in '68 we would go to the ticket window, and we got to know a ticket seller who would say, "Come back in a half hour, and I'll be able to sell tickets on the third deck over the Tiger dugout." That perspective was kind of cool. You just put your elbows on that little shelf and looked down on everything. I don't know if it was a seat [from which] you would like to see a lot of baseball, but it was pretty cool. When I later umpired at Tiger Stadium, I remember always looking up at those third-deck seats, which brought back a lot of memories.

My most vivid memory of umpiring at Tiger Stadium was the 1984 World Series, which was the first World Series that I worked. My parents and brothers were in the stands, so it was very fulfilling. I was slated to work Game Six behind the plate, but as you know, the Tigers won the championship in five.

I remember working third base, where I had two really close calls. After those plays, [Hall of Fame umpire] Doug Harvey came down and said, "Kid, I know this is a thrill for you, but this is just another game for me."

I was at first base when Gibson hit those two home runs in Game Five. It was kind of a neat experience. It was not your typical game when you look down in the last inning and there are policemen on horses lined up. It was kind of an event. When the game ended, all the umpires celebrated too because the umpiring was outstanding. I remember walking back through the tunnel later in the evening, and there was no grass in the infield. The sad part was a lot of cars were turned over, and there was vandalism. I remember the Tiger clubhouse manager Jim Schmakel gave the umpires a bat when we left the stadium in case we needed it if something happened. We went back to the Dearborn Hyatt with our families, but later I called Jimmy Butsicaris at the Lindell AC bar, who was a good friend of ours, and asked what it was like, and he said, "Great, come on down." So we went back to the Lindell and celebrated some more.

The tiny umpire room at Tiger Stadium was terrible; it was so small. We had a rule that you did your "number two" back at the hotel. The ones we have now are five times that size.

The tough ground rule at Tiger Stadium was the flagpole, where if you hit it above the yellow line it was a home run, but I never saw a ball hit the flagpole. We did have that overhang in right, which was a little tougher. But actually, the older ballparks like Tiger Stadium were a little easier because the fans couldn't reach over and interfere with a potential home run ball.

In the late afternoon when you were behind home plate, there was a very, very dark shadow cast by the light standards between the pitcher's mound and home plate, and that made it a little difficult for the hitter, the catcher, and the umpire to see the ball. You would see the ball in the sunlight from the mound then it would go into a tunnel of darkness, so your eyes had to focus back on it and pick it up. I remember many games where I was hoping that it would get cloudy or someone would win the game before it got to that point of the day.

The seats were so close at Tiger Stadium, but you really didn't pick up the individual catcalls, and when there was a big play, it was more or less of a roar.

I don't think there are any better baseball fans than the ones in Detroit, especially when they have a good ball club. It was better for me when they didn't have a good club because I didn't have so many traffic problems going home to Battle Creek.

In 1999, baseball asked me if I wanted to work the last game at Tiger Stadium, but my family had scheduled a trip out west, so I passed on it. I kind of regret that now, because I would have liked to have said I worked the last game there.

"The Biggest House in the Neighborhood"
Living Near Tiger Stadium

Frank Rashid

Tiger Stadium was situated between Corktown, directly south across Michigan Avenue, and North Corktown, sometimes called the Briggs Community, separated from the stadium by the Fisher Freeway (I-75) after it was built in the late 1960s. The area was first settled by Irish immigrants in the 19th century and later by Germans, Maltese, and Mexicans as well as migrants from the American South. The oldest surviving neighborhood in the city, it is now home to an ethnically and economically diverse population.

We contacted longtime residents to find out what life was like in the area when it was home to Tiger Stadium. Jim Brazeau, now retired, has lived in Corktown since 1989. Mark Crowley, an elementary school science teacher in the Detroit Public Schools, has lived there since 1986. Patricia Muldoon, who works in media relations, and her husband, Brian, an upholsterer, have lived there since 1987. Mario Muscat, a storage warehouse manager, has lived his entire 54 years in the same Church Street house in sight of Tiger Stadium. And lifelong Detroiter John Prusak, a retired teacher and a filmmaker, moved to Corktown in 1985.

What drew you to the neighborhood?

John Prusak: At the time, I was doing a lot of freelance work in cinematography, and I liked the central location. I can be anywhere in Metro Detroit in about a half hour. When you live in Corktown, you're usually driving the opposite way of heavy traffic.

Patricia and Brian Muldoon: We're native Detroiters and were looking to stay in the city. We both grew up within two miles of here and were familiar with the neighborhood. The architecture of the homes definitely intrigued us the most. Some of the homes date back to the Civil War. Our home is a 113-year-old simple Queen Anne style.

Jim Brazeau: The opportunity to have an older home in a historic neighborhood.

Mark Crowley: Proximity to family, work, and downtown; the ethnic mix; and, believe it or not, the excitement of being around baseball.

Mario Muscat: Conception. I had no say in the matter!

What keeps you in the neighborhood?

Mark Crowley: All of the above, except there's a lot less baseball now. And the hope that someday we'll at least break even on our home's investment.

Patricia and Brian Muldoon: This is our home. We raised our two sons here, we work here in the city, and a lot of our family and friends are in the area. We love the diversity in the neighborhood and the overall commitment of our neighbors to stay and make it work in a pretty tough city. We love the city of Detroit.

John Prusak: Corktown is a very convenient location. There are also some amazing people that live here. It's a tight-knit community.

Jim Brazeau: It's a great community.

Mario Muscat: Family, friends, and work.

How did living near Tiger Stadium affect your everyday life?

John Prusak: You shared your neighborhood with the public. When 30 or 40 thousand people came down to watch a baseball game, most parked their cars on the streets surrounding the stadium. Many times you would see the same people attending a game and parking in front of your house. People had a sharing attitude when fans came down for a game.

Patricia and Brian Muldoon: I always thought of TS as the biggest house in the neighborhood, which had 80-some parties a year. During the season, we just had to plan a little if we were leaving during a game and figure into our plans getting back into the neighborhood before the games let out. If we were having people over, parking was always a challenge. Having a schedule on the refrigerator was not for the purpose of attending games; it was for knowing when the Tigers had home games.

Mark Crowley: We always had to plan our arrivals, departures, and family gatherings at our home according to the baseball schedule, because of game-day traffic.

Jim Brazeau: At first, the parking problem was an issue; with no garage or driveway, finding a place to park after work, even with the paid parking pass, was a problem.

Mario Muscat: I worked at the stadium as a clubhouse boy, stands sweeper, and batboy for the Tigers; for the Lions as a clubhouse boy, ball boy, sideline gopher, and message runner for coach play calling.

Parking was a problem on game days. In the '80s, more drunkenness and disorderly conduct started, and more younger people, who didn't necessarily care about baseball or the neighborhood, started coming to party more than to watch baseball.

What did you most like about living near Tiger Stadium?

Jim Brazeau: The whole atmosphere during ball season, hearing the National Anthem being sung by the fans, being able to just walk over and take in a game anytime, getting to know all of the ushers and other stadium workers, including Paws.

Mario Muscat: The exciting atmosphere; making money working in the stadium and later selling souvenirs and parking cars around the neighborhood; different events that happened there like Fireman and Policeman Field Day, professional soccer games back in the late sixties, staging the National Guard for patrols during the '67 riot.

Patricia and Brian Muldoon: We liked the energy it brought, the feeling that something was alive. You could hear the echo of the crowds roar through the neighborhood. You knew if the Tigers were winning or losing just by the sound or lack of sound vibrating from within the walls. The glow from the stadium lights was somehow a warming comfort on the streets. Even from a distance around the city, the ring of light in the sky let you know the Tigers were in town. The radiance of the light always projected a welcoming presence in the night sky. Our kids were little when they started Fireworks Fridays at the stadium, and they'd dig sitting in their pajamas on the porch watching them or hanging out with the neighborhood kids on the corner across from the stadium to see them even better.

A Corktown parking lot in 1984 (Frank Rashid).

Mark Crowley: The stadium did generate a lot of excitement in the neighborhood and was a boon to many mom-and-pop parking lot and concession owners, many of whom are still our current neighbors. It was a real easy commute to the games, and parking for us was no problem with our resident parking passes for street parking. Friends always had extra tickets to share with us for a parking spot. [It was] easy to walk across the street and bring our kids and others to games for a couple bucks after the fifth inning.

John Prusak: Close proximity to the baseball game. Some people came great distances just to attend. We could walk to the games just like they did a hundred years ago.

When I first moved to Corktown, I talked to an elderly woman who grew up on Wabash. Her name was Thelma, and she was probably born at the turn of the 20th century. Her father would come home from work and had Thelma walk down to the ballpark to get the final scores of the games. I thought that was odd until I realized this little ritual happened before there was radio! Back then, it was the only way you could find out how the Tigers did.

Another thing she told me…. The banners that had all the club names on flagpoles along the perimeter of the ballpark had a logical pattern to them. The banner at the corner of Michigan and Trumbull belonged to the visiting baseball club that was there currently. The groundskeeper rotated the banners in order of the games to be played. They were rotated in a clockwise direction so you always knew what team had played there last, who was in town (the banner at Michigan and Trumbull), and what teams would be arriving in the future. That was before radio and telephones. So, the passing people would know who was playing.

What did you most dislike about it?

Jim Brazeau: The disrespect shown by the fans, leaving litter all over, including their parking tickets.

John Prusak: You had to be patient driving to or from your house on game days. Luckily, I have a garage, so there was always a place for the car.

Mark Crowley: The litter and disorderly conduct of some fans—urinating, defecating, yelling, and sometimes fighting. Fan car thefts and car break-ins were a common occurrence during the games. Noise and traffic, especially if it were a hot summer night without air conditioning and you were trying to get to bed early.

Mario Muscat: As I said, parking was tight. Some fans would park in my handicapped parking space. People urinated in the streets and lots and left their litter behind—starting more in the '80s, as I said—as celebrations spilled over across the street into the neighborhood.

Patricia and Brian Muldoon: Only on game days were there issues with parking and just the crowds' general lack of respect from the fans who seemed not to understand that this was a residential neighborhood. The drunken behavior. The cleanup afterwards could be a little annoying. Street parking was a big issue at one point. Resident parking was put into place, which really helped resolve that problem. From a political standpoint, you sometimes felt, though, that the owners of the Tigers came first. Downtown and the residents were an afterthought on matters that affected the neighborhood. At times this would be frustrating, in that you had to remind the powers that be that people live here too.

What is your favorite memory about living near Tiger Stadium?

Mark Crowley: (1) The Nelson Mandela visit. I bartered parking passes for tickets in order to be inside the stadium to witness this historic event. We even hosted a Mandela tailgate party at our house. (2) Our daughter's birthday party in the upper bleachers with family and grade school classmates. Monaghan's preppy-looking security even let us bring the birthday cake in with us. (3) Being at the final game of the season in '87 when Frank Tanana threw a complete game to beat Toronto and clinch the AL East and then the relatively peaceful celebration that followed. But Detroit's Finest were out in full force that night after learning the ugly lessons from the '84 World Series melee.

Jim Brazeau: The concerts, especially Rod Stewart and the Eagles. Getting all the benefits of the music without having to pay!

John Prusak: We would listen to Ernie Harwell on the radio doing the play-by-play report of the game. When it got to the seventh inning stretch, we would walk over to the ballpark and enter for free. The exits were all open, and no one ever stopped us from entering. If we were lucky, the game would go into extra innings, so it was like seeing a whole game for free.

Another memory was how the sound traveled. If you were listening to the radio, you could hear Lou Whitaker hit a home run. Then the crowd would all yell, "LOU!" Then about six seconds later, you heard the live version as it traveled through the air. Quite a phenomenon.

Patricia and Brian Muldoon: It was getting involved with the Tiger Stadium Fan Club, the group that was hoping to save it. We met an extraordinary group of folks that we would have never known otherwise, especially the friendships that resulted with Catherine Darin and Eva Navarro. These two incredible women had love and passion not only for Tiger Stadium and baseball but also for doing what is right in this world socially. A lot of time and effort went into this; we were engaged with not only our neighbors but also so many people beyond the boundaries of TS. This time will always be a most cherished memory.

Mario Muscat: Working at the stadium, meeting the players and other celebrities, Ernie Harwell and his staff, the World Series, being in front of 53,000 people as a batboy, and shagging batting practice.

What is your least favorite memory?

Patricia Muldoon: It's not so much a memory, but the realization of how much housing stock was taken for parking lots and that loss of history in this neighborhood. This has always bothered me.

John Prusak: People urinating on the side of the house. I suspect they wouldn't like us to do that in their neighborhood.

Mark Crowley: Watching the first hole being punched into the center field bleachers wall on the first day of demolition.

Mario Muscat: The last game, and then when they started to tear it down.

Jim Brazeau: The way the relocation was done, the disregard for the neighborhood's input, the teardown. And this is still going on.

Did you notice any difference in the atmosphere or in the behavior of crowds for different kinds of events?

Patricia and Brian Muldoon: Yes, Opening Day or when the Tigers made the playoffs or the series were always more electrifying. When the Three Tenors and Nelson Mandela came, it was a different vibe, more subdued. The music concerts just brought out their own unique nuttiness. It seemed when it wasn't a baseball crowd, though, the stadium was more a destination only, and the neighborhood restaurants and bars were not utilized as much.

John Prusak: The baseball crowds seemed to be the best. Probably because it seemed more cross-generational. All ages attended the baseball games.

Jim Brazeau: Most of the fans were just overly jubilant. Opening Day was always exciting.

Mark Crowley: I never lived in the neighborhood during the Lions' tenure but did witness many other events, such as I mentioned with Mandela. Heard a few concerts from our backyard—Eagles, Rod Stewart, the Three Tenors. Was an extra behind home plate for Billy Crystal's movie *61**. Also saw a women's baseball game right after the Tigers moved to Comerica. All these events had a totally different feel to a ball game. Mandela was the most different atmosphere that I ever experienced at Tiger Stadium. It was more akin to being in church than at a ballpark. The atmosphere was a very spiritual one. Whoever might have been sitting next to you at that event, you knew you had something in common with them. This was also the only time when I was in the stadium when the crowd was predominantly African American. Although it was a very multiethnic crowd, it was a much different demographic than that who showed up for a ball game. It was the most peaceful setting I've been in with 45,000 or so people.

In your view, how has life in the neighborhood changed since the Tigers left Tiger Stadium?

Mark Crowley: There's a lot less public urinating and litter, except on [the St. Patrick's Day] Parade Day of course. (My hunch is that it has something to do with the overconsumption of alcohol!) Ironically, it isn't quieter because of an increase in the rock and dance club scene that has picked up since the days of the stadium. In fact, the noise is more of a problem now because it carries on into the early morning hours, sometimes until dawn.

John Prusak: I miss the parties on Opening Day. Neighbors would have "open houses," and everyone would come early for hot dogs and liquid refreshment.

Mario Muscat: It was a lot quieter during the season. Neighborhood people lost [a] source of income, businesses struggled, and the north wind blows much stronger onto Church Street and the noise from the I-75 freeway [is louder].

Jim Brazeau: The change is all good. Love seeing all the new businesses and the new neighbors. Things have gotten a whole lot better, with all the new traffic coming into the neighborhood. There isn't the litter or the trash that the ballpark fans brought with them.

Patricia and Brian Muldoon: From a resident living in the neighborhood, not at all. Yes, the energy, the noise, that vibe is gone and missed by some, but not all. The divide in the neighborhood was in thirds: some loved it, some hated it, and some prospered from it. The Tiger organization never did much to enhance the neighborhood, so there was no sense of loss from that perspective. The businesspeople in the neighborhood were probably more affected financially. There were quite a few residents that were employed by the Tigers or local businesses. So, yes, there were some casualties. Others,

Corktown today: Church Street (Frank Rashid).

though, have figured out ways to be a part of it still. They park cars and run shuttles downtown. The bars run their own shuttle buses with special offers to the games. For many people, their memories of TS include being in this neighborhood. So coming back to their favorite pub, having a beer and burger before they hop on the bus to the game is just how they do it now. People adapt.

In your view, how has life in the neighborhood changed since Tiger Stadium was demolished?

Mark Crowley: Most families, in particular the three-generational ones, have stayed. New families have established themselves in the neighborhood with their young children. The big question is: How long will they stay? The pattern has been usually until schools become an issue, especially as kids move into middle and high school.

While still catering to baseball fans, the neighborhood is redefining itself as an entertainment district destination with the establishment of several new bars, restaurants, and a club or two. For the most part, this has been positive, except for some of the reasons I've already stated above. It's become a very desirable place for young professionals to live. In fact, we are at 100 percent residential occupancy with a need for more living spaces.

Mario Muscat: The neighborhood started seeing new businesses and more outside

Corktown today: Bagley Street (Frank Rashid).

people moving here to live and work and more people coming to see the neighborhood as tourists rather than as fans.

Jim Brazeau: Things are only getting better. I'd like to have the area remain a ballpark with historical markers and statues dedicated to all the players. It's an attraction like the Michigan Central Railroad Station and needs to be highlighted that way.

John Prusak: It's quieter and there's less congestion, although I miss the crowds. It made the neighborhood feel vibrant. It still bothers me that the city spent all that money to demolish the stadium, and what do we have now? A vacant field full of memories. One good thing about the absence of the stadium is that people can play baseball on that hallowed ground. Every day I see people playing catch or having a pickup game. People are taking care of the old ballfield, and The Corner is still a destination.

A few weeks ago, I stopped southbound on Trumbull waiting for the traffic light at Michigan to change. I noticed a police car parked on Michigan in front of the park. There were about 15–20 people having a pickup game, and two cops were on the first base sideline. One cop was pointing out towards center field, and the other cop was bent over laughing…. Everyone, including the cops, was having a great time. It looked like a Norman Rockwell painting. Everyone left their troubles outside of the fence, and they were just playing ball!

Patricia Muldoon: The neighborhood hums along like always. The street vendors are gone; a couple of stores have closed. Most of the bars and restaurants are still thriving, and new ones are opening. But more interesting was what did happen. At first, it was just getting used to this foreign, open, exposed landscape. So many people remarked how they thought it would look bigger, emptier. Quickly, it seemed too small for the stadium even to have ever fit there. Overgrown grass and garbage came fast. The realization that this would be one more abandoned, unkempt city property was pretty apparent. Then that first fall and spring after it was gone, there were these daily pilgrimages starting to happen. You'd always see people just walking around talking, pointing at emptiness, like they lost something and were looking for it. This was constant, not random; it was like watching from a distance a wake that just wasn't going to end. Then little things started to happen. A small group of people started taking care of cutting the grass and picking up the garbage. I'm only guessing here now, that it was the baseball gods that somehow sent a movie crew there to shoot a film. They hauled in some sand and, boom, the field was back. The measuring sticks came out, chalk lines went down. A sign was tied on the fence in tribute to Ernie Harwell, declaring it Ernie Harwell Park. A flag went up the flagpole. Pretty soon people were out there playing catch with their kids, then groups of people, then bigger groups of people that looked like work or bar leagues. Then kids' baseball leagues held practice there. Even the Salvation Army bussed in large groups for a field trip to play baseball. The people started to return, to take back their park, not needing the constraints of man-made walls. This could lead you to surmise that TS was really always separate from the neighborhood. We just shared the same boundaries. On my route home, passing this daily, it just charms me. How simple, the people came back for the sole purpose of playing ball.

Is there anything else you would like to say? Anything else that you would like readers to know about life near Tiger Stadium?

Mario Muscat: I hope they do something with the site, like keeping part of the field with some retail and restaurants surrounding it.

Mark Crowley: Many of the multigenerational families that made their livelihoods from parking, souvenirs, bars, and restaurants around the stadium are now slowly accepting the reality that there can be life after the stadium, as I outlined above. We have to continue to think beyond the stadium's traditional eight-month neighborhood economy. There's an empty hole at The Corner now.

A big politically charged question remains as to what is going to happen to The Corner. George Jackson and the DEGC [Detroit Economic Growth Corporation] control the chessboard as Olympia Entertainment and Ilitch Holdings whisper into their collective ear. The consensus of the neighborhood seems to be that we would like to see a mixed-use development—residential and commercial—with some portion of the field preserved for use. To me, it doesn't seem realistic to keep the field's original dimensions and to develop the site in a manner that will generate year-round revenue. A lot of the current property owners' anxiety is being generated by the uncertainty being perpetuated by the moves–or lack of–of the DEGC. Potential investors of any Corktown project are holding their cards close to their chests because of this power play being acted out. The Old Tiger Stadium Conservancy is also a player in this scenario as the clock ticks away on Senator Levin's earmarked development funds for the stadium site.

Patricia Muldoon: As this book goes to press, the city of Detroit is filing for bankruptcy. The arguments continue as what to do with this parcel of historic land. Five years, ten years from now, what we see at Michigan and Trumbull will not be the same as what we see today. I feel TS was the silent force that somehow protected this neighborhood. Corktown is the oldest established neighborhood in the city, where our city's growth started. It'll play that role again. I'd like Tiger Stadium to be remembered as serving as the gateway to this neighborhood, going back before Bennett Park was built. From its beginnings as a hay and agricultural trade market, Michigan and Trumbull has always been a place where people gathered, and I think always will. The people are returning it naturally again to that. My best friend always tells me that hope dies last.

The signature lettered sign of Tiger Stadium, 1999 (© Rebecca Cook).

The Stadium
An Essay in Memory of George Cantor

TOM DeLISLE

Being part-Irish and all-Detroit, I am reminded of the sad state of affairs every time I am forced to view what to me remains a ghastly scar that decorates the face of our city at the junction of Michigan and Trumbull just northwest of downtown.

That vacant lot, a cemetery without a proper tombstone, was once both the joy of our youth and the comfort of our old age across 100 years of shared emotional investment in the city's greenest parcel of land. To have stumbled into the 21st century without Tiger Stadium still available to succeeding generations of Detroiters seems so wrong, so short-sighted. It is an indictment of the vision, and heart, of the city "fathers" who willed us the collective inheritance of an empty lot where a church of common faith and imagination had stood, a site where our shared dreams once came true, where light and magic held our hearts and graced our town.

Nothing in Detroit was as dear, and no location ever spoke to us as our stadium did. It will forever remain Briggs Stadium to me and my buddies who grew up after World War II on the city's east side. Just as it was Navin Field to my dad who was born here as America was planning to enter World War I, and Bennett Park to my grandfather who came from Michigan's Thumb at the very beginning of the previous century, arriving in time to see Detroit's Tigers take the field at Michigan and Trumbull a few seasons before young Georgian Ty Cobb was ready to join the club.

A contemporary aside: An early 2013 issue of *Sports Illustrated* contains the personal column of a writer yearning for the onset of the new baseball season, framing it as the certain relief from the storms that battered America's east coast in winter months. The piece highlights the stirrings of fan interest and team activities at the Red Sox home ballpark, despite the unseasonal chill in Boston, and an excited anticipation in Chicago as an improving team—yes, really—and the final touches of a facelift wrought by over $300 million in renovations of the Cubs' ancient and nationally beloved home field augur solace for long-suffering locals.

But while Boston's Fenway Park opened in 1912 on the same day as Detroit's Navin Field and Chicago's Wrigley Field opened in 1916, it is worth noting that baseball had been played every season on that same Michigan and Trumbull field since 1896 and that Detroit officially entered the American League there on Opening Day at Bennett Park, April 25, 1901.

Local big shots and Tigers management closed that field for all time at the end of September 1999, after it had been in continuous operation for "only" 104 years. That it had been the repository of the dreams and communal unity of generations of Detroiters, seeing them through year after year, decade upon decade, of excitement and entertainment and yearning and hope and outrageous bad fortune and jaw-dropping, tear-inducing victory attained against all odds, uniting the local community in a mass glorification and celebration of the home team, that it had brought us together for all that—you might think—should have spared our stadium the opportunists' axe, allowed our place the benefit of some doubt.

But no. Toss in that it was the most gorgeous of ballparks, with its greenest of green grasses across its wide expanse. Add that its towering fan sections seemed to be perched just over the action on that field, allowing an intimacy unmatched in sports—and certainly not remotely copied by its Styrofoam and plastic successor—and you must wonder at its destruction. Its dull gray workingman's exterior gave way to the visual magic of an Oz-like bright interior with perfect white lines framing that sea of green. Sunshine that clearly illuminated the perfect white uniforms of Tiger players—yeah, that's him, young Kaline, out there in right, watch him throw, like a cannon—might have, should have, given our stadium the care and protection it deserved, after what it gave us over the years.

When we were kids, we knew someone who had a friend who knew someone who claimed to have actually walked on the perfect green table that was the field. That someone, in our minds, was royalty.

My mom took me and some of my friends to see Ted Williams play his final game in 1960. She saw it in the paper and said, "Hey, whatta ya say? Let's go." It was a sunny afternoon in September. We sat in the upper deck above third base and watched the inimitable Williams unwind out of his perfect stance and cork one into the upper deck in right in his last appearance on our field of dreams. You could hear the "wows" echo around the stadium. It was one special day at the most special of ballparks.

We dreamed, letting our young minds soar above the concrete "fields" of our northeast Detroit streets, where we played on rectangular diamonds lined by cement curbs on both sides. And every so often a game ended when our ball crashed through a neighbor's picture window, and once when Mike Carabio leapt for a line drive that curved over the curb towards the sidewalk and which he might have snagged had he not laid open his forehead on the stiff metal guy wire that supported a nearby phone pole. Sauer Avenue was our Briggs Stadium, and instead of concrete, we wondered what the real deal must have looked like spread out in greenest green from deep center field. We could only imagine and settled instead for Sauer. And Carabio, a gamer and a hell of a glove man, was back at third on our cement grounds the following spring. Scar and all.

That they topped Briggs with majestic rising lights in the late 1940s took nothing from the stadium's appeal. At night under their glow, it seemed ethereal, literally heavenly. It was about as close to heaven as a Detroit kid could get. Its only local competition might have been the street windows of the J. L. Hudson Department store at Christmas. What else could match the splendor? Ford Motor had its fabulous Rotunda showroom at Christmas before it burned in 1962. And trips to Bob-Lo Island, down the Detroit River on a Great Lakes pleasure steamer, were a kick for generations of locals. But nothing matched the attraction, the magic, the feel of that stadium. Has any other spot in Michigan ever held so many memories, so many dreams, or meant so much to the millions who found themselves proud to be associated with our town, our state as part of the home team sharing World Series wonder in 1935, 1945, 1968, and 1984?

To discard that singular locale's legacy, reduce those memories, subject them to the wrecking ball was a sin against a place and its people. The bastards.

Detroit has never been an ethereal city. Thus its stadium was muscular and direct and tough, like the factories and auto shops that sprawled along the spoked byways that spread out northwest and northeast of the city's downtown riverfront locale. It didn't pamper its fans. I was convinced as a child that there was no spot on earth colder or windier than the upper deck of Briggs Stadium on those freezing Friday nights in late November when the Detroit high school football championships were contested in the annual Goodfellows games: Catholic versus public schoolboy showdowns. I thought the very concrete of those upstairs passageways trapped and held the cold in anticipation of us arriving those steely nights. It was like walking through an icebox, accounting for the achingly numb feet throughout the stadium by the beginning of the third quarter.

(Our city's charity tradition of those Goodfellows Classics, held for decades to the theme of "No Kiddie Without a Christmas," had to be suspended in the 1960s. The games kept ending in riots. So much for charity. What the hell: It was Detroit.)

A Detroit Lion game in December bore little resemblance, of course, to the season-opening contests played in sunny and often balmy September. Our stadium offered no escape, no comfort, for its year-round fans. Ours is a city designed for determined folks, and our stadium reflected its surroundings. To be among those throngs of football fans clogging its entrances before kickoff on a late fall Sunday afternoon, with men in gray and brown hats puffing on pungent cigars, the deep and expectant rumble circulating through the corridors and aisleways as the mob filtered its way to their seats, you felt you belonged, you were part of the home team, familiar among what seemed to be the inhabitants of an entire city, attired in three sweaters, two coats, two pair of long underwear, three pair of socks jammed into what we called galoshes. That was the Detroit of another, special era. Our city in another time. And as tough as it was, it somehow felt so right.

There were perfect spots in that stadium. Most fans had their favorites. Mine was on the concrete ramp that ran outside the ballpark's southern rim, rising above Michigan Avenue. Taking crowds up its walkway to the second deck, it afforded a fan the opportunity for a bird's-eye view around and above its gray walls. The best of perfect views, for me, came upon that ramp on an autumn night, when the lights above the stadium blended with those along Michigan, with the car lights shining along its lanes. Across the street from the ramp was a giant moving billboard that faced the stadium, showing a heroic Bobby Layne, the legendary Lion quarterback of the championship years, in his classic blue Lions 22 jersey, gripping a football that was about the size of a Buick with that ball constantly dipping forward and back in his hand. I was absolutely in awe of the sight.

I fail to recall what product Number 22's glorious moving sign was endorsing, but it should have been Cutty Sark. Stars who make commercial endorsements ought to be, in the interests of fairness, intimately familiar with the products they sell, and Layne's legendary thirst likely had Cutty stock running up there with the Big Three automotive giants. He actually was the inspiration for a local brewery, Goebel 22 Beer, sponsors of what else? Detroit Lion football. And his "impaired" driving arrests were the stuff of local legend.

Along that ramp, amid those crowds, up the sidewalks of what was then the "Skid Row" of Michigan Avenue that spread about a half mile east of the stadium, we were led, steered, directed to our sporting castle in the '50s and '60s by my dad. When we were immersed in a crowd, he grabbed us by our collars, pulling us to him and then pushing us this way and that, aiming us where we were supposed to go, and never allowing us to stray out of arms' reach. "We" were my older brother and I. And we inherited our love of Briggs Stadium from my father. A Naval veteran of World War II, he returned from the south Pacific after two years at sea to bring his sons to these communal gatherings, introducing us to Detroit's main assembly point in a repetition of a tradition that his father had shown to him.

Maybe the biggest Lion game at Briggs Stadium—bigger possibly than even the victorious NFL Championship contests that were played there in 1953 and 1957—was the 1962 Thanksgiving game with the then-champion Green Bay Packers. The whole town was in an uproar. In all the years before or since, I've never seen the town at such fever pitch. The Lions felt they were better than the champion Packers that year, which of course they were, and felt they had been cheated out of an earlier victory over them by the whimsical football gods, which of course they were, outplaying the Pack in muddy Green Bay earlier in the season yet losing 9–7. They would show the Packers who the better team was back here in Detroit on Thanksgiving, which of course they did.

My dad rarely got tickets to games; he worked six days a week, often seven, as an accountant and could not afford the time or luxury of sports attendance. But, miracle of miracles, he was given two seats to that 1962 Game of the Century. My brother and I had a revolving system: If there were only two tickets to a game, depending on who had gone last, the other would attend with my father.

It was my luck that in 1962 my brother's turn was next. I was devastated but obedient to our system, so I tried to hide my disappointment. I'm sure I clearly failed in that effort. But after a short week of sheer anxiety, on that cold Thanksgiving morning, my father suddenly announced that *both* of us should dress in three sweaters, two pair of long underwear, and the rest of the typical Lion fan outfit and prepare to go to the big game.

I was frantic on our drive downtown and crazed on our long familiar walk along Michigan Avenue to the stadium. Dad had made a secret call before we left home. What was his plan? How was he going to get all three of us into the game? Whom had he called?

By the time we were amid the throng that pushed towards the turnstiles near Michigan Avenue, I was completely confused and wildly anxious. What had he arranged? Surely he couldn't talk us past the ticket-takers; he wasn't that kind of dad. Scrupulously honest, he would never try to sneak me in. What could be his plan?

When we got to the front of the long surging line, being pushed and shoved to the left and right, barely moving amid all the jabbering big men in their brown and gray coats, their stunning cigar smoke everywhere in the air around us, slowly making our way right up to the turnstiles, the uniformed Briggs Stadium men with their hands stuck out at us—"Tickets please"—and with me on the edge of a nervous breakdown, my dad suddenly said, "Here" and pressed both the tickets into my brother's hand. "You guys have a good time and enjoy the game. I'm gonna go to work, and I'll pick you up on the corner out there 15 minutes after the final gun."

Before either of us could say a word, before I could insist that he not deprive himself of that memorable afternoon, knowing that he wanted to see that game probably as much or more than either of us did, he had turned and quickly was out of sight amid the massive crowd. All I saw of him as he plunged ahead—the only person heading out of the stadium, bucking the surging fans coming in—was the dopey fake leather brown hat with wool earflaps that my mom always made him wear on cold days. He looked silly in that hat, and he knew it. And we loved to kid him about it. But there he went, in that foolish hat, attired in three sweaters and two pair of pants and clumsy galoshes, the entire traditional get-up, off to a Thanksgiving afternoon at work, while my brother and I proceeded to what was, in fact, truly the Lions' Game of the Century.

My father was never honored in his life, for anything. For me, if it had ever been in my power, I would have erected a "Father of All Time" statue to him, depicting him wearing that silly hat, moving out of that crowd that Thanksgiving morning, and I would put it right there at the locally legendary corner of Michigan and Trumbull, outside of what was once Briggs Stadium, our Briggs Stadium.

Tom with his father Charlie DeLisle, spring 1957 (courtesy Tom DeLisle).

Detroit has always been a neighborhood city, not a downtown-based metropolis. At one point, it had more privately owned homes than any city in America. In such a place, where those neighborhoods spread out for miles beyond a small downtown area, a stadium like ours means more than a ballpark in cosmopolitan towns like New York or Los Angeles. I can't believe that any city felt as affectionately or as intimately about its stadium as Detroit did about Bennett Park, Navin Field, Briggs Stadium, and Tiger Stadium. Maybe in cities like Cleveland or Chicago, the inhabitants loved their fields as much as we did ours, but nowhere could they have loved them more.

Which begs the question: How could a city as tested, as difficult, as prideful, as yearning, as Detroit allow some misguided planners, opportunists, profit seekers, politicians, and businessmen to destroy the one location in our town that meant so much to so many? Detroiters deserved more.

Yes, Tiger Stadium was old. Sections of it were surrendering to time. The modern "needs" of franchise ownership were not being served. There were problems in terms of structure, design, and the comfort of the teams and fans who brought our stadium to life each year, each season.

Yes, problems. The ills that confront any old stadium site, just as in Boston and Chicago. They fixed their problems there and preserved their heritage. We dodged our problems here and destroyed our history.

On that glorious evening of September 27, 1999, after the final game of that final season when the Tigers brought out their former team stars who lit up all our lives, all our tender years, there were fans all around that jammed ballpark who wept. Some sniffled surreptitiously; some had great tears rolling down their cheeks as the curtain was dropped on over 100 years of sports play, of our community gathering, at our glorious stadium. Those who cried were the ones who understood what was happening and what was being lost that night.

In September of 1999, as the curtain was in its final stages of being lowered on Tiger Stadium, with the dreadful deed almost finally done, I had what I considered the personal opportunity of a lifetime. Working as a producer for local television station Channel 50, which broadcast Tiger games that season, I was asked to prepare a closing show about the stadium. With the assignment, I was given an all-areas, anytime pass around the park during its final week. We shot tape in every part of that glorious site. We worked on a day when the Tigers were out of town and we were about the only people in the park. I got the chance to stand in that deep center field, in that lush grass, and slowly take it all in. What was the feel? How did it look? Magnificent. I was truly awed. At last I had arrived. But too late.

We even shot a final scene that would be broadcast on the stadium's final night, of Al Kaline, the greatest Detroit Tiger of the past 70 years, the idol of our youth, emerging from the Tiger dugout into a completely empty stadium, under the blazing lights of the towers and slowly walking to home plate. We filmed his journey twice, both up close and all the way from the deepest recess of the center field bleachers. We then saw him as he circled home plate and took a long last look, a 360-degree turn, at the stadium that had been his home for 21 marvelous and unforgettable years. Al made one last turn and headed out of the field up towards an open gate just off home plate and went through the nearest exit and into the dark that took him out of Tiger Stadium forever. I had goose bumps producing and shooting it and still hold that memory close to my heart.

But there had been one other moment during that week of bidding farewell to that beautiful stadium that stands out in my mind to an even greater degree. Earlier that same day, I took a solitary walk up the concrete ramp that ran outside the south side of the stadium to the upper deck. My favorite stadium site didn't disappoint on my last visit.

As I looked towards Michigan Avenue, imaging in my mind's eye the Bobby Layne billboard that had stood out there so many years ago and the surging crowds that we had navigated on so many summer days and autumn evenings all those years ago, I stepped out of the sunlight and into the interior shadows of the old ballpark. And as I turned off the ramp to head down an interior corridor, I felt someone grab me by the back of my jacket. At my neck.

I turned to greet whoever of our crew had put his strong hand on my collar. The touch I had felt was unmistakable, jarring, a shock, but when I looked, I saw no one. I quickly glanced in all directions. But there was no one there. Not a soul.

No, check that. I was mistaken. I'm sure it was a soul after all.

For the Love of the Game

Karen Elizabeth Bush

In September of 1999, Tiger Stadium hosted its last major league baseball game and part of my life went away. I didn't actually despair that much at the time. So much already was gone. So much of what the old ballpark meant belonged to a different era. Still, the closing of Tiger Stadium gave a kind of finality to the very changes in the game that helped bring about the park's demise. Perhaps partly because of this, in those final days before the last pitch, baseball fans everywhere treated the grand old stadium to a wake fit for a hero of the game.

As part of the citywide mourning and celebration, I found myself asked again and again to list my favorite ballpark memories—to identify just what I thought I would miss most about a heap of concrete that had been the epicenter of the existence of so many people. It's time to say it again.

The 40 or 50 years that I spent watching baseball down at The Corner blur when I try to think about them. My memories are a series of vignettes: watching Frank Lary charge off the mound to seize a bat Jimmy Piersall had "slipped" up the middle, and then—as the hushed crowd erupted in laughter—seeing Lary drop the thing ... and saunter airily back to the rubber; marveling with a retired Paul Foytack over the fact that this new kid pitcher Fidrych seemed to like the game better than the money he was mak-

Karen Elizabeth Bush, "The Lady in Blue," in her regular seat by the grounds crew, c. 1984 (courtesy Karen Elizabeth Bush).

244

ing; seeing Dick McAuliffe slide headfirst into first base on a dropped third strike; hearing our beloved Hank Aguirre call out in mock scorn, "Is all I got GIRLS?" as he watched his brood swarm over the top of the dugout during a father-son game (which his son Rance caught, by the way); seeing Al Kaline, and later Mickey Stanley, defy gravity to scale the fence after fly balls ... and watching Al spin and throw a strike to third base to hold a runner.

The area next to the visitor's clubhouse was initially a loading area, and it seems to me that it also served as a stage for some of the greater dramas of the ballpark. It was in that cavernous place that a frantic Luke Appling caught up with a fan club president named Barbara McConchie and me. "Girls!" he called. "Have you seen Jim Campbell?" Luke had heard that Mayo Smith was about to be signed to manage the club. "I gotta talk to him! I don't want to see Jim get burned." I guess he didn't need to worry.

I stood in that cavern the day Denny McLain won number 30, and Joe Garagiola introduced me to Dizzy Dean, and Dean turned and introduced me to Hank Greenberg.

I miss taking for granted being able to pick up the flight of the ball from any seat in the house. I miss being able to appreciate the intricacies of infield play without twisting around in my seat. I miss the proximity of the playing field. I miss hearing infield chatter. I miss hearing outfielders call for the ball. I miss the idiosyncrasies of the playing field itself—the shadows across the infield; the tumble home that put an extra spin on a ball hit near the warning track.

But what do I miss most about Tiger Stadium? That's the only question that's easy to answer. The people. The vendors, the stile men, the ushers, the media guys, the

The Tigers taking the field, 1999 (© Rebecca Cook).

matrons, the grounds crew, the old front office staff, many of the players—the people who make up baseball, all of whom, over the last half century, have become my good friends. Some are gone now. Many of the rest did not travel to Comerica Park, and of those who made the move, the majority are screened from fan contact by the design of the park itself.

And so, today's fan will never be able to watch baseball in the way fans once did, but Navin Field and Briggs Stadium and Tiger Stadium still live on in the stories told whenever people gather to remember the days when baseball was played—and watched—for the love of the game.

Closer

Todd Jones

The farewell to Tiger Stadium started in spring training of 1999, when our equipment manager Jim Schmakel showed us the special Tiger Stadium patch we would wear on our jerseys. Randy Smith the general manager, John McHale the club president, and our manager Larry Parrish explained the different things that were going to happen at the ballpark as we worked our way to the final game. We weren't a very good team, so this was something to break up the season, and we were excited if for nothing else that it would take the focus off how bad we were.

I was just getting into the teeth of my career, and Detroit had embraced me like no other city ever had, so I was having the time of my life watching the closing months, weeks, and days of our old friend, Tiger Stadium.

In the top of the right field upper deck, there was a banner with a countdown for every home game that was completed. A. J. Sager and I had the best seats in the house in the bullpen. We would sit out there each night and count them down. Like me, A. J. was thankful to be pitching for Detroit. He helped me to relax and get me through the pressure of being a young closer. The bench outside the submarine that I called our bullpen dugout gave us a good perspective, but we had no idea what perspective was until the night of the last game.

As the season wound down, the home games became bigger and bigger and took on a whole new meaning that I wasn't prepared for. I remember especially in September that, at the end of each game, fans would just sit and stare out at the field, while others took pictures of the ballpark. But the cool thing was that fans would save their beer cups from the night and then hundreds would get scoops of dirt from along the sides of the walls down near us and all along the field. It was like a pilgrimage. At first, security would try to do what they could to discourage fans from doing that, but the fans would come down with tears in their eyes, sometimes with their grandparents and parents. They just wanted a keepsake for themselves, perhaps a way to connect with their childhood.

But the eerie part was that it was done in dead silence. Fans would come down to the side of the walls, look around, say a prayer, or pause for a moment, scoop some dirt, touch the ground, say goodbye, and leave just as calmly and respectfully as if they were at a funeral service. This happened every night. That's when I realized this is going be one of the biggest things any of us had ever been a part of before.

The cool part for me was after the game I would walk real slow from the bullpen to the dugout and catch glimpses of people's lives. I would see a grown man crying his eyes

248   Part II: Memories

A fan scoops a souvenir cup of dirt during the last season at Tiger Stadium, 1999 (© Rebecca Cook).

out because he hadn't been able to get to Tiger Stadium since his dad died, because the ballpark reminded him too much of his father, but he wanted to come down one last time to reconnect with his dad. Or there would be a dad with a kid on his shoulder saying to him or her, "Never forget this moment."

At the beginning of the last week at Tiger Stadium, Randy Smith explained to us that after the final game there would be an on-field ceremony and that we would have to stay for it. We were all like, "That sucks. We have to go to Minnesota for a game the next day. We're thinking we can beat the traffic and get to the airport, and no one will ever know we're gone." He said, "Absolutely not. You're staying." He was the boss, so we said OK.

It turned out to be a great decision.

The next day I went to see Randy Smith in his office, the PR guy Tyler Barnes, and [manager] Larry Parrish. I told them I thought we could honor the players of the past by not wearing our numbers but the numbers of former players who made their positions famous. For instance, whoever played right field should wear Al Kaline's number 6. So we did that, but as it turned out, I wore my number 59 to represent the current players, and for that I was greatly honored.

After the meeting, I stayed in the skipper's office and made sure he knew that I wanted to pitch in the final game no matter what. I was the closer, and one of the perks would be that I would be the last pitcher to ever pitch at Tiger Stadium. Looking back, it was one of the top things I ever did in baseball.

September 27, 1999, was a very hectic day for us, to say the least. I woke up early and saw they were broadcasting live on all the local channels from Tiger Stadium. I got to the park early. It was like Opening Day, but it was closing day. There were some people protesting, but for the most part there was a good vibe in the air. That day, we signed everything that we were told to sign. Balls, bats, hats, posters of all kinds. Some players were discussing what they were going to take from the stadium. My friend Ernie Harwell always joked about getting the visitors' urinal and using it as a planter for [his wife] Lulu's flowers in her garden. I was able to get a stadium seat and a home plate that was used during that final season.

When batting practice came around, Tiger president John McHale walked into the clubhouse. His dad was a former GM of the club, and John himself had played football at Notre Dame, so he was someone who demanded respect.

He came walking in very fast and bothered and said, "Men, I don't want to take up much of your time, but it sure would be nice if you would win tonight." We all kind of laughed at him. Then he said, "MAYBE I DIDN'T MAKE MYSELF CLEAR. YOU GUYS BETTER WIN TONIGHT!" Well, that was just flat-out shocking. We knew what was on the line. We knew this city—this state—was ready to celebrate, and a win would make it all flow.

But for the first time we could actually chip in and do our part. For the whole season, our part was to stay out of the way and let people say their goodbyes, and now we could help out and win. Lucky for us, we did. Thank you, Robert Fick!

After the pregame ceremony, I decided to take Al Kaline's glove out with me for the national anthem. He and I had been close, and this was such a big day, so it was a way to pay respect to him.

In the fifth inning, Kaline took down the final number in the upper deck, kissed his hand, and then touched the side of the stadium and waved to the crowd.

In the eighth inning, the phone rang in the bullpen, and I am in the game. My heart pounded like it had never pounded before. We were up, 4–2, to start the eighth inning. Jeff Montgomery of the Royals had the same idea that I had because he wanted to be the last one to pitch at Tiger Stadium. I don't remember how, but Robert Fick came to the plate with the bases loaded. This was dumb, but I wanted it to come down to the game on the line and a save opportunity. But then, boom, Fick hits a moon-shot grand slam, and the place went crazy as the stadium shook for the last time.

It was then 8–2 when I came in to pitch the ninth inning, so I knew I could relax and enjoy the moment.

As I walked to the mound it hits me, "What do I do?" I was blessed to be part of the moment. I knew I wasn't going to be allowed to keep the final ball because Jim Schmakel's son was the batboy that day.

I ran out there, but I couldn't feel my fingers, and then my mouth was so dry that I couldn't spit. It had just hit me that I was in the middle of something bigger than anything this ol' Georgia boy had ever been a part of. I thought my heart was racing in the bullpen, and now I was pretty sure I was going to have a heart attack on the mound.

Somehow as the inning started, I was OK. I can't remember who I faced, but the next thing I noticed were these flashbulbs going off. When I say flashbulbs, I mean it was like fireworks but with no booms. Then I realized I had two outs in the middle of the coolest thing I had ever been a part of. And then I realized I was facing Carlos Beltran, who was the Rookie of the Year, so he was no easy out.

By this time, there were 40,000 flashbulbs, so neither one of us could see, but the flashbulbs gave me the advantage. I had two strikes on him, and I was thinking "Throw him the curve," so I threw the curve, he swung over it, and it was over.

I'm the last guy to ever throw a pitch in Tiger Stadium. I was shocked when the game ended, like everyone else. I had not done anything to embarrass myself or the club or Tiger Stadium. I had been fighting on what to do if I got the last out. Do I celebrate and jump up and down or not do anything? All I wanted to do was not mess up, just let it happen and get out of the way. I think I did that. I just shook my catcher Brad Ausmus' hand. I couldn't have the ball, so I stole the rosin bag off the mound, and I gave it to my dear friend, longtime Tiger fan Mike Fezzey, who was then the general manager of WJR radio in Detroit.

When the closing ceremony started, I was in awe as players from Tiger history walked onto the field from the center field area. It was like seeing ghosts from the past as the club even brought back the oldest living former Tiger [Eldon Auker]. All the fans I saw were sobbing.

As it turned out, Ron LeFlore was wanted by the police for back child support, and he had shown up for the closing ceremony. After he got off the field, he was taken and put in a police car and carried off to jail. "It was worth it," he told one of his teammates. The police were nice enough to let him go onto the field and tip his cap one last time. As the night went on, the names got bigger. Fidrych, Freehan, Parrish, Tanana, Lolich, Gibson, Fielder, Kaline, and then Trammell and Whitaker all walked to their positions. They dug up home plate and took it over to the new ballpark.

A bunch of us decided to spend that night in the clubhouse. We were going to camp out in tents in the outfield, but the brass got word of it and

Todd Jones celebrates after throwing the final pitch at Tiger Stadium on September 27, 1999 (© Rebecca Cook).

asked us not to do that. About ten of us, including me, Brian Moeller, and Robert Fick slept in the training room on the tables with towels as blankets and pillows. We didn't get much sleep, but it was worth it.

Before I went to sleep, I took a walk around the stadium and went one block to Nemo's bar. It was packed, and there was a cool vibe. I just sat there and hung out. Nemo's made the best burger in town, and I was starving. So I had a couple and chilled out. I was spent and so tired because I had been through the most intense day of my life. By 11 or 12, I collapsed in the training room and slept until about eight, when guys arrived at the ballpark to ride the bus to the airport. Needless to say, it had been an incredible 24 hours.

Reflections on the Closing of Tiger Stadium

*The Final Opener** by Kim Stroud

Tiger Stadium, 1912–1999: Yesterday was opening day here. I live in the neighborhood, and I was home for lunch just before the game started. Opening day is how you know spring has arrived in Corktown—all the people you haven't seen much of all winter and some who come in just for the season are back. Everyone's out—not all baseball fans, but for some it's good business, and others are drawn out by the excitement and noise to stand on their porches and talk with neighbors and keep a closer eye on their kids playing. It's a beautiful, sunny and almost warm day, with daffodils and magnolias blooming, goldfinches still at the feeder, and the sound of helicopters, flyover planes, and music from the bars up on the avenue linking us all together. Lots of people are driving around, figuring out where to park and walking through to Tiger Stadium. A few are partying at tailgate parties in our vacant lots. The noise goes all the way into the house, but I like it and leave the doors open. Tish, the neighborhood cat, isn't in her usual place on the porch next door—she probably doesn't like the hubbub. On my way back to work, I remember that a few friends are going to the game—one guy stood in line for hours to get tickets to this last opening day, and I vaguely look for him in the lot at St. Peter's Church, where I know he parks. The street vendors are back, with their folding tables and peanuts (cheaper here than inside) at their usual spots. The police are everywhere, directing all kinds of traffic. They've created a little staging area for the mounted division's beautiful horses on the Trumbull Avenue Bridge.

Next year, it will be a corporate opening day, and our little community will be a regular, struggling Detroit neighborhood. The suburban jocks in their SUVs won't have to navigate our narrow streets to get to our scattered private parking lots, which will probably be more convenient for them. It will also cost them more, but I don't really think they care.

*Originally published in *Here*, a 'zine edited by Neil deMause in 1999. Reprinted with permission.

The Final Week by Judy Davids

September 25, 1999: A week before the last game at Tiger Stadium, a friend called me at work to see how I was doing. He figured it must be a difficult time for me. I'm on the executive committee of the Tiger Stadium Fan Club. I told him I was holding up. Later, I choked back tears as I relayed the phone conversation to a colleague.

Yes, I felt bad. But the more I thought about how bad I felt, the better it made me feel. I feel bad because something mattered in my life.

A place where I spent happy summer nights with my sisters on Family Night will be gone. A place where my fifth grade teacher regularly took the girls on the softball team to Ladies and Retirees Day with money out of her own pocket; a place I skipped high school to go to on Opening Day in 1976, 1977 and 1978; a place where my husband and I held hands in the upper deck bleachers and fell in love with each other and a baseball team; a place where my husband, while still a college student, redesigned the owner's box for Mr. Tom Monaghan, and where he so graciously allowed us to sit on opening day in 1984 with the lovely Louise Kaline (and, oh yeah, I should mention that her husband Al was with her); a place where that same year we watched the Tigers clinch their division, the pennant, and the World Series from our bleacher seats; a place where a superstar right fielder named "Gibby" gave our friend and son's godfather, John "Baseball John" Miramonti, a landscaping job through the right field bleacher fence; a place where we exchanged jokes through that same fence with George Brett for ten years, and where we introduced our two-month-old son Dylan to the eventual Hall of Famer; a place where we got Reggie Jackson, Don Sutton, Harmon Killebrew, and many others to autograph baseballs we caught during batting practice; a place where we convinced a bunch of Minnesota Twins during batting practice to meet us at St. Andrew's Hall in downtown Detroit, and they did, and we all jumped up on stage with the Polish Muslims and sang "We Are the World"; a place we fought so desperately to save for nearly nine years of our lives, and ended up meeting the greatest group of people in the world, the members of the Tiger Stadium Fan Club; and a place where we take our little boys, Dylan and Willie Mays, to play under the center field scoreboard and chase the team mascot, Paws, through the bleachers for a photograph.

This place will be gone forever.

Yes, I have many reasons to feel bad, and I wouldn't trade a single one of them to feel better. Just the other day Willie, who is four, said he wanted me to write down all the things he loved the most. The list was about 15 items long. Number one was Tiger Stadium and number two was Paws. I saved that list. Unfortunately, Willie is probably too young to remember Tiger Stadium for his whole life as I will. Now that really makes me sorry, but not as sorry as I feel for those who will not miss it at all. They really missed a lot.

The Navin Field Grounds Crew by John Davids

The last sections of Tiger Stadium were demolished on September 26, 2009. But something very special occurred there in the spring and summer of 2010: something unprecedented, something unexpected, something spiritual, something magical.

Tom Derry was one of those people that made the Tiger Stadium Fan Club work. Tom was always there to do whatever needed to be done. He loved the ballpark, and everyone in the fan club loved Tom. As he drove down Michigan Avenue that spring after the ballpark was razed, he was troubled by the tall weeds and garbage that had taken over the site he loved so much. He decided he had to do something about it, so he made a few calls to see who might be willing to come down and clean up the site. Thankfully, one of the calls he made was to Judy and me.

The evening of May 10 about a dozen of us met at The Corner. Tom brought his riding mower; the rest of us brought shovels, rakes, and hoes. We began picking up garbage, cutting the grass, and trying to find home plate, the pitcher's mound, and the baselines. After a couple of hours, we had made a big difference: you could actually see the mound, the baselines, and the edge of the infield skin. It was possible to determine where the seating decks had stood as well because grass had never grown in those areas, so all that existed there were weeds, very tall, very healthy weeds that grew to the size of small trees. The areas of the field that had been grass were actually in pretty good shape. I'm sure the grass that had been planted on the field was of a very high quality and, even after ten years of neglect, the grass was pretty magnificent.

The feelings I had that evening were very intense. I believe in ghosts. Really. Our house has had a ghost from the day we moved in. That evening at the ballpark I felt the presence of many ghosts. It was spectacular. When we got home, Judy and I both mentioned the ghosts at the same time. She had felt their presence, too. She felt like the geese in the outfield were reincarnated fans or players. The presence of these spirits made me feel like we were embarking on something worthwhile. They made me feel appreciated and loved.

Many people came out to The Corner that summer: to reclaim and maintain the field, to play ball, to get their pictures taken on the mound. Every time I was there, people would drop by. The most interesting were the older couples who would just happen to be driving down Michigan Avenue and see us out on the field. They would park their cars and find their way in through the gate nearest first base. As they approached us, they would invariably ask, "Is this where Tiger Stadium was?" Their reactions varied but were typically pretty emotional. Those who had cameras would have us take their pictures on the mound, first base, home plate. I suppose it reflected who their favorite player had been. Many were in tears as they walked the field and reminisced, and I was often in tears myself. I felt good that we had tried so hard to see that this place was not abandoned and forgotten.

Of all Detroit buildings, Tiger Stadium held a unique place in people's hearts. The Fan Club always made the point that Tiger Stadium held more memories for Michiganders than any other building in the state. I don't think any other building even comes close. Fans in Boston and Chicago love their ballparks, too. Fenway's and Wrigley's charms are obvious and immediate. Tiger Stadium's charm was more subliminal; it was such a great ballpark because it worked so well as a ballpark. No other park put fans so close to the field. The amazing proximity to the field was a product of daring cantilevers that put the upper deck on top of the field. You always felt close to the game, and to baseball, when you watched the Tigers play at home. Our love of baseball was a product of that closeness.

The experiences we had that summer really brought our personal Tiger Stadium journey full circle. Tiger Stadium had been the place where Judy and I fell in love in the summer of 1978. Before that, it had been the place that held Judy's fondest memories of her grandfather, who brought her to many games, always sitting in the same bleacher section. During our courtship and first years of marriage, we attended hundreds of games and got to know many of the players during batting practice. Tiger Stadium became the center of our lives for several years as we fought to save it. The fight to save our special place led us to meet the most incredible people we had ever known: the Tiger Stadium Fan Club. When we eventually lost the fight, however, Tiger Stadium became a very bitter place for us. The fight cost us dearly. Along with the ballpark, we lost our love for professional baseball. We had forced ourselves to believe we could prevail; I think that was the only way any of us could have dedicated ourselves so completely to our cause. When the stadium was abandoned it hurt. When the stadium was demolished it hurt all over again.

But then Tom Derry saved everything for us. Tom made the corner of Michigan and Trumbull special again. It is really a perfect thing that has happened at The Corner over the past three summers. The Navin Field Grounds Crew continues to maintain the field as volunteers. People still come by and walk the field in wonderment. People play ball on the field nearly every day. A Detroit high school team even uses the park as its practice field. It is, after all, one of the finest fields in the city. Tiger Stadium once more belongs to the people who love her. They are drawn there because they have some kind of connection to this piece of land. There is no more pain there for us, no bitter fighting, no anguish. Tiger Stadium lives again, bringing pure joy to so many people, just as she did for 88 years.

An old-time baseball game at the site of the old ballpark: June 14, 2014 (Frank Rashid).

Elegy for Tiger Stadium BY JIM DANIELS

Wrap yourself in nostalgia's blankets
it's cold outside.

But even the blanket's moth-eaten,
ragged with grief.
For today Tiger Stadium comes down.
*

Oh, the old green wooden seats
banging to start up a rally

Oh, the corrupt ushers
in their crooked ties

barking at kids sneaking down
to the good seats

Oh, the long urinal troughs in the men's room
the lineup of drunks and young boys on tiptoe

Oh, the bullpens along the baselines
watching the wonderfully evil Goose Gossage
warm up, the ball exploding in the catcher's mitt.

Oh, the waxy plastic beer cups stacking up
beneath the bleacher benches

Oh, my three-year-old daughter in her sundress
smiling in her Tiger hat that last season, last game.

Michigan and Trumbull, Michigan and Trumbull.
Cochrane and Kaline, Cochrane and Kaline.
*

Oh, so you want me to wrap things up do you?
A game permanently shortened by rain.

Just remember stepping through shadows
up the narrow fenced ramp
into the upper deck
and into the explosion of sunshine on green grass.
Sunshine and green grass.

Squint and be a good boy.
Squint, and don't cry.

Remember your first game ever
before anyone lied to you.

Let me call them out: Harmon Killebrew,
Boog Powell, Dick McAullife, #3,
with the stance of a mad scientist
trying to kill his creation.

Come on back for your cup of coffee
in the bigs, Purnal Goldy.

Come back for your one good season
Champ Summers. Let me say it again,

Champ Summers. Gates Brown.
Earl Wilson, the pitcher who pinch-hit,

Ron LeFlore, the ex-con. Jim Northrup,
grand-slam king. Bases loaded, dude.

Ray Oyler, come on back and crack .200.
Stormin' Norman Cash come on back
and hit .361 again and show it was no fluke.

A high foul ball. A major league pop-up
and Freehan has the mask off, and Lance
Parrish has the mask off, and Mickey Cochrane
has the mask off.

Oh, big Frank Howard hitting one over the roof.
Oh, Dave Rozema karate-kicking his way
out of baseball just because he was young
and excitable.

Okay, Bird, I know you've been waiting,
come on back and tell the ball a few things
you forgot to say.

Bleachers or General Admission
Ladies/Retirees Day. Polish
American Night.

50,000 kids with free bats bouncing them
off concrete. Bring back the father-son games

Charlie Dressen is my grandfather. Mayo Smith
my great uncle. Billy Martin the dark sheep.
Al Kaline, kind uncle. Gibby, the cousin
the parents worried about.

Roll off the tarp, drag the infield.
Herbie do the Shuffle one more time

Bring back Jake Wood and Jerry Lumpe.

Mickey Lolich, come back in from the Donut Shop.
Denny McLain, come back from prison one last time.
*
Did I say I was going to stop? The rain's letting up some.
The Orioles are in town with the Robinsons.
The Yanks are in town with Mantle and Maris
and did McLain really groove one to Mantle in '68?

Just an organ in between innings.
No rock and roll scoreboard hi-jinks razzamatazz.
Ernie, take the mike.
We'll all pull up a Stroh's and stay awhile.
We'll come down from Paradise to catch a foul ball.

Charlie Maxwell, come on back from Paw Paw.
It's baseball. Nobody's died. They're all still alive.

Rust and cracks in memory's stadium.
It didn't have to be this way.
Trammell and Whitaker have one more double play
to turn.

Sock it to 'em Tigers.
Bless you, Boys.

I'm squinting into the sun.
All my life I've never seen such green.

The Tiger Stadium field in 2015 (Tom Derry).

Appendix 1
161 Baseball Hall of Famers Who Played at the Tiger Stadium Site

Bill Dow

Today, the ball field where Tiger Stadium once stood is being taken care of by some very dedicated fans who appreciate the historical significance of this hallowed ground. It is no wonder that folks like to participate in pickup games or just play catch on the site where nine World Series ('07, '08, '09, '34, '35, '40, '45, '68, '84), three major league All-Star games ('41, '51, '71), and two NFL championship games('53, '57) were held.

It is where Babe Ruth hit his 700th home run and Lou Gehrig ended his famous streak of consecutive games played.

And it is also the site—as Bennett Park, Navin Field, Briggs Stadium, or Tiger Stadium—where almost 75 percent of the players enshrined in the National Baseball Hall of Fame played in a regular-season game (including interleague play), a World Series game, or an All-Star game.

Or to be more specific, of the 215 men who played in the majors and who were inducted into the Hall of Fame as players, 161 performed at The Corner—and this number does not include individuals who may have played there but who were inducted as major league executives or managers. Nor does it include Negro League inductees who did not play in the majors.

Here is the list of those Hall of Famers:

Hank Aaron	Jim Bottomley	Roberto Clemente
Roberto Alomar	Lou Boudreau	Ty Cobb
Luis Aparicio	George Brett	Mickey Cochrane
Luke Appling	Lou Brock	Eddie Collins
Richie Ashburn	Mordecai Brown	Jimmy Collins
Earl Averill	Jim Bunning	Earle Combs
Jeff Bagwell	Jesse Burkett	Stan Coveleski
Frank Baker	Roy Campanella	Sam Crawford
Johnny Bench	Rod Carew	Joe Cronin
Chief Bender	Steve Carlton	George Davis
Yogi Berra	Orlando Cepeda	Andre Dawson
Craig Biggio	Frank Chance	Dizzy Dean
Bert Blyleven	Jack Chesbro	Ed Delahanty
Wade Boggs	Fred Clarke	Bill Dickey

Joe DiMaggio	Willie Keeler	Cal Ripken, Jr.
Larry Doby	George Kell	Phil Rizzuto
Bobby Doerr	Joe Kelley	Robin Roberts
Hugh Duffy	Harmon Killebrew	Brooks Robinson
Dennis Eckersley	Ralph Kiner	Frank Robinson
Johnny Evers	Chuck Klein	Jackie Robinson
Red Faber	Barry Larkin	Ivan Rodriguez
Bob Feller	Tommy Lasorda	Red Ruffing
Rick Ferrell	Tony Lazzeri	Babe Ruth
Rollie Fingers	Bob Lemon	Nolan Ryan
Carlton Fisk	Freddie Lindstrom	Ray Schalk
Elmer Flick	Ernie Lombardi	Red Schoendienst
Whitey Ford	Ted Lyons	Tom Seaver
Nellie Fox	Mickey Mantle	Joe Sewell
Jimmie Foxx	Heinie Manush	Al Simmons
Frankie Frisch	Juan Marichal	George Sisler
Lou Gehrig	Pedro Martinez	Enos Slaughter
Charlie Gehringer	Eddie Mathews	Duke Snider
Bob Gibson	Willie Mays	Tris Speaker
Lefty Gomez	Willie McCovey	Willie Stargell
Joe Gordon	Joe McGinnity	Don Sutton
Goose Goslin	Joe Medwick	Frank Thomas
Goose Gossage	Johnny Mize	Jim Thome
Hank Greenberg	Paul Molitor	Sam Thompson
Ken Griffey, Jr.	Joe Morgan	Joe Tinker
Lefty Grove	Jack Morris	Alan Trammell
Tony Gwynn	Eddie Murray	Dazzy Vance
Gabby Hartnett	Stan Musial	Arky Vaughan
Harry Heilmann	Hal Newhouser	Rube Waddell
Rickey Henderson	Phil Niekro	Honus Wagner
Billy Herman	Mel Ott	Bobby Wallace
Harry Hooper	Satchel Paige	Ed Walsh
Rogers Hornsby	Jim Palmer	Zack Wheat
Waite Hoyt	Herb Pennock	Hoyt Wilhelm
Catfish Hunter	Tony Perez	Billy Williams
Reggie Jackson	Gaylord Perry	Ted Williams
Ferguson Jenkins	Eddie Plank	Vic Willis
Hughie Jennings	Kirby Puckett	Dave Winfield
Randy Johnson	Tim Raines	Early Wynn
Walter Johnson	Pee Wee Reese	Carl Yastrzemski
Addie Joss	Jim Rice	Cy Young
Al Kaline	Sam Rice	Robin Yount

Appendix 2
The 15 All-Star Game Home Runs Hit at Briggs/Tiger Stadium

Bill Dow

1941

Arky Vaughan off Sid Hudson in the 7th inning
Arky Vaughan off Eddie Smith in the 8th inning
Ted Williams off Claude Passeau in the 9th inning

1951

Stan Musial off Ed Lopat in the 4th inning
Bob Elliott off Ed Lopat in the 4th inning
Vic Wertz off Sal Maglie in the 4th inning
George Kell off Sal Maglie in the 5th inning
Gil Hodges off Fred Hutchinson in the 6th inning
Ralph Kiner off Mel Parnell in the 8th inning

1971

Johnny Bench off Vida Blue in the 2nd inning
Hank Aaron off Vida Blue in the 3rd inning
Reggie Jackson off Dock Ellis in the 3rd inning
Frank Robinson off Dock Ellis in the 3rd inning
Harmon Killebrew off Ferguson Jenkins in the 6th inning
Roberto Clemente off Mickey Lolich in the 8th inning

Appendix 3
The Lions' Most Memorable Games at Tiger Stadium
Bill Dow

In their last Tiger Stadium game program, the Lions listed their most memorable games played at Michigan and Trumbull.

September 9, 1938: In their first game at Briggs Stadium, the Lions beat the Pittsburgh Pirates, 16–7, before 17,000 fans. [Editors' Note: Actually, the first Lions' game at Briggs Stadium occurred on October 16, 1938, when Detroit lost 7–5 to the Washington Redskins in front of a crowd of 42,855. The September 9, 1938, game was played at the University of Detroit's home field, Titan Stadium, and depending on the source, the attendance was either 17,000 or 18,000.]

November 7, 1943: The Lions and the New York Giants struggle through a scoreless tie seen by 16,992 spectators, the last 0–0 tie in the National Football League (NFL).

December 21, 1952: The Lions win 31–21 over the Los Angeles Rams to take the National Conference title and earn the right to play the Cleveland Browns for the NFL championship (which they capture the next week in Cleveland).

December 27, 1953: A 17–16 victory over the Cleveland Browns gives the Lions their second straight NFL championship. Bobby Layne hits Jim Doran with a 33-yard touchdown pass and Doak Walker kicks the extra point with 2:08 left to play.

October 20, 1957: Down 27–10 to the Baltimore Colts with eight minutes left, John Henry Johnson runs for a TD and Bobby Layne throws two touchdown passes to Hopalong Cassady, the last coming with only 46 seconds left.

December 29, 1957: The Lions annihilate the Cleveland Browns, 59–14, to win their fourth and last NFL championship.

November 22, 1962: In the "Thanksgiving Day Massacre," the Lions trample the Green Bay Packers, 26–14, as a smothering defense led by linebacker Joe Schmidt and the "Fearsome Foursome" of linemen Alex Karras, Roger Brown, Darris McCord, and Sam Williams sack quarterback Bart Starr 11 times. [Editors' Note: Most sources agree that Starr was sacked 11 times, but "Green Bay Packers 14 at Detroit Lions 26," www.pro-football-reference.com says that Starr was sacked "only" ten times, and the National Football League records do not include Detroit's performance on their list of teams that have had 11 sacks in a game.]

December 20, 1970: The Lions shut out the Packers, 20–0, in front of 57,387 fans to clinch their first playoff berth since 1957.

A Select Bibliography of Works About Tiger Stadium

Compiled by Frank Rashid

Books, Articles and Documentary Films

Adair, Lori, and Edward Neuwirth. *Shared Treasures: The Battle for Tiger Stadium.* Ann Arbor: Fatman Films/Prime Time Productions, 1992. Video.

Austin, Richard H. "Tiger Stadium: Corner of Michigan Avenue and Trumbull Avenue, Detroit, Wayne County." Lansing: Michigan History Division, Michigan Department of State, 1978.

Bachelor, Lynn W. "Stadiums as Solution Sets: Baseball, Football and the Revival of Downtown Detroit." *Review of Policy Research* 15, no.1 (1998): 125–40. Reprinted in *The Economics and Politics of Sports Facilities*, edited by Wilbur C. Rich, 89–102. Westport, Connecticut: Quorum Books, 2002.

Bak, Richard. *A Place for Summer: A Narrative History of Tiger Stadium.* Detroit: Wayne State University Press, 1998.

_____, and Charlie Vincent. *The Corner: A Century of Memories at Michigan and Trumbull.* Chicago: Triumph Books, 1999.

Benson, Michael. *Ballparks of North America: A Comprehensive Historical Reference to Baseball Grounds, Yards, and Stadiums, 1845 to Present.* Jefferson, NC: McFarland, 1989.

Betzold, Michael. "The House That Frank Built." *Detroit Free Press Sunday Magazine*, April 19, 1992.

_____. *Tiger Stadium: Where Baseball Belongs.* Detroit: Tiger Stadium Fan Club, 1988.

_____, and Ethan Casey. *Queen of Diamonds: The Tiger Stadium Story.* 2nd ed. West Bloomfield, Michigan: Northmont Publishing Company, 1997. First edition published by Altwerger and Mandelin, 1992.

Buckley, James, Jr. *America's Classic Ballparks: A Collection of Images and Memorabilia.* San Diego: Thunder Bay Press, 2013.

_____. *Classic Ballparks.* New York: Barnes & Noble, 2004.

Casey, Ethan. "The Malling of Major League Baseball: *The Sporting News* and the Media/Corporate Assault on Classic Ballparks." *Elysian Fields Quarterly* 11, no. 1 (1992).

_____. "Volunteers Working to Preserve Tiger Stadium." *Metro Times*, March 24, 2014.

Cauffiel, Lowell. "Squeeze Play." *Detroit Monthly* (May 1988).

Cohen, Irwin J. *Tiger Stadium.* Charleston, South Carolina: Arcadia, 2003.

_____. *Tiger Stadium, Comerica Park: History & Memories.* Laingsburg, Michigan: Boreal Press, 2011.

Colatosti, Camille. "Sports Stadium Ripoffs: Building Neighborhoods or Building Profits." *Dollars & Sense* July-August 1996: 17+. Academic OneFile.

Daniels, Jeff, host. *America's Classic Ballparks.* 20th Anniversary Collector's Edition. Produced by Bruce Lixey. Directed by Bob Hercules. Chicago: Questar Video, 2010. DVD. First edition produced as *Baseball's Heirlooms: The Classic Ball Parks* [sic]. Arlington, Virginia: WETA-TV, 1991. Video.

Davids, John, Judy Davids, and Harijs Krauklis. *The Cochrane Plan.* Detroit: John Davids, 1991.

deMause, Neil, and Joanna Cagan. "Deus ex Pizza." *Field of Schemes: How the Great Stadium Swindle Turns Public Money into Private Profit.* Revised edition. Monroe, ME: Common Courage, 2008. First edition published in 1998.

Detroit Design Team. *Detroit Stadium Study: Final Report.* Detroit: HOK 1989.

Detroit News. *Home, Sweet Home: Memories of Tiger Stadium.* Champaign, IL: Sports Publishing LLC, 1999.

Downtown Development Authority. *"The Corner": What's Next? Request for Proposal, an Invitation.* Detroit: City of Detroit, 1999.

A Select Bibliography of Works About Tiger Stadium

Enders, Eric. *Ballparks Then and Now*. San Diego: Thunder Bay Press, 2002.
Falls, Joe. *Echoes of Tiger Stadium*. Southfield, Michigan: Primeau Productions, 1999. Audio cassette.
_____, and Irwin Cohen. *So You Love Tiger Stadium Too (Give It a Hug)*. Grand Ledge, MI: Connection Graphics, 1999.
Fair, James. *The Tigers' Current Stadium Lease: An Evaluation*. Chicago: Heartland Institute, 1992.
The Final Game: September 27, 1999. New York: PSP, 1999. Commemorative program.
Foster, Margaret. "Tiger Stadium Demolition Resumes." *Preservation Magazine*, June 9, 2009. http://www.preservationnation.org/magazine/2009/todays-news/tiger-stadium-demolition.html.
Gillette, Gary, Eric Enders, Stuart Shea, and Matthew Silverman. *Big League Ballparks: The Complete Illustrated History*. New York: Metro Books, 2009.
Glaser, Gary, Richard Bak, Peter Comstock Riley, and Chris Felcyn. *Stranded at the Corner: The Battle to Save Historic Tiger Stadium*. Detroit: Michigan & Trumbull, 2006. DVD.
Grant, Adam. "Tiger Stadium: The Cochrane Plan and Why It Failed." Unpublished paper. Archival Material, 2001.
Gruber, Michael P. "Tiger Stadium." *The Literary Map of Detroit*. Ed. Frank D. Rashid. Detroit: Marygrove College Institute for Detroit Studies, 2004.
Guyette, Curt. "A Hole in the Heart: Corktown's Lost Field of Dreams." *Metro Times*, August 6, 2003.
Harrigan, Patrick. *The Detroit Tigers: Club and Community, 1945–1995*. Toronto: University of Toronto Press, 1997.
Harwell, Ernie, and Tim Rayborn. *Michigan and Trumbull: The History of Tiger Stadium*. Detroit: The Detroit Tigers, 1999. Video and audio cassette.
_____, May Krager, and Al Carmichael. *Michigan and Trumbull: Reminiscences of the History of Tiger Stadium*. Detroit: Ernie Harwell, 1999. Compact Disc.
Jacoby, Andy. "Demolition by Neglect in Detroit and the Battle to Save Historic Tiger Stadium: Lessons for Baseball Park Preservationists." *University of Denver Sports and Entertainment Law Journal* 1, no. 1 (2010): 46–75.
Kelin, John. "Last Look: RIP Tiger Stadium." *Elysian Fields Quarterly* 25, no. 3 (2008).
Long, Rebecca M. "Detroit's Field of Dreams: The Grassroots Preservation of Tiger Stadium." MA Thesis, Clemson University and the College of Charleston, 2012. http://tigerprints.clemson.edu/all_theses/1371/.
Lowry, Philip J. *Green Cathedrals: The Ultimate Celebration of Major League and Negro League Ballparks*. Revised edition. New York: Walker, 2006. Originally published as *Green Cathedrals*. Cooperstown: Society for American Baseball Research, 1986; republished as *Green Cathedrals: The Ultimate Celebration of All 271 Major League and Negro League Ballparks, Past and Present*. Reading, MA: Addison-Wesley, 1992.
McCarthy, John. "Entertainment-Led Regeneration: The Case of Detroit." *Cities* 19, no. 2 (April 2002): 105–111.
McGraw, Bill. "One Hundred Years of Baseball in Detroit: Remembrance and Celebration." *Detroit Free Press Magazine*. April 5, 1981.
Michigan at Trumbull: Turning the Corner. Ann Arbor: A. Alfred Taubman College of Architecture and Urban Planning, University of Michigan, 2000.
Moss, Richard J. *Tiger Stadium*. Lansing: John M. Munson Michigan History Fund, Michigan History Division, Michigan Department of State, 1976.
Okkonen, Marc. *Baseball Memories 1900–1909: An Illustrated Chronicle of the Big Leagues' First Decade*. New York: Sterling, 1992.
_____. *Baseball Memories 1930–1939: A Complete Pictorial History of the "Hall of Fame" Decade*. New York: Sterling, 1994.
_____. *Baseball Memories 1950–1959: An Illustrated Scrapbook of Baseball's Fabulous 50's*. New York: Sterling, 1993.
Official Souvenir Magazine: Farewell to Tiger Stadium, 1912–1999 [*Detroit Tigers Magazine*]. New York: Professional Sports Publications, 1999.
Panzenhagen, Tom. *Corner to Copa: The Last Game at Tiger Stadium, the First at Comerica Park*. Detroit: Detroit Free Press, 2000.
Pastier, John. "The Business of Baseball." *Inland Architect* 33, no. 1 (1989): 56–62.
_____. "Diamonds Aren't Forever." *Historic Preservation* 45, no. 4 (1993): 26.
_____. *Historic Ballparks*. Edison, NJ: Chartwell Books, 2006.
_____. "Rescue Operation: Plans to Save Tiger Stadium." *Inland Architect* 35, no. 5 (1991): 42–49.
Pastier, John, et al. *Ballparks: Yesterday and Today*. Edison, NJ: Chartwell Books, 2007.
Pierce, Charles P. "The End of the Line for Tiger Stadium." *Esquire*, August 1, 1999. http://www.esquire.com/features/the-game/ESQ0899-AUG_GAME.
A Proposal to Redevelop Detroit's Tiger Stadium. Detroit: The Navin Field Consortium, 2002.
Rashid, Frank D. "Against the Empire: The Lost Struggle to Save Tiger Stadium." *The Elysian Fields Quarterly* 16, no. 1 (1999): 6–8.
_____. "Baseball, Scholarship, and the 'Duty to Justice.'" In *Baseball/Literature/Culture 2002–2003: Selected Papers*, 93–105. Ed. Peter Carino. Jefferson, NC: McFarland, 2004.

_____. "Testimony Prepared for the Subcommittee on Domestic Policy, Committee on Oversight and Government Reform." Build It and They Will Come: Do Taxpayer-Financed Sports Stadiums, Convention Centers and Hotels Deliver as Promised for America's Cities? Hearing before the Subcommittee on Domestic Policy of the Committee on Oversight and Government Reform, House of Representatives, 110th Congress. Washington, D.C.: US Government Printing Office, 29 March 2007.
Reed, Lawrence W. *Stadium Subsidies Strike Out*. Midland, Michigan: Mackinac Center for Public Policy, 1995.
Reid, Lloyd B. *Tiger Stadium Parking and Traffic Survey*. Detroit: L. B. Reid, 1961.
Reidenbaugh, Lowell. *Take Me Out to the Ballpark*. St. Louis: The Sporting News, 1983.
Roche, Jason. *Stealing Home*. Detroit: Jason Roche, 2013. Video.
Rushlow, John, and Tom DeLisle. *Tiger Stadium: The Final Farewell, a Day to Remember*. Detroit: WKBD-TV, 1999. Video.
Sanders, Tom. "Treasure at Michigan and Trumbull." *Elysian Fields Quarterly* 23, no. 1 (2006), 58–62.
Selter, Ronald M. *Ballparks of the Deadball Era: A Comprehensive Study of Their Dimensions, Configurations, and Effects on Batting, 1901-1919*. Jefferson, NC: McFarland, 2008.
Shannon, Bill and George Kalinsky. *The Ballparks*. New York: Hawthorn Books, 1975.
Smith, Ron, and Kevin Belford. *The Ballpark Book*. Revised edition St. Louis: The Sporting News, 2003.
Spiegel, Craig. *Tiger Stadium: Detroit, Michigan*. Detroit: Lawrence Technological University, 1990.
Sports Illustrated Presents Tiger Stadium: A Celebration. Special Collector's Edition. New York: Time, 1999.
Stanton, Tom. *The Final Season: Fathers, Sons, and One Last Season in a Classic American Ballpark*. New York: Thomas Dunne Books/St. Martin's, 2001.
Tackach, James, and Joshua B. Stein. *The Fields of Summer: America's Great Ballparks and the Players Who Triumphed in Them*. New York: Crescent Books, 1992.
Tiger Stadium Fan Club v. Governor, Docket no. 194133. 553N.W.2d7 (1996).
Uberti, David. "How American Sports Franchises Are Selling Their Cities Short." *The Guardian*, September 22, 2014. http://www.theguardian.com/cities/2014/sep/22/-sp-how-american-sports-franchises-sell-cities-short?CMP=share_btn_fb.
Unobstructed Views: A Tiger Stadium Fan Club Publication. Detroit: Tiger Stadium Fan Club, 1988–1996.
Voelker, Don. "Michigan and Trumbull Before Baseball." *Michigan History* 73, no. 4 (July/August, 1989): 24–31.
Von Goeben, Robert. *Ballparks: Major League Stadiums Past and Present*. New York: Barnes & Noble, 2004.

Fiction, Poetry and Music

Daniels, Jim. *The Long Ball*. Pittsburgh: Pig in a Poke Press, 1988.
Evers, Crabbe. *Tigers Burning: A Duffy House Mystery*. New York: William Morrow, 1994.
Hagy, Alyson Carol. "Stadia." *Michigan Quarterly Review* 25.2 (1986): 351–62.
Hassenger, Ben. "The Corner." BQuiet Music, 2008. Lyrics, recording, and video. http://www.reverbnation.com/benhassenger.
Indigo, Susannah. "Tiger Stadium: October 1968." *Slow Trains* 2, no. 2 (2002).http://www.slowtrains.com/vol2issue2/indigovol2issue2.html.
Markowski, Ed. "Section 408 Tiger Stadium" and "Tiger Baseball Late July 1967." *Slow Trains* 3, no. 3 (2003). http://www.slowtrains.com/vol3issue3/markowskivol3issue3.html.
Monger, Timothy. "Michigan and Trumbull." *H.O.M.E.S. Volume 1*. Telegraph, 2001.
Mordenski, Jan. "Like Colavito." *Abandon Automobile: Detroit City Poetry 2001*. Ed. Melba Joyce Boyd and M.L. Liebler. Detroit: Wayne State University Press, 2001.
Perry, Rachael. "Tiger Stadium." *Elysian Fields Quarterly* 17, no. 3 (2000), 13. Reprinted in Perry, Rachael. *How to Fly*. Pittsburgh: Carnegie Mellon University Press, 2004.
Sharp, Thom. "Don't Tear It Down." Mike Ridley, 1991.
Sinclair, John. "Let's Call This." *Metro Times*, April 7, 2010 (originally published in 1982).

Films Featuring Tiger Stadium

Burton, LeVar, and Stanford Whitmore. *One in a Million: The Ron LeFlore Story*. Directed by William A. Graham. EMI Films, 1978.
Shapiro, Alan, and Bobby Fine. *Tiger Town*. Directed by Alan Shapiro. Disney, 1983.

About the Contributors

Michael Betzold's older sister, Peggy Swift, took him to his first Tigers games on Ladies' Days in the late 1950s. She also stoked his love of words, and he worked for the *Detroit Free Press* and wrote several books, including *Queen of Diamonds: The Tiger Stadium Story* with Ethan Casey. He was one of the five founders of the Tiger Stadium Fan Club in September 1987.

Known to Detroit baseball as J.P. McCarthy's "Lady in Blue," **Karen Bush** traces her baseball roots back to the day when, as a toddler, she was expected to know that "Charlie Gehringer lives here" whenever her parents drove her through Fowlerville, Michigan. Writer, editor, semi-retired college instructor, Karen presently heads up the Eddie Lake Society, whose members have given a large part of their lives to baseball, on and off the field.

Jim Daniels has written fourteen poetry collections, four fiction collections, and three produced screenplays. He received the Brittingham Prize for Poetry, the Tillie Olsen Prize, the Blue Lynx Poetry Prize, and two fellowships each from the National Endowment for the Arts and the Pennsylvania Council for the Arts. A Detroit native, Daniels now lives in Pittsburgh and is the Thomas Stockham Baker Professor of English at Carnegie Mellon University.

John Davids is an architect at Kingscott Associates. In the 1970s he and his wife Judy fell in love in the lower deck bleachers at Tiger Stadium. When the stadium was threatened, they volunteered to help the Tiger Stadium Fan Club show how remodeling could meet the needs of the team and the fans, and in 1990, they produced *The Cochrane Plan* for renovating Tiger Stadium. These days he avoids major league baseball.

Judy Davids is an interior architect, performer, author of *Rock Star Mommy*, and community engagement specialist for the City of Royal Oak, Michigan.

Tom DeLisle is a former *Detroit Free Press* reporter, who was part of the staff that won a Pulitzer Prize in 1968 for the paper's coverage of the 1967 Detroit riot. He later served as executive assistant to Detroit Mayor Roman Gribbs, before becoming a producer for several Detroit radio and television shows. He also was a producer at WABC in New York and was a writer for the *Tonight Show with Johnny Carson* when Richard Dawson served as a substitute host.

Neil deMause is co-author of *Field of Schemes: How the Great Stadium Swindle Turns Public Money into Private Profit* and runs the website fieldofschemes.com. He is a contributing editor for *City Limits* magazine, a contributing writer for *Extra!Magazine*, and a frequent contributor to the *Village Voice*, *Slate*, and numerous other publications.

Freelancer **Bill Dow** has been a regular contributor on Detroit sports history with the *Detroit Free Press* and *Baseball Digest*. Dow became an Al Kaline and Detroit Tigers fan in 1962 at the age of seven prior to attending his first game that year at Tiger Stadium. During the 1990s he helped fight to save the historic ballpark as a member of the Tiger Stadium Fan Club.

As a Tiger Stadium Fan Club board member, **Michael P. Gruber** wrote the nomination that eventually secured the stadium's listing on the *National Register of Historic Places*. He grew up in Detroit

About the Contributors

and attended the University of Detroit and Duke University. A retired teacher of English at Mercy High School in Farmington Hills, he lives in Detroit.

Todd Jones had a major league career that spanned 16 seasons. He pitched for the Tigers from 1997 to 2001 and from 2006 to 2008 and is the franchise's all-time save leader. He threw the last pitch at Tiger Stadium on September 27, 1999.

Jerry Lemenu's courtroom drawings have appeared on all major television networks and news services as well as locally on WDIV-TV. In the 1980s his sports cartoons were featured in the *Detroit News*. He teaches art at Ferndale High School and the Center for Advanced Studies and the Arts (CASA). He is a founding member of the Tiger Stadium Fan Club.

Born and raised in Southwest Michigan, **Rebecca Long** is passionate about Detroit's architectural history. A graduate of Clemson University/College of Charleston's Masters of Historic Preservation program, she dedicated much of her graduate studies to Michigan, in particular to Detroit-based subjects, and wrote her graduate thesis about Tiger Stadium preservation efforts. She currently lives in Grand Rapids, Michigan, where she works in Community Development.

John Pastier is a professionally trained architecture critic who has written about ballparks for more than 40 years in professional, preservation, baseball, and general-interest periodicals and in several baseball books, including *Ballparks Yesterday and Today* (Chartwell, 2007). He was a consultant on Camden Yards, Petco Park, and Safeco Field and received a USA Fellowship from the National Endowment for the Arts. He saw his first Tiger Stadium game in 1971. He lives in San Jose.

Lifelong Detroiter **Frank Rashid** is professor emeritus of English and a founding member of the Institute for Detroit Studies at Marygrove College. He edits the online *Literary Map of Detroit* and has published essays on the poetry of Emily Dickinson, Robert Hayden, and Lawrence Joseph and on Detroit literature, culture, and politics. He is one of the founders of the Tiger Stadium Fan Club.

Kim Stroud, an urban planner and licensed realtor, is the mortgage, land contract, and tax foreclosure counselor with United Community Housing Coalition, a 45-year-old non-profit legal services organization in Detroit. She lived in Corktown from 1997 until 1999, and now lives with her husband Frank Rashid in northwest Detroit.

Index

Numbers in *bold italics* indicate pages with illustrations

Aaron, Hank 173, 259, 261
Achkar, Alan 127n16
Aguirre, Hank 244
Aguirre, Rance 244
Al Kaline Day 173
Alan, Marc 51–52
All-Star Game *see* Major League Baseball All-Star Game
Allen, Tim 195
Allenson, Maureen 150n23
Allenson, Tom 150n23
Allison, Carl 150n23
Alomar, Roberto 259
altitude, effect on home runs 102, 119n170
American Institute of Architects, Detroit chapter 111
American League 11, 36, 39, 43, 47, 59, 73, 79, 112, 121; pennant 4, 6n3, 14, 15–16, 26–27, 38, 49, 53, 87, 89, 223, 252; playoffs 52, 176, 232, 233, 252
American League East division championship: (1972) 52; (1984) 6n3, 252; (1987) 232
American Sportscasters Association 216
Anaheim Stadium 84
Anderson, Sparky 55, 57, 58, 174, 176, 184, 198, 212, 215, 216, 226
Anderson, William 196
Angell, Roger vi, 2
Angus, Samuel 12–13
Ann Arbor, MI 112, 179, 190
Aparicio, Luis 223, 259
Appling, Luke 245, 259
Archer, Dennis 123, 135, 139–40, 141, 142, 143, 145, 147, 150n20, 152n63, 155
Arlington 110; *see also* Ballpark at Arlington
Armour, Bill 13
Arthurhultz, Philip 139
Ashburn, Richie 259
Astroturf 219
AT&T Park (San Francisco) 63n26, 86, 102, 118n112
Atlanta 110

Atlanta Braves 126
Atlanta Crackers 45
Atlanta Falcons 126
Auker, Eldon 167, 189, 250
Ausmus, Brad 250
Austin, Dan 115n3
Avanti Press **26**, **27**, **32**, **36**, **37**, **38**, **39**, **80**, **90**, **92**
Averill, Earl 259

Baade, Robert 150n29
Babson, Steve: *Working Detroit: The Making of a Union Town* 62n1
Bachelor, Lynn W. 149n10
Bagwell, Jeff 259
Baim, Dean 150n29
Bak, Richard 29n7, 62n2, 63n8, 63n9, 67n1, 67n3, 115n14, 115n31, 116n65, 116n66, 119n151, 119n157, 119n160, 120n204, 120n205
Baker, Frank 259
Baker, Genevieve 167
Baker, Joe 199–201
Baker Bowl 36, 70, 77, 84, 85, 101, 102, 103, 104, 117n74, 119n57, 119n157
ballot initiative (1992) and referendum (1996) 135, 139, 140, 141, 143–44
The Ballpark at Arlington 87, 104, 117n90, 118n111
Ballpark Digest 158, 164n36, 164n37, 164n38, 164n42, 164n45
ballpark names 97, 119n155, 143, 151n41
Baltimore 86
Baltimore Colts 225, 262
Baltimore Orioles 11, 46, 122, 127n5, 256
Barber, Red 199
Barnes, Tyler 248
Barney, Lem 175, 218–19, 225
Baseball/Literature/Culture 2002–2003: Selected Papers, edited by Peter Carino 149
Baseball Magazine 80, 81, 117n88
baseball season: (1961) 220, 221;

(1968) 183, 223, 227; (1984) 177, 179, 201, 213, 224; (1987) 202; (1989) 202; (1999) 184–85, 247
Bat Day 257
batting practice 194, 199–201, 205, 207, 210, 223, 225, 227, 252, 253
Battle Creek, MI 227, 228
Beatles 54
Beck, Jason 63n15
Beer, Louis 140, 150n28
Behm, Richard 186; "Getting Al Kaline's Autograph" 182
BEI, Inc. 111
Beinke & Wees 117n75
Bell, Burt 67n5
Belle Isle Aquarium 163n16
Beltran, Carlos 249
Bench, Johnny 173–74, 259, 261
Bender, Chief 259
Bengal Bar 204
Bennett, Charlie 10, 17
Bennett Park (1896–1911) **9**, 9–17, **15**, 19, 23, 68, 70–75, 86, 100, 162, 188, 237, 238, 242; attendance 15; concerts 70; expansions 74; fireworks 70; first major league game 12, 29n16; ice-skating 70; night baseball 70; seating capacity 11, 29n14, 73, 116n59; site plan, c. 1910 **74**, **77**; standing room **9**, 14; structural elements 70; "wildcat" bleachers 10, **11**, 73–74, **75**, 76, 89
Bensky, Alex 150n28
Benson, Michael: *The Ballparks of North America: A Comprehensive Historical Reference to Baseball Grounds, Yards, and Stadiums, 1845 to Present* 29n12
Berberet, Lou 205
Berra, Yogi 259
Bess, Philip: *City Baseball Magic: Plain Talk and Uncommon Sense About Cities and Baseball Parks* 118n103
Betzold, Michael 15n19, 28n5, 63n8, 63n16, 149n8, 116n58,

269

116n64, 119n151, 119n161, 120n193, 127–28n20
Bevacqua, Kurt 176
Bielfield, Jay 125
Big Bird, *Sesame Street* 53; *see also* Fidrych, Mark
Big Brothers/Big Sisters 201
Big Three 240
Biggio, Craig 259
Biletnikoff, Bill 219
Bing, Dave 148
Birkerts, Gunnar 110, 137, 139
Birkerts-O'Neal Plan 111, 137, 138, 139
Birmingham, MI 223
Black Bottom 130
Black Sox 19, 195
Blanchard, James 139
bleacher sections in MLB parks 91, 118n128
Bloomfield Hills, MI 190
Blue, Vida 174, 189, 261
Blyleven, Burt 259
Bob-Lo Island 239
Boggs, Wade 259
Boileau, Lowell **61**, **156**; *The Fabulous Ruins of Detroit* 62, 63n24
Bond Clothes 188
Bonds, Barry 103
Book Cadillac Hotel 221; *see also* Sheraton Cadillac Hotel
Boros, Steve 172
Boston 242, 253
Boston Red Sox 17, 19, 40, 122, 127, 192, 210, 213, 214, 221, 223–24
Boswell, Thomas vi
Bottomley, Jim 259
Boudreau, Lou 259
Boulevard Park 8
Boyer, Cletis 205
Boyle, Eugene 174
Bradley, Bill 152n54
Braves Field (Boston) 79, 82, 117n82, 117n80
Brazeau, Jim 229–237
Brett, George 252, 259
Bridges, Tommy 214
Briggs, Spike 39, 41, 42
Briggs, Walter O. 3, 19, 22, 23, 26, 30–41, 43, 47, 53, 64, 93, 96–99, 162
Briggs community 50, 229; *see also* Corktown, North Corktown
Briggs Manufacturing Company
Briggs Stadium (1938–1961) 1, 3, **25**, 30–43, **31**, **36**, **42**, **44**, 45 64–66, 93–104, 106, 168, 169–70, 179, 187, 194, 206, 221, 222, 238, 239, 241, 242, 245, 262; architectural drawings and documents 120n208; boxing at **25**; capacity 35, 63n5, 72, 116n43; clubhouse **39**; cross-sections through stands, 1938 **98**, **99**; expansions (1937–38) 96; field configurations and outfield dimensions **108**; Kaline's Corner 47, **48**, 106, **107**; lower-deck plan **97**; name

of 97, 119n157; night baseball 39, **40**, 63n8, 106, 188, 194, 239; 1938 reconfiguration of 1936 right-center-field stands **97**; office and ticket building (re-designed 1951) **107**; outfield configuration 120n181; picketers **31**; scoreboard **37**, **38**; smells 197; street-side projection **31**, **95**; upper-deck plan **97**; ushers 197; *see also* Michigan and Trumbull; Navin Field (1912–1937); Tiger Stadium (1912–2009)
Briggs Stadium Boycott Commission 40
Brock, Lou 49, 60, 195, 259
Brookens, Tom 208
Brookings, Ron 214
Brookings Institution 149n4
Brooklyn Dodgers 39, 45, 190
Brooks Lumber Company 159–60
Brown, Bill 105, 120n185
Brown, Gates 47, 48, 169, 255
Brown, Kenyon 43
Brown, Mordecai 259
Brown, Roger 66, 190, 262
Brush Stadium (New York) 119n157; *see also* Polo Grounds
Bruske, Paul H. 76, 81, 116n68, 117n89
Bruton, Billy 45, 172
Buchta, Robert 133
Buck, Jack 216
Bud Bowl 163n13
Bufford, Dennis 201
Bugbee, Gordon 150n27
Build It and They Will Come: Do Taxpayer-Financed Sports Stadiums, Convention Centers and Hotels Deliver as Promised for America's Cities? 149
Bunning, Jim 222, 259
Burke, Kathy 150n23
Burke, Nancy 150n23
Burkett, Jesse 259
Burns, James D. 12
Burns Park 12
Burns Security Company 192
Burton, LeVar 225
Burton Historical Collection, Detroit Public Library *see* Ernie Harwell Sports Collection
Bush, Karen Elizabeth **244**, 244–46
Butkus, Dick 174
Butsicaris, Jimmy 229
Butzel Field 226

Caddel, Ernie 64
Cadillac (Kennedy) Square 150n16
Cagan, Joanna: *Field of Schemes: How the Great Stadium Swindle Turns Public Money into Private Profit* 127n3, 127n14, 128n25, 128n28, 151n47
Camden Yards (Baltimore) *see* Oriole Park at Camden Yards
Campanella, Roy 259

Campbell, Jim 55, 57, 112, 197, 223, 245
Canadian Football League 121
Candlestick Park 80, 84
Canseco, Jose 200
Cantor, George 238
Carabio, Mike 239
Carew, Rod 208, 259
Carey, Paul 212, 213–15
Carlton, Steve 259
Carolina Panthers 126
Carrigan, Bill 18
Cartwright, Alexander 7
Casey, Ethan 28n5, 63n8, 63n16, 149n8, 116n58, 116n64, 119n151, 119n161, 120n193, 127–28n20
Casey's Bar 208
Cash, Norm 1, 7, 45, 49, 63n11, 102, 105, 170, 172, 173, 181, 191, 195, 201–2, 209–10, 210, 217, 221, 225, 256
casino gambling 130, 144, 146
Cass Technical High School 169
Cassady, Hopalong 262
Castillo, Marty 176
Cauffiel, Lowell 134
Cavanaugh, Jerry 50
A Century of Progress: Meeting the Challenges of the Times: A History of the Osborn Engineering Company, 1892–1992 120n209
Cepeda, Orlando 259
Chance, Frank 259
Channel 50 (WKBD-TV) 242
Cherry Street 10, 87, 89, **89**, **90**, **91**, **92**, 93, 96, 115n25, 115n27, 173, 187; *see also* Kaline Drive
Chesbro, Jack 259
Chevrolet, offer to maintain and refurbish the field 160, 164n47
Chicago, IL 140, 242, 253
Chicago Bears 174
Chicago Cubs 14, 27, 38, 47, 56, 126
Chicago Tribune 127, 128n29, 128n30
Chicago White Sox 19, 47, 122, 125, 136
Church Street 229
Chylak, Nestor 208
Cicotello, David: *Forbes Field: Essays and Memories of the Pirates' Historic Ballpark* 117n73
Cigar Aficionado 128n23
Cincinnati 110, 129, 204
Cincinnati Bengals 126, 219
Cincinnati Reds 8, 19, 70
Citizens' Bank Park 84, 86
Clark, Earl "Dutch" 64
Clark, Tony 105, **171**
Clarke, Fred 259
classic ballparks' proximity to downtown 70
Clay, Gil 204
Clem, Andrew 117n91, 120n190; *Clem's Baseball: Our National Pastime* 29n27, 115n22, 115n25, 117n93, 117n94, 117n95, 117n100,

117*n*101, 118*n*104, 118*n*106, 118*n*108, 119*n*159, 119*n*172
Clemente, Roberto 173, 195, 259, 261
Cleveland, OH 110, 179, 242, 117*n*86, 120*n*208
Cleveland Browns 65, 217, 262
Cleveland Cavaliers 124
Cleveland Gateway complex 124
Cleveland Indians 39, 43, 47, 53, 67*n*3, 122, 124, 127*n*6, 170, 179, 187, 198, 207, 221
Cleveland Municipal Stadium 35, 79, 100
Cleveland Plain Dealer 124, 127*n*16
Clinton, IA 226
Clotworthy, Dennis 209–10
Cobb (film) 29*n*21
Cobb, Ty 7, 13–15, 17–20, 22, 23, 29*n*21, 52, 73, 80, 112, 119*n*174, 121, 153, 157, 185, 188, 197, 202, 203, 204, 213, 217, 238, 259
Cobo Hall 66
Coca-Cola 204
Cochrane, Mickey 26, 52, 110, 116*n*43, 168, 176, 208, 256, 259
Cochrane Avenue 167, 212, 214, 255 *see also* National Avenue
Cochrane Plan 4, 57, 99, 110–111, 137, 138, 139, 140; cross-section showing luxury seats *99*; lower-deck design *110*; upper-deck seating plan 99
Cockrel, Sheila 155
Cogdill, Gale 66
Cohen, Richard M.: *The Scrapbook History of Baseball* 117*n*78
Colavito, Rocky 43, 170, 171, 172, 179, 189, 205, 221
Coleman, Ken 67*n*5
Collins, Charles "Rip" 167–68
Collins, Eddie 259
Collins, Jimmy 259
Colorado Rockies 104
Colt Stadium (Houston) 117*n*90
Columbus Senators 10
Combs, Earle 259
Comerica Bank 143
Comerica Park 3, 61, 62, 71, 100, 105–106, 111, 112, 124, 148, 149*n*6, 156, 194, 197, 201, 206, 209, 245; acreage/space 3, 6*n*4; attendance 61, 63*n*23; cost 145, 151*n*48; financing 143; naming rights 143, 151*n*41; parking 163*n*1; public subsidies 146; ticket prices 146, 152*n*57
Comiskey Park 32, 78, 79, 81, 84, 96, 117*n*87, 119*n*157, 120*n*179, 121, 122, 125, 136; *see also* New Comiskey Park
Committee to Rebuild Detroit and Wayne County 145
Common Ground Coalition 139, 143–44
concession areas, demand for 124
Conroy, Joe 139
Conway, Mary 193

Conyers, John 139
Cook, Rebecca **5**, *46*, *48*, *69*, *83*, *132*, *159*, *171*, *177*, *185*, *188*, *195*, *200*, *201*, *207*, *211*, *214*, *237*, *245*, *248*, *250*
Cooperstown 7
Coors Field 84, 104
Corktown 8, 16, 73, 130, *131*, 158, 203, 209, 212, 229–37, *231*, *234*, *235*; advantages of living near the Stadium 230–31; central location 229; disregarded by City and Tigers 232, 233, 234; disrespect from baseball fans 230, 232, 233; diversity 230; entertainment district 234, 235; historic homes 229, *234*, *235*; life after the Tigers 234–36; parking lots *231*
Corktown Citizens District Council (CCDC) 154, 155
"Corn Flakes Reilly" *see* Reilly, Mike
"The Corner" *see* Michigan and Trumbull
Cornerstone Charter Schools 160
Corrigan, Maura 152*n*55
County Stadium (Milwaukee) 84, 102, 113
Couzens, Frank 87
Coveleski, Stan 259
Cowboys Stadium 126
Crain's Detroit Business 116*n*49
Crawford, "Wahoo" Sam 13, 14, **15**, 259
Creevy, Patrick 181
Cronin, Joe 173, 259
Crosley Field 79, 84, 104, 117*n*80, 119*n*157, 120*n*183
Crowley, Carmen 150*n*23
Crowley, Mark 150*n*23, 229–37
Cruz, Deivi *177*
Crystal, Billy 163*n*13, 197, 233; *see also* 61*
Cubs Park *see* Wrigley Field
Cutty Sark 240
Cy Young Award 222

Daniels, Jim 179–84, *181*, 186, 254–55; "Baseball Cards #1" 181; "The Bookkeepers Talk Baseball" 183; "Elegy for Tiger Stadium" 255–56; "Extra Innings, Tiger Stadium, 1982" 184; "The Fat Man at the Ballgame" 179–80; "Getting Al Kaline's Autograph" 182; "New Words" 182; "Nightmare" 181; "Play by Play" 181; "Polish American Night, Tiger Stadium" 183; "Stormin' Norman" 181; "31–6" 182; "Time, Temperature" 180; "Willie the Wonder" 180; "World Series 1968" 183
Dapper, Cliff 45
Darin, Catherine 1, 2, 150*n*23, 161, 203, 232–33
Darvas, Robert 134, 137
Davids, Dylan 252

Davids, John 3, 6*n*4, 111, 137, 252–53
Davids, Judy 111, 137, 251–52, 253
Davids, Willie Mays 252
Davis, George 259
Davis, Zachary Taylor 76, 120*n*170
Dawson, Andre 259
Deadball Era 14, 20, 22, 49, 73, 104, 117*n*99, 122, 119*n*174
Deadline Detroit 165*n*53
Dean, Bill 118*n*118, 119*n*173
Dean, Dizzy 245, 259
Dearborn, MI 210
Dearborn Press and Guide 210
Delahanty, Ed 259
Delaney, Kevin: *Public Dollars, Private Stadiums* 125, 28*n*24
Delaware River baseball rubbing mud 207
DeLisle, Charlie 241–43
DeLisle, Tom 238–43, *242*
deMause, Neil 127*n*7, 127*n*10, 127*n*17, 127*n*19
deMause, Neil: *Field of Schemes: How the Great Stadium Swindle Turns Public Money into Private Profit* 127*n*3, 127*n*14, 128*n*25, 128*n*28, 151*n*47
Denver Broncos 170, 175
Derry, Sarah **203**, 212
Derry, Tom 149*n*9, 150*n*23, 150*n*27, 159, 160–61, 164*n*44, 201–3, **203**, 212, 253–54
The Designated Hatter 213; *see also* Detroit Athletic Company
Detroit: 134, 138, 139, 141, 143, 145, 154, 162, 202, 213, 230, 239, 242; bankruptcy 148, 237, Building Authority 149*n*15; City Council 87, 140, 141, 155–56, 156, 157–58, 162; civic leaders 129, 130, 138, 140–41, 147, 161, 238, 239, 240, 242; deindustrialization 129, 149*n*1; downtown **69**, 137, 143, 198; emergency manager 148; image 130–2, 153, 240; life 179; 1967 civil disturbance 47–48, 130, 180, 182, 230; population growth, 1900–1950 72–73, 116*n*53, 116*n*54; Recreation Department 148; redevelopment 130, 133, 134, 138, 142, 146; response to proposals for reuse of Tiger Stadium 156–58, 163*n*8; 250th birthday 107
Detroit Athletic Company 156, 167, 212; *see also* The Designated Hatter
Detroit Chamber of Commerce 50
Detroit Convention Center 130
Detroit Council of Churches 36
Detroit Department of Planning and Development 154
Detroit Economic Growth Corporation (DEGC) 157, 158, 160, 164*n*39, 164*n*46, 237
Detroit Fire and Police Department Field Days 201, 230

Detroit Free Press 28n1, 66, 115n19, 133, 145, 154, 157, 163n2, 163n4, 163n5, 163n24, 163n25, 167, 177, 203, **206**
Detroit/Hamtramck Assembly Plant ("Poletown Plant") 130, 146
Detroit Heralds 100
Detroit High School Football Championships 240
Detroit Incinerator 130, 149n7
Detroit Lions 36, 41, 50, 51, 52, 55, 64–67, 99–100, 133, 135, 144, 168, 174–75, 181, 190, 192, 205, 207, 216–219, 225, 239, 240, 241; African American fans 51; All-Time Team 218; Detroit Medical Center 152n63
Detroit Metro Times 63n19, 154, 157, 163n3, 163n7, 163n9–11, 163n13–18, 163n21–24
Detroit Mounted Police **27**, **31**, 228, 251
Detroit News 116n38, 134, 157, 163n23, 118n124, 174, 203, **107**; see also Avanti Press
Detroit Panthers 100
Detroit Pistons 54, 55, 135
Detroit Police 232, 251; Athletic League (PAL) 161–63, 165n55
Detroit Public Schools 142, 229
Detroit Public Television 160
Detroit Red Wings 54, 55, 57, 150n21
Detroit River **131**, 239
Detroit Stars 36
Detroit Sunday Journal 60, 63n20
Detroit Symphony Orchestra 136
Detroit Tigers 147, 168, 192, 196, 213–14, **245**; African American fans 1, 3, 30, 34, 39–40, 43, 45, 47, 49, 136; African American players 43, 45, 47, 180, 219–20; attendance at Comerica Park 61, 63n23; final season at Tiger Stadium 247; franchise value 146, 148, 152n56; maintenance of Tiger Stadium 155–56; management 134–35, 138, 141, 239; naming 12, response to proposals for reuse of Tiger Stadium 155–57; uniform vi, 16, 220, 224, 239; world championships 175–77, 224
Detroit Tigers (football team) 100
Detroit Tigers Media Guide 116n46, 116n47, 120n187
Detroit Tigers Radio Network 213
Detroit Times **65**
Detroit Wolverines 8, 10, 73
Detroiters for Jobs & Development 125
Deutsch, Jordan A.: *The Scrapbook History of Baseball* 117n78
Devil Restaurant 212
DeWitt, Frank 43
Dickey, Bill 259
Dickson, Paul: *The Dickson Baseball Dictionary* 29n26

DiMaggio, Dom 214
DiMaggio, Joe 103, 224, 260
Dinan Field 64; see also Titan Stadium; University of Detroit
Dixon, Jennifer 163n2
Doby, Larry 39, 40, 43, 260
Dodger Stadium (Los Angeles) 117n84
Doerr, Bobby 260
Domino's Pizza 55, 109
Donovan, "Wild" Bill 13
"Don't Tear It Down" 194, 195–96
The Doors 172
Doran, Jim 217, 262
Doubleday, Abner 7
Douglasville, GA 204
Dow, Bill 142, 150n28, 158,
Dowty, Stuart, 150n28
Doyle, Vince 192
Dressen, Charlie 256
Dudley, Linnea (resources) **24**
Duffy, Hugh 260
Duggan, Joseph E. 44
Duggan, Michael 139, 140, 141, 144, 147, 152n63, 161
Dyersville, IA 213

The Eagles 232, 233
Eastern Market 8
Ebbets Field (Brooklyn) 16, 76, 78, 81, 84, 85, 102, 104, 117n80, 118n114, 119n157, 120n182, 216, 219
Eckersley, Dennis 260
Eckstein, Rick: *Public Dollars, Private Stadiums* 125, 28n24
Economic Club of Detroit 109
Eleven Most Endangered Historic Places see National Trust for Historic Preservation
Elliott, Bob 261
Ellis, Art 139, 147, 152n63
Ellis, Doc 174, 261
Elysian Fields, Hoboken, NJ 8
Elysian Fields Quarterly 149
eminent domain 146, 149n6
Engel, Clyde 13
Engler, John 139, 144, 151n45, 152n63
Ernie Harwell Day 182; see also Harwell, Ernie
Ernie Harwell Park 236
Ernie Harwell Sports Collection **9**, **11**, **15**, **21**, **28**, **37**
ESPN Magazine 203
Estleman, Loren D. 178, 186; *Jitterbug* 186; *King of the Corner* 186
Evans, Darrell 56
Evers, Crabbe (pseud. William Brashler and Reinder Van Til) 178, 186; *Tigers Burning* 178
Evers, Hoot 189
Evers, Johnny 260
Ewing-Cole Architects, Philadelphia 118n109
Exhibition Stadium (Toronto) 117n90

Faber, Red 260
The Fabulous Ruins of Detroit see Boileau, Lowell
Facebook 159
Falb, Kent 174
Falls, Joe 187, 189
fan clubs 191
fantasy camp at Tiger Stadium 201
Farmer, Sam 128n26
Farr, Mel 218
Fasano, Emery 189
"Fathers Playing Catch with Sons" see Hall, Donald
Faust, Scott 134
Fear Strikes Out 222; see also Piersall, Jimmy
Fearsome Foursome 190, 262
Feliciano, Jose 49, 171–72; "Feliz Navidad" 172
Feller, Bob 168, 224, 260
Fenway Park 16, 17, 34, 57, 59, 62, 68, 77, 79, 82, 87, 89, 101, 104, 117n84, 117n87, 118n114, 120n184, 121, 126, 127, 136, 197, 213, 221, 223, 238, 253
Ferkovich, Scott 115n14
Fernandez, Chico 172, 221, 225
Ferrell, Kerry 196–98; *Rick Ferrell, Knuckleball Catcher: A Hall-of-Famer's Life Behind the Plate and in the Front Office* 196
Ferrell, Rick 43, 196–98, 260
Fetzer, John 43, 46, 47, 51, 54, 55, 106, 108, 173
Fezzey, Mike 250
Fick, Robert 60, 249, 250
Fidrych, Mark 2, 53–54, 55, 153, **195**, 197, 226, 244–45, 250, 256
"Field of Dreams" 213
Field of Dreams (film) 195, 225
Field of Schemes: How the Great Stadium Swindle Turns Public Money into Private Profit 151n47
Fielder, Cecil 52, 102, 105, 250
Final Four 147, 148
The Final Season see Stanton, Tom
Fine, Sidney: *Violence in the Model City: The Cavanagh Administration, Race Relations, and the Riot of 1967* 63n14
Finegood, Steven 150n28
Fingers, Rollie 260
Finn, John & Son 113
fire resistance in stadiums 75–76, 78–79, 82
Fisher Freeway (I-75) 229
Fisk, Carlton 260
Flick, Elmer 260
Flood, Curt 49
football at Michigan and Trumbull 3, 36, 41, 45, 50, 64–67, 68, 96, 99–100, 175, 181, 186n10, 190, 192–93, 216–19, 225, 240, 241, 262; see also Detroit Lions
Forbes, Chuck 136–37
Forbes Field 63n25, 70, 75, 76, 77, 78, 81, 84, 91, 102, 117n73, 117n80, 117n83, 117n85, 118n131

Ford, Henry 16, 18
Ford, Whitey vi, 260
Ford, William Clay 50, 51, 66
Ford Field 66, 148; public financing campaign and cost 145; ticket prices 146, 152n57
Ford Frick Award 215, 216
Ford Motor Company 148
Ford Rotunda 239
Fort, Rodney 150n29; *Hard Ball: The Abuse of Power in Pro Team Sports* 152n51
Fort Pontchartrain 8
foul lines and outfield stands in classic ballparks 117n80
Fox, Nellie 260
Fox Theatre 58, 59, 124, 137
Foxtown 112
Foxx, Jimmy 23, 29n32, 103, 260
Foytack, Paul 244
Free Lunch: How the Wealthiest Americans Enrich Themselves at Government Expense (and Stick You with the Bill) 152n58
Freedom of Information Act request 134
Freehan, Bill 47, 49, 169, 173, 191, 192, 199, 250, 256
Freund, David M.P. 149n1
Fricker, Daniel G. 154, 163n4-5
Frisch, Frankie 260
Frontier League 61, 155
Fryman, Woody 192
Fundaro, Bill 206-8
Future Shock 224

Gaedel, Eddie 41, 63n10
Gaetti, Gary 101
Gallagher, John 163n24-27
gambling and baseball 22, 143, 151n42, 182
Garagiola, Joe 176, 215, 216, 245
Garver, Ned 221
Gaye, Marvin 172; "Sexual Healing" 184
Gehrig, Lou **37**, 153, 260
Gehringer, Charlie 26, 123, 153, 173, 208, 224, 260
General Electric 113
General Motors 130
German Americans in the Briggs Community 229
Gibson, Bob 49, 260
Gibson, Kirk 55, 56, 105, 169, 175-77, 184, 194, 208, 211, 216, 224, 227, 228, 250, 252, 256
Giddings, James 144
Giffels & Vallett Inc., L. Rossetti, Associated Engineers and Architects 96, 113
Giuliani, Rudy 123
Glaser, Gary 163n16
Goebel 22 Beer 240
"golden age of ballparks" vi
Goldy, Purnal 255
Gomez, Lefty 260
Goodfellows game 240
Gordon, Joe 260
Goslin, Goose 26, 28, 176, 260

Gossage, Goose 56, 169, 176, 216, 255, 260
Graham, Billy 22, **25**, 29n31
Grand Canyon 195
Grand Circus Park 214
Grand Rapids, MI 224
Gratiot Ave. 191
Gratz, Roberta Brandes 142, 152n60
Great Depression 87, 118n114
Great Lakes Aerial Photos 164n41
Great Lakes Summer Collegiate League 61
Green, Pumpsie 40
Green Bay Packers 66, 67n9, 218, 262
Green Cathedrals: The Ultimate Celebration of All 271 Major League and Negro League Ballparks, Past and Present (Philip J. Lowry) *see* Lowry, Philip J.
Greenberg, Hank 1, 5, 36, 38, 87, 102, 103, 123, 153, 157, 167-68, 187, 197, 199, 208, 224, 245, 260
Greene, Sam 69, 86, 115n8, 118n113
Greening of Detroit 160
Greensboro, NC 196
Greiner, Claude 159, 164n44
Gretsky, Wayne 197
Gribbs, Roman 173
Griffith Stadium 70, 76, 78, 79, 84, 85, 117n80, 117n87, 119n157, 120n208, 221
Griffey, Ken, Jr. 260
Grilli, Steve 226
Grosse Pointe, MI 174
"Ground from the Mound" 163n19; *see also* Tiger Stadium, dirt
Grove, Lefty 260
Grubb, Johnny 208
Gruber, Michael P. 1, 133
Guise, Edward 174
Gumbleton, Bishop Thomas 150n23
Gutowsky, Ace 64
Guyette, Curt 63n19, 149n7, 150n25, 151n40, 154, 155-56, 163n3, 163n7-11, 163n13-18, 163n21-22
Gwynn, Tony 175, 260

Hagy, Alyson Carol 186; "Stadia" 184
Hake, Harry 76
Hale, Sammy 187
Hall, Donald 186, 190; *Dock Ellis: In the Country of Baseball* 190; "Fathers Playing Catch with Sons" 179; *Fathers Playing Catch with Sons: Essays on Sport (Mostly Baseball)* 190; "Football: The Goalposts of Life" 181; "Poem with One Fact" 190
Hall of Fame *see* National Baseball Hall of Fame; Pro Football Hall of Fame
Hall of Famers 13, 36, **46**, 55, 111, 113, 150n26, 157, 168, 173, 175, 176, 181, 182, 196, 216, 252, 259-60; *see also* National Baseball Hall of Fame; Pro Football Hall of Fame
"Hall of Heroes" 162-63
Hamilton Anderson Associates 158
Hamtramck 36
Hand, John 170, 209
Hanson, Jason 218
Harris, Ned **38**
Hart, George 139
Hart, Leon 64
Hartnett, Gabby 260
Harvard University 124
Harvey Doug 228
Harwell, Ernie 45-47, **46**, 49, 58, 63n12, 139, 157-58, 171-72, 172, 175, 181, 185, 188, 190, 193, 201, 202, 205, 209, 211, 212, 213, 225, 227, 232, 233, 236, 248, 256; *Tuned to Baseball* 63n12; *see also* Ernie Harwell Day; Ernie Harwell Park
Harwell, Lulu 249
Hastings Street 130
Hatfield, Fred 222
The Haymarket 10, 237
Heilbronner Baseball Bureau 116n43
Heilmann, Harry 202, 214, 215, 260
Heisman Trophy 64, 175
Helyar, John: *Lords of the Realm: The Real History of Baseball* 127n2
Henderson, Rickey 260
Henderson, Stephen 160, 164n48
Henning, Lynn 174
Henning, William H.: *Detroit's Street Railways: City Lines, 1922-1956* 116n61
Henry Ford Hospital 174
Herman, Billy 260
Hernandez, Willie 176, 177
Herndon, Larry 175, 202
Herts, Henry B. 76
Hiller, John 183, 224
Hobbs, Roy 196
Hodges, Gil 261
Hodges, Russ 46
Hogan, Rosemary 136, 150n23
HOK Sport 79, 117n96, 118n107; *see also* Populous
Holmes, Dan 29n19
home-road home run splits of leading Tigers sluggers 102-3
The Home Run Encyclopedia: The Who, What, and Where of Every Home Run Hit Since 1876 29n30
home-run-friendly classic ballparks 103-4
home runs: cumulative totals in selected old ballparks 101; minimum lengths in MLB ballparks 101-2
Hood, Morris III 160
Hooper, Harry 260
Hornsby, Rogers 260

274 Index

Horton, Willie 45, 49, 60, 63n15, 102, 103, 105, 120n189, 162, 169–70, 172, 180, 195, 201, 202, 223
Houk, Ralph 226
House of David 22
Houston, TX 110
Houston Astrodome 50
Houtteman, Art 169
Howard, Frank 105, 191, 256
Howard Johnson's (Washington Boulevard and Michigan) 192
Howe, Gordie 173, 209
Hoyt, Waite 260
Hubbell, Carl 13
Hudson, Sid 261
Hughes, Chuck 174–75, 190, 217
Hugs *see* Tiger Stadium Hugs
Humphreys, Brad 150–51n29
Hunkin and Conkey 16, 113
Hunter, Catfish 260
Hutchinson, Fred 261
Hyatt Regency, Dearborn 228
Hygrade Ball Park Franks 179

Ilitch Holdings 237
Ilitch, Marian 139, 148; casino ownership 143, 151n42
Ilitch, Mike 3, 55, 58–59, 61, 63n19, 63n20, 112, 120n202, 125, 133, 137, 138, 139, 140, 143, **144**, 151n41, 151n42; wealth 145–46, 148, 152n50, 152n63, 157, 223
Ilitch, Ronald Tyrus 120n203
Ilitches 56, 140, 146, 141n42, 155–56, 213
Ingham County Circuit Court 144
Inkster, MI 189
Inland Architect 120n201
inside-the-park home runs 119n174
Irish American residents of Corktown 229

Jack Murphy Stadium 84
Jackson, Austin 52
Jackson, George 158, 160, 164n40, 164n48, 237
Jackson, Reggie 52, 169, 173–74, 189, 223, 252, 260, 261
Jackson, Shoeless Joe 19, 195
Jackson State Penitentiary 225
Jacobs, Jane 136, 152n60
Jacobs Field 84, 122
James, Bill 63n17
Jarry Park (Montreal) 117n90; *see also* Parc Jarry
Jeffries Projects 169
Jeffsan Corp. 111
Jenkins, Ferguson 260, 261
Jenkinson, William J. 22, 29n30
Jennings, Hughie 11, 14, 18, 20, 80, 260
"jewel box" ballparks 76
J.L. Hudson Department Store 239
Joe Louis Arena 54, 150n21
John C. Lodge Freeway (M-10) 182, 219
Johnson, Alex 170

Johnson, Ban 11, 12, 14
Johnson, David Kay 147, 155n58
Johnson, John Henry 262
Johnson, Randy 260
Johnson, Roland T.: *The Scrapbook History of Baseball* 117n78
Johnson, Walter 13, 260
Jones, David: "Frank Navin" in *Deadball Stars of the American League* 29n18
Jones, Todd 247–50, **250**
Joss, Addie 260

Kaffer, Nancy 164
Kaline, Al 4, 44, **46**, 49, 102, 105, 106, 112, 120n188, 170, 172, 173, 174, 181, 182, 185, 195, 198, 199, 202, 204, 209, 211, 221, 223, 225, 239, 243, 245, 248, 249, 250, 252, 256, 260
Kaline, Louise 252
Kaline Drive 173, 212, 255; *see also* Cherry Street
"Kaline's Corner" 47, **48**, 106, **107**, 195
Kalinsky, George: *The Ballparks* 116n43, 119n156
Kansas City, MO 120n198
Kansas City Athletics 170, 205
Kansas City Royals 56, 176, 249
Karras, Alex 66, 190, 218, 225, 262
Kates, Maxwell 63n11
Kavanaugh, Kelli B. 155
Keating, Tom 204
Keeler, Willie 260
Kell, George **46**, 168–69, 171, 260, 261
Keller, Charlie 171, 221
[Kellerman], Jeanie Wylie 149n6
Kelley, Joe 260
Kelly, John 139, 150n28
Kelsey, John 19, 22
Kennedy, Robert 49
Kennedy, Ted 197
Kennedy Square 212
Keri, Jonah 63n26
Kevorkian, Jack 60
Khalil, Dave 212
"Kids at the Corner" 162
Kiersh, Edward 128n23
Killebrew, Harmon 105, 173, 252, 255, 260, 261
Kilpatrick, Kwame 141, 155, 157
Kiner, Ralph 260, 261
King, Martin Luther, Jr. 49
Kingdome (Seattle) 84, 102, 118n105, 118n112
Kittides, Christopher 111
Klein, Chuck 260
Knorr, Fred 41, 43
Kochevar, Tony 204
Korean War 168
Kowalkowski, Bob 66
Kubek, Tony 172
Kuenn, Harvey 43, 170, 173, 179, 195, 222
Kuhn, Bowie 173
Kukula, Patricia 111

"The Lady in Blue" *see* Bush, Karen Elizabeth
Lajoie, Bill 226
Lake Erie Monarchs 61
Lakeland (FL) Ledger 119n166
Lambeau Field 175
Landis, Kenesaw Mountain 19, 22, 27, 89
Landon, Alf 22, **24**
Landry, Greg 190
Lane, Night Train 225
Lansing, MI 202
Lapides, Max 187–89
Larkin, Barry 260
Larson, Gary 161
Lary, Frank 172, 222, 244
Lasorda, Tommy 260
lawsuits to prevent public stadium subsidies 135, 144, 151n45; *see also* Taxpayers of Michigan Against Casinos
Layne, Bobby 41, 64, 217, 240, 243, 262
Lazzeri, Tony 260
A League of Their Own 197
League Park (Cleveland) 78, 79, 81, 84, 85, 102, 117n80, 117n87, 118n117
League Park (Detroit) 70; *see also* Boulevard Park
Lear Corporation 162
Leavitt, Charles W., Jr. 76
LeBeau, Dick 219
Lee, Bill "Spaceman" 223–24
LeFlore, Ron 225–6, 250, 255
Lemenu, Jerome **144**, 150n23
Lemon, Bob 260
LeRoy, Greg: *The Great American Jobs Scam* 127n13
Lessenberry, Jack 163n16
Levin, Carl 139, 158, 160, 161, 162, 163n8, 237
Levine, Philip 178–79, **179**
Leyland, Jim 226
"Light My Fire" 172
Lindell Athletic Club 49, 217, 223, 228
Lindstrom, Freddie 260
Linn, Thomas 161, 164n39
Lis, Wally 195
Little Caesars Arena 152n54
Little Caesars Pizza 55, 58, 60, 112
little league baseball 160
Livingston, Harold 178
Lolich, Mickey 47, 49, 173, 198, 201, 250, 256, 261
Lombardi, Ernie 260
Long, Judith Grant 151–52n48; *Public/Private Partnerships for Major League Sports Facilities* 124, 128n27
Lopat, Ed 261
Los Angeles 195, 242
Los Angeles Dodgers 126, 216
Los Angeles Memorial Coliseum 83, 102, 104, 117n90, 120n180
Los Angeles Rams 217, 262
Los Angeles Times 63n12, 128n26, 198

Lou Gehrig's Disease 192
Louis, Joe **25**
Love, Ed 145
Lowry, Philip J. 29n14, 115n19, 115n23, 115n28, 115n35, 116n37, 116n39, 116n41, 116n44, 116n45, 116n47, 116n48, 116n50, 120n190, 120n191
Lubinger, Bill 127n16
Luisa, Angelo: *Forbes Field: Essays and Memories of the Pirates' Historic Ballpark* 117n73
Lukow, Kevin 63n22
Lumpe, Jerry 256
Lyons, Ted 260

Mack, Connie 26
Mack, Gene **44**, 45
Mack Park 36
Madonna: "It Used to Be My Playground" 197
Maglie, Sal 261
Mahaffey, Maryann 138–39, 156
Maher, Bruce 217
Maher, Marianne 150n27
Major League Baseball 129, 133, 141, 147
Major League All-Star Game 148; balloting at Tiger Stadium 192; home runs 261; 1941 game at Briggs Stadium 38, 63n6; 1951 game at Briggs Stadium 40, 173; 1971 game at Tiger Stadium 52, 173–74, 189, 195, 223; 1976 game at Veterans Stadium 54; 2005 game at Comerica Park 147
Maltese American residents of Corktown 229
Mandela, Nelson 22, 232, 233
Mann, Erroll 192
Mantle, Mickey 45, 105, 170, 182, 202, 205, 217, 256, 260
Manush, Heinie 260
March of Dimes Walkathon 192
Marichal, Juan 260
Maris, Roger 45, 170, 205, 256
Mark Ridley's Comedy Castle 195
Martha and the Vandellas 157–68
Martin, Billy 52, 191, 207, 210, 225, 256
Martin, Jim 65
Martin, Len: *Forbes Field: Build It Yourself* 118n131
Martinez, Pedro 260
Marty, John 126
Marygrove College **179**; Library **24**
Mason, Hodges 136
Massey Ferguson 225
Matchick, Tommy 48–49
Mathews, Eddie 260
Maxwell, Charlie 172, 181, 195, 256
Mayo Smith Society 195
Mays, Willie 173, 260
McAuliffe, Dick 47, 245, 255
McCarthy, Eugene 22, 49
McCartney, Bill 65
McCord, Darris 66, 190, 262
McCovey, Willie 260

McDevitt, John 109, 133–34
McGinnis, Jim 204–5
McGinnity, Joe 260
McGraw, Bill 63n20, 177
McGraw, John 11
McGwire, Mark 103, 105
McHale, John, Jr. 140, 147, 152n63, 247, 249
McKenna, Brian 63n10
McKonchie, Barbara 245
McLain, Denny 47, 49, 52, 182, 190, 203, 222–23, 245, 256
McLaughlin, Charles E. 76
McNamara, Edward 139, 140, 152n63
media, role of 135, 141, 151n30, 157, 163n24
Medwick, Joe ("Ducky") 2, 27, 29n13, 34, 60, 89, 92, 103, 260
Memorial Stadium (Baltimore) 84, 102
Merle Alvey Dixieland Band 172, 224
Mesrey, Dave 226
Metrodome 121, 123
Metropolitan Stadium (Bloomington, MN) 84–86, 117n99, 117n101, 118n110
Mexican Americans living near Tiger Stadium 229
Meyer, the Rev. John 150n23
Miami Dolphins 126
Michigan and Trumbull ("The Corner") (1896–) 17, 62, 68–73, 76–77, 86, 100–101, 104–5, 112–113, 150n23, 159, 160, 162–63, 168, 176, 178, 192, 193–94, 198, 199, 210, 212, 213, 236, 237, 238, 242, 244, 253, 255, **255**; after the Tigers 233–37; ashes of fans 5, 161, 203; building industry firms active over time 113–14; central location 69, 70, 106; fireworks 70, 230; growth of ballpark site area and seating density 71; largest crowd 19–20; musical performances 22, 23, 24, 68, 70, 206, 232, 233; old-time baseball **254**; opera 22, **23**, **24**; orientation of playing fields on the site 73, 75, 76; political rallies, demonstrations, and speeches 19–20, 22, 24, **31**, 49, 68, 232, 233; public transit service to 69, 71, 116n61; religious gatherings 19–20, 22, 25; sacred ground 203; seating capacities 72, 73, 76, 95; size of site 71, 73, 77; *see also* Bennett Park; Briggs Stadium; Navin Field Grounds Crew; Tiger Stadium
Michigan and Trumbull LLC 155
Michigan Avenue 7, 8, 29n25, 62, 188, 189, **193**, 194, 198, **214**, 221, 222, 240, 241, 252
Michigan Avenue bus 199
Michigan Central Railroad Station 236
Michigan Chronicle 151n37

Michigan Court of Appeals 144, 146, 147
Michigan Central Railroad Station 236
Michigan State Legislature 139, 144
Michigan, State of 138, 139
Michigan State University 55, 162, 170, 176
Michigan Strategic Fund 139, 143, 144, 146, 151n44
Michigan Supreme Court 139, 144, 146, 147, 149n6, 152n55
Michigan's Thumb 238
Michnuk, Joe 210–13
Miller Park (Milwaukee) 84
Milliken, William 51, 173
Milwaukee Brewers 12
Milwaukee County Stadium 113
Miner, Craig 66
Minneapolis 110
Minneapolis Federal Reserve 123
Minnesota Twins 57, 61, 123, 126, 173, 208, 252
Minnesota Vikings 123
Miramonti, "Baseball John" 252
Mitchell, Houston 63n12
Mize, Johnny 260
Mlive.com 163n24
Moeller, Brian 250
Molitor, Paul 260
Monaghan, Tom 54–58, 109, 111, 112, 125–26, 133, 138, 139, 252
Montgomery, Jeff 249
Monthly Detroit 134
Montreal 110
Montreal Expos 125, 223
Moon, Charles 150n28
Moore, Lenny 225
Mordenski, Jan 186; "Like Colavito" 179
Morgan, Joe 260
Moriarty, George 18
Morris, Jack 55, 211, 211, 260
Moroz, Betty 150n23, 191–94
Moroz, Dave 150n23
Moroz, Mary 150n23, 191–94, **193**
Mossi, Don 172
Most Valuable Player (MVP) 222
Mothers' Day 201
Motor City Marauders 61
Motor City Muckraker 165n53
Motown Records 157
Mount Clemens 2, 195
Moynes, James A. 113
Muldoon, Brian 150n23, 229–37
Muldoon, Patricia 150n23, **193**, **196**, 229–37
multideck major league ballparks 82, 117n90
multisport stadiums 85, 118n112
Mumford, Lewis 1
Municipal Stadium (Cleveland) 79, 84, 91, 100, 102, 117n87, 119n155
Municipal Stadium (Kansas City) 84
Munsey, Paul 128n27
Munson, Thurman 200

Murphy, Ruth 45
Murray, Eddie 260
Muscat, Mario 200, 229–37
Musial, Stan 260, 261

naming rights 143
The Nation 127n15, 165n53
National Anthem 171–72, 230
National Association 8
National Avenue 74, 77; *see also* Cochrane Avenue
National Baseball Hall of Fame 19, 173, 189, 190, 215, 216; *see also* Hall of Famers
National Basketball Association 55
National Football conference championship 262
National Football League 36, 41, 64, 65, 99–100, 175, 176, 262
National Football League Championship games: (1952) 262; (1953) 217, 241, 262; (1954) 217; (1957) 217, 241, 262
National Guard 230
National Geographic Society 189
National League 8, 11, 12, 13, 43, 79, 198, 217
National Preservation Magazine 203
National Public Radio 203
National Register of Historic Places 1, 57, 109, 137
National Street 10, 167
National Trust for Historic Preservation 57, 109, 150n27
Nationals Park 85
Naughty Marietta 24
Navarre Farm 8
Navarro, Eva 1, 2, 150n23, 161, **193**, 203, 232–33
Navin, Frank 12–28, 29n18, 61, 62, 73, 75, 93, 212
Navin, Jim 212
Navin, Thomas, Jr. 13
Navin Field (1912–1937) 16–29, **21, 24, 26, 27, 28**, 31, **32**, 33, 34, 35, 62, 68, 71, 76–97, 100, 117n87, 123, 157, 158, 160–61, 162, 167, 168, 187, 213, 238, 242, 245, **255**; architectural drawings and documents 120n208; attendance 19; "a ballpark to compare with the best in the land" 80; bleacher expansion, 1935-6 **93**; box seats 81–82; composite image **90**; configurations 17, 29n27; cross-section 1912 **78**; expansions 75–78, 87, 118n114; "the finest baseball field in the country" 76; fire-resistance 75, 76, 78, 79; ground rules 187; internal circulation and exiting, 81–82, 95; Labor Day tradition 187; lower-deck plans **81, 88, 89, 91, 94**; name 119n157; office and ticketing building 17, 77, 78, 79, **80**; opera 22, 23, 24; parking 18, **92**;

parochial school rally 19, **20**, 29n28; playing field configurations and outfield dimensions **108**; right-field exit **28**; right field overhang **94, 95**; scoreboard 17, **26, 27, 28, 32, 38**; seating expansion, 1936 **93**; site plan, 1912 **77**; standing-room-only **26**, 197; steam-heated dugout 81; steel and concrete construction 76–79, 82; telephone pole sitters **27**; temporary 1936 configuration **93**, 94; temporary World Series bleachers (1934, 1935) **27, 91, 92**, 187; ticket prices **90**, 90–91; upper deck plans **82, 94**; viewing distances and intimacy 82–87; *see also* Bennett Park (1896–1911); Briggs Stadium (1938–1960); Michigan and Trumbull; Tiger Stadium (1912–2009)
Navin Field Consortium 156, 163n1 2
Navin Field Grounds Crew 4, 159, 160, 161, 185, 194, 201–3, 210–12, 226–227, **227**, 252–53
NBC *Game of the Week* 215, 216
NBC-TV 172, 174, 176, 216
Neft, David S.: *The Scrapbook History of Baseball* 117n78
Negro League baseball in Detroit 36, 62n2
Nemo's Bar 250
New Comiskey Park 80, 84, 122; *see also* Comiskey Park
New England Patriots 217
new stadium: costs 145, 146; cost vs. benefits 138, 147, 152n51; development rationale 141; impact 147, 148; promotion and broken promises 142–43, 145, 146–47, 151n34; subsidies 138, 140, 146, 148
New Yankee Stadium 52, 85 *see also* Yankee Stadium
New York Bulldogs 64
New York City 198, 242; Parks and Recreation 164n49
New York Giants (football) 218, 262
New York Highlanders 15
New York Knights 196
New York Post 128n21
New York Stock Exchange 123
New York Times 127n4, 145, 147, 203
New York Yankees 116n43, 127, 181, 189, 205, 210, 213–14, 225, 256
Newhouser, Hal 153, 260
Neyer, Rob 122, 63n17
Niekro, Joe 192
Niekro, Phil 260
no-hitters 168–69, 201–2
Noll, Roger 150–51n29
Nonrahs-Sinacola Stadium Redevelopment, LLC 154–5, 163n9
North Corktown 229; *see also*

Corktown and Briggs Community
Northrup, Jim 47, 49, 192, 201, 209, 255
Northwestern High School 45, 169–70, 180
Notre Dame High School 192

Oakland, CA 110
Oakland Athletics 52, 126, 173
Obama, Barack 190
O'Connell, Mary 150n24
Okkonen, Marc 29n18, 115n19, 117n76; *Baseball Memories: 1900–1909* 116n61; *Baseball Memories 1950–1959: An Illustrated Scrapbook of Baseball's Fabulous Fifties* 120n192, 120n194
Olbermann, Keith 158, 164n40
Old City Hall 149–50n16
Old Tiger Stadium Conservancy 4, 62, 149n9, 157, 158, 159–60, 161, 163n9, 237
Olympia Entertainment 143, 237
Olympia Stadium 54, 63n18
Onassis Coney Island (Michigan and Trumbull) 153
One in a Million: The Ron LeFlore Story 225
O'Neal, Joe 110, 137, 139
Oosting, Jonathan 164n47, 165n50
"An Open Letter to Mayor Anthony Williams and the DC City Council from 90 Economists on the Likely Impact of a Taxpayer Financed Baseball Stadium in the District of Columbia" 127n18
Opening Day 17, 63n5, 191, 193, 197, 233, 234; (1896) 9; (1901) 12, 29n16, 238; (1912) 17, 76; (1949) **36**; (1958) 204; (1976) 252; (1977) 252; (1978) 252; (1983) 210; (1984) 252; (1999) 251; (2010) 212
opera boxes 83
Opera Under the Stars 22, **23, 24**
Orchestra Hall 136
The Origins of the Urban Crisis: Race and Inequality in Postwar Detroit see Sugrue, Thomas J.
Oriole Park at Camden Yards 63n26, 86, 122
Osborn, Frank C. 113
Osborn, Ken 113
Osborn Engineering Company 16, 31, 33, 76, 79–80, 81, 93–94, 96, 109, 113, 115n22, 115n25, 115n27, 115n28, 116n42, 117n75, 117n87, 117n97, 117n98, 118n122, 118n133, 118n134, 119n135, 118n136, 118n137, 119n138, 119n144, 119n154, 119n155, 120n208; 134; scope of ballpark work 79, 113
Ott, Mel 214, 215, 260
Ourlian, Robert 63n20
overflow crowds in early baseball 81, 116–17n71; *see also* standing-

Index 277

room-only in Bennett Park (1896–1911); Tiger Stadium (1912–2009)
Owen, Marv 27, 89
Owens, Steve 66, 175, 219
Oyler, Ray 256

Pacific Institute, Seattle 176
Paige, Satchel 260
Palace of Auburn Hills 111
Palace of the Fans 78, 81, 117n74
Palm, Kristin 152n52
Palmer, Jim 260
Paradise, MI 256
Paradise Valley 130
Parc Jarry (Montreal) 91; see also Jarry Park
Parker, Jim 225
Parker, Raymond 64
Parnell, Mel 261
Parrish, Lance 55, 194, 250, 256
Parrish, Larry 247, 248
Passeau, Claude 261
Pastier, John vi, 3, 6n4, 132, 198–99
Pastor, Bob **25**
Patek Philippe 205
Patrick, Van 67n5, 214, 215
Paw Paw, MI 256
Paws (Tigers mascot) 230, 252
Pennock, Herb 260
The People's Champion: Willie Horton 169
Pepitone, Joe 172
Perez, Tony 260
Perkins, Dave 128n26
Perry, Gaylord 207, 260
Perry, Jim 191
Petco Park (San Diego) 84, 86
Peters, Ricky 210
Peterson, Harold: *The Man Who Invented Baseball* 28n4
Petroskey, Dale 189–90
Petry, Dan 55, 211
Philadelphia, PA 110, 129
Philadelphia Athletics **9**, 23
Phillips, Tony 101
A Piece of the Field LLC 156
Piedmont Park (Atlanta) 29n26
Piersall, Jimmy 43, 204, 221–22, 244
Piluras, Tom 150n23
Pitt, Michael 150n28
Pittsburgh, PA 12, 50, 63n25, 76, 110, 121, 129
Pittsburgh Pirates 15, 215
Pittsburgh Pirates (football) 67n3, 262
A Place for Summer: A Narrative History of Tiger Stadium see Bak, Richard
Plank, Eddie 260
playing field dimensions 100–101
playoffs 233
Plum Street 167
Poet Laureate of the United States 190
Poletown 130, 149n6

Poletown: Community Betrayed 149n6
Poletown Lives! 149n6
Polish American 198
Polish-American Night 183, 192, 256
Polish Muslims 252
Polo Grounds (New York) 69, 78–79, 84, 89, 91, 96, 100–1, 104, 105, 117n87, 118n126, 119n155, 120n208
Pontiac, MI 100
Pontiac Metropolitan Stadium (Silverdome) 36, 54, 66, 147; ticket prices 152n57, 175, 219
Populous 79; see also HOK Sport
Porterfield, Bob 168
Portman, John 130
Portsmouth Spartans 64
Powell, Boog 255
Prebenda, Ron 51–52
premium seating sections in baseball stadiums 85
Presley, Elvis 54
Pre-World War II ballparks 127
Princeton and Syracuse streets (Dearborn) 210
Pro Football Hall of Fame 216, 218
Proposal S 145
Provenzano, Frank 150n25
Prusak, Barbara 150n23
Prusak, John 150n23, 229–37
Public Dollars, Private Stadiums 125
public transit in Detroit 69, 71
Puckett, Kirby 260

Queen of Diamonds 109
Queen of Diamonds: The Tiger Stadium Story see Betzold, Michael; Casey, Ethan
Quirk, James 150n29; *Hard Ball: The Abuse of Power in Pro Team Sports* 152n51

Raines, Tim 260
Rambeau, David 136
Rashid, Anne **193**
Rashid, Frank 150n20, **193**, 202
Rashid, Frederick 1, 2
Rashid, Kevin 150n23
Ravitz, Mel 138–39
Reagan, Ronald 122, 123, 189
"rebellion" 1967 see Detroit 1967, civil disturbance
Recreation Park 8
Red Sox Hall of Fame 223
Redland Field 77, 79, 91
Redmond, Herbie 256
Reed, Jack 189, 221
Reese, Pee Wee 260
Reeves, Martha 157–58
Reidenbaugh, Lowell: *Take Me Out to the Ballpark* 115n19, 115n34, 115n36, 116n39, 116n43, 120n195
Reilly, Mike 227–28
Reinsdorf, Jerry 125

Renaissance Center 130
Republican Convention, 1980 130, 147
Requests for Proposals (RFPs) 154–55
Retrosheet 198
Ricciardi, J.P. 126
Rice, Jim 224, 260
Rice, Sam 260
Rich, Wilbur C.: *The Economics and Politics of Sports Facilities* 145, 149n10, 149n11, 152n49
Richard, Gabriel 133
Richards, G.A. 64
Richie, Tim 161–62, 165n55
Ricketts, Tom 127
Riley, Peter Comstock 4, 155–57, **156**, 158, 161, 165n54
"riot" 1967 see Detroit 1967, civil disturbance
Ripken, Cal Jr. 37, 158, 260
Ripken and Associates 158
riverfront dome project 50–52, 54, 66, 150n21
Riverview High School 65
Rizzuto, Phil 260
Roberts, Emory S. 116n40, 118n119
Roberts, Robin 260
Robinson, Brooks 192, 199–200, 256, 260
Robinson, Frank 173, 256, 260, 261
Robinson, Jackie 34, 39, 180, 219, 260
Robison Field (St. Louis) 117n75
Rockwell, Norman 236
Rodriguez, Ivan 260
Roesink, John 36
Roesink's Pant Store **27**
Rogell, Billy 7
Rogers, John N. "Trey" 162
Rogers, Phil 127, 128n30
Rogers Centre 126
Rolnick, Arthur 123, 127n11
Roman Coliseum 211
Rookie of the Year 54, 249
Roosevelt Stadium (Jersey City) 117n90
Rosa Parks Boulevard 180
Rosentraub, Mark 150n29
Rosetti, Gino 111, 113
Rosetti Associates 54, 57, 116n67, 107
Rote, Tobin 65, 217
Royal Oak, MI 173
Royals Stadium 84
Rozema, Dave 203, 224–25, 256
Rubin, Neil 163n23, 163n24
Ruffing, Red 214, 260
Ruth, Babe 18, 22, 23, 29n29, 36, 45, 82, 103, 112, 121, 122, 153, 169, 195, 203, 209, 213, 217, 224, 227, 259, 260
Ryan, Nolan 201, 260

SABR see Society for American Baseball Research
Safeco Field 84
Sager, A. J. 247

St. Andrew's Hall 252
St. George Cricket Grounds 70
St. John, Paige 63n20
St. Leo's Catholic Church 150n23
St. Louis, MO 110, 129
St. Louis Browns **26**, 41, 215
St. Louis Cardinals 49, 124, 126, 168
St. Louis Rams 126
St. Patrick's Day Parade **193**, 233
St. Paul Saints 61, 63n22
St. Peter's Episcopal Church 150n23, 251
St. Rocco 189
Salvation Army 236
Sam the Tailor 167
Samojeden, Michael 150n27
San Antonio, TX 175
San Diego Padres 56, 175–77, 216
San Francisco, CA 110; rejection of stadium subsidies 136
San Francisco Giants 126
Sanborn Insurance Company map (1897) 78, 115n18, 116n60, 116n62, 117n81, 118n132,
Sanders, Charlie 174
Sanders, Heywood 149n4
Sanderson, Allen R. 150n29
Sauer Avenue 239
Sauk Trail 8
Save Fenway Park 150n24
Save Our Sox 136, 150n24
Schaefer, Germany 13, 14, 29n19
Schalk, Ray 260
Scheffing, Bob 45, 172, 221
Scheider, Roy 197
Schembechler, Bo 57–58, 109, 125, 135, 139, 141
Schmakel, Jim 212, 228, 246, 249
Schmidt, Joe 65–66, 216–17, 225, 262
Schoendienst, Red 260
Schramm, Jack: *Detroit's Street Railways: City Lines, 1922-1956* 116n61
Scott, Ron 136
Scully, Vin 176, 216
Seals Stadium (San Francisco) 117n90
Seattle, WA 110
Seattle Mariners 122
Seattle Times 127n1
Seaver, Tom 260
Seifman, David 128n21
Selter, Ronald: *Ballparks of the Deadball Era: A Comprehensive Study of Their Dimension, Configurations and Effects on Batting, 1901-1919* 29n22; "Bennett Park Historical Analysis" 29n9, 115n17, 115n19, 115n20, 115n21, 115n23, 115n31, 115n33, 115n34, 115n36, 116n62, 116n63
Sewell, Joe 260
Shannon, Bill: *The Ballparks* 116n43, 119n156
Sharp, Thom 194–96, **196**
Sheraton Cadillac Hotel 222; *see also* Book Cadillac Hotel

Shibe Park 36, 75–78, 81, 84, 105, 119n157
Sick's Stadium (Seattle) 91, 102, 117n90
Siebern, Norm 205
Simmons, Al 260
Sinatra, Frank 54
single-deck ballparks 77, 82, 83
Sisler, George 260
61* 60, 163n13, 193; *see also* Crystal, Billy
"Skid Row" 221, 222, 241; *see also* Michigan Avenue
Skowron, Bill 205
SkyDome (Toronto) 84, 121, 122, 126
Slate 127n17
Slaughter, Enos 260
Slayback, Bill 191
Smith, Eddie 261
Smith, Mayo 47, 49, 245, 256
Smith, Randy 247, 248
Smulyan, Jeff 122
Snead, David L. 142
Snider, Duke 260
Snorton, Matt 170
Snyder, Rick 148
soccer: at recent major league baseball parks 118n112; at Tiger Stadium 230
Society for American Baseball Research (SABR) 29n30, 117n84, 119n164, 119n175, 119n176, 119n177
Soos, Troy 181
Sosa, Sammy 103
Southern Methodist University 64
Sparma, Joe 171
Speaker, Tris 22, 87, 202, 260
Spenser and Wycoff 20
Spicer, Gary 157–58
spitball 207
Spivey, Andre 162
Splendid Splinter *see* Williams, Ted
Sporting Life 70, 71, 75, 76, 115n10, 115n13, 115n15, 115n16, 116n59, 116n68, 116n69, 116n70, 117n74, 117n77, 117n89
The Sporting News 86, 115n8, 115n24, 116n37, 118n113, 118n121, 218, 224
Sports Illustrated 65, 66, 176, 238
Sports, Jobs, and Taxes: The Economic Impact of Sports Teams and Stadiums 151n29
Sportservice 143, 172
Sportsman's Park (St. Louis) 77, 79, 84, 101–2, 104, 117n72, 117n75, 117n80, 117n87, 119n163, 120n208
Stade Olympique (Montreal) 84, 118n104
Stanley, Mickey 47, 200, 224, 225, 245
Stanton, Tom 186; *The Final Season* 184–85
Stargell, Willie 260
Starr, Bart 66, 67n9, 262

State Fair Coliseum 66
State of Michigan Historic Site 109
Steinbrenner, George 52
Stewart, Rod 232, 233
Stirling, James 109, 120n196
streetcars 188
Stroh's Beer 256
Stroud, Joe 145
Stroud, Kim 144–45, 150n23, 251
Studstill, Pat 217–18
Subcommittee on Domestic Policy, Committee on Oversight and Government Reform, U.S. House of Representatives 149n
suburbanization 46–47
Sugrue, Thomas J. 63n13, 147, 149n1
Sullivan, Neil 150n29
Sumitomo Bank 143
Summer, Champ 255
Super Bowl 147, 148
Suppes, Corry 128n27
Surdam, David G.: *How Baseball Outlasted the Great Depression* 116n43
Sutton, Don 252, 260
Swackhamer, Robert 114
Swearingen, Dale 134
Sweeney, Ed **15**
Swift, Peggy **193**

Tampa Bay Rays 126
Tanana, Frank 202, 232, 250
Tax Reform Act (1986) 124
Taxpayers of Michigan against Casinos (TOMAC) 146, 152n55; *see also* lawsuits to prevent public stadium subsidies
Telenews Theater 214
Templeton, Gary 176
Tentler, Leslie Woodcock: *Seasons of Grace: A History of the Catholic Archdiocese of Detroit* 29n28
Tettleton, Mickey 7, 105
Texas Rangers 33, 104
Thanksgiving Day Lions game 218; (1953) 217; (1961) 218; (1962) 66, 189–90, 225, 241–42, 262; (1968) 66; (1970) 219; (1974) 66, 175
Thanksgiving Day Parade 161
This Week in Baseball 211
Thomas, Frank 260
Thomas, June Manning 149n2, 149n3, 149n5
Thomas, Steve 156, 212–13
Thome, Jim 260
Thompson, Bobby 46
Thompson, Jason 105, 227
Thompson, Richard 174
Thompson, Sam 260
Thorn, John 28n2; *Baseball in the Garden of Eden: The Secret Early History of the Game* 28n3
Three Tenors 233
Throneberry, Marv 205
"Tiger Joe" 213

Tiger Stadium (1912–2009) 1, 2, 3, 4, 43–62, 77, 101–2, 106, 108–11, 117n84, *132*, 154, **156**, **188**, 189, 190, 197, 213, 242, 246, 252; acreage/space of 3, 6n4; African Americans in 39–40, 233; architects, designers, engineers, and builders 75, 88, 96, 112, 113–14; attendance 56, 68–69, 73–74, 78, 87, 89, 97, 106, 179; autograph collecting at 170–71, *171*, 172, *177*, 210, 221; ball man 206–8; banners 231; baseball catching and retrieving 190, 199–201, 210, 212, 215, 252; base-sweepers 192; bat boys 200, 209–10, 230, 233; bleachers 6n2, 33, *42*, **48**, 87, 89–91, 93, 96–97, 119n156, 181, 182, **183**, 184, 198, 199, **200**, 202, 207, 208, 210, **211**, 216, 224, 225 232 252, 255, 256; box seats 197, 199, 207; broadcast booths *32*, 45, 54, 58, 188, 213, 215–16; bullpens 120n185, 179, 192, 223–24, 226, 227, 255; capacity 35, 63n5, 100; center field 17, 100, 102, 119n171, 225, 226, 242; commissary 191; "common ground" 180, 181, 238, 239; concerts 206, 232, 233; concession areas 33, 34, 40, 54, 110, 137, 191; concourses 3, 16, 32, 33, 34, 35, 38, 95, 96, 125, 134, 175, 197, 210; demolition of 133, 157, 158–59, **159**, 194, 202 198, 201, 223, 233, 240, 253, 254, 256; Detroit Lions' final game at 175; dirt 156, 195, 247, **248** (*see also* "Ground from the Mound"); disappointment experienced in 182–83; distinctive atmosphere of 130–32, 153–4, 194, 197, 198–9, 208, 210, 215, 217, 228, 230, 239; drinking in 181, 184, 190, 204; dugout(s) 2, 27, 28, 35, *37*, 48, *83*, 199n58, 157, 158, 168, 169, 177, 179, 182, 189, 192, 197, 200, 202, 207, 208, 209, 210, 223, 225; empty 189, 192, 198–99, 208, 215; expansions 75–78, 96; exterior 130, 179, 238, 239; family 227, 248, 252; fathers and sons in 153, 185, 190, 208, 241–42, 247–48, 256; field configurations and outfield dimensions (1935, 1936, 1938, 1955) **108**; final Tigers' game at (1999) 189, 190, 193, 195, **195**, 202, 206, 208, 209, 220, 224–5, 226, 227, 228, 233, 242, 248–50, 255; final Tigers' pitch 249–50, *250*; fire (1977) 54; Fireworks Fridays 230; first experiences at 189, 191, 194, 196–97, 198, 199, 201, 208, 210, 213–14, 215, 217, 218, 219–20, 224, 225, 255; flagpole *42*, 47, 62, 153, 159–60, 164n44, 194, 196, 217, 228, 236; gambling 204; gate 13 213; general admission (grandstand) 34, 179–80, 182, 183, 191, 194, 199, 200, 256; grass 161–3, 175, 179, 182, 189, 202, 218, 239, 253, 255, 256; ground rules 228; grounds crew 191, 204–5, 213, 217, 220, 246; height of 120n207; historic designation 202; historic significance 140, 153–54, 197, 209, 213; hitting background 220, 221; home run distances 87–88, 89, 100–1, 118n116, 119n149; home runs at 68, 100–5; hot dogs 226; Ladies/Retirees Day 252, 256; largest sports crowd (59, 203) 100; lease (1977–78) 60, 137; lights *40*, 106, 230, 239; in literature 178–86; locker room(s) (clubhouses) 39, 168, 170, 172, 209–10, 210, 211, 214, 215, 218, 225, 227; lower deck 199; maintenance of 155; marquee *56*; memorabilia, sale or auction of 157; minor league baseball at 154–57; naming of 179; Negro League games at 62n2; night baseball at 39, *40*, 188, 194, 239; obstructed views 21, 75, 86, 110; office and ticket building 17, 77, 78, 79, *80*, 106, *107*; office annex (8th Ave.) 133; organ 256; outfield depth, average over time 100; outfield dimensions 119n171; overhang (right-field) 32–33, 34, **48**, *82*, **94**, 95, 96, **98**, 101, 104–5, 110, 221, 228; owner's box 252; parking 143, 163n1, 178, 223, 230, **231**, 233; players' parking lot 191, 196, 220; preparation for life 182; preservation 132; preservation/renovation proposals 154–57, 160–2; press box *32*, 35, 54, 107, 190, 201; professional soccer 230; race and racism 1, 3, 30, 34, 39–40, 43, 45, 47, 49, 63n4, 136, 219–20, 233; rain delays 35, 194, 210; ramps 34, 54, 79–80, 81, 96, 191, 199, 215, 240–41, 243, 255; refuge 1, 180, 201; renovation 133, 140; renovations (1977–1984) 54–55, 107–108, 111; romance 1, 153, 184, 252, 253; roof 201; "rusted girder" 109; "salt damage" 133–34; scoreboard 17, **26**, **27**, **28**, *32*, *37*, **38**, 202, 214, 252; seating density and capacities over time, 71, 76, 96, 115n28, 115n29, 115n30; seating proximity vi, 19, 82–87, 132, 137, 188, 215, 216, 228, 239, 245, 253; security guards 191, 192, 200, 210–12, 232; smells 189, 190, 210; sounds 202, 217, 219, 228, 230, 232; souvenirs of 172–73, 191, 205–6, 212–13, 224; standing-room-only 37–38, 90, 116n43, 195; steel and concrete construction 76–79, 82; street-side projection (Trumbull Ave.) *31*, 96, **98**, 120n199; structural elements, systems, and quirks 76, 79, 82, 94–96, 110; structural soundness of 134–35, 137, 140; tarp 204, 210, 256; therapeutic role of 184–85; third-deck *32*, 35, 227–28; ticket booth **211**; ticket office 17; ticket prices 38, 42–43, **90**, 191, 210, **211**; ticket sellers 187, 227; ticket surcharge 54, 55, 60, 61, 63n20, 155; ticket takers 241, 245; "Tiger Plaza" 56, 58, 112, 138, **214**; 22-inning game (1962) 189, 221; umpires 69, 76, 192, 215, 227–28; umpires' locker room 228; upper-deck (second deck) vi, **114**, 194, 199, 200, 210, 221, 239, 240, 255; urinals 225, 249, 255; ushers 185, 189, 200, 206, **207**, 210, 230, 245, 255; vendors 184, 191, 205–206, 208–9, 221, 224, 245; violence and unruliness 2, 6n3, 10, 18, 40, 43, 181, 190, 193, 210–11, 222, 228, 230, 232; VIP seating 197; The Wave 2, 6n2; in winter 192, 199; "worst seat in baseball" 198; *see also* Briggs Stadium, 1938–1960; Michigan and Trumbull; Navin Field, 1912–1937

Tiger Stadium Fan Club (TSFC) 1, 4, 57, 58, 109, 111, 127, 132–48, 149n9, 151n45, 152n55, 157, 159, 191, 193, 194, 195–96, 198, 199, 202, 213; activities and projects 135, 150n26, 193; African American involvement 136, 142; historic designation committee 137, 150n27, 202; legal committee 137; membership 135–6, 137–8, opening day protest (1990) 193, 232–33, 252

Tiger Stadium Hugs 135, 137, 193

Tiger Stadium Renovation: Phase III Study 149n15

TIGER STADIUM signs 201, **237**

Tiger Stadium: State of Michigan Historic Site Plaque **196**

Tiger Stadium: Where Baseball Belongs 29n8

Tigers' "cookie girls" 191

Tigers fans 2, 12, 40, 47, **95**, 173, 192, 198, 220, 221, 222, 223, 224, 225, 228, 232–33, 247–48, 250

"Time, Temperature" *see* Daniels, Jim

Tinker, Joe 260

Tish 251

Titan Stadium 262; *see also* Dinan Field; University of Detroit

Toffler, Alvin 224

Toledo Blade 128n22, 163n24, 164n29, 164n32–35

Torme, Mel 173

Toronto Argonauts 121

Toronto Blue Jays 57, 121, 122, 126, 127n4, 176, 202, 232

Toronto Star 128n26

280 Index

Trammell, Alan 55, 171, 176, 208, 250, 256, 260
Traverse City, MI 211
Tremain, Brian 150*n*23, 198
"trickle-down urbanism" 147
Tropicana Field (St. Petersburg) 102, 125
Trucks, Virgil 168–69
Trumbull, John 8
Trumbull Avenue 27, *31*, 32, **80**, **95**, 96, 99, 120*n*199, 167, 188, 198, *214*
Turner, Edward, MD 136
Turner Construction 134, 149*n*15
Tyrus Raymond Cobb, Greatest Tiger of All: A Genius in Spikes plaque **196**
Tyson, Ty **32**, 168

Unitas, Johnny 225
U.S. Cellular Field 122
U.S. Census 117*n*79
U.S. Marine Corps 168
U.S. Postal Service 205
University of Colorado 65
University of Detroit 64, 67*n*3, 262; *see also* Dinan Field; Titan Stadium
University of Detroit Mercy *see* University of Detroit
University of Detroit Titans 64
University of Michigan 88, 109, 169, 190
University of Notre Dame 249
Unobstructed Views 133, 137, 149*n*12, 149*n*13
upper-deck viewing distances of baseball stadiums, 1895–2013 84–85
USA Today 127*n*6, 212
Utley, Jerome A. 88, 93–94, 113, 118*n*120

Van Buskirk, Clarence R. 76
Vance, Dazzy 260
Vanderbeck, George 8–9, 70–71
Van Dyke–Lafayette bus 199
Vaughan, Arky 260, 261
Veeck, Bill 41
Veryzer, Tom 191
Veterans Stadium (Philadelphia) 54, 84
Village Voice 127*n*7
Vincent, David 119*n*164, 119*n*165, 119*n*167
Vinyard, JoEllen: *For Faith and Fortune: The Education of Catholic Immigrants in Detroit, 1805–1925* 29*n*28
Virgil, Ozzie 40, 180, 225
Vitruvius 78
Voelker, Donald 150*n*27; "Michigan and Trumbull Before Baseball" 28*n*6
Vonnegut, Kurt 224

Wabash Street 231
Waddell, Rube 260
Wagner, Honus 15, 260
"A Walk with Tom Jefferson" *see* Levine, Philip
Walker, Doak 64, **65**, 262
Walker, Wayne 218
Walker & Co. 113
Wall Street Journal 145
Wallace, Bobby 260
Walsh, Ed 260
Walter P. Reuther Library, Archives of Labor and Urban Affairs, Wayne State University 23, 24, 25, *31*, *42*, *131*, *183*
WARM Training Center 160
Warner, Doug 149*n*23
Warner, Patty 149*n*23
Warren, MI 191, 199
Washington Boulevard 192
Washington Redskins 262
Washington Senators 13, 168–69
Watkins, Walter 156
Watson, JoAnn 1, 2
"The Wave" 2
Wayne County 138, 141, 144–45
Wayne County Commission 144–45
Wayne County Stadium Authority 51, 144
Wayne State University 50, 66, 174
WDET-FM 145, 151*n*30
WDTR-FM 142
"We Are the World" 252
Weeghman Park (Chicago) 79, 119*n*157
Wells, Marvin 205–6, **206**
Wert, Don 183
Wertz, Vic 168–69, 261
West, Troy 63*n*25
Western League 8, 11, 73
Western Market 8
Wheat, Zack 260
Whitaker, Lou 55, 176, 203, 232, 250, 256
Whiting, Margaret 172
Whitman, Walt 96, 119*n*152
"wildcat bleachers" 10, **11**
Wilhelm, Hoyt 260
William Steele & Sons 76
Williams, Anthony 125
Williams, Billy 260
Williams, Dick 56, 176
Williams, Sam 190, 262
Williams, Ted 103, 105, 112, 169, 194, 205, 214, 220, 221, 224, 239, 260, 261
The Willie Horton Field of Dreams 162
Willis, Vic 260
Wilson, Earl 47, 48, 255
Wimmer, Robert 63*n*18
Windsor Star 163*n*24
Winfield, Dave 210, 260
Witkosky, Art 208–9
WJR radio 46, 64, 213, 214–15, 250
Wockenfuss, John 203, 226–27, **227**
women's baseball 233
Wood, Jake 45, 172, 181, 219–20, **220**, 225, 256

Wood, Wilbur 199
Woodbridge, Dudley 8
Woodbridge, William 8
Woodbridge Grove 8, 10, 73
Woods, Cassandra 163*n*8
The World Almanac and Book of Facts 116*n*43, 116*n*44, 116*n*45
World Series 147, 148, 176, 227, 232, 233; (1907) 14, 19, 73; (1908) 14, 74; (1909) 15; (1934) 27, 60, 87–89; (1935) 4, 27–28, **28**, 87, 90–93, 101, 176, 239; (1940) 35, 37–38; (1945) 38, 239; (1968) 2, 49, 60, 183, 189, 195, 239; (1984) 2, 6*n*3, **56**, 56–57, 157, 175–77, 189, 193, 194, 208, 209, 211–12, 216, 227, 228, 232, 239, 252; (2006) 147; (2007) 213; (2012) 147; (2013) 213
World War I 19, 122, 238
World War II 4, 35, **38**, 38, 49, 62*n*2, 102, 103, 106, 129, 150*n*23, 168, 178, 238, 241
Worman, Thomas D.: *Detroit's Street Railways: City Lines, 1922–1956* 116*n*61
Wornley, Bradford 116*n*49
Wright, Travis 164*n*39
Wrigley Field 31, 34, 38, 39, 57, 59, 68, 79, 82, 84–87, 91, 101, 104, 106, 117*n*80, 118*n*114, 119*n*157, 119*n*158, 120*n*179, 126, 127, 136, 140, 223, 238, 253; *see also* Cubs Park
Wrigley Field (Los Angeles) 103, 104, 120*n*179
The Wrong Stuff 223; *see also* Lee, Bill "Spaceman"
WXYZ-TV (Channel 7) 193
Wynn, Early 260

Yankee Stadium 18, 60, 62, 69, 79, 82, 84, 89, 91, 101, 113, 117*n*84, 117*n*87, 118*n*114, 118*n*122, 118*n*133, 119*n*142, 119*n*143, 121, 122, 125, 126, 127, 127*n*8, 136, 160, 164*n*49, 119*n*155169; 1970s reconstruction 84–85, 118*n*106; *see also* New Yankee Stadium
Yastrzemski, Carl 192, 210, 224, 260
Yawkey, Thomas A. 13
Yawkey, William C. 12–13
Yawkey, William H. 13, 14, 17, 19
York, Rudy 102
Yost, Eddie 172, 204
Young, Coleman 54, 55, 57, 109, 123, 125, 139, 150*n*21, 152*n*63
Young, Cy 112, 260
Yount, Robin 260

Zachary, Chris 191
Zachary and Associates 158
Zeiler, Peter 157
Zetlin, Lev 134
Zielinski, Susan 150*n*27, 150*n*28
Zimbalist, Andrew 150–51*n*29

www.ingramcontent.com/pod-product-compliance
Lightning Source LLC
Chambersburg PA
CBHW081544300426
44116CB00015B/2745